Photographer's Guide to the
Sony a6400

Photographer's Guide to the Sony a6400

Getting the Most from Sony's Advanced Mirrorless Camera

Alexander S. White

WHITE KNIGHT PRESS
HENRICO, VIRGINIA

Published by
White Knight Press
9704 Old Club Trace
Henrico, Virginia 23238
www.whiteknightpress.com
contact@whiteknightpress.com

ISBN: 978-1-937986-82-7 (paperback)
         978-1-937986-83-4 (ebook)

To my wife, Clenise.

Contents

CHAPTER 4: THE CAMERA SETTINGS1 MENU   39

Chapter 5: The Camera Settings2 Menu   112

CHAPTER 6: PHYSICAL CONTROLS   145

CHAPTER 7: PLAYBACK 158

CHAPTER 8: THE SETUP MENU AND MY MENU 171

Chapter 9: Motion Pictures   192

CHAPTER 10: WI-FI, BLUETOOTH, AND OTHER TOPICS   215

APPENDIX A: LENSES AND ACCESSORIES   229

INTRODUCTION

Since 2009, I have been writing and publishing guide books for advanced compact cameras, such as the Sony RX100 series and RX10 series, several Nikon Coolpix models, and other models from Panasonic, Leica, Canon, and Fujifilm. All of my books up to this point have covered cameras with fixed lenses, rather than cameras with interchangeable lenses. With this guide for the a6400, I have moved into the area of interchangeable-lens models. I was attracted to this model because of my familiarity with other Sony cameras, and because this model has all of the features that I would look for in a general-purpose camera. (Although the official name of the camera is the ILCE-6400 or the α6400, using the Greek letter alpha, I am calling it the a6400 in this book for simplicity.)

The a6400 is quite compact, but it uses an APS-C sensor, the same size as is found in many DSLR and other sophisticated cameras. This large sensor allows the camera to achieve a blurred background quite easily, and to create images that can be enlarged to generous sizes without losing details. The camera also has advanced focusing capabilities, excellent continuous-shooting features, and, in a departure from previous practice in cameras for this market segment, the ability to shoot video without an arbitrary time limitation, usually about 29 minutes for many compact cameras.

There have been some criticisms of the a6400, as there are with any camera model, but they do not involve major problems. The camera does not have in-body optical stabilization, so there is no SteadyShot feature to minimize motion blur from camera shake, unless you are using a Sony lens that includes that feature. There are several lenses that do include SteadyShot, and in other cases you can use a fast shutter speed or a tripod

to avoid motion blur. In addition, the camera's rotating LCD monitor can flip 180 degrees forward for selfies, but the camera's hot shoe is positioned so an accessory in the shoe will block most of the screen when the monitor is rotated like that. I will discuss that issue in Appendix A, where I discuss accessories, including a bracket for relocating an accessory to the side of the camera.

My goal with this book is to provide a thorough guide to the camera's features, explaining how they work and when you might want to use them. The book is aimed largely at beginning and intermediate photographers who are not satisfied with the documentation that comes with the camera and who prefer a more complete explanation of the camera's controls and menus. For those seeking more advanced information, I discuss some topics that go beyond the basics, and I include in the appendices information about additional resources. I will provide updates at my website, whiteknightpress. com, as warranted.

One note on the scope of this guide: I live in the United States, and I bought my camera here. I am not very familiar with the variations for cameras sold in Europe or elsewhere, such as different chargers. The photographic functions are generally not different, so this guide should be useful to photographers in all locations. I should note that the frame rates for video recording are different in different areas. In North America, Japan, and some other areas, the NTSC video system is generally used, whereas in Europe and elsewhere, the PAL system is in use. In this book, I discuss video frame rates in the context of the NTSC system. Also, I have stated measurements of distance and weight in both the Imperial and metric systems, for the benefit of readers in various countries around the world.

CHAPTER 1: PRELIMINARY SETUP

When you purchase your Sony a6400, the box should contain the camera itself, battery, charger/AC adapter, shoulder strap, micro USB cable, body cap, and brief instruction pamphlets. Sony also lists as included items the protective cap that is inserted into the accessory shoe and the eyepiece cup that is intended to be attached to the viewfinder. There may also be a warranty card and some advertising flyers. Of course, if you purchase the camera as a kit, there will be a lens included as well. With cameras sold outside the United States and Canada, there should be a power cord that connects to the battery charger.

There is no CD with software or a user's guide; the software programs and user's guide supplied by Sony are accessible through the Internet. To install PlayMemories Home, the Sony software for viewing and working with images and videos, go to the following Internet address: https://www.sony.net/disoft, where the program can be downloaded for Macintosh or Windows-based computers.

At the same site, you also can install Sony's Imaging Edge software. That software suite provides remote shooting, Raw image development, and editing functions. The Sony user's guide and related documents are available at https://www.sony.com/electronics/support/e-mount-body-ilce-6000-series/ilce-6400m/manuals. You also can get access to Sony help and tutorial materials at http://rd1.sony.net/help/ilc/1810/h_zz/ and at https://www.sony.net/tutorial/ilc/.

One of the other basic requirements for using this camera is to attach a lens. This is a simple operation, but you need to be careful to minimize the possibility of letting any dust or other foreign matter get inside the camera's body. You should arrange the camera and lens together in a safe area, such as on a bed or table, with both caps on the lens and the body cap on the camera. When you are ready, remove all of the caps, and hold the camera with the lens mount pointing downward,

to avoid exposing it to dust or other items from above. Line up the index mark on the lens with the white index mark on the camera's lens mount, press the lens firmly into place against the lens mount, and twist the lens clockwise until it catches and locks into place.

You might want to attach the shoulder strap to the a6400 body as soon as possible, so you can support the camera with the strap over your shoulder or around your neck. You also should attach the eyepiece cup by sliding it onto the viewfinder window, if you plan on using the viewfinder. Otherwise, you may want to leave it off, because it can interfere with your ability to place accessories in the camera's hot shoe, and it can partially block your view of the LCD monitor when the monitor is tilted up to a horizontal position.

Charging and Inserting the Battery

The Sony battery for the a6400 is the NP-FW50. With this camera, the standard procedure is to charge the battery while it's inside the camera. To do this, you use the supplied micro USB cable, which plugs into the camera and into the supplied Sony charger or another power source, such as a USB port on your computer or a standard USB charger.

There are pluses and minuses to charging the battery while it is inside the camera. On the positive side, you don't need an external charger, and the camera can charge automatically when it's connected to your computer. You also can find many portable charging devices with USB ports, and many newer automobiles have USB slots where you can plug in your a6400 to keep up its charge.

One drawback is that you cannot charge another battery outside of the camera using this system. A solution to this situation is to purchase at least one extra battery and a device to charge your batteries externally. However, with the a6400, you can use the supplied battery charger as an AC adapter that will power the camera.

So, if your battery runs completely down, you don't have to wait until you have recharged it to start using the camera again. You can plug the charger into the camera and into an AC outlet or USB power supply, and operate the camera directly from that power source, as long as there is a partially charged battery inserted in the camera. However, the battery will not be charged in that situation. I'll discuss batteries, chargers, and other accessories further in Appendix A.

Figure 1-1. Battery Lined Up to Go into Camera

Figure 1-2. Battery Going into Camera

Figure 1-3. Battery Secured by Latch

To insert the battery, open the battery/memory card compartment door on the bottom of the camera. Then look for the rectangular set of connectors on the battery, and insert the battery so those connectors are positioned close to the front of the camera as the battery goes into the compartment, as shown in Figure 1-1 and Figure 1-2. You may have to nudge aside the blue latch that holds the battery in place, as shown in Figure 1-3, to get the battery fully inserted.

With the battery inserted and secured by the latch, close the battery compartment door and slide the ridged latch on the door to the closed position. Then plug the larger, rectangular end of the micro USB cable into the corresponding slot on the provided AC charger, which is model number AC-UUD12 in the United States. Plug the smaller end of the cable into the micro USB port. This port, which is labeled the Multi port, is located under a small door on the lower part of the camera's left side as you hold it in shooting position, as shown in Figure 1-4.

Figure 1-4. Charger Connected to Camera

Plug the charger's prongs into a standard electrical outlet. A small orange lamp below the camera's Multi port will light up steadily while the battery is charging; when it goes out, the battery is fully charged. The full charging cycle should take about 150 minutes. (If the charging lamp flashes, that indicates a problem with the charger or a problem with the temperature of the camera's environment.)

Choosing and Inserting a Memory Card

The a6400 does not ship with a memory card. If you turn the camera on with no card inserted, you will see the error message "NO CARD" flashing in the upper left corner of the screen. If you ignore this message and press the shutter button to take a picture, you will be able to capture one image, if the Release w/o Card option on screen 4 of the Camera Settings2 menu is set to Enable.

However, even if you can capture an image, don't be fooled into thinking that the camera is storing the image in internal memory, because that is not the case.

Actually, the camera will temporarily store the image and play it back if you press the Playback button, but the image will not be permanently stored. (I did manage to save a NO CARD image by using a video capture device to capture the image from the camera's HDMI port to my computer while it was still on the screen, but that is not a process I would want to do often.) Some other camera models have a small amount of built-in memory so you can take and store a few pictures even without a card, but the a6400 does not have any such safety net.

Therefore, you need to purchase and insert a memory card. The a6400 uses two basic types of memory storage cards. First, it can use all varieties of SD cards, which come in several capacities; some examples are shown in Figure 1-5.

Figure 1-5. Memory Cards of Various Capacities

The standard card, called simply SD, comes in capacities from 8 MB (megabytes) to 2 GB (gigabytes). A higher-capacity card, SDHC, comes in sizes from 4 GB to 32 GB. The newest, and highest-capacity card, SDXC (for extended capacity) comes in sizes of 48 GB, 64 GB, 128 GB, 256 GB, 512 GB, and 1 TB (terabyte); this version of the card can have a capacity up to 2 TB, theoretically, and SDXC cards generally have faster transfer speeds than the smaller-capacity cards.

The a6400 also can use micro SD cards, which are smaller cards, often used in smartphones and other small devices. These cards operate in the same way as SD cards, but you have to use an adapter that is the size of an SD card to insert this tiny card in the a6400 camera, as shown in Figure 1-6.

In addition to using various types of SD cards, the a6400, being a Sony camera, also can use Sony's

proprietary storage devices, known as Memory Stick cards. These cards are similar in size and capacity to SD cards, but with a slightly different shape, as shown in Figure 1-7. Memory Stick cards come in various types. The ones that can be used in the a6400 are the Memory Stick PRO Duo and the Memory Stick PRO-HG Duo.

Figure 1-6. Micro SD Card and Adapter

Figure 1-7. Sony Memory Stick Card

There are some important limitations on your choice of a memory card. If you want to record video using either of the camera's two XAVC S formats (XAVC S 4K and XAVC S HD), which provide the highest quality, you have to use an SDHC or SDXC card rated in Speed Class 10, UHS Speed Class 1, or faster. If you want to record in the XAVC S formats using the highest quality of 100 megabits per second, you have to use a card rated in UHS Speed Class 3.

If you are using Memory Stick cards, the only one that can record XAVC S video is the Memory Stick PRO–HG Duo. Sony does not list any Memory Stick card as being able to record XAVC S video using the formats at 100 megabits per second.

These specifications are not just recommendations; if you try to record in a video format on a card that does not meet the requirements for that format, the camera will display an error message, as shown in Figure 1-8, and will not record the video.

The XAVC S options are worth using for many purposes, so it is a good idea to get one of the high-powered cards that can support their use. Figure 1-9 shows five cards I have tested that can handle all video formats on the a6400—the SanDisk Extreme Pro 32 GB SDHC card, the Lexar Professional 64 GB SDXC card, the SanDisk Extreme 256 GB SDXC card, the SanDisk Extreme Pro

512 GB SDXC card, and the Lexar Professional 1 TB SDXC card, all of which are rated in UHS Speed Class 3.

Figure 1-8. Error Message for Using Wrong Card for Video Format

Figure 1-9. Memory Cards Rated in UHS Speed Class 3

If you decide to use a Memory Stick card, be sure you have a card reader that can accept those cards, which, as noted above, are not the same shape as SD cards and require readers with compatible slots.

Once you have chosen a card, open the door on the bottom of the camera that covers the battery/memory card compartment, and slide the card into the slot until it catches. You insert an SD card with its label next to the open door, as shown in Figure 1-10; insert a Memory Stick card the opposite way, with its label pointing outward so it is visible.

Push the card firmly into the slot until it catches and stays in place, then close the compartment door and make sure it is firmly latched. To remove either type of card, push down on its edge until it releases and springs out, so you can remove it.

Although a card may work well when newly inserted in the camera, it's a good idea to format a card when first using it in the camera, so it will have the correct file structure and will have any bad areas blocked off from use. To do this, turn on the camera by moving the power switch to the On position, then press the Menu button on the upper area of the camera's back. Next, press the Right button (right edge of the control wheel on the camera's back) multiple times until the toolbox icon, the next to last icon at the top right of the screen, is highlighted, and the heading below that icon says

Setup5, as shown in Figure 1-11.

Figure 1-10. SD Card Going into Camera

Figure 1-11. Screen 5 of Setup Menu

(I will refer to the other three edges of the control wheel as the Left, Up, and Down buttons, and to the button in the middle of the wheel as the Center button.)

The orange highlight bar should already be positioned on the top line of the menu, on the PC Remote Settings command. Press the Down button, or turn the control wheel, so the Format command is highlighted by the orange bar.

Press the Center button when the Format line is highlighted. On the next screen, seen in Figure 1-12, highlight Enter and press the Center button again to carry out the command.

Figure 1-12. Format Confirmation Screen

Setting the Date, Time, and Language

You need to make sure the date and time are set correctly before you start taking pictures, because the camera records that information invisibly with each image and displays it later if you want. It is, of course, important to have the date (and the time of day) correctly recorded with your archives of digital images. The camera should prompt you to set these items the first time you turn it on. If not, or if you need to change the settings, follow these steps:

1. Turn the camera on, then press the Menu button. Press the Right button enough times to display the Setup5 screen while the Setup menu's toolbox icon is highlighted.

2. Press the Down button to move the orange highlight bar to the Date/Time Setup line on the menu screen, as shown in Figure 1-13, and press the Center button to select that option, which leads to the screen shown in Figure 1-14.

Figure 1-13. Date/Time Setup Highlighted on Setup Menu

Figure 1-14. Date/Time Setup Options Screen

3. Highlight the Date/Time option, press the Center button, and then, by pressing the Left and Right buttons or by turning the control wheel, move left and right through the month, day, year, and time settings, as shown in Figure 1-15.

Figure 1-15. Date and Time Settings Screen

4. Change the values by pressing the Up and Down buttons or by turning the control dial (the ridged dial at the extreme right of the camera's top). When everything is set correctly, press the Center button to confirm. Then use a similar method to adjust the Daylight Savings (On or Off) and Date Format options, if necessary.

5. If you need to change the language the camera uses for menus and other text, press the Menu button and navigate to the Language item, which is one line above the Date/Time Setup item, as shown earlier in Figure 1-13. Press the Center button to select it. You then can select from the available languages on the menu, as shown in Figure 1-16.

Figure 1-16. Language Selection Screen

CHAPTER 2: BASIC OPERATIONS

Now that the Sony a6400 has the correct time and date set and a charged battery inserted along with a memory card, I'll discuss the steps to get your camera into action and to capture a usable image to your memory card.

Introduction to Main Controls

Before I discuss settings, I will introduce the camera's main controls to give a better idea of which button or dial is which. I won't discuss the controls in detail here; there is more information in Chapter 6. For now, I will include images showing the buttons, switches, and dials of the a6400. You may want to refer back to these images for a reminder about each control as you go through this book. Some of these illustrations show the camera with the 18-135mm kit lens mounted on it. Other lenses will differ in appearance from this one, and may have different controls.

TOP OF CAMERA

On top of the camera are some of the most important controls and dials, as shown in Figure 2-1. You use the mode dial to select a shooting mode for stills or video. For basic shooting without making many other settings, turn the dial so the green AUTO label is next to the white marker; this will set the camera to one of its most automatic modes.

The shutter button is used to take pictures. Press it halfway to evaluate focus and exposure; press it all the way to take a picture. You can change its behavior through various options on the Camera Settings1 and Camera Settings2 menus. The on/off switch turns the camera on and off.

The control dial, just to the right of the mode dial, is used to adjust shutter speed in Shutter Priority mode and to adjust aperture in Aperture Priority and Manual exposure modes. It makes similar adjustments in Movie mode, when shutter speed or aperture can be adjusted.

In Program mode, it adjusts Program Shift. This dial also is used to navigate through various screens and options for camera settings. It can be programmed to perform other functions using the My Dial Settings option on screen 8 of the Camera Settings2 menu and the Dial/Wheel EV Compensation item on screen 9 of that menu.

Figure 2-1. Controls on Top of Camera

The Multi Interface Shoe functions as a flash shoe to hold an external flash unit, and it also accepts certain other Sony accessories that communicate with the camera through the shoe, such as microphones and flash triggers, as discussed in Appendix A. The built-in flash unit is stored inside the top of the camera; it pops up when you press the flash pop-up button. The sensor plane indicator marks the plane of the camera's digital sensor, in case you need to measure the exact distance from the sensor to your subject for a closeup shot.

The C1 button (Custom Button 1) can be programmed to perform any one of numerous camera operations, such as adjusting ISO, White Balance, or Drive Mode, using the Custom Key options on screen 8 of the Camera Settings2 menu.

Figure 2-2 shows the controls on the camera's back. The viewfinder window is where you look into the viewfinder when you want to view the scene at eye level, with your eye shaded from the sun. You can attach the included eyepiece cup to shade the view more completely. The diopter adjustment wheel is used to adjust the viewfinder for your vision. The eye sensor, a small slot to the right of the viewfinder, senses when your head is near, and can switch the camera between using the LCD screen and using the viewfinder.

BACK OF CAMERA

Figure 2-2. Controls on Back of Camera

The red Movie button, at the extreme right side of the camera's back, starts and stops the recording of a video sequence. The Menu button calls up the camera's system of menu screens with settings for shooting, playback, and other options, such as control button functions, audio features, and others.

In shooting mode, the Function (Fn) button calls up a menu of camera functions for easy access. It also can be used to lock the operation of the control wheel and control dial, if it is set to do that using the Dial/Wheel Lock option on screen 9 of the Camera Settings2 menu. In playback mode, pressing this button can send an image to a smartphone or tablet. The Playback button places the camera into playback mode, so you can view your recorded images and videos. The C2/Delete button (Custom Button 2), marked by a trash can icon, acts as the Delete button in playback mode, for erasing images. In shooting mode, this button can be programmed to carry out any one of numerous functions.

The control wheel is a rotary dial for navigating through menu screens and other screens with camera settings. In Shutter Priority and Manual modes, it adjusts shutter speed; in Aperture Priority mode, it adjusts aperture. It makes corresponding adjustments in Movie mode, when possible. In Program mode, it adjusts Program Shift. It also can be programmed to adjust one of several settings, such as exposure compensation, White Balance, or ISO, using options on screens 8 and 9 of the Camera Settings2 menu. In addition, each of the wheel's four edges acts as a direction button when you

press it in, for navigating through menu screens and moving items such as the focus frame.

The button in the center of the wheel (Center button) is used to confirm selections and for some miscellaneous operations. The top edge of the wheel (Up button) also acts as the Display button. You can press this button to choose the various display screens in either shooting or playback mode. In addition, the Left, Right, Center, and Down buttons can each be programmed through the Custom Key options on screen 8 of the Camera Settings2 menu to handle any one of numerous functions.

The LCD monitor—which displays the scene viewed by the camera along with the camera's settings and plays back your recorded images—tilts up or down to allow you to hold the camera in a high or low position to view a scene from unusual angles. It also can rotate forward 180 degrees for self-portraits or vlogging (video blogging).

In addition, the LCD has limited touch screen capabilities: You can touch the screen to move the focus frame, to set a new focus point, or to take a picture. You can tap the screen twice in playback mode to enlarge an image, and then scroll the enlarged image with your finger. You also can tap twice to enlarge the screen to assist with focusing when using manual focus.

The AF/MF/AEL switch lever lets you set the function of the button inside the switch. If the switch is set to the top position, that button functions as the AF/MF button in shooting mode. With that setting, the button can be used to select manual focus (MF) when the camera is using autofocus mode, or autofocus (AF) when the camera is using manual focus mode. The AF/MF button also can be assigned to another function, as discussed in Chapter 5, using the Custom Key options on screen 8 of the Camera Settings2 menu.

If the AF/MF/AEL switch lever is set to the AEL position, the button inside the switch lever functions as the AEL button. In that case, the button can be used to lock the exposure of images in shooting mode, or it can be programmed to any one of numerous other functions in shooting mode, as discussed in Chapter 5.

In playback mode, pressing this button enlarges a still image that is being displayed on the LCD or in the viewfinder. That function is assigned to this button in playback mode regardless of the position of the AF/MF/

AEL switch lever. No other function can be assigned to this button in playback mode.

The flash pop-up button, to the left of the Menu button, is used to pop up the camera's built-in flash unit so it will be available for use. In order to use that flash, you have to first pop it up with this button.

FRONT OF CAMERA

There are several items to point out on the camera's front, as shown in Figure 2-3.

The AF Illuminator/Self-timer Lamp lights up to signal the operation of the self-timer and to provide illumination so the camera can use its autofocus system in dark areas. The infrared remote sensor receives signals from a compatible remote control to operate the camera's shutter and to start and stop movie recording. Remote controls are discussed in Appendix A.

Figure 2-3. **Items on Front of Camera**

The lens mount is where you attach a compatible lens. This camera is designed to use Sony's E mount lenses, but it also can accept other lenses with an appropriate adapter, as discussed in Appendix A. The lens mounting index is a white dot that needs to be lined up with a similar white dot on the lens you are attaching, before twisting the lens into place.

The lens release button is pressed when you need to remove a lens from the camera body. The lens contacts are where the camera communicates electronically with an attached lens. The image sensor, inside the camera's body, is where the image is formed by the light that strikes the sensor. It is important to protect the sensor from dust and any other sort of contamination. The two small openings above the lens mount are where the built-in microphone receives sound to be recorded for videos.

On the left side of the camera is a small door that covers the jack for connecting an external microphone for video recording, and the Multi and HDMI ports, as seen in Figure 2-4 with the door closed and Figure 2-5 with the door open.

The top port, called the Multi Terminal port, is where you connect the micro USB cable that is supplied with the camera to charge the battery or power the camera, or to connect the a6400 to a computer to upload images.

You also can connect other accessories that use the Multi connector, such as Sony or non-Sony remote controls, as discussed in Appendix A. Using Sony's Imaging Edge software, you can connect the camera to a computer using the USB cable, and control the camera from that software, as discussed in Chapter 8. The middle port, the HDMI port, is for connecting the camera to an HDTV to view your images and videos. You also can use this port to send a "clean" HDMI signal to an external video recorder or monitor, as discussed in Chapter 9.

Figure 2-4. **Left Side of Camera with Door Over Ports Closed**

Figure 2-5. **Left Side of Camera Showing Ports**

The microphone jack accepts a standard 3.5mm stereo microphone that will record sound for video recordings.

RIGHT SIDE OF CAMERA

The one item of note on the right side of the camera, shown in Figure 2-6, is the NFC active area, designated by a fancy letter N. You can touch another device that uses near field communication, such as an Android smartphone or tablet, to that spot to activate a wireless connection to the camera, as discussed in Chapter 10. (The red Movie button is located partly on the right side and partly on the back of the camera; I discussed it earlier with other controls on the back of the camera.)

Figure 2-6. Right Side of Camera

VIEW OF CAMERA WITH LENS

In Figure 2-7, the a6400 camera is shown with a lens attached—the Sony E 18-135mm f/3.5-5.6 OSS kit lens.

Figure 2-7. Sony a6400 Camera with 18-135mm Kit Lens

This view shows the two ridged rings on the lens. The larger ring, closer to the camera's body, is the zoom ring. You turn that control to zoom the lens in and out between the 18mm (wide-angle) setting and the 135mm (telephoto) setting. The smaller ring, closer to the end of the lens, is the focus ring. You turn that control to focus the lens when the camera is using manual focus instead of autofocus. This lens has an AF/

MF switch, which switches the lens between autofocus and manual focus modes. Not all lenses have that switch, and some lenses have other controls in addition to that switch. In this view, the camera's built-in flash unit is shown in its popped-up position, ready to fire.

BOTTOM OF CAMERA

Finally, as shown in Figure 2-8, on the bottom of the camera are the tripod socket, the battery/memory card compartment, and the access lamp.

Figure 2-8. Items on Bottom of Camera

The battery/memory card compartment door has a small flap that opens to make room for the cord from an AC adapter, if you use that optional accessory, as discussed in Appendix A. The small access lamp near the hinge of the battery/memory card compartment door glows red when the camera is writing data to a memory card, indicating that you should not interrupt this activity by trying to turn the camera off or remove the memory card.

Taking Pictures in Intelligent Auto Mode

Now I'll discuss how to use these controls to start taking pictures and videos. First, here is a set of steps for taking still photos if you want to let the camera make most decisions for you. This is a good approach for quick snapshots without fiddling with too many settings. I used the Sony 18-135mm kit lens for these steps; you may have to make some adjustments if you are using a different lens.

1. Remove the lens cap. Locate the AF/MF switch on the left side of the lens and make sure it is set to AF, as shown in Figure 2-9.

Figure 2-9. AF/MF Switch on 18-135mm Lens

2. Move the on/off switch on top of the camera to the On position. The LCD screen will illuminate to show that the camera has turned on. (If you see a message about creating an image database file, that means the memory card contains some images recorded by another camera. Select Enter to dismiss the message and then proceed.)

3. Find the mode dial on top of the camera at the right, and turn it so the green AUTO label is next to the white indicator mark, as shown in Figure 2-10. This sets the camera to the Intelligent Auto shooting mode. If you see the help screen that describes the mode (called the Mode Dial Guide by Sony), shown in Figure 2-11, press the Center button twice to dismiss it. (I'll explain how to dispense with that help screen altogether in Chapter 8.)

Figure 2-10. Mode Dial at AUTO Position

Figure 2-11. Mode Dial Guide Screen for Auto Mode

4. If you're indoors or in an area with low light, press the flash pop-up button, located on the upper part of the camera's back to the left of the Menu button, to release the flash unit and cause it to pop up. If you don't do this, the flash cannot be fired.

5. Press the Menu button at the upper area on the camera's back to activate the menu system. As I discussed in Chapter 1, navigate through the menu screens by pressing the Right and Left buttons. The Camera Settings1 and Camera Settings2 menus are headed by a camera icon with a number 1 or 2; the Network menu by the globe icon; the Playback menu by the triangular Playback symbol; the Setup menu by the toolbox icon; and the My Menu option by the star icon.

6. The icon for the currently active menu system is highlighted with a color background and is outlined by a gray line. You can tell which numbered screen of that menu system is active by looking at the numbers separated by a slash mark at the upper right corner of the display, such as the numbers 1/14 shown in Figure 2-12, meaning the camera is displaying the first of 14 menu screens. You also can tell what menu screen is currently displayed by looking at the line of dots at the very bottom of the screen. One of those dots will be orange, to indicate which screen is displayed.

Figure 2-12. Screen 1 of Camera Settings1 Menu

7. When a given menu screen is selected, navigate up and down through the options on that screen by pressing the Up and Down buttons or by turning the control wheel right or left. When the orange selection bar is on the option you want, press the Center button to select that item. Then press the Up and Down buttons or turn the control wheel to highlight the value you want for that option, and press the Center button to confirm it. You can

then continue making menu settings; when you are finished with the menu system, press the Menu button to go back to the live view, so you can take pictures.

8. Using the procedure in Step 7, make the settings shown in Table 2-1 for the Camera Settings1 menu. For menu options not listed here, any setting is acceptable for now.

Suggested Settings for Camera Settings1 Menu in Intelligent Auto Mode

Menu Option	Setting
File Format (Still Images)	JPEG
JPEG Quality	Extra Fine
JPEG Image Size	L: 24M
Aspect Ratio	3:2
Color Space	sRGB
Lens Compensation	All values at Auto
Auto Mode	Intelligent Auto
Drive Mode	Single Shooting
Bracket Settings	No Setting Needed
Interval Shooting Function	Interval Shooting Off
Memory	No Setting Needed
Register Custom Shooting Setting	No Setting Needed
Focus Mode	Single-shot AF
Priority Set in AF-S	Balanced Emphasis
Priority Set in AF-C	Balanced Emphasis
Focus Area Limit	Leave all options checked
AF Illuminator	Auto
Face/Eye AF Settings	Subject Detection=Human; Right/Left Eye Select=Auto; Face Detect Frame Disp=On; Animal Eye Display=Off
AF w/Shutter	On
Pre-AF	Off
AF Area Registration	Off
Del. Reg. AF Area	No Setting Needed
AF Area Auto Clear	Off
Disp. Cont. AF Area	On
Circulation of Focus Point	Does Not Circulate
AF Micro Adjustment	AF Adjustment Setting=Off
ISO Setting	ISO Range Limit = 100-102400
Spot Metering Point	Center
Exposure Step	0.3EV
AEL w/Shutter	Auto
Exposure Std. Adjust	No Setting Needed

Menu Option	Setting
Flash Mode	Autoflash
Exposure Compensation Setting	Ambient & Flash
Red Eye Reduction	Off
Soft Skin Effect	Off
Shutter AWB Lock	Off
Focus Magnifier	No Setting Needed
Focus Magnification Time	No Limit
Initial Focus Magnification	x1.0
AF in Focus Magnification	On
MF Assist	On
Peaking Setting/Display	On
Peaking Setting/Level	Mid
Peaking Setting/Color	Yellow
Face Registration	No Setting Needed
Registered Faces Priority	Off
Smile Shutter	Off
Auto Obj. Framing	Off
Self-portrait/ -timer	On

9. If you don't want to make all of these settings, don't worry; you are likely to get usable images even if you don't adjust most of these settings at this point. I have not included any recommendations for the Camera Settings2, Setup, or other menus; the default settings should work well in Intelligent Auto mode. I will discuss all of the menu options later in the book.

10. Press the Menu button again to make the menu disappear, if it hasn't done so already.

11. Aim the camera to compose the picture. If you are using a zoom lens, use the zoom ring or other zooming mechanism to set the focal length of the lens as you want, to include more of the scene or to zoom in for an enlarged view.

12. Once the picture looks good on the display, gently press the shutter button halfway and pause in that position. You should hear a beep and see a group of green focus brackets or blocks on the LCD screen indicating that the subject will be in focus, as shown in Figure 2-13.

Figure 2-13. Green Blocks Indicating Focus is Sharp

Figure 2-14. Focus Mode Menu Options Screen

13. You also should see a green dot in the extreme lower left corner of the screen. If that green dot lights up steadily, the image is in focus; if it flashes, the camera was unable to focus. In that case, you can re-aim and see if the autofocus system does better from a different distance or angle.

14. After you have made sure the focus is sharp, push the shutter button all the way to take the picture.

VARIATIONS FROM FULLY AUTOMATIC

Although the a6400 takes care of several settings when it's set to Intelligent Auto mode, the camera still lets you make a number of adjustments to fine-tune the shooting process.

Focus

With some cameras, you have few or no options for focus settings in the most automatic shooting mode. With the a6400, you can make several focus-related settings in this mode, as long as you are using a lens with compatible autofocus capability. I will give a brief overview of focus options here, with further discussion in the chapters that discuss the various menu options and physical controls.

Focus Modes

There are five focus modes available for shooting still images with the a6400, as indicated by the five settings for the Focus Mode item on screen 5 of the Camera Settings1 menu (AF-S, AF-A, AF-C, DMF, and MF), which are shown in Figure 2-14. Those settings are single-shot autofocus, automatic autofocus, continuous autofocus, direct manual focus, and manual focus. (For movies, the only usable options are the AF-C and MF settings.)

With the AF-S setting, the camera starts to focus when you press the shutter button halfway down. At that point, it tries to achieve sharp focus on an object in the focus area. If it can focus sharply, it beeps and displays one or more green focus frames or blocks and a solid green disk. The focus stays locked at that distance as long as you hold the shutter button halfway down; you can then press the button the rest of the way down to take the picture.

With the AF-A setting, the camera combines the AF-S and AF-C settings. That is, it locks focus and keeps it locked if the subject is not moving, as is the case with the AF-S setting. However, if the subject (or the camera) starts to move, the camera operates as if it were using the AF-C setting, discussed below, and continuously adjusts the focus as necessary to keep the subject in focus.

With the AF-C setting, when you press the shutter button halfway, the camera attempts to focus on an object in the focus area, but it continues to adjust the focus as needed, if the camera or the subject moves. The camera does not lock the focus setting until you press the button all the way down to take the picture. The green dot appears in the lower left of the display when focus is achieved, but it is surrounded by curving lines to indicate that the camera is continuing to adjust focus.

With the DMF setting, the camera lets you use both the autofocus capability of single autofocus and the manual focusing capability. With this combination of two focus modes, you can press the shutter button halfway to let the camera use autofocus, and then continue to adjust focus on the lens manually. You have to keep the shutter button pressed halfway down while you adjust the focus manually. (DMF is not available with all lenses that can be used with this camera.)

Finally, with the MF setting, focusing is entirely up to you. You adjust focus manually on the lens to bring the image into sharp focus. You might use manual focus in a dark or reflective environment where the camera would have difficulty, or in a situation where the camera might not focus on the subject that is most important to you. Another use of manual focus is for extreme closeup shots, when you need to adjust the focus distance very precisely. As I will discuss in Chapter 4, you can set the camera to assist with manual focusing through several menu options.

My preference is to use the AF-S setting for single autofocus in most situations. In tricky focusing environments, such as taking macro images or pictures of the moon, I often use manual focus with the focus-assisting aids provided by the camera. Continuous autofocus is useful when you are taking pictures of subjects that are moving unpredictably, such as animals or children at play, or sports competitors.

You also can touch the screen to tell the camera where to direct its autofocus. For this feature to work, turn on the touch screen using the Touch Operation option on screen 3 of the Setup menu. Then, below that option, make sure that either the Touch Panel + Pad option or the Touch Panel Only option is turned on. On Screen 9 of the Camera Settings2 menu, set Function of Touch Operation to Touch Focus. Then, when you touch an area on the screen, the camera will place a focus frame at that point. Press the shutter button down halfway to focus at that area and press it all the way down to capture the image. I will discuss the Touch Focus option and other touch operations of the LCD monitor in Chapter 6, where I discuss the camera's physical controls.

Other Settings

There are several other items that can be adjusted in Auto mode, but not many that will have an immediate and noticeable effect on your photography. For example, you can adjust items such as the aspect ratio (shape) of your images as well as the file format, image size, and quality. Those options are important when you want to have more control over your images, but, for general picture-taking in Intelligent Auto mode, they are not critical. I have set forth recommended menu settings in Table 2-1, and I will discuss details of those options in Chapter 4.

However, there are a few menu options you might want to take advantage of when you first use the a6400 in Intelligent Auto mode, and I will discuss those briefly.

You might want to use the Soft Skin Effect option, so the camera will use processing to soften the appearance of skin tones. That option is located on screen 12 of the Camera Settings1 menu. It is effective only when face detection is turned on and a face is detected. (Face detection is automatically turned on in Auto mode.) When the effect is turned on, you can set it to Lo, Mid, or Hi using the Left and Right buttons.

Another setting you might want to try for basic shooting is the Auto Mode option, the first item on screen 3 of the Camera Settings1 menu. Normally, this option is set to Intelligent Auto. If you select the other available setting, Superior Auto, the camera will use the same settings and functions as with Intelligent Auto, but it will go one step further. In appropriate conditions, the camera will use its special multiple-shot capability. That is, if the environment is dark or lighted from behind (backlit), the camera may take a rapid burst of shots using a high ISO setting, and combine those shots internally to produce a composite image of higher quality than otherwise would be possible. I will discuss that option in Chapter 3.

Flash

You may want to use the a6400's built-in flash unit if you take pictures in dim lighting or need flash to soften shadows. In Chapter 4 I'll discuss the Flash Mode settings, Flash Compensation, and the prevention of "red-eye." In Appendix A, I'll discuss the use of external flash units.

It's important to remember that the built-in flash unit cannot pop up on its own, even if Flash Mode is set to Fill-flash, which requires the flash to fire. You have to use the flash pop-up switch on the back of the camera to release the flash before it can fire.

For this discussion, I'm assuming the camera is set to Intelligent Auto mode. In some other situations, such as with some of the Scene mode settings, the Flash Mode menu will not appear; you will see an error message if you try to use the Flash Mode menu option when the shooting screen is active.

In Intelligent Auto mode, with the flash unit popped up, go to screen 10 of the Camera Settings1 menu and select Flash Mode. Then press the Up and Down buttons or turn the control wheel to select a flash mode from that list. Press the Center button to confirm the selection.

Figure 2-15. Flash Mode Menu

The vertical menu at the left of the screen, shown in Figure 2-15, has icons for the five flash modes—a lightning bolt with the "no" sign crossing it out, for Flash Off; a lightning bolt with the word "Auto," for Autoflash; a lightning bolt alone, for Fill-flash (meaning the flash will always fire); a lightning bolt with the word "Slow," for Slow Sync; and a lightning bolt with the word "Rear," for Rear Sync. When the camera is in Intelligent Auto mode, the last two choices will be dimmed; if you highlight one of them and press the Center button, the camera will display a message saying you cannot make that selection in this shooting mode.

I discussed earlier how to set the flash unit to the Autoflash mode. If, instead of Autoflash, you choose Fill-flash, you will see the lightning bolt icon on the screen at all times (if the flash is popped up and no other setting interferes), and the flash will fire regardless of whether the camera's exposure system believes flash is needed. You can use this setting when you are certain that you want the flash to fire, such as in a dimly lighted room. This setting also can be useful in some outdoor settings, even when the sun is shining, such as when you need to reduce the shadows on your subject's face. There is an illustration of the use of Fill-flash in Figure 4-78 in Chapter 4.

With some settings, such as continuous shooting, the flash will fire if you set it to do so, but the use of flash will limit the use of the other setting. In other words, instead of doing rapid continuous shooting, the camera will take multiple images but at a reduced rate, because the flash cannot recycle fast enough to fire repeatedly in rapid succession. In some situations, such as with

the Night Scene setting of Scene mode, the Flash Mode menu option cannot be selected; that line will be dimmed on the menu screen.

If you set the mode dial to P, for Program mode, and then use the menu system to select a flash mode, you will see the same five options for Flash Mode on the menu, but this time the Autoflash option will be dimmed because that selection is available only in the more automatic modes. In addition, the Flash Off option will be dimmed; that option is available only in Auto mode and with some settings in Scene mode. Of course, if you don't want the flash to fire, you can just leave the flash unit retracted.

In summary, when using Intelligent Auto mode, if you don't want the flash to fire because you are in a museum or similar location, you can select the Flash Off mode. If you want to leave the decision whether to use flash up to the camera, you can select Autoflash mode. If you want to make sure the flash will fire no matter what, you can select Fill-flash mode. In Chapter 4, I'll explain the other Flash Mode options—Slow Sync and Rear Sync—and I'll discuss other flash-related topics.

Drive Mode: Self-Timer and Continuous Shooting

The Drive Mode menu option provides more adjustments you may want to make when using Intelligent Auto mode. Select this menu item from screen 3 of the Camera Settings1 menu, and the camera will display a vertical menu for Drive Mode, as shown in Figure 2-16. You also can select this menu by pressing the Left button on the control wheel, unless it has been reset to a different function using the Custom Key (Still Images) menu option.

Figure 2-16. Drive Mode Menu

You navigate through the options on this menu by pressing the Up and Down buttons or by turning the control wheel.

I will discuss the Drive Mode options more fully in Chapter 4. For now, you should be aware of a few of the options. (I will skip some others.) If you select the top option, represented by a single rectangular frame, the camera is set for single shooting mode; when you press the shutter button, a single image is captured. With the second option, whose icon looks like a stack of images, the camera is set for continuous shooting, in which it takes a rapid burst of images while you hold down the shutter button. Use the Left and Right buttons or turn the control dial to choose Hi+, Hi, Mid, or Lo for the speed of shooting. With the Hi+ setting, the camera can shoot up to 11 frames per second.

If you choose the third option, whose icon is a dial with a number beside it, the camera uses the self-timer. Use the Left and Right buttons or control dial to choose two, five, or ten seconds for the timer delay and press the Center button to confirm. Then, when you press the shutter button, the shutter will be triggered after the specified number of seconds.

The ten-second delay is useful when you need to place the camera on a tripod and join a group photo; the two-second or five-second delay is useful when you want to make sure the camera is not jiggled by the action of pressing the shutter button. This option helps when you are taking a picture for which focusing is critical and you need to avoid shaking the camera, such as an extreme closeup or a time exposure. I will discuss the use of the self-timer and other Drive Mode options in more detail in Chapter 4.

Overview of Movie Recording

Now I'll discuss recording a short movie sequence with the a6400. Once the camera is turned on, turn the mode dial to select the green AUTO icon, for Intelligent Auto mode. There is a special Movie mode setting marked by the movie film icon on the mode dial, but you don't have to use that mode for shooting movies; I'll discuss the use of that option and other details about video recording in Chapter 9.

On the first screen of the Camera Settings2 menu, highlight File Format and press the Center button to go to the submenu with three choices for the format of movie recording. For now, be sure the third option, AVCHD, is highlighted, as shown in Figure 2-17; that format provides high quality for your videos without

requiring a special memory card. (As discussed in Chapter 1, if you select XAVC S 4K or XAVC S HD for the movie format, you have to use a memory card in Speed Class 10 or greater.)

Figure 2-17. AVCHD Highlighted for File Format

Go to screen 5 of the Camera Settings1 menu, to the Focus Mode item. Select AF-S for single autofocus, AF-A for automatic autofocus, AF-C for continuous autofocus, or DMF for direct manual focus. With any of those settings, the camera will use continuous autofocus for recording movies.

For the rest of the settings, I will provide a table like the one included earlier in this chapter for shooting still images. The settings shown in Table 2-2 are standard ones for shooting good-quality movies. All of these settings are found on the Camera Settings2 menu.

Table 2-1.   **Suggested Camera Settings2 Menu Settings for Movies in Intelligent Auto Mode**

FILE FORMAT	AVCHD
RECORD SETTING	60i 24M (FX)
S & Q SETTINGS	NO SETTING NEEDED
AF DRIVE SPEED	NORMAL
AF TRACKING SENSITIVITY	STANDARD
AUTO SLOW SHUTTER	ON
INITIAL FOCUS MAGNIFICATION	x1.0
AUDIO RECORDING	ON
AUDIO LEVEL DISPLAY	ON
WIND NOISE REDUCTION	OFF
MARKER DISPLAY	OFF
MARKER SETTINGS	NO SETTING NEEDED
MOVIE W/ SHUTTER	OFF
STEADYSHOT	ON
ZOOM	NO SETTING NEEDED
ZOOM SETTING	OPTICAL ZOOM ONLY
FINDER/MONITOR	AUTO

Zebra Setting	Off Unless Needed
Grid Line	Off Unless Needed
Exposure Settings Guide	Off Unless Needed
Function of Touch Operation	Touch Focus
Movie Button	Always
Audio Signals	On

Settings not listed above can be ignored for present purposes, or set as you want. There are some other settings you can make for still images on the Camera Settings1 menu that will affect movie recording; I will discuss that topic in Chapter 9. You can leave the other items set as they were for shooting still images, as listed in Table 2-1.

After making these settings, aim the camera at your subject, and when you are ready to start recording, press and release the red Movie button at the right edge of the camera's back. (If you see an error message, go to screen 9 of the Camera Settings2 menu, and make sure the Movie Button option is set to Always.)

The screen will display a red REC icon in the lower left corner of the display, above a counter showing the elapsed time in the recording, as shown in Figure 2-18.

Figure 2-18. **Shooting Screen During Video Recording**

The camera will also display recording-level indicators to show the volume of sound being recorded for channel 1 and channel 2, if you have set all of the menu options as listed above. Hold the camera as steady as possible (or use a tripod), and pan it (move it side to side) smoothly if you need to. The camera will keep shooting until you press the red Movie button again to stop the recording, or until the camera stops on its own because of overheating. According to Sony, the camera should record in any mode for at least 30 minutes, but that limit is not pre-determined; it depends on factors such as the environment you are working in and the format you are using.

The camera will automatically adjust exposure as lighting conditions change. You can zoom the lens in and out as needed, but you should do so sparingly if at all, to avoid distracting the audience and to avoid recording sounds of zooming the lens on the sound track. If the Touch Operation features are turned on through screen 3 of the Setup menu and the camera is set for autofocus and Touch Focus, you can touch the screen where you want the camera to direct its focus. When you are finished recording, press the Movie button again, and the camera will save the footage.

Those are the basics for recording video clips with the a6400. I'll discuss movie options in more detail in Chapter 9.

Viewing Pictures

Before I cover more advanced settings for taking still pictures and movies, as well as other matters of interest, I will discuss the basics of viewing your images in the camera.

REVIEW WHILE IN SHOOTING MODE

Each time you take a still picture, the image will show up on the LCD screen (or in the viewfinder) for a short time, if you have the Auto Review option on screen 7 of the Camera Settings2 menu set to turn on this function. I'll discuss the details of that setting in Chapter 5. By default, the image will stay on the screen for two seconds after you take a new picture. If you prefer, you can set that display to last for five or ten seconds, or to be off altogether.

REVIEWING IMAGES IN PLAYBACK MODE

To review images taken previously, you enter playback mode by pressing the Playback button—the one with the small triangle icon to the lower left of the control wheel. To view all still images and movies for a particular date, go to screen 3 of the Playback menu and set the View Mode option to Date View. If you prefer, you can set View Mode to show only stills, only AVCHD movies, only XAVC S HD movies, or only XAVC S 4K movies.

Once you choose a viewing option, you can scroll through recorded images and movies by pressing the Left and Right buttons or by turning the control wheel or control dial. Hold down the Left or Right button to move more quickly through the images. You can enlarge the view of any still image by pressing the AF/MF/AEL button, located on the back of the camera under the mode dial, and you can scroll around in the enlarged image using the four direction buttons. You also can enlarge an image by selecting the Enlarge Image option on screen 2 of the Playback menu.

In addition, you can enlarge an image by tapping quickly twice on the LCD screen, if the touch screen features of the LCD are enabled through the Touch Operation item on screen 3 of the Setup menu. After double-tapping the screen, you can scroll the enlarged image around with your fingers, and you can return it to normal size by double-tapping again.

If you press the Center button or the Menu button, an enlarged image will return to normal size. If you press the Down button when an image is normal-sized, you will see an index screen with a number of thumbnail images (either 12 or 30, depending on a Playback menu option). If you move the highlight to the far left of the index screen and press the Center button, the camera will display a calendar screen, with thumbnail images on any date for which images or videos are present on the memory card. You can select images from the index and calendar screens by pressing the Center button on a highlighted thumbnail image. I'll discuss other playback options in Chapter 7.

Playing Movies

To play movies, move through the files by the methods described above until you find the movie you want to play. You should see a triangular playback icon inside a circle, as shown in Figure 2-19.

Figure 2-19. Movie Ready to Play in Camera

Press the Center button to start the movie playing. Then, as seen in Figure 2-20, you will see icons at the bottom of the screen for the controls you can use, including the Center button to pause and resume play.

Figure 2-20. Initial Movie Playback Control Icons

(If you don't see the controls, press the Display button until they appear.) You also can press the Down button to bring up a more detailed set of controls on the screen, as shown in Figure 2-21.

Figure 2-21. Movie Playback Control Icons from Control Panel

To change the volume, pause the movie and press the Down button to bring up the detailed controls; then navigate to the speaker icon, next to last at the right of those controls, and press the Center button to select it. Then use the control wheel, the control dial, or the Right and Left buttons to adjust the volume. To exit from playing the movie, press the Playback button. I'll discuss other movie playback options in Chapter 9.

If you want to play movies on a computer or edit them with video-editing software, you can use the PlayMemories Home software that is provided through the Sony web site. You also can use any program that can deal with AVCHD and XAVC S video files, such as Adobe Premiere Elements, Adobe Premiere Pro, Final Cut Express, Final Cut Pro, iMovie, or Windows Movies and TV, depending on what type of computer you have.

Chapter 3: Shooting Modes for Still Images

Until now, I have discussed the basics of setting up the camera for quick shots, using Intelligent Auto mode to take pictures with settings controlled mostly by the camera's automation. As with other advanced cameras, though, with the Sony a6400 there is a large range of other options available. To explain this broad range of features, I need to discuss shooting modes and the Camera Settings1 and Camera Settings2 menu options. In this chapter, I'll discuss the shooting modes; in Chapters 4 and 5, I'll discuss the Camera Settings1 and Camera Settings 2 menus.

In order to capture still images, you need to select one of the shooting modes available on the mode dial: Intelligent Auto, Program Auto, Aperture Priority, Shutter Priority, Manual exposure, Memory Recall, Sweep Panorama, or Scene Selection. (The other two modes on the dial are for movies, which I will discuss in Chapter 9.) So far, I have discussed primarily the Intelligent Auto mode. Now I will discuss the others, after some review of the first one.

Intelligent Auto Mode

I've already discussed this shooting mode in some detail. This is a good choice if you need to take a quick shot and don't have much time to fuss with settings such as ISO, White Balance, aperture, shutter speed, or focus. It's also a good mode to select when you hand the camera to someone else to take a photo of you and your companions. For example, I used Intelligent Auto mode for a quick shot of a man examining his possessions in a public park, as seen in Figure 3-1.

To make this setting, turn the mode dial to the green AUTO label, as shown in Figure 3-2. When you select this mode, the camera makes several decisions for you and limits your options in some ways. The camera will select the shutter speed, aperture, and ISO setting, along with several other settings over which you will have no control.

Figure 3-1. Intelligent Auto Mode Example

Figure 3-2. Mode Dial at AUTO Position

For example, you can't set White Balance to any value other than Auto, and you can't choose a metering method or use exposure bracketing. You can, however, use quite a few features, as discussed in Chapter 2, including Flash Mode, some settings of Drive Mode, Focus Mode, and others. You also can use sophisticated options such as the Raw format, which I will discuss in Chapter 4 when I discuss the items on the Camera Settings1 menu.

One interesting aspect of this mode is that the camera tries to figure out what sort of subject or scene you are shooting. Some of the subjects the camera will attempt to detect are Infant, Portrait, Night Portrait, Night Scene, Landscape, Backlight, Low Light, and Macro. It also will try to detect certain conditions, such as whether a tripod is in use, and it will display appropriate icons for those situations. So, if you see different icons when you aim at various subjects in this shooting mode, that means the camera is evaluating the scene for factors such as brightness, backlighting, the presence of human subjects, and the like, so it can use the best possible settings for the situation.

For Figure 3-3, the camera evaluated a scene with a human face and appropriately used its Portrait setting. A Portrait icon is in the upper-left corner of the screen.

Figure 3-4 shows the use of automatic scene recognition for a small bell located closer to the lens. The camera interpreted the scene as a macro, or closeup shot, and switched automatically into macro mode, indicated by the flower icon.

Figure 3-3. Scene Recognition - Portrait

Figure 3-4. Scene Recognition - Macro

Of course, scene recognition depends on the camera's programming, which may not interpret every scene the same way that you would. If that becomes a problem, you may want to make individual settings using one of the more advanced shooting modes, such as Program, Aperture Priority, Shutter Priority, or Manual. Or, you can turn the mode dial to the SCN position and select a scene setting that better fits the current situation.

SUPERIOR AUTO MODE

With the a6400, Sony has included a second automatic mode, but has not given it a separate position on the mode dial. Instead, you have to go to screen 3 of the Camera Settings1 menu and select the Auto Mode menu option. When you select that item, you will see a screen for choosing Intelligent Auto or Superior Auto. If you select the lower icon for Superior Auto, as shown in Figure 3-5, the camera will be set to that mode.

Figure 3-5. Superior Auto Mode Icon Highlighted on Menu

Superior Auto mode includes all features of Intelligent Auto mode, but adds an extra function. In Superior Auto mode, as with Intelligent Auto mode, the camera uses its scene recognition capability to try to determine what subject matter or conditions are present, such as a portrait, a dimly lit scene, and the like.

For many scenes, the camera will function just as it does in Intelligent Auto mode. However, in a few specific situations, when lighting is dim, the camera takes a different approach: It captures a rapid burst of shots and combines them internally into a single composite image.

The camera is likely to raise the ISO setting to a fairly high level in order to permit the use of a fast enough shutter speed to capture the scene clearly. The use of this high ISO setting introduces visual "noise" into the image. By taking multiple shots and combining them, the camera averages out and cancels some of the noise, increasing the quality of the final image.

One problem with this system is that you have no control over when the camera decides to use this burst shooting technique. The camera will automatically use this approach when it detects a scene with dim lighting or backlighting. In those cases, the a6400 fires a burst of shots. You will hear the rapid firing, then it will take longer than usual for the camera to process the multiple shots into a single composite image; you will likely see a message saying "Processing" on a black screen for several seconds. When the camera is using this feature, you will see a message saying the camera is taking three shots, as shown in Figure 3-6.

Figure 3-6. Message When Camera Using Multi-shot Feature in Superior Auto Mode

The camera will not use this multiple-shot feature when File Format (Still Images) is set to Raw or Raw & JPEG.

I have not found much advantage in using the Superior Auto setting. However, there may be cases when the burst-shooting feature will improve image quality, so it is not a bad idea to use Superior Auto mode when shooting in low light or backlit conditions. As a general rule, though, I prefer to use a mode such as Program, discussed below, and set my own values for items such as DRO, HDR, ISO, and Metering Mode.

If you want to use Superior Auto mode, there is an easier way to get access to it than selecting Auto Mode from screen 3 of the Camera Settings1 menu. Instead, use the Function Menu Settings option on screen 8 of the Camera Settings2 menu, and set one of the 12 settings for the Function menu to Shoot Mode. Then, whenever you turn the mode dial to the AUTO setting, just press the Function button when the shooting screen is displayed, and you will see on the Function menu the icon for the current setting for Auto Mode, either Intelligent Auto or Superior Auto. At this point, move the highlight block to that icon using the direction buttons, and, when the icon is highlighted, turn the control wheel to cycle through the choices. When your new selection (either Intelligent Auto or Superior Auto) is highlighted, press the Function button to exit to shooting mode.

If the camera has used the multiple-shot feature of Superior Auto mode, you can extract single images from the burst of shots using the Superior Auto Image Extraction menu option, discussed in Chapter 4.

Program Mode

Choose this mode by turning the mode dial to the P setting, as shown in Figure 3-7.

Figure 3-7. Mode Dial at Program Position

Program mode (sometimes called Program Auto mode) lets you control many of the settings available with the a6400, apart from shutter speed and aperture, which the camera chooses on its own. You still can adjust the camera's automatic exposure to a fair extent by using exposure compensation and bracketing, as discussed in Chapter 4, and Program Shift, discussed later in this section. You don't have to make a lot of decisions if you don't want to, because the camera will make reasonable choices for you as defaults.

The camera can choose a shutter speed as long as 30 seconds or as short as 1/4000 second.

The Program Shift function, which is available only in Program mode, works as follows. Once you have aimed the camera at your subject, the camera displays its chosen settings for shutter speed and aperture in the lower left corner of the screen. At that point, you can turn the control dial or the control wheel, and the values for shutter speed and aperture will change, if possible under current conditions, to select different values for both settings while keeping the same overall exposure of the scene.

With this option, the camera "shifts" the original exposure to your choice of any of the matched pairs that appear as you turn the wheel or dial. For example, if the original exposure was f/2.8 at 1/30 second, you may see equivalent pairs of f/3.2 at 1/25, f/3.5 at 1/20, and f/4.0 at 1/15, among others. When Program Shift is in effect, the P icon in the upper left corner of the screen will have an asterisk to its right, as shown in Figure 3-8.

To cancel Program Shift, turn the control wheel or the control dial until the original settings are in effect or move the mode dial to another mode, then back to

Program. You also can cancel by pressing the flash pop-up button to raise the flash; Program Shift cannot function with flash in use.

Figure 3-8. Asterisk Indicating Program Shift in Use

Program Shift is useful if you want a slightly faster shutter speed to stop action or a wider aperture to blur the background, or you might have some other creative reason. This option lets the camera quickly evaluate the exposure, but gives you the option to tweak the shutter speed and aperture to suit your current needs.

Of course, if you need to use a specific shutter speed or aperture, you probably are better off using Aperture Priority, Shutter Priority, or Manual exposure mode. However, having Program Shift available is useful when you're taking pictures quickly using Program mode, and you want a fast way to tweak the settings somewhat.

Another important aspect of Program mode is that it expands the choices available through the Camera Settings1 menu, which controls many of the camera's settings that directly affect your images. You will be able to make choices involving ISO sensitivity, metering mode, DRO/HDR, Creative Style, Picture Effect, and others that are not available in the Auto modes. I won't discuss those settings here; if you want to explore that topic, see the discussion of the Camera Settings1 menu in Chapter 4 for information about the many selections that are available.

Aperture Priority Mode

You select Aperture Priority shooting mode by turning the mode dial to the A setting, as shown in Figure 3-9.

In this mode, you select the aperture and the camera chooses a shutter speed for proper exposure. With this mode, you can exercise control over depth of field of your shots. When you select a narrow aperture, such

as f/16.0, the depth of field will be broad, with the result that more items will appear to be in sharp focus at varying distances from the lens. On the other hand, with a wider aperture, such as f/2.8, the depth of field will be relatively shallow, and you may be able to keep only one subject in sharp focus.

Figure 3-9. Mode Dial at Aperture Priority Position

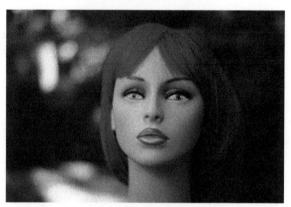

Figure 3-10. Aperture Set to f/1.8

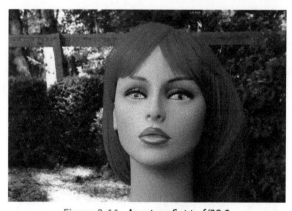

Figure 3-11. Aperture Set to f/22.0

In Figures 3-10 and 3-11, I took two pictures using the Sony DT 50mm f/1.8 lens, which is mounted to the a6400 using Sony's Mount Adaptor because it is an A-mount lens. The settings were the same except for aperture values. For Figure 3-10, I set the aperture to f/1.8, the widest possible for this lens. With this setting, because the depth of field at this aperture was quite shallow, the items in the background are fairly blurry. I took Figure 3-11 with the aperture set to f/22.0, the narrowest possible setting, resulting in a broader depth of field, making the background appear considerably sharper.

These photos illustrate the effects of varying aperture by setting it wide (low numbers) to blur the background or narrow (high numbers) to enjoy a broad depth of field and keep subjects at varying distances in sharp focus. A need for shallow depth of field arises often in the case of outdoor portraits or photographs of subjects such as flowers. If you can achieve a shallow depth of field by using a wide aperture, you can keep the subject in sharp focus but leave the background blurry, as in Figure 3-10.

This effect is sometimes called "bokeh," a Japanese term for a pleasing blurriness of the background. In this situation, the fuzzy background can be an asset, minimizing distraction from unwanted objects and highlighting the sharply focused portrait of the subject.

Here is the procedure for using this shooting mode. With the mode dial at the A setting, use the control wheel or the control dial to select the aperture value. The available settings depend on the lens you are using and the setting of the Exposure Step option on screen 8 of the Camera Settings1 menu. For example, using the Sony 18-135mm kit lens with Exposure Step set to 0.5EV, the available settings are f/3.5, f/4.0, f/4.5, f/5.6, f/6.7, f/8.0, f/9.5, f/11.0, f/13.0, f/16.0, f/19.0, and f/22.0.

When you set the aperture, as seen in Figure 3-12, the f-stop (f/5.6 in this case) will appear at the bottom of the screen next to the shutter speed. If you turn on the Exposure Settings Guide option on screen 6 of the Camera Settings2 menu, you will see a graphic display of the aperture values on a moving band as you turn the control wheel, as shown in Figure 3-13.

Figure 3-12. Normal Display of Aperture Setting

Figure 3-13. Graphic Display of Aperture Setting

The camera will select a shutter speed that will result in a normal exposure given the aperture you have set. The camera can choose shutter speeds from 30 seconds to 1/4000 second.

Although in most cases the camera will be able to select a corresponding shutter speed that results in a normal exposure, there may be times when this is not possible. For example, if you are taking pictures in a very bright location with the aperture set to f/3.5, the camera may not be able to set a shutter speed fast enough to yield a normal exposure. In that case, the fastest possible shutter speed will flash on the display to show that a normal exposure cannot be made using the chosen aperture. The camera will let you take the picture, but it may be too bright to be usable.

Similarly, if conditions are too dark for a good exposure at the aperture you have selected, the slowest possible shutter speed (30", meaning 30 seconds) will flash.

If conditions are too bright or dark for a good exposure, the camera's display may become bright or dark, giving you notice of the problem. This will happen if the Live View Display item on screen 7 of the Camera Settings2 menu is set to Setting Effect On. If that option is set to Setting Effect Off, the display will remain at normal brightness, even if the exposure settings would result in an excessively bright or dark image. I will discuss that menu option in Chapter 5.

One more note on Aperture Priority mode: Depending on the lens you are using, not all apertures may be available at all times. For example, with the 18-135mm kit lens, the widest aperture, f/3.5, is available only when the lens is zoomed out to its wide-angle setting. As soon as the lens is zoomed in slightly beyond the 18mm focal length, the widest aperture available is f/4.0. At the highest zoom levels, the widest aperture available is f/5.6.

Some zoom lenses, however, are constant-aperture lenses, which maintain their widest aperture at all zoom levels. For example, the Sony E 10-18mm f/4 OSS lens provides a constant aperture of f/4.0 throughout its zoom range. Lenses of that sort tend to be fairly expensive, but it may be worthwhile to have the constant aperture, so you can blur the background and shoot in relatively dim light. Of course, you also may use a lens with a fixed focal length, such as 35mm or 50mm, in which case the aperture will be constant because the lens does not zoom.

Shutter Priority Mode

In Shutter Priority mode, you choose the shutter speed you want and the camera will set the corresponding aperture to achieve a proper exposure of the image.

Figure 3-14. Mode Dial at Shutter Priority Position

In this mode, designated by the S position on the mode dial, as shown in Figure 3-14, you can set the shutter to be open for a time ranging from 30 seconds to 1/4000 of a second.

If you are photographing fast action, such as a bird in flight, a baseball swing, or a hurdles race at a track meet, and you want to freeze motion with a minimum of blur, you should select a fast shutter speed, such as 1/2000 of a second. For Figure 3-15 and Figure 3-16, I used different shutter speeds for images of a group of colored beads as I poured them into a clear plastic pitcher.

In Figure 3-15, I used a shutter speed setting of 1/2000 second. In this image, you can see the individual beads clearly. In Figure 3-16, with the shutter speed set to 1/60 second, the beads blur together into what looks almost like a continuous stream.

You select this shooting mode by turning the mode dial to the S indicator, as shown in Figure 3-14. Then you

select the shutter speed by turning the control wheel or the control dial.

Figure 3-15. Shutter Speed Set to 1/2000 Second

Figure 3-16. Shutter Speed Set to 1/60 Second

If you turn on the Exposure Settings Guide option on screen 6 of the Camera Settings2 menu, you will see a graphic display of the shutter speeds on a moving band as you turn the control wheel or dial, similar to the display of aperture settings, shown earlier in Figure 3-13.

Although the a6400 uses the letter "S" to stand for Shutter Priority on the mode dial and to designate this mode on the live view screen, it uses the notation "Tv" on the Shooting mode display in Shutter Priority mode, next to the control dial and control wheel icons, as shown in Figure 3-17. Tv stands for time value, a term often used for shutter speed.

As you cycle through various shutter speeds, the camera will select the appropriate aperture to achieve a normal exposure, if possible. As I discussed in connection with Aperture Priority mode, if you set a shutter speed for which the camera cannot select an aperture that will yield a good exposure, the aperture reading at the bottom of the display will flash. The flashing aperture means that proper exposure at the selected shutter speed is not possible at any available aperture, according to the camera's calculations.

Figure 3-17. Tv Label for Shutter Speed on Shooting Screen

For example, if you set the shutter speed to 1/320 second in a fairly dark indoor environment, the aperture number (which will be the widest setting for the lens in use, if the lens is at its wide-angle setting) may flash, indicating that proper exposure is not possible. As I discussed for Aperture Priority mode, you can still take the picture if you want to, though it may not be usable. A similar situation may take place if you select a slow shutter speed (such as four seconds) in a relatively bright location. (This situation is less likely to happen in Aperture Priority mode, because of the wide range of shutter speeds the camera can use to achieve a good exposure.)

If the current settings in this mode would result in an image that is excessively dark or bright, the LCD display will grow dark or bright to show that effect, but only if the Live View Display option on screen 7 of the Camera Settings2 menu is set to Setting Effect On. If that option is set to Setting Effect Off, the display will show a normal image even in unusually bright or dark conditions.

Manual Exposure Mode

The technique for using this mode is similar to what I discussed for the Aperture Priority and Shutter Priority modes. To control exposure manually, set the mode dial to the M indicator, as shown in Figure 3-18. You now have to control both shutter speed and aperture by setting them yourself. To set the aperture, turn the control dial; to set the shutter speed, turn the control wheel. (You can reverse the roles of the dial and wheel using the Dial/Wheel Setup option on screen 8 of the Camera Settings2 menu.)

The values you set will appear at the bottom of the display, as shown in Figure 3-19. You can turn on the Exposure Settings Guide option on screen 6 of the Camera Settings2 menu to display two moving bands showing the aperture and shutter speed as they are adjusted.

As you adjust shutter speed and aperture, a third value, to the right of the aperture, also may change. That value is a positive, negative, or zero number. The meaning of the number is different depending on the current ISO setting.

Figure 3-18. Mode Dial at Manual Position

Figure 3-19. Aperture and Shutter Speed Values in Manual Mode

In Chapter 4, I'll provide more details about the ISO setting, which controls how sensitive the camera's sensor is to light. With a higher ISO value, the sensor is more sensitive and the image is exposed more quickly, so the shutter speed can be faster or the aperture more narrow, or both.

Figure 3-20. ISO Menu

To set the ISO value, from the shooting screen, press the Right button to bring up the ISO menu, as shown in Figure 3-20, and scroll through the selections using the Up and Down buttons or by turning the control wheel or the control dial. (You also can bring up the ISO menu through the ISO Setting item on screen 8 of the Camera Settings1 menu.)

Choose a low number like 100 to maximize image quality when there is plenty of light; use a higher number in dim light. Higher ISO settings are likely to cause visual "noise," or graininess, in your images. Generally speaking, you should try to set ISO no higher than 800 to ensure the highest image quality.

If the ISO value is set to a specific number, such as 125, 200, or 1000, then, in Manual exposure mode, the icon at the bottom center of the display is a box containing the letters "M.M.," which stand for "metered manual," as shown in Figure 3-19.

In this situation, the number next to the M.M. icon represents any deviation from what the camera's metering system considers to be a normal exposure. So, even though you are setting the exposure manually, the camera will still let you know whether the selected aperture and shutter speed will produce a standard exposure.

If the aperture, shutter speed, and ISO values you have selected will result in a darker exposure than normal, the M.M. value will be negative, and vice-versa. This value can vary only by +2.0 or -2.0 EV (exposure value) units; after that, the value will flash, meaning the camera considers the exposure excessively abnormal.

Of course, you can ignore the M.M. indicator; it is there only to give you an idea of how the camera would meter the scene. You very well may want part or all of the scene to be darker or lighter than the metering would indicate to be "correct."

As with the Aperture Priority and Shutter Priority modes, the camera's display will become unusually bright or dim to indicate that current settings would result in an abnormal exposure, but only when the Live View Display option on screen 7 of the Camera Settings2 menu is set to Setting Effect On.

If, instead of a specific value, you have set ISO to Auto ISO, the icon at the bottom center of the screen

changes. In this situation, the camera displays the exposure compensation icon, which contains a plus and minus sign, as shown in Figure 3-21. The reason for this change is that, when you use Auto ISO in Manual exposure mode, the camera can likely produce a normal exposure by adjusting the ISO. There is no need to display the M.M. value, which shows deviation from a normal exposure.

Instead, when ISO is set to Auto ISO, the camera lets you adjust exposure compensation, so you can set the exposure to be darker or brighter than the camera's autoexposure system would produce.

Figure 3-21. Shooting Screen in Manual Mode Using Auto ISO

To set exposure compensation in Manual mode, press the Down button and adjust exposure compensation using the scale that appears. Or, if you prefer, you can assign exposure compensation to the C1, C2, Center, Left, Right, AF/MF, AEL, or Focus Hold button (if the lens you are using has a Focus Hold button). You make that assignment using the Custom Key (Still Images) option on screen 8 of the Camera Settings2 menu, as discussed in Chapter 5. You also can use the Function menu to adjust exposure compensation, if that option has been included in that menu, as also discussed in Chapter 5, or you can adjust it with the Exposure Compensation item on screen 8 of the Camera Settings1 menu.

With Manual exposure mode, the settings for aperture and shutter speed are independent of each other. When you change one, the other one stays unchanged until you adjust it manually. But the effect of this system is different depending on whether you have selected a specific value for ISO as opposed to Auto ISO.

If you select a numerical value for ISO, which can range from 100 to 102400, the camera leaves the creative decision about exposure entirely up to you, even if the resulting photograph would be washed out by excessive exposure or underexposed to the point of near-blackness.

However, if you select Auto ISO for the ISO setting, then, as discussed above, the camera will adjust the ISO to achieve a normal exposure if possible. In this case, Manual exposure mode becomes like a different shooting mode altogether. You might call this the "aperture and shutter speed priority mode," because you are able to set both aperture and shutter speed but still have the camera adjust exposure automatically by changing the ISO value.

The ability to use Auto ISO in Manual exposure mode is very useful. For example, suppose you are taking photographs of a craftsman using tools in a dimly lighted area. You may want to use a narrow aperture such as f/8.0 to achieve a broad depth of field and keep the tools and other items in focus, but you also may want to use a fast shutter speed, such as 1/250 second, to freeze action. If you use Aperture Priority mode, the camera will choose the shutter speed; with Shutter Priority mode, the camera will choose the aperture, and with Program mode, the camera will choose both values. Only by using Manual exposure mode with Auto ISO can you choose both aperture and shutter speed and still have the camera find a good exposure setting automatically.

Even with the ability to use Auto ISO, though, there may be situations in which the camera cannot produce a normal exposure. This could happen if you have limited the scope of the Auto ISO setting by setting a narrow range between the Minimum and Maximum settings for Auto ISO. It also could happen if you have chosen extreme settings for aperture and shutter speed, such as 1/500 second at f/16.0 in dark conditions. In such situations, the ISO setting label and the exposure compensation value at the bottom of the display will flash, indicating that a normal exposure cannot be achieved with these settings.

The range of shutter speeds in Manual mode is the same as for Shutter Priority mode: 1/4000 second to 30 seconds, with one important addition. In Manual exposure mode, you can set the shutter speed to the Bulb setting, just beyond the 30-second mark, as shown in Figure 3-22. With the Bulb setting, you have to press and hold the shutter button to keep the shutter open. You can use this setting to take photos in dark conditions by holding the shutter open for a minute or more.

Figure 3-22. Bulb Setting for Shutter Speed in Manual Mode

One problem is that it is hard to avoid jiggling the camera, causing image blur, even if the camera is on a tripod. In Appendix A, I discuss using a remote control to trigger the camera. After the exposure ends, the camera will process the image for the same length of time as the exposure, to reduce the noise caused by long exposures. You will not be able to take another shot while this processing continues. (You can disable this setting with the Long Exposure Noise Reduction option on screen 2 of the Camera Settings1 menu.)

The Bulb setting is not available when some other options are in use, including Smile Shutter, Auto HDR, the HDR Painting or Rich-tone Monochrome setting for Picture Effect, the Multi Frame Noise Reduction setting for ISO, the Drive Mode settings of continuous shooting, continuous self-timer, or continuous bracketing, or Silent Shooting.

Another feature available in the Manual shooting mode is Manual Shift, which is similar to Program Shift, discussed earlier. To use Manual Shift, you first have to assign one of the control buttons (Custom 1, Custom 2, Center, AF/MF, AEL, or Focus Hold) to the AEL (autoexposure lock) Hold or AEL Toggle function using the Custom Key (Still Images) option on screen 8 of the Camera Settings2 menu, as discussed in Chapter 5. (The Left, Right, or Down button can be assigned to AEL Toggle, but not to AEL Hold.)

Then, after making your aperture and shutter speed settings, change the aperture setting while pressing the button assigned to the AEL function. (If you selected AEL Toggle, you don't have to hold down the button; just press it and release it.)

When you do this, the camera will make new settings with equivalent exposure, if possible. For example, if the original settings were f/3.5 at 1/160 second, when you select Manual Shift and change the aperture to f/3.2, the camera will reset the shutter speed to 1/200 second, maintaining the original exposure. In this way, you can tweak your settings to favor a particular shutter speed or aperture without affecting the overall exposure. An asterisk will appear in the lower right corner of the display while you activate the button that controls AEL.

I use Manual exposure mode often, for various purposes. One use is to take images at different exposures to combine into a composite HDR (high dynamic range) image. I will discuss that technique in Chapter 4.

I also use Manual mode when using a third-party external flash, as discussed in Appendix A. In that case, the flash does not interact with the camera's autoexposure system, so I need to set the exposure manually. Manual mode also is useful for some special types of photography, such as making silhouettes, as shown in Figure 3-23.

Figure 3-23. Silhouette Captured Using Manual Mode

Scene Mode

Scene mode, represented by the SCN setting on the mode dial, as shown in Figure 3-24, is different from the other shooting modes I have discussed. With this mode, you are telling the camera what sort of environment the picture is being taken in and what type of image you are looking for, and you are letting the camera make the decisions as to what settings to use to produce that result.

With most of the Scene mode settings, you cannot select many options that are available in Program, Aperture Priority, Shutter Priority, and Manual exposure mode, such as ISO, DRO, Creative Style, Picture Effect, Metering Mode, and White Balance.

There also are some menu settings and control options that are available with certain scene settings but not others, as discussed later in this chapter.

Figure 3-24. Mode Dial at Scene Position

Although some photographers may not like Scene mode because it takes creative decisions away from them, I find it useful in various situations. You don't have to use these scene types only for their labeled purposes; you may find that some of them offer a group of settings that is well suited for shooting scenarios that you regularly encounter. I'll discuss how Scene mode works, and you can decide for yourself whether you might take advantage of it on occasion.

Select Scene mode by turning the mode dial to the SCN indicator, as in Figure 3-24. Now, unless you want to use the setting that is already in place, you need to select from the list of nine scene options. There are several ways to do this, depending on current settings. If the Mode Dial Guide is turned on through screen 2 of the Setup menu, then, whenever you turn the mode dial to the SCN setting and press the Center button, the Scene Selection menu, shown in Figure 3-25, will appear.

Figure 3-25. Scene Selection Menu

If the Mode Dial Guide is not in use, or if the camera is already set to Scene mode, you can go to screen 3 of the Camera Settings1 menu and call up the Scene Selection item, which produces the same menu as shown in Figure 3-25.

Figure 3-26. Sports Action Icon on Shooting Screen

Figure 3-27. Scene Mode Icon on Function Menu

Once the Scene Selection menu is on the display, scroll through the nine selections on that menu using the Up and Down buttons, the control wheel, or the control dial. Press the Center button to select a setting and return to the shooting screen. You will then see an icon for that setting in the upper left corner of the LCD display. For example, Figure 3-26 shows the display when the Sports Action setting is selected.

One helpful point about the Scene mode menu system is that each scene type has a main screen with a brief description of the setting's uses as you move the selector over it, as shown in Figure 3-25, so you are not left trying to puzzle out what each icon represents.

As you keep pushing the Up or Down button or using the control wheel or control dial to move the selector over the scene type icons, when you reach the bottom or top edge of the screen, the selector wraps around to the first or last icon and continues scrolling.

As I discussed earlier for Intelligent Auto mode, there is an easier way to select the sub-modes, such as Portrait, Landscape, and the like. On screen 8 of the Camera Settings2 menu, choose the Function Menu Settings option, and assign the Shoot Mode option to one of the 12 slots for the Function menu. Then, whenever the mode dial is set to Scene, you can press the Function button from the shooting screen to bring up the Function menu with the icon for the current Scene mode setting displayed, as shown in Figure 3-27.

Highlight that icon by moving to it with the direction buttons and turn the control wheel to scroll through the available settings (Portrait, Landscape, Sunset, etc.). When your choice is highlighted, press the Function button to return to the shooting screen.

There is one more, even easier way to switch among the various scene types: Turn the control dial while the shooting screen is displayed in Scene mode, and the camera will cycle through the scene selections. The scene-type icon will change, in the upper left of the display. (This does not work if the dial has been set to control exposure compensation using the Dial/Wheel EV Compensation option on screen 9 of the Camera Settings2 menu. That setting will override the scene mode function, even though exposure compensation is not available in Scene mode.)

Those are the methods for selecting a scene type. But you need to know something about each option to decide whether it's one you would want to use. In general, each scene setting carries with it a variety of values, including things like flash options, Drive Mode settings, emphasis on various colors, and others. Some settings are designed for certain types of shooting rather than particular subjects such as sunsets or portraits. For example, the Anti Motion Blur and Hand-held Twilight settings are designed for difficult shooting environments, such as dimly lighted areas.

With that introduction, I will discuss the main features of each of the nine choices, with a sample image for each of the settings.

PORTRAIT

The Portrait setting is designed to produce flesh tones with a softening effect, as shown in Figure 3-28. You should be fairly close to the subject and use a focal length of 80mm or more if you are using a lens with that focal length, so as to blur the background if possible; the camera will try to use a wide aperture to assist in this blurring.

You may want to pop up the flash and use the Fill-flash setting, as I did with this image, to reduce shadows. If you want to improve the lighting, consider using off-camera flash. You cannot use Sony's wireless flash settings for that purpose, because the Wireless Flash setting is not available in Scene mode, but you can trigger an off-camera optical slave flash using the on-camera flash.

Figure 3-28. Portrait Example

If you are shooting a portrait in front of a busy background, such as a house, try to position the subject's head in front of a plain area, such as a light-colored wall, so the head will be seen clearly.

You can use the self-timer for single shots, but you cannot use the self-timer for multiple shots, or bracketing or continuous shooting.

Sports Action

The Sports Action setting is for use when lighting is good and you need to freeze the action of your subjects, such as athletes, children at play, pets, or other subjects in motion. Depending on conditions, the camera may set a high ISO value so it can use a fast shutter speed to stop action. The camera sets itself for continuous shooting, so you can hold down the shutter button and capture a burst of images. In that way, you increase your chances of capturing the action at a perfect moment.

You can switch to a different speed of continuous shooting if you want, but you cannot set Drive Mode to single shooting and you cannot use the self-timer or any form of bracketing. You can use flash if you wish, but that will slow down the speed of the continuous shooting, which you cannot disable.

In Figure 3-29, the camera set itself to f/5.6 with an ISO setting of 1000, and a shutter speed of 1/2000 second to freeze the action. Using the high-speed continuous shooting setting, I took a burst of several shots to catch this one of a young man jumping into the river on a hot summer afternoon.

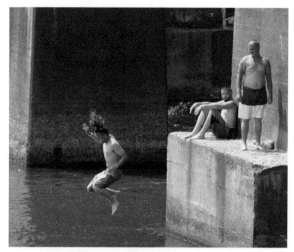

Figure 3-29. Sports Action Example

Macro

With the Macro setting, the a6400 sets itself to take closeups. Though you can focus at close range in other shooting modes, it is convenient to use this setting with its options that are suited for taking extreme closeups of flowers, insects, or other small objects.

When you select the Macro option, the camera will let you use the self-timer, but you cannot turn on continuous shooting or exposure bracketing. You can use the flash if you pop it up.

With the a6400, there is no special setting for macro focus. The minimum focus distance depends on the lens you are using. For example, with the Sony 18-135mm kit lens, the closest distance for focusing is 1.48 foot (0.45 meter), or about 18 inches (45 cm). That is not very close if you want to take a true macro image, in which the image is roughly the same size as the subject itself. If you need to take many macro shots, you should consider purchasing a lens with macro specifications, such as the Sony FE 50mm f/2.8 macro lens, which can focus as close as 6.3 inches (16 cm).

When the camera is set to the Macro setting in Scene mode, you can still use the manual focus option. This can be an excellent approach when using Macro because you can fine-tune the focus, which becomes critical and hard to measure precisely when you are photographing insects or other objects in extreme closeups. To use manual focus, set Focus Mode on screen 5 of the Camera Settings1 menu to MF, or use the AF/MF switch on the lens, if the lens has such a switch. Then use the focusing mechanism on the lens to adjust focus. You also can use the direct manual focus option, if it is available on the lens you are using; I will discuss focus options further in Chapter 4.

Figure 3-30. Macro Example

In Figure 3-30, I used the Macro setting to take a picture of a flower using the 16-50mm kit lens. I focused as close to the subject as I could, using the single-autofocus mode.

LANDSCAPE

Landscape is a Scene mode setting that I use often. It is convenient to turn the mode dial to the SCN position and pull up the Landscape setting when I'm taking pictures at a scenic location. The camera lets you use Fill-flash in case you want to shoot an image of a person close to the camera in front of a building or other attraction, and it boosts the brightness and intensity of colors somewhat. You cannot use continuous shooting or exposure bracketing, but you can use the self-timer.

Figure 3-31. Landscape Example

Figure 3-31 is an example taken using this setting to capture a view of people gathered at a swimming area on the James River in Richmond, Virginia.

SUNSET

This setting is designed to capture the reddish hues of the sky as the sun rises or sets. You can use Fill-flash if you want to, so you can take a portrait of a person with the sunset or sunrise in the background. You cannot use continuous shooting or exposure bracketing, but you can use the self-timer. The main feature of this setting is that the camera boosts the intensity of the reddish colors in the scene.

Of course, as I noted earlier, you don't have to limit the use of this, or any Scene mode setting, to the subject its name implies. For example, if you are photographing red and orange leaves of trees that are changing colors in autumn, you might want to try the Sunset option to create an enhanced view of the brightly colored foliage. In Figure 3-32, I used this setting for a view of the sky a few minutes after sunset.

Figure 3-32. Sunset Example

NIGHT SCENE

The Night Scene option is designed to preserve the natural look of a nocturnal setting. The camera disables the flash; if the scene is dark, you should use a tripod, if possible, to avoid motion blur during the long exposure that may be needed. You can use the self-timer, but not continuous shooting or exposure bracketing. This setting is good for outdoor scenes after dark when flash would not help. The camera does not use multiple shots, as it does with some other modes used in dim lighting, such as Hand-held Twilight.

Figure 3-33. Night Scene Example

In Figure 3-33, I used the Night Scene setting to photograph office buildings and a downtown highway using the 18-135mm kit lens. The camera used a shutter speed of 1/30 second with an aperture of f/3.5 and set ISO to 6400.

HAND-HELD TWILIGHT

This Scene mode setting gives you an option for taking pictures in low light without flash or tripod. In dim lighting, blurring can happen when the camera uses a slow shutter speed to expose the image properly, because it is hard to hold the camera steady for an exposure longer than about 1/30 second.

To counter the effects of blurring, with Hand-held Twilight the camera raises the ISO to a higher-than-normal level so it can use a fast shutter speed and still admit enough light to expose the image properly. Because higher ISO settings result in increased noise, the a6400 takes a burst of four shots and combines them through internal processing into a single composite image with reduced noise.

Hand-held Twilight is useful for a landscape or other static subject at night when you cannot use a tripod or flash. If you can use a tripod, you might be better off using the Night Scene setting, discussed above. Or, if you don't mind using flash, you could just use Intelligent Auto, Program, or one of the more ordinary shooting modes. Hand-held Twilight is a very useful option when it's needed, but it will not yield the same overall quality as a shot at a lower ISO with the camera on a steady support.

With Hand-held Twilight, the flash is forced off. You can use the self-timer, but not continuous shooting or bracketing. If File Format is set to Raw, the camera

will change it to JPEG temporarily. You can set JPEG Quality to Extra Fine if you want to.

Figure 3-34. Hand-held Twilight Example

In Figure 3-34, I used this setting for a shot of a group of rafters out for an evening excursion just before sunset. The camera shot this image at f/5.6 and set the ISO to 1600, with a shutter speed of 1/250 second, fast enough to hand-hold the camera without noticeable motion blur. As I noted above, this setting is excellent for hand-held shots of motionless or slow-moving subjects in dim light. If there is brisk motion involved, you may do better with the Anti Motion Blur setting, discussed later in this section.

NIGHT PORTRAIT

This night-oriented setting is for taking a portrait when you are willing to use flash. With Night Portrait, the camera takes only one shot and it activates the flash in Slow Sync mode. I will discuss the Slow Sync setting and provide an example in Chapter 4. Basically, with this Flash Mode setting, the camera uses a slow shutter speed, so that as the flash illuminates the portrait subject in the foreground, there is enough time for the natural light to illuminate the background also. You cannot use the Flash Off setting for Flash Mode, though you can leave the flash unit retracted, and the camera will still let you take the picture.

You can use the self-timer, but not continuous shooting or exposure bracketing. Because of the slow shutter speed, you should use a tripod if possible, to avoid motion blur.

In Figure 3-35, which was taken outdoors at night, the camera used a shutter speed of 1/4 second, an exposure long enough to allow the lights in the background to show up clearly. For this shot, I used the Sony HVL-

F32M flash and the 18-135mm kit lens, and I had the camera on a tripod. With this setting, you should advise the subject not to move during the relatively long exposure.

Figure 3-35. **Night Portrait Example**

ANTI MOTION BLUR

Like other night-oriented options, this last Scene mode setting is not meant for a particular subject, but for dim lighting, using a technique similar to that used by the Hand-held Twilight setting, discussed above. Just as with Hand-held Twilight, with Anti Motion Blur the camera raises the ISO to a higher-than-normal level and combines a burst of four shots into a single composite image with reduced noise. In addition, the camera counteracts blur from motion of the subject to a fair extent, by analyzing the shots and rejecting those with motion blur as much as possible. For Figure 3-36, I used this setting for a shot of two joggers on a pedestrian bridge across the river shortly before sunset.

Figure 3-36. **Anti Motion Blur Example**

Because it was getting dark, the camera used an ISO setting of 1600 with a shutter speed of 1/250 second at f/5.6. The Anti Motion Blur setting is likely to use a higher ISO setting than Hand-held Twilight, to maximize the camera's ability to capture the scene in dim light. Anti Motion Blur is useful as the light is fading if you don't want to use flash.

You should not expect good results if you use this setting with fast-moving subjects, because the camera will not be able to eliminate the motion blur. With slower-moving subjects, though, the a6400 can do a good job of minimizing blur. With this setting, you can use the self-timer, but not continuous shooting or exposure bracketing, and the flash is disabled. As with Hand-held Twilight, if File Format is set to Raw, the camera will change it to JPEG while this setting is in use. You can set JPEG Quality to Extra Fine.

Sweep Panorama Mode

The next setting on the mode dial is designed for the shooting of panoramic images. When you use this shooting mode, if you follow the fairly simple steps involved, the camera will stitch together a series of images internally to produce a final result with a dramatic, wide (or tall) view of a scenic vista or other appropriate subject.

Figure 3-37. **Mode Dial at Sweep Panorama Position**

To shoot a panorama, turn the mode dial to select the icon that looks like a long, squeezed rectangle, as shown in Figure 3-37. You will immediately see a message telling you to press the shutter button and move the camera in the direction of the arrow that appears on the screen. (If the Mode Dial Guide option is turned on, you will have to press the Center button to dismiss the screen that describes Sweep Panorama mode before this message appears.) At that point, you can follow the directions and likely get good results. However, the camera allows you to make a number of choices for your panoramic images using the Camera Settings1 menu.

Press the Menu button, and you will go to the menu screen that is currently active.

Navigate to the Camera Settings1 menu, which limits you to fewer choices than in most other shooting modes because several options are not appropriate for panoramas. For example, the File Format (Still Images), JPEG Quality, JPEG Image Size, and Aspect Ratio settings are dimmed and unavailable. Also, options such as Drive Mode, Focus Area, and Flash Mode are of no use in this situation and cannot be selected.

You will, however, see two options on screen 1 of the Camera Settings1 menu that are not available for selection in any other shooting mode: Panorama Size and Panorama Direction, as shown in Figure 3-38.

Figure 3-38. **Panorama Options on Camera Settings1 Menu**

If you select Panorama Size, you will see two options, Standard and Wide.

With Standard, a horizontal panorama will have a size of 8192 by 1856 pixels, which is a resolution of about 15 megapixels (MP). If you choose Wide, a horizontal panorama will have a size of 12416 by 1856 pixels, resulting in a resolution of about 23 MP.

A vertical panorama at the Standard setting is 3872 by 2160 pixels, or about 8.3 MP; a vertical panorama at the Wide setting is 5536 by 2160 pixels, or about 12 MP.

The Panorama Direction option lets you choose Right, Left, Up, or Down for the direction in which you will sweep the camera to create the panorama. There is a shortcut for choosing the direction. Turn the control dial while the panorama shooting screen is displayed, and the direction arrow will change to a different position. You can cycle through all four positions with turns of the dial. (This does not work if the dial has been assigned to control exposure compensation using

the Dial/Wheel EV Compensation option on screen 9 of the Camera Settings2 menu.)

Also, you can use the Direction setting with various orientations of the camera to get different results than usual. For example, if you set the direction to Up and then hold the camera sideways while you sweep it to the right, you will create a horizontal panorama that has 2160 pixels in its vertical dimension rather than the standard 1856.

Those are the main settings for panoramas. There are other options that are available for selection in this mode on the Camera Settings1 menu, including Metering Mode, White Balance, Creative Style, and others. I will discuss all of these menu options in Chapter 4. You can set the focusing method using the Focus Mode menu option, though you cannot select automatic autofocus or continuous autofocus. Table 3-1 provides suggested settings for the Camera Settings1 menu options in Sweep Panorama mode, as a starting point.

Table 3-1. **Suggested Camera Settings1 Menu Options for Panoramas**

PANORAMA SIZE	STANDARD
PANORAMA DIRECTION	RIGHT
COLOR SPACE	sRGB
LENS COMPENSATION	ALL VALUES AT AUTO
BRACKET SETTINGS	NO SETTING NEEDED
INTERVAL SHOOTING FUNCTION	INTERVAL SHOOTING = OFF
MEMORY	NO SETTING NEEDED
REGISTER CUSTOM SHOOT. SETTING	NO SETTING NEEDED
FOCUS MODE	SINGLE-SHOT AF
PRIORITY SET IN AF-S	BALANCED EMPHASIS
PRIORITY SET IN AF-C	BALANCED EMPHASIS
FOCUS AREA LIMIT	ALL VALUES SELECTED
AF ILLUMINATOR	AUTO
FACE/EYE AF SETTINGS	NO SETTING NEEDED
AF W/SHUTTER	ON
PRE-AF	OFF
AF AREA REGISTRATION	OFF
DELETE REGISTERED AF AREA	NO SETTING NEEDED
AF AREA AUTO CLEAR	OFF
DISPLAY CONTINUOUS AF AREA	ON
CIRCULATION OF FOCUS POINT	DOES NOT CIRCULATE
AF MICRO ADJUSTMENT	NO SETTING NEEDED
EXPOSURE COMPENSATION	ADJUST IF NEEDED
ISO SETTING	NO SETTING NEEDED

Metering Mode	Multi
Spot Metering Point	Center
Exposure Step	0.3EV
AEL w/Shutter	Auto
Exposure Standard Adjustment	No Setting Needed
Exposure Compensation Setting	Ambient & Flash
Red Eye Reduction	Off
White Balance	Auto
Priority Set in AWB	Standard
Creative Style	Standard
Shutter AWB Lock	Off
Focus Magnifier	No Setting Needed
Focus Magnification Time	No Limit
Initial Focus Magnification	x1.0
MF Assist	On
Peaking Setting/Display	On
Peaking Setting/Level	Mid
Peaking Setting/Color	Yellow
Face Registration	No Setting Needed
Registered Faces Priority	Off

One setting you can make when shooting panoramas is exposure compensation, using the exposure compensation button, assuming the Down button or some other control is assigned to that function. (You also can use the Function menu, or the Exposure Compensation menu item on screen 8 of the Camera Settings1 menu, as noted in the above table.) I will discuss that function in Chapter 4. This feature can be useful for panoramas because the camera will not change the exposure if the camera is pointed at areas with varying brightness.

For example, if you start sweeping from a dark area on the left, the camera will set the exposure for that area. If you then sweep the camera to the right over a bright area, that part of the panorama will be overexposed and possibly washed out in excessive brightness. To correct for this effect, you can reduce the exposure using exposure compensation. In this way, the initial dark area will be underexposed, but the brighter area should be properly exposed. Of course, you have to decide what part of the panorama is the one you most want to have properly exposed.

Another way to deal with this issue is to point the camera at the bright area before starting the shot and press the shutter button halfway to lock the exposure,

then go back to the dark area at the left and start sweeping the camera. In that way, the exposure will be locked at the proper level for the bright area.

Once you have made all of the settings you want for your panorama, follow the directions on the screen. Press and release the shutter button and start moving the camera at a steady rate in the direction you have chosen. I tend to shoot my panoramas moving the camera from left to right, but you may have a different preference. You will hear a steady clicking as the camera takes multiple shots during the sweep of the panorama. A white box and arrow will move across the screen; your task is to finish the camera's sweep at the same moment that the box and arrow finish their travel across the scene. If you move the camera too quickly or too slowly, the panorama will not succeed; if that happens, try again.

Panoramas generally work best when the scene does not contain moving objects such as cars or pedestrians, because, when items are in motion, the multiple shots are likely to capture images of the same object more than once in different positions.

It is advisable to use a tripod if possible, so you can keep the camera steady in a single plane as it moves. If you don't have a tripod available, you might try using the electronic level that Sony provides with the a6400. You have to activate the level using the Display Button option on screen 6 of the Camera Settings2 menu, as discussed in Chapter 5. Then press the Display button until the screen with the electronic level appears. Make sure the outer tips of the level stay green as much as possible, and the resulting panorama should benefit from the level shooting.

You cannot use the camera's Touch Focus features in Sweep Panorama mode; touching the screen will have no effect in this mode for purposes of autofocus. (You can use manual focus in this mode, and tapping the screen twice with manual focus in effect will magnify the display, but it's not likely that that feature would be useful for panorama shooting.)

When a panoramic shot is played back in the camera, it is initially displayed at a small size so the whole image can fit on the display screen. You can then press the Center button to make the panorama scroll across the display at a larger size, using the full height of the screen.

Figure 3-39 is a sample panorama, shot from left to right using the Standard setting, hand-held.

Figure 3-39. Sample Panorama: James River, Richmond, Virginia

Memory Recall Mode

There is one more shooting mode to discuss, apart from Movie mode and S & Q Motion mode, both of which I will discuss in Chapter 9. This last mode, called Memory Recall, is a powerful tool that gives you expanded options for your photography.

Figure 3-40. Mode Dial at Memory Recall Position

When you turn the mode dial to the MR position (shown in Figure 3-40) and then select one of the seven groups of settings that can be stored there, you are, in effect, selecting a custom-made shooting mode that you create with your own favorite settings.

You can set up the camera as you want it—with stored values for items such as shooting mode, shutter speed, aperture, White Balance, ISO, and other settings—and later recall all of those values instantly just by turning the mode dial to the MR position and selecting one of the seven stored memory registers on the Memory Recall screen. With the a6400, unlike some other camera models, you can store settings for any shooting mode, including the Intelligent Auto and Scene modes.

Here is how this works. First, set up the camera with the settings you want to recall. For example, suppose you are going to do street photography. You may want to use a fast shutter speed, say 1/250 second, in black and white, at ISO 800, using continuous shooting with

autofocus, Large and Extra Fine JPEG images, and shooting in the 1:1 aspect ratio.

The first step is to make all of these settings. Set the mode dial to Shutter Priority and use the control dial to set a shutter speed of 1/250 second. Then press the Menu button to call up the Camera Settings1 menu and, on screen 1, select JPEG for File Format, Extra Fine for JPEG Quality, L for the image size, and 1:1 for Aspect Ratio.

Then move to screen 3 and choose continuous shooting set to Hi speed for Drive Mode. On screen 8, under ISO Setting, set ISO to 800, then on screen 11 set White Balance to Daylight. Next, scroll down three positions below White Balance to the Creative Style option and select the B/W setting, for black and white. You can set any other available Camera Settings1 menu options as you wish, but the ones listed above are the ones I will consider for now.

On the Camera Settings2 menu, go to screen 7 and set the Live View Display item to Setting Effect On.

Once these settings are made, navigate to the Memory item, shown in Figure 3-41, which is the second item on screen 4 of the Camera Settings1 menu.

Figure 3-41. Memory Item Highlighted on Menu

After you press the Center button, you will see a screen like the one in Figure 3-42, showing icons and values for all of the settings currently in effect.

Figure 3-42. Memory Settings Screen

The word Memory appears at the upper left of the screen, and the indicators 1, 2, 3, M1, M2, M3, and M4 at the upper right. In the example shown here, the number 1 is highlighted. Now press the Center button, and you will have selected register 1 to store all of the settings you just made. Registers 1, 2, and 3 are stored in the camera's internal memory. Registers M1, M2, M3, and M4 are stored on the memory card that is currently inserted in the camera.

Note the short gray bar at the right side of the Memory screen shown in Figure 3-42. That bar indicates that you can scroll down through other screens to see additional settings that are in effect, such as High ISO Noise Reduction, Color Space, Interval Shooting, Pre-AF and several others. Use the Up and Down buttons to scroll through those screens.

Next, to check how this worked, try making some very different settings, such as setting the camera to Manual exposure mode with a shutter speed of one second, File Format set to Raw, Aspect Ratio set to 16:9, continuous shooting turned off, ISO set to Auto ISO, and Creative Style set to Vivid. Then turn the mode dial back to the MR position and press the Center button while the number 1 is highlighted for Register 1. You will see that all of the custom settings you made have instantly returned, including the shutter speed, Aspect Ratio, and other menu settings. You can then continue shooting with those settings.

This is a very useful feature, and it is more powerful than similar options on some other cameras, which can save menu settings but not values such as shutter speed, or can save settings only for the less-automatic shooting modes, but not the Scene and Auto modes. In addition, if you now switch back to Manual exposure mode, the camera will restore the settings that you had in that mode before you turned to the MR mode.

You can store some, but not all, settings from the Camera Settings1 and Camera Settings 2 menus, including items such as White Balance, exposure compensation, ISO, Live View Display, Zebra, Grid Line, Auto Review, and others, as well as the aperture and shutter speed values, provided, of course, that you are using a lens that communicates properly with the camera. You also can recall Scene mode settings. So, for example, you could set up one of the seven memory registers to recall Scene mode using the Macro setting. In that way, you could be ready for closeup shooting on a moment's notice. You cannot save Program Shift.

Note that you can recall the M1, M2, M3, or M4 settings only if the memory card that has those settings saved is inserted in the camera. On the positive side, this means that you can build up an inventory of different groups of settings, and store them in groups of four on different memory cards. If those cards are clearly labeled or indexed, you can select a card with the four groups of settings you may need for a particular shooting session. However, whenever you format a card, the stored settings will be lost.

If you call up a group of settings using Memory Recall mode, you need to remember to make any other settings that require the use of a physical control. For example, you would need to make sure the switch on the Sony 18-135mm kit lens is set to the AF position in order to use any autofocus settings.

Overall, though, this feature is powerful and useful. With a twist of the mode dial and the press of a button, you can call up a group of settings tailored for a particular type of shooting. It is worthwhile to experiment with this feature and develop various groups of settings that work well for your shooting needs.

CHAPTER 4: THE CAMERA SETTINGS1 MENU

The a6400 has six menus: Camera Settings1, Camera Settings2, Network, Playback, Setup, and My Menu. The first two contain settings that affect images and videos, as well as some other options that affect the functioning of various controls, such as the buttons, wheel, and dial. The Network menu has settings that govern the operation of the camera's Wi-Fi and Bluetooth features for remote control and transferring images. The Playback menu includes items for controlling playback of images and videos. The Setup menu has options that affect the camera's operation but that do not affect the image-making and video-recording operations directly, such as settings for camera sounds, monitor brightness, and the formatting of memory cards. Finally, the My Menu system lets you add your most-used menu options to a customized, short menu of favorites.

I will discuss all of these menus in the various chapters of this book. In this chapter, I will discuss only the Camera Settings1 menu, which mainly offers ways to control the appearance of still images and how you capture them. The available options on this menu will change depending on the setting of the mode dial. For example, if the camera is set to Intelligent Auto mode, the Camera Settings1 menu options are limited because that mode is for a user who wants the camera to make many decisions without input. If the camera is in Sweep Panorama mode, the Camera Settings1 menu options are limited because of the specialized nature of that mode. For this discussion, I'm assuming you have the camera set to Program mode, because with that mode you have access to most of the options on the Camera Settings1 menu.

Turn the mode dial on top of the camera to P, which represents Program mode, as shown in Figure 4-1.

Figure 4-1. Mode Dial at Program Position

Enter the menu system by pressing the Menu button. When the orange highlight bar is visible on a menu screen, you can navigate through the various screens of that menu by pressing the Right or Left button or by turning the control dial at extreme right of the camera's top. As you press either of those buttons or turn the dial, you will see an orange dot at the very bottom of the screen move through a line of gray dots, indicating which screen of the current menu system you are viewing. You also will see a pair of numbers separated by a slash mark at the top right of the menu screen. Those numbers also indicate which screen of the menu is now displayed.

Figure 4-2. Screen 7 of Program Menu

For example, Figure 4-2 shows screen 7 of the Camera Settings1 menu when the camera is in Program mode. The orange dot is in the seventh position from the left at the bottom of the screen, and the numbers at the top right are 7/14, meaning the current screen is the seventh of fourteen screens of this menu system.

When the menu system first appears, the camera will display the last menu screen that was viewed. If you need to move to a different screen or a different menu, press the Right and Left buttons or turn the control dial to navigate to that screen. As you keep pressing the direction buttons or turning the control dial, the cursor will move through all numbered screens of the various menu systems.

As you move through the menu screens on the a6400, after the Camera Settings1 menu comes the Camera Settings2 menu, then the Network menu, headed by a globe icon. The last three menus are the Playback menu, marked by a triangle icon; the Setup menu, marked by a toolbox icon; and, finally, the My Menu option, marked by a star icon.

To navigate quickly through these six menu systems, you can press the Up button or turn the control wheel to move the highlight block into the line of icons at the top of the screen. When one of those icons is highlighted, and the long, orange highlight bar has disappeared from the screen, you can use the Left and Right buttons or the control dial to move directly from one menu system to another without going through the various screens of each menu.

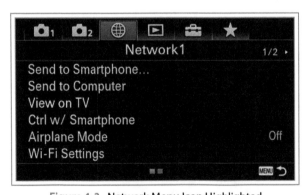

Figure 4-3. Network Menu Icon Highlighted

For example, in Figure 4-3, the Network menu icon is highlighted. From there, you can press the Left button twice or turn the control dial to the left to move the highlight to the camera icon for the Camera Settings1 menu at the far left, as shown in Figure 4-4.

Then you can press the Down button or turn the control wheel to move the highlight into the list of items on screen 1 of the Camera Settings1 menu.

In this chapter, I will discuss only the Camera Settings1 menu; I will discuss the other five menus in Chapter 5

(Camera Settings2), Chapter 7 (Playback), Chapter 8 (Setup and My Menu), and Chapter 10 (Network).

Figure 4-4. Camera Settings1 Menu Icon Highlighted

The Camera Settings1 menu has many options on 14 numbered screens. In most cases, each option (such as JPEG Image Size) occupies one line, with its name on the left and current setting (such as L: 24M) on the right. Some items on the menu screens are dimmed and have only a dash at the right side, such as the Auto Mode, Scene Selection, and Superior Auto Image Extraction options in Figure 4-5, for example.

Figure 4-5. Screen 3 of Camera Settings1 Menu

This means those options are not available for selection in the current context. In this case, the camera was set to Program mode, in which those three options cannot be used.

Some items are preceded by an icon that indicates whether they are used for still images, movies, or Slow & Quick Motion movies, among other items. For example, Figure 4-6 shows screen 6 of the Camera Settings1 menu, on which all but one of the items are preceded by the icon showing they are applicable only for still images.

Figure 4-7 shows screen 1 of the Camera Settings2 menu, which has three settings (Exposure Mode, File Format, and Record Setting) that apply only for normal-speed movies, two settings (S & Q Exposure Mode and S & Q Settings) that apply only for S & Q Motion recording, and one setting (Proxy Recording) that applies only for proxy recording.

Figure 4-6. Screen 6 of Camera Settings1 Menu

Figure 4-7. Screen 1 of Camera Settings2 Menu

To follow the discussion below of the options on the Camera Settings1 menu, leave the shooting mode set to Program, which gives you access to most of the items on that menu. (I'll also discuss the options that are available only in other modes as I come to them.) I'll start at the top of screen 1 and discuss all of the options on each of the 14 screens of this menu.

Screen 1 of the Camera Settings1 menu is shown in Figure 4-8.

Figure 4-8. Screen 1 of Camera Settings1 Menu

File Format (Still Images)

This first option on the Camera Settings1 menu lets you make the important choice of whether to shoot still images using the Raw format, as JPEG files, or in both formats at the same time, as shown in Figure 4-9.

Figure 4-9. File Format Menu Options Screen

As is the case with most camera manufacturers, Sony offers its own special Raw format, which is a file type that preserves as much as possible of the raw data received by the camera through its lens for each still image. If you want to shoot images with the highest possible quality, choose Raw for this menu option. If you want to shoot images that are easier to edit and to share, choose JPEG, which is an industry-standard format that is compatible with a wide range of photo editing programs, email programs, and other software. However, there are some other factors to consider in making this choice.

Raw files are larger than other files, so they take up more space on your memory card, and on your computer, than JPEG files. But Raw files offer advantages over JPEG files. When you shoot in the Raw format, the camera records as much information as it can about the image and preserves that information in the file it saves to the memory card.

When you open the Raw file later on your computer, your software can process that information in various ways. For example, you can change the exposure or white balance of the image when you edit it on the computer, just as if you had changed your settings while shooting. In effect, the Raw format gives you what almost amounts to a chance to travel back in time to improve some of the settings that you didn't get quite right when you pressed the shutter button.

For example, Figure 4-10 is an image I took with the a6400 using the Raw format, with the exposure purposely set too dark and White Balance set to Incandescent, even though I took the picture outdoors during daylight hours.

Figure 4-10. Raw Image Captured with Abnormal Settings

Figure 4-11 shows the same image after I opened it in Adobe Camera Raw software and adjusted the settings to correct the exposure and white balance. The result was an image that looked just as it would have if I had used the correct settings when I shot it.

Figure 4-11. Raw Image After Adjustments in Software

Raw is not a cure-all; you cannot fix bad focus or excessive exposure problems. But you can improve some exposure-related issues and white balance with Raw-processing software. You can use Sony's Imaging Edge software to view or edit Raw files, and you also can use other programs, such as Adobe Camera Raw, that have been updated to handle Raw files from this camera.

Using Raw can have disadvantages, also. The files take up a lot of storage space; Raw images taken with the a6400 are about 24 MB in size, while Large JPEG images I have taken are between about 6 and 17 MB, depending on the settings used. Also, Raw files have to

be processed on a computer; you can't take a Raw image and immediately share it through social media or print it; you first have to use software to convert it to JPEG, TIFF, or some other standard format for manipulating digital photographs. If you are pressed for time, you may not want to take that extra step. Finally, some features of the a6400 are not available when you are using the Raw format, such as the Auto HDR, Picture Effect, Soft Skin Effect, and Digital Zoom options.

If you're undecided as to whether to use Raw or JPEG, you have the option of selecting Raw & JPEG, the second choice for the File Format (Still Images) menu item. With that setting, the camera records both a Raw and a JPEG image when you press the shutter button.

The advantage with that approach is that you have a Raw image with maximum quality and the ability to do extensive post-processing, and you also have a JPEG image that you can use for viewing, sharing, printing, and the like. Of course, this setting consumes storage space more quickly than saving your images in just Raw or JPEG format, and it can take the camera longer to store the images, so there may be a slowdown in the rate of continuous shooting, if you are using that option. You also cannot use some menu options that conflict with the Raw setting.

When you choose Raw & JPEG, you can select a JPEG Quality setting and a JPEG Image Size setting (both discussed below) that will apply only to the JPEG image; the Raw image is always at the maximum size and quality.

The best bet for preserving the quality of your images and your options for post-processing and fixing exposure mistakes later is to choose Raw files. However, if you want to use features such as Sweep Panorama mode, the Scene mode types of Hand-held Twilight and Anti Motion Blur, the Picture Effect menu option, and others, which are not available with Raw files, then choose JPEG. If you choose JPEG, I recommend using Large size and Extra Fine quality, unless you have an urgent need to conserve storage space on your memory card or on your computer. If you want Raw quality and are not concerned about storage space or speed of shooting, choose Raw & JPEG. However, you will still not be able to use Picture Effect and some other options.

JPEG Quality

The second option on this menu, JPEG Quality, is available for selection at any time, though it takes effect only when you are shooting JPEG images. The choices are Extra Fine, Fine, and Standard, as shown in Figure 4-12.

Figure 4-12. JPEG Quality Menu Options Screen

The term "quality" in this context concerns the way in which digital images are processed. In particular, JPEG (non-Raw) images are digitally "compressed" to reduce their size without losing too much information or detail from the picture. However, the more an image is compressed, the greater the loss of detail and clarity in the image.

The Extra Fine setting provides the least compression. Images captured with the Fine or Standard setting undergo increasingly more compression, resulting in smaller files with somewhat reduced quality. I recommend always using the Extra Fine setting for JPEG files, unless you have a need to preserve storage space or are taking numerous images that do not need to be of high quality, such as images for photo ID cards or for an inventory of possessions.

JPEG Image Size

This setting controls the size in pixels of a JPEG still image recorded by the camera. (Raw images are always recorded at the maximum image size.) The Sony a6400 has a relatively large digital sensor for a compact camera, and that sensor has a high maximum resolution, or pixel count. The sensor is capable of recording a still image with 6000 pixels, or individual points of light, in the horizontal direction and 4000 pixels vertically. When you multiply those two numbers

together, the result is 24 million pixels, often referred to as megapixels, MP, or M.

The resolution of still images is important mainly when it comes time to enlarge or print your images. If you need to produce large prints (say, 8 by 10 inches or 20 by 25 cm), then you should select a high-resolution setting for JPEG Image Size. You also should choose the largest setting if you may need to crop out a small portion of the image and enlarge it for closer viewing.

For example, if you are shooting photos of wildlife and the animal or bird you are interested in is in the distance, you may need to enlarge the image digitally to see that subject in detail. In that case, you should choose the highest setting (L) for Image Size.

The available settings for JPEG Image Size are L, M, and S for Large, Medium, and Small, as shown in Figure 4-13.

Figure 4-13. JPEG Image Size Menu Options Screen

When you select one of these options, the camera displays a setting such as L: 24M, meaning Large: 24 megapixels. The number of megapixels changes depending on the Aspect Ratio setting, discussed below. This is because when the shape of the image changes, the number of horizontal or vertical pixels changes also, to form the new shape.

For example, if the Aspect Ratio setting is 3:2, the maximum number of pixels is used because 3:2 is the aspect ratio of the camera's sensor. However, if you set Aspect Ratio to 16:9, the number of horizontal pixels (6000) stays the same, but the number of vertical pixels is reduced from 4000 to 3376 to form the 16:9 ratio of horizontal to vertical pixels. When you multiply those two numbers (6000 and 3376) together, the result is about 20 million pixels, which the camera states as 20M, as will be shown on screen 1 of the Camera Settings1 menu.

One of the few reasons to choose a JPEG Image Size setting smaller than L is if you are running out of space on your memory card and need to keep taking pictures in an important situation. Table 4-1 shows approximately how many images can be stored on a 64 GB memory card for various settings.

Table 4-1.   **Number of Images that Fit on a 64 GB Card (Image Size vs. Quality at 3:2 Aspect Ratio)**

	Large	Medium	Small
Raw & JPEG (Extra Fine)	1400	1700	2100
Raw	2400	-----	-----
Extra Fine	3400	5500	8600
Fine	6800	9999+	9999+
Standard	9999+	9999+	9999+

As you can see, if you are using a 64 GB memory card, which is a fairly common size nowadays, you can fit about 1400 images on the card even at the maximum settings of 3:2 for Aspect Ratio, Large for Image Size, and Raw & JPEG (Extra Fine) for Quality. If you limit the JPEG image quality to Fine, with no Raw images, you can fit about 6800 images on the card. If you reduce the JPEG Image Size setting to Small, you can store more than 10,000 images. I am unlikely ever to need more than about 300 or 400 images in any one session. And, of course, I can use a larger memory card or multiple memory cards.

If space on your memory card is not a consideration, I recommend you use the L setting at all times. You never know when you might need the larger-sized image, so you might as well use the L setting and be safe. Your situation might be different, of course. If you were taking photos purely for a business purpose, such as making photo identification cards, you might want to use the Small setting to store the maximum number of images on a memory card and reduce expense. For general photography, I rarely use any setting other than L for Image Size. (One exception could be when I want to increase the focal length reach of the lens without losing image quality; see the discussion of Smart Zoom and related topics in Chapter 5.)

Aspect Ratio

This third option on the Camera Settings1 menu lets you choose the shape of your still images. The choices are the default of 3:2, as well as 16:9 and 1:1, as shown in Figure 4-14. These numbers represent the ratio of the units of width to the units of height. For example, with the 16:9 setting, the image is 16 units wide for every 9 units of height.

Figure 4-14. Aspect Ratio Menu Options Screen

The aspect ratio that uses all pixels on the image sensor is 3:2; with any other aspect ratio, some pixels are cropped out. So, if you want to record every possible pixel, you should use the 3:2 setting. If you shoot using the 3:2 aspect ratio, you can always alter the shape of the image later in editing software such as Photoshop by cropping away parts of the image. However, if you want to compose your images in a certain shape and don't plan to do post-processing in software, the aspect ratio settings of this menu item can help you frame your images in the camera using the appropriate aspect ratio on the display.

For each of the aspect ratios discussed below, I am including an image I took using that setting in the same location at the same time, to show what the different aspect ratios look like. The default 3:2 setting, used for Figure 4-15, includes the maximum number of pixels, and is the ratio used by traditional 35mm film. This aspect ratio can be used without cropping to make prints in the common U.S. size of six inches by four inches (15 cm by 10 cm).

The 16:9 setting, illustrated in Figure 4-16, is the "widescreen" option, like that found on many modern HD television sets. You might use this setting when you plan to show your images on an HDTV set. Or, it might be suitable for a particular composition in which the subject matter is stretched out in a horizontal arrangement. With this setting, some pixels are cropped out at the top and bottom, though none are lost at the left or right.

Figure 4-15. Aspect Ratio Set to 3:2

Figure 4-16. Aspect Ratio Set to 16:9

The 1:1 ratio, illustrated in Figure 4-17, produces a square shape, which some photographers prefer because of its symmetry and because the neutrality of the shape leaves open many possibilities for composition. With the 1:1 setting, the camera crops pixels from the left and right sides of the image.

Figure 4-17. Aspect Ratio Set to 1:1

The Aspect Ratio setting is available in all shooting modes except Sweep Panorama. However, although you can set Aspect Ratio when the camera is in Movie mode or S & Q Motion mode (mode dial turned to movie-film icon or S & Q), that setting will have no effect until you switch to a mode for taking still images, such as Program mode. When the mode dial is set to the Movie position or the S & Q position, you cannot take still images.

Panorama Size and Panorama Direction

The next two commands on this screen of the menu are available only when the mode dial is at Sweep Panorama mode. I discussed these settings in Chapter 3, in connection with that mode. You should not need the Panorama Direction menu option often, because you can set the panorama direction by turning the control dial when the camera is in Sweep Panorama mode (unless you have set the dial to control exposure compensation using the Dial/Wheel EV Compensation option on screen 9 of the Camera Settings2 menu). You do need the Panorama Size option in order to set the size of the Panorama to Standard or Wide.

Screen 2 of the Camera Settings1 Menu is shown in Figure 4-18.

Figure 4-18. Screen 2 of Camera Settings1 Menu

Long Exposure Noise Reduction

This option uses processing to reduce the "noise" that affects images during exposures of one second or longer. This setting is turned on by default. When it is turned on, the camera processes your shot for a time equal to the time of the exposure. So, if your exposure is for two seconds, the camera will process the shot for an additional two seconds after the image is captured, creating a delay before you can shoot again.

In some cases, this processing may remove details from your image. In addition, in certain situations you may prefer to leave the noise in the image because the graininess can be pleasing in some cases. Or, you may prefer to remove the noise using post-processing software. If you want to turn off this option, use this menu item to do so.

This option is not available for adjustment when the camera is set for continuous shooting, Multi Frame Noise Reduction, exposure bracketing, or in the Auto, Sweep Panorama, or Scene modes. The camera will select a setting for Long Exposure Noise Reduction in those cases. For example, the camera will turn this option off with the Sports Action, Hand-held Twilight, and Anti Motion Blur Scene mode settings, but turn it on with the Portrait and Macro settings.

I recommend you make this setting based on the type of shooting you are doing. If you're taking casual shots or don't want to do post-processing, I suggest you leave this option turned on. But, if you are shooting with Raw quality and want to do processing with software, I recommend turning it off.

High ISO Noise Reduction

This next menu entry has three settings: Normal, Low, or Off; the default is Normal. This option removes noise caused by the use of a high ISO level. One problem with this sort of noise reduction is that it takes time to process your images after they are captured. You may want to set this option to Low or Off to minimize the delay before you can take another picture. If File Format (Still Images) is set to Raw, this option will be unavailable on the menu because this processing is not available for Raw images. It is not available for adjustment on the menu in the Auto, Scene, or Sweep Panorama modes; it is always set to Normal in those modes.

Color Space

With this option, you can choose to record your still images using the sRGB "color space," the more common choice and the default, or the Adobe RGB color space. The sRGB color space has fewer colors than Adobe RGB; therefore, it is more suitable for producing images for the web and other forms of digital display than for printing. If your images are likely to be printed commercially in a book or magazine or it is critical that you be able to match a great many color variations, you might want to consider using the Adobe RGB color

space. I always leave the color space set to sRGB, and I recommend that you do so as well unless you have a specific need to use Adobe RGB, such as a requirement from a printing company that you are using to print your images.

If you are shooting your images with the Raw format, you don't need to worry so much about color space, because you can set it later using your Raw-processing software.

Lens Compensation

The final item on screen 2 of the Camera Settings1 menu, labeled Lens Comp., provides three sub-options that you can turn on to adjust the appearance of images by correcting for three problems that are inherent in camera lenses: Shading Compensation, Chromatic Aberration Compensation, and Distortion Compensation. This menu option is available only when you are using a lens that permits this sort of automatic compensation. Sony includes this feature with many of its lenses; a list of compliant lenses is available at https://www.sony.com/electronics/support/articles/00016553.

Figure 4-19. Lens Compensation Menu Options Screen

Each of this menu item's sub-options, shown in Figure 4-19, can be set to either Off or Auto. When one of the settings is set to Auto, the camera uses its digital processing to correct the image for that particular type of problem. There are some differences in how these settings operate, as described below.

SHADING COMPENSATION

This problem involves a darkening in the corners of images. If you set this option to Auto, the camera will automatically apply processing to compensate for that darkening. I recommend you leave it set to Auto, unless you have a particular reason to deal with it in post-processing software. According to my tests, this option provides corrections for Raw images as well as JPEG images, unlike the other two, which appear to affect JPEG images only.

CHROMATIC ABERRATION COMPENSATION

This correction involves the distortion of colors in images because of the characteristics of the lens. I recommend leaving it set to Auto unless you want to address chromatic aberration in post-processing software.

DISTORTION COMPENSATION

This last option corrects for the effect by which the lens bends or curves straight lines. It could not be disabled on my a6400 camera when using either the 18-135mm or 16-50mm kit lens, but it could be disabled with the Sony FE 100-400mm f/4.5-5.6 GM OSS lens and with the Sony DT 50mm f/1.8 lens. Even if you are using a lens for which this option can be disabled, I recommend leaving it set to Auto unless you are certain you want to deal with distortion in post-processing software.

If you generally use a program such as Adobe Photoshop Lightroom to apply lens corrections, you can leave the above options set to Off (except for Distortion Compensation with some lenses) and apply any needed corrections using your post-processing software. According to Sony, if you want to apply corrections to Raw files, you may need to use Sony's Imaging Edge software. See https://www.sony.com.sg/electronics/support/articles/00018031. (This article says to use Image Data Converter software, but that software has been replaced by Imaging Edge.)

The items on screen 3 of the Camera Settings1 menu are shown in Figure 4-20.

Auto Mode

This option is available for selection only when the mode dial is set to the AUTO position. This menu item lets you choose either Intelligent Auto or Superior Auto for the shooting mode, as discussed in Chapter 3. If the Mode Dial Guide option is turned on through screen 2 of the Setup menu, the screen for choosing between these two modes is automatically displayed whenever you turn the mode dial to the AUTO position and press the Center

button when the guide screen appears. If that option is not turned on or the mode dial is already at the AUTO position, you can use the Auto Mode option to choose one or the other of the Auto modes. You also can change between Intelligent Auto and Superior Auto using the Function menu, if the Shoot Mode option appears on that menu, as discussed in Chapter 5.

Figure 4-20. Screen 3 of Camera Settings1 Menu

Scene Selection

As discussed in Chapter 3, this option is used only when the camera is set to Scene mode. You use this menu item to select one of the settings in that shooting mode, including Portrait, Anti Motion Blur, Sunset, Night Scene, and others. Note that you also can use the control dial to change scene types when the shooting screen is displayed (unless the dial has been assigned to adjust exposure compensation using the Dial/Wheel Setup option on screen 9 of the Camera Settings2 menu).

In addition, the Scene Selection menu screen appears automatically when you turn the mode dial to the SCN position and press the Center button, if the Mode Dial Guide option on screen 2 of the Setup menu is turned on. Also, as with Auto Mode, discussed above, you can choose a scene type using the Shoot Mode option on the Function menu, if that option is included in that menu system.

Superior Auto Image Extraction

This next option lets you control how the camera handles images captured with the burst-shooting feature of Superior Auto mode. As I discussed in Chapter 3, in that mode, when lighting is dim or involves backlighting, the camera may decide to shoot a burst of images at a high ISO value and combine them internally into a single image that is processed so as to remove noise. With this menu option, you can set the camera so it saves all of those continuous shots as individual images, or operates as usual, and creates only one single, composite image.

If you set this option to Auto, the camera behaves as you would expect it to do normally with Superior Auto mode: it takes a rapid burst of images, and then combines them into a single, final image. If you set it to Off, the camera takes the same rapid burst, but displays the several images in the burst individually.

I prefer to leave this option set to Auto, to get the benefit of the special processing of Superior Auto mode. If I wanted multiple images, I would prefer to use continuous shooting. However, if for some reason you want the camera to save the multiple shots from Superior Auto mode as individual images, this option is available.

Drive Mode

This next option on screen 3 of the menu gives access to features of the a6400 for shooting bursts of images, bracketing exposures, and using the self-timer.

Figure 4-21. **Drive Mode Menu**

When you highlight this option and press the Center button, a menu appears at the left of the screen as shown in Figure 4-21, with eight choices represented by icons: Single Shooting, Continuous Shooting, Self-timer (Single), Self-timer (Continuous), Continuous Exposure Bracketing, Single Exposure Bracketing, White Balance Bracketing, and DRO Bracketing. Scroll through this menu using the Up and Down buttons or the control wheel. When the icon for an option is highlighted, you can select sub-options by pressing the Left and Right buttons or by turning the control dial. (You have to scroll down to see all of the choices on the menu.)

Details for the Drive Mode settings are discussed below.

SINGLE SHOOTING

This is the normal mode for shooting still images. Select this top choice on the Drive Mode menu to turn off all continuous shooting. In some cases, having one of the continuous-shooting options selected will make it impossible to make other settings, such as Soft Skin Effect or Long Exposure Noise Reduction. If you find you cannot make a certain setting, try selecting single shooting to see if that removes the conflict and fixes the problem.

As noted in Chapter 3, this option is not available with the Sports Action setting of Scene mode.

CONTINUOUS SHOOTING

Continuous shooting, sometimes called burst shooting, is one of the most useful features of the a6400, which provides speeds up to 11 frames per second (fps), with focus and exposure adjusted for each shot. This capability is useful in many contexts, from shooting an action sequence at a sporting event to taking a series of shots of a person in order to capture changing facial expressions. I often use burst shooting for street photography to increase my chances of catching an interesting scene.

Figure 4-22. **Continuous Shooting Icon Highlighted on Menu**

To activate burst shooting, scroll down to the second icon on the Drive Mode menu, which looks like a stack of overlapping frames, as shown in Figure 4-22. When that icon is highlighted, press the Left or Right button or turn the control dial to select the speed of shooting—Hi+, Hi, Mid, or Lo. The Hi+ setting provides speeds up to 11 fps; Hi offers speeds as high as 8 fps; Mid has speeds up to 6 fps; and the Lo setting is rated at up to 3 fps. Once a speed is selected, press and hold the shutter button to fire off a burst of shots. The camera will shoot at the selected speed level until its memory buffer fills up, at which point the shooting will change to a considerably slower pace.

With the Hi+ setting, the camera does not provide a real-time live view of the scene it is shooting, although it does provide images that lag the shooting somewhat. If you need a constantly updated live view, you should choose the Hi option rather than Hi+. Otherwise, I usually choose Hi+ for the added speed of shooting.

If Focus Mode is set to AF-S for single autofocus, the camera will not adjust its focus during the burst of shots. But, if you set Focus Mode to AF-C for continuous autofocus or AF-A for automatic autofocus, the camera will adjust focus for each shot, as long as the aperture value is no higher than f/11.0. The reason for this limitation is that the camera's ability to adjust focus during continuous shooting depends on its use of phase-detection autofocus, which uses 425 special autofocus points covering most of the area of the image sensor.

This phase-detection system cannot function at apertures more narrow than f/11.0, such as f/12.0 and f/16.0. At those narrower apertures, the camera reverts to using contrast-detection autofocus, which is quite accurate but considerably slower than the phase-detection process. So, if you need to take bursts of continuous shots with autofocus adjustments for all images, you need to ensure that the camera is using an aperture of f/11.0 or lower.

In addition, you need to check the setting of the Priority Set in AF-C menu option on screen 5 of the Camera Settings1 menu. As discussed later in this chapter, that setting controls whether the camera emphasizes quick release of the shutter as opposed to accurate autofocus, or puts a "balanced emphasis" on both. When I tested continuous shooting using my Sony 18-135mm lens, I found that, when this option is set to Release or Balanced Emphasis, the camera and lens did not focus well when using the Hi+, Hi, or Mid setting for continuous shooting.

When I changed the setting to AF, meaning the camera should take its time to get the focus sharp, the autofocus performance during high-speed continuous shooting improved dramatically, although the speed of shooting slowed down significantly while the camera focused. With continuous shooting set to its Lo speed,

I found that autofocus worked well with continuous shooting, even with the Balanced Emphasis setting for Priority Set in AF-C.

Also note that autofocus will not be accurate in all situations during burst shooting. If the subject is one that is difficult to focus on, the camera may not always focus sharply. But when conditions are reasonably good, the autofocus works very well during burst shooting, provided you use the AF setting for Priority Set in AF-C.

If you want the camera to adjust its exposure during the series of continuous shots, you need to go to screen 9 of the Camera Settings1 menu and check the setting of the AEL w/Shutter menu item. If that item is set to On, the camera will lock exposure when you press the shutter button, and exposure will be locked throughout the burst as it was set for the first image, even if the lighting changes dramatically.

However, if you set AEL w/Shutter to Off, the camera will adjust its exposure as needed during the burst of shots. If you set AEL w/Shutter to Auto, the camera will adjust exposure during continuous shooting if Focus Mode is set to continuous autofocus or automatic autofocus. If it is set to single autofocus, the camera will keep the exposure locked. (Of course, if you want the camera to adjust exposure automatically, you have to use an exposure mode in which the camera normally controls exposure. If you use Manual mode with a fixed ISO value, the exposure will not change.)

Although you can turn on the flash when the Continuous Shooting option is selected, and the camera will take a series of shots with flash as you hold down the shutter button, the time between shots may be one second or longer, because the flash cannot recycle quickly enough to take a more rapid series of shots.

After taking a burst of shots, it can take the camera a while to save them to the memory card. The access lamp on the bottom of the camera lights up in red while the camera is writing to the card. In addition, the camera will display a series of small vertical lines along with a series of changing numbers in the upper left corner of the display, indicating the number of images remaining to be written from the buffer to the memory card. While the access lamp is illuminated and the buffer-emptying display is active, be sure not to remove the battery or the memory card. While the buffer is being emptied, you can take additional shots, you can enter playback mode to view images that have already been written to the memory card, and you can use the menu system.

When you have captured a series of continuous shots, the way they are displayed in playback mode depends on a menu setting called Display as Group, on screen 3 of the Playback menu. If that option is turned on, as it is by default, then, once the burst of shots is captured and written to the memory card, the camera will display all of the shots in the group as a single item that appears like a stacked group of images. In the lower right corner of the display, the camera displays the word Expand next to a round icon, as shown in Figure 4-23. These indications mean you can press the Center button to open up the group to see the individual images inside it.

Figure 4-24. Group of Continuous Shots Expanded as Individual Items

Figure 4-25. Image Taken with Continuous Shooting

Continuous shooting is not available in Sweep Panorama mode, in Scene Selection mode (except for the Sports Action setting), with certain Picture Effect settings, with Auto HDR turned on, with ISO set to Multi Frame Noise Reduction, or when the Smile Shutter is turned on.

SELF-TIMER

The next icon down on the menu of Drive Mode options represents the self-timer, as shown in Figure 4-26.

Figure 4-23. Group of Continuous Shots Displayed as Single Item

If you don't press the Center button, the group, which may contain hundreds of images, will behave like a single image for purposes of scrolling through images and deleting them. If you press the Center button, the group opens up and you can view each individual image within the group. The camera will display a set of numbers in the upper right corner of the display, such as 1/16, indicating which image is being viewed out of how many total images in the group, as shown in Figure 4-24. To end the expansion and group the images back into a single item, press the Center button again.

For Figure 4-25, I used continuous shooting to take a series of images of birds at our backyard feeder, with the goal of catching one of them in flight. After capturing many images, I selected this one showing a bird on the wing. It was shot with the Sony FE 100-400mm f/4.5-5.6 GM OSS lens at 1/1000 second, at ISO 8000 and f/5.6.

Figure 4-26. Self-timer Icon Highlighted on Menu

The self-timer is useful when you need to be the photographer and also appear in a group photograph. You can place the a6400 on a tripod, set the timer for five or ten seconds, and insert yourself into the group before the shutter clicks. The self-timer also is helpful when you don't want to cause blur by jiggling the camera as you press the shutter button.

For example, when you're taking a macro shot very close to the subject, focusing can be critical, and any bump to the camera could cause motion blur. Using the self-timer gives the camera a chance to settle down after the shutter button is pressed, before the image is recorded.

The self-timer option presents you with three choices: ten seconds, five seconds, or two seconds. When the self-timer icon is highlighted, press the Left or Right button or turn the control dial to highlight one of these options, and press the Center button to select it. After you make this selection, the self-timer icon will appear in the upper left corner of the display with the chosen number of seconds (10, 5, or 2) displayed next to the icon, as shown in Figure 4-27. (If you don't see the icon, press the Display button until the screen with the various shooting icons appears.)

Figure 4-27. Self-timer Icon on Shooting Screen

Once the self-timer is set, when you press the shutter button, the timer will count down for the specified number of seconds and then take the picture. The reddish lamp on the front of the camera will blink, and the camera will beep during the countdown. You can cancel the process by pressing the shutter button again or by pressing the Left button, assuming it is still assigned to Drive Mode.

The self-timer is not available in Sweep Panorama mode, with the Sports Action setting of Scene mode, when the Smile Shutter is activated, or for recording

a movie, and you cannot select continuous autofocus when the self-timer is turned on. To use the self-timer with bracketing, you need to use the Self-timer During Bracket menu option, discussed later in this chapter.

SELF-TIMER (CONTINUOUS)

The next item down on the Drive Mode menu, shown in Figure 4-28, is another variation on the self-timer. With this option, you can set the timer to take multiple shots after the countdown ends. You can choose any of the three time intervals, and you can set the camera to take either three or five shots after the delay. When you highlight this option, you will see a horizontal triangle indicating that, by pressing the Left and Right buttons or turning the control dial, you can select one of six combinations of the number of shots and the timer interval. For example, the option designated as C3/2s sets the camera to take three shots after the timer counts down for two seconds; C5/10s sets it for five shots after a ten-second delay.

Figure 4-28. Self-timer (Continuous) Icon Highlighted on Menu

This option is useful for group photos; when a series of shots is taken, you increase your chances of getting at least one shot in which everyone is looking at the camera and smiling. You can choose any settings you want for File Format, JPEG Quality, and JPEG Image Size, including Raw & JPEG, and you will still get three or five rapidly fired shots, though the speed of shooting will decrease slightly when using the Raw format. You cannot use continuous autofocus with this option.

CONTINUOUS EXPOSURE BRACKETING

This next option on the Drive Mode menu, shown in Figure 4-29, sets the camera to take three, five, or nine images with one press of the shutter button but with a different exposure level for each image, giving you a greater chance of having one image that is properly exposed.

When you highlight this option, you will see a horizontal triangle meaning that you can use the Left and Right buttons or the control dial to select one of 16 combinations of the difference in exposure value and the number of images in the bracket. The first 12 choices include exposure value (EV) intervals of 0.3, 0.5, 0.7, or 1.0, each with a bracket of three, five or nine exposures. The other four choices are for EV intervals of 2.0 or 3.0 EV, each with a bracket of three or five exposures.

Figure 4-29. Continuous Exposure Bracketing Icon Highlighted on Menu

The decimal numbers represent the difference in EV among the multiple exposures (three, five, or nine) that the camera will take. (With the larger EV intervals of 2.0 or 3.0 EV, the available numbers of shots are three or five; there is no option for choosing nine shots, because the overall exposure range would be too great, given the larger EV interval.)

For example, if you select 0.7 EV as the interval for three exposures, the camera will take three shots— one at the metered exposure level; one at a level 0.7 EV (or f-stop) below that, resulting in a darker image; and one at a level 0.7 EV above that, resulting in a brighter image. If you want the maximum exposure difference among the shots, select 3.0 EV as the interval for the three or five shots.

Once you have set this option as you want it and composed your scene, press and hold the shutter button and the camera will take the three, five, or nine shots in rapid succession while you hold down the button.

If you set this option for three exposures, the first one will be at the metered value, the second one underexposed by the selected interval, and the third

one overexposed to the same extent. If you set it for five exposures, the first three shots will have the values noted above, the fourth will have the most negative EV, and the fifth will have the most positive EV. With nine exposures, the pattern will be similar, with the final two exposures having the most negative and positive EV settings, respectively. (You can change this order using the Bracket Settings menu option, discussed later in this chapter.)

You can use exposure compensation, in which case the camera will use the image with exposure compensation as the base level, and then take exposures that deviate under and over the exposure of the image with exposure compensation.

If you pop up the flash and set it to fire, using the Fill-flash setting for example, the flash will fire for each of the bracketed shots and the exposure will be varied, but you have to press the shutter button for each shot, after the flash has recycled. (The orange dot to the right of the flash icon on the screen shows when the flash is ready to fire again.) With this approach, the camera will vary the output of the flash unit rather than the exposure value of the images themselves.

When using Manual exposure mode with ISO set to Auto, the camera adjusts the ISO setting to achieve the different exposure levels for the multiple images. If ISO is set to a specific value, the camera varies the shutter speeds for the multiple shots.

Single Exposure Bracketing

The next option is similar to the previous one, except that, with this selection, you have to press the shutter button for each shot; the camera will not take multiple shots while you hold down the shutter button. You have the same 16 choices for combinations of EV intervals and numbers of exposures. You might want to choose this option when you need to pause between shots for some reason, such as if you are using a model who needs to have some costume or makeup adjustments for each exposure. It also could be useful if you want to look at the resulting image after each shot to see if you need to make further adjustments to your settings.

Apart from using individual shutter presses, this option works the same as continuous exposure bracketing. For example, you can use flash and you can change the order of the exposures using the Bracket Settings menu option.

None of the bracketing options—exposure, White Balance, or DRO—is available in the Auto, Scene, or Sweep Panorama shooting mode.

WHITE BALANCE BRACKETING

The next option on the Drive Mode menu, White Balance Bracketing, whose icon is highlighted in Figure 4-30, is similar to Continuous Exposure Bracketing, except that only three images can be taken and the value that is varied for the three shots is white balance rather than exposure.

Figure 4-30. White Balance Bracketing Icon Highlighted on Menu

Using the Left and Right buttons or the control dial, select either Lo or Hi for the amount of deviation from the normal White Balance setting. Then, when you press the shutter button (you don't have to hold it down), the camera will take a series of three shots—one at the normal setting; the next one with a lower color temperature, resulting in a "cooler," more bluish image; and the last one with a higher color temperature, resulting in a "warmer," more reddish image. When you use this form of bracketing, unlike exposure bracketing, you will hear only one shutter sound because the camera takes just one image, with one quick shutter press, and then electronically creates the other two exposures with the different White Balance values.

You can change the order of the exposures using the Bracket Settings menu option, discussed later in this chapter.

DRO BRACKETING

This final option on the Drive Mode menu sets the a6400 to take a series of three shots at different settings of the DRO (dynamic range optimizer) option.

I'll discuss DRO later in this chapter. Essentially, DRO alters the a6400's image processing to even out the contrast between shadowed and bright areas. It can be difficult to decide how much DRO processing to use, and this option gives you a way to experiment with several different settings before you decide on the amount of DRO for your final image.

As with White Balance Bracketing, you can select Hi or Lo for the DRO interval. Also, as with White Balance Bracketing, you only need to press the shutter button once, briefly; the camera will record the three different exposures electronically. The order of these exposures is not affected by the Bracket Order menu option.

Bracket Settings

The next option on this menu screen includes two settings for how bracketed exposures are taken. When you select Bracket Settings, you will see two sub-options: Self-timer During Bracket, and Bracket Order, as shown in Figure 4-31.

Figure 4-31. Bracket Settings Menu Options Screen

The Self-timer During Bracket option lets you use the self-timer with bracket shooting. Without this option you could not use bracketing and the self-timer at the same time, because they are selected by different options on the Drive Mode menu.

With this menu item you can have the self-timer set for two, five, or ten seconds before the first bracket shot is triggered, or you can leave the self-timer turned off. This setting turns on the self-timer for any type of bracket shooting you choose from the Drive Mode menu—exposure, White Balance, or DRO.

The second sub-option, Bracket Order, lets you alter the sequence of the bracketed shots. There are two choices. The first one, shown selected in Figure 4-31, is the default setting, with which the first shot is at the normal setting, the next is more negative (or with lower color temperature), the one after that is more positive (or with higher color temperature), and so on, ending with the most negative setting and, finally, the most positive setting. If you choose the second option, the images are shot in a strictly ascending series, moving from the most negative setting to the most positive setting.

The Bracket Order option affects the order for exposure bracketing and White Balance bracketing, but not for DRO bracketing.

Interval Shooting Function

This option lets you set up the camera to shoot a series of still images at a specified interval in order to create a time-lapse sequence that is played back like a movie. The end result is a movie that is greatly speeded up, usually in order to show a long process, such as the sun setting, a flower unfolding, a parking lot filling up with cars, or a building being constructed, in a much shorter period of time, such as five or ten seconds.

With the a6400, you can capture the series of shots using the Interval Shooting Function menu option, but you cannot create the final movie in the camera. Instead, you have to use Sony's Imaging Edge software, which can be downloaded for free from Sony.

Here are the steps to use for this process:

1. Select the Interval Shooting Function option on screen 3 of the Camera Settings1 menu and press the Center button to select it.

2. On the first screen of sub-options, shown in Figure 4-32, set Interval Shooting to On.

Figure 4-32. First Screen of Sub-options for Interval Shooting

3. Set Shooting Start Time to a value from 1 second to 99 minutes and 59 seconds. This period of time represents the delay from when you press the shutter button to when the interval shooting series starts. Unless you have a reason to delay the start of shooting, pick 1 or 2 seconds, so the sequence will get started immediately.

4. Set Shooting Interval to a value from 1 second to 60 seconds, which represents the time between shots. The larger this value, the faster the action will appear in the final movie. If you choose 1 second, the action will be speeded up about 30 times, if you use the standard 30 frames per second (fps) speed for the final movie. If you choose 10 seconds, it will be speeded up 300 times; if you choose 60 seconds, it will be speeded up 1800 times. So, for a very long process, such as building a house, you may want to choose the maximum interval of 60 seconds, to keep the length of the final movie at a reasonable length.

5. Set Number of Shots to a value from 1 to 9999. If you set this value to 9999 and use 60 seconds for the interval between shots, the camera can record an event that lasts for about one week. Of course, if you record a sequence for one week, you can then reset the camera to start another sequence, if you are recording an event that lasts more than one week, as long as you are able to continue supplying power to the camera and making sure the memory card does not fill up.

6. Set AE Tracking Sensitivity to High, Mid, or Low. This setting controls how readily the camera changes its exposure settings when lighting conditions change. The value you use for this setting depends on the subject you are recording. For example, if you are recording a construction project, you may not want the exposure to change every time a cloud passes over the sun. In that case, set this option to Low. On the other hand, if you are recording the sunset, it is natural for the exposure to change constantly as the sky darkens. In that case, you may want to choose High. As you work with this feature, you may find which setting produces the results you prefer.

7. On the second screen of sub-options, set Silent Shooting in Interval to On or Off. This setting depends on your needs. If you are recording a

sequence in an area where you want to minimize the sounds of the camera operating, choose On; if you would prefer to hear the shutter being operated for each shot, choose Off.

8. For the last sub-option, set Shooting Interval Priority to On or Off. This setting controls what happens when the camera is set to Program or Aperture Priority mode, in which the camera selects the shutter speed. In that situation, it is possible that, if the lighting of the subject dims, the shutter speed the camera selects will become longer than the shooting interval that is set. For example, if the shooting interval is set to three seconds but the lighting becomes so dim that the camera needs to choose a shutter speed of four seconds, a problem arises. If Shooting Interval Priority is turned on, in that situation the camera will reduce the shutter speed in order to maintain the shooting interval as set. If it is turned off, the camera will use the longer shutter speed, regardless of the shooting interval that was set.

9. On screen 1 of the Camera Settings1 menu, set Aspect Ratio to the desired value: 3:2, 16:9, or 1:1. If you are going to be using Sony's Imaging Edge software to create the final movie, you may want to choose 16:9, because that is the aspect ratio of the movie that will be created by that software. If you choose one of the other settings, there will be black bars at the sides of the movie frame.

10. Make any other settings you need. For example, you may want to select a preset value for White Balance, rather than using Auto White Balance, in order to avoid changes in the coloration of the images as the lighting changes. I have found it a good idea to shoot only JPEG images, because the software had difficulty creating a movie with Raw files, even though it should be possible.

11. When you are ready, set the camera on a sturdy tripod, make sure it has a steady supply of power that is sufficient for the planned duration of the sequence, and press the shutter button.

Once the images have been captured, they will appear in the camera as a group, similar to how a group of continuous shots appears, as discussed earlier in this chapter. You can view a preview of how the final movie will look. To do that, go to screen 2 of the Playback menu and select Continuous Playback for Interval.

The camera will display a screen with the notation Continuous Playback in the lower right corner, with a white disc to the left, indicating that you press the Center button to activate continuous playback for interval shots.

Then, navigate to the group of interval shots you just captured, and press the Center button. The camera will play back the group of interval shots quickly, giving you an approximate idea of how the final sequence will look. To play it again, press the Down button. You can adjust the speed of this playback by turning the control wheel during playback, or by using the Playback Speed for Interval option on screen 2 of the Playback menu. When you have finished previewing the sequence in continuous playback mode, press the Center button to exit to normal playback.

If you want to create a final time-lapse movie from a group of interval shots, follow these steps:

1. Download Sony's free Imaging Edge and PlayMemories Home software packages. The download sites are https://support.d-imaging.sony.co.jp/app/disoft/en/ and https://www.sony.net/pm/, respectively. Install both of those programs on your computer.

2. Using a card reader, load the memory card with the interval shots into the computer. In the Imaging Edge Viewer module, select the images you want to include in the time-lapse movie.

3. Go to the Imaging Edge Viewer's Tools menu, and select Create Time-Lapse Movie. Select values as indicated on the computer screen for items such as Output Method, File Settings, and Trimming, then select Next at the bottom of the screen.

4. The PlayMemories Home software on your computer should start automatically, with the selected images loaded into the video-editing screen. Make any other desired settings, then click Next at the bottom of the screen, and save the movie in the desired format.

For more detailed instructions on this process, see Sony's support website at https://support.d-imaging.sony.co.jp/support/tutorial/ilc/en/ilce-6400/08.php.

Screen 4 of the Camera Settings1 menu is shown in Figure 4-33.

Figure 4-33. Screen 4 of Camera Settings1 Menu

Recall

The Recall option is used only when the mode dial is set to MR. Using this option, you can recall the camera settings that you stored to one of the seven slots for the Memory Recall mode, as discussed in Chapter 3.

When the mode dial is first turned to MR, this option's main screen appears on the camera's display with one of the seven indicators at the upper right highlighted, as shown in Figure 4-34. (If the Mode Dial Guide option is turned on through screen 2 of the Setup menu, the Mode Dial Guide screen will appear first; you then have to press the Center button to make this screen appear.)

Figure 4-34. Memory Recall Screen

If the mode dial is already at MR and you want to change to another memory register, you can use this menu option. Once the Memory Recall screen is displayed, either by turning the mode dial to MR or by using this menu option, use the direction buttons, the control wheel, or the control dial to select register 1, 2, 3, M1, M2, M3, or M4 at the upper right of the screen. The settings for registers 1, 2, and 3 are stored in the camera's internal memory; the settings for registers M1 through M4 are stored on a memory card. Of course, you have to make sure the appropriate memory card is in the camera if you want to use M1 through M4.

When the register whose saved settings you want to recall for use is highlighted, press the Center button, and the new group of settings stored to that register will take effect.

Memory

The second option on screen 4 of the Camera Settings1 menu, Memory, was discussed in Chapter 3 in connection with the Memory Recall shooting mode. Once you have set up the a6400 with the settings you want to store to a register of the MR mode, select the Memory option and choose one of the seven numbered registers.

Press the Center button, and the current settings will be stored to that register for the Memory Recall mode. You can recall those settings at any time by turning the mode dial to the MR position (or selecting the Memory Recall menu option if the mode dial is already at that position) and selecting register 1, 2, or 3, or M1, M2, M3, or M4. As noted above, the contents of the first three registers are stored to the camera's internal memory, while the contents of M1 through M4 are stored to a memory card in the camera.

With either the Recall or Memory option, you can scroll to additional screens using the Down button to see other settings currently in effect.

Register Custom Shooting Settings

This final option on screen 4 provides a useful feature for quick recall of a group of shooting settings for the a6400. In order to take advantage of this option, you have to use this menu item as well as the Custom Key (Still Images) option on screen 8 of the Camera Settings2 menu, which I will discuss in Chapter 5. With that option, you can assign a particular control button, such as the C1, C2, Left, Right, Center, Down, AF/ MF, or AEL button, to carry out one operation of your choice from a long list of options, such as bringing up the ISO, Drive Mode, or White Balance menu, activating Eye AF, or locking exposure or focus.

Among the many options that can be assigned to a control button are three options called Recall Custom Hold 1, 2, and 3. For example, if you assign a control button to the Recall Custom Hold 1 option, then, when you press that button in shooting mode, the camera will immediately put into effect all of the settings that are stored for the Recall Custom Hold 1 option. (This feature works only when the camera is set to one of the PASM shooting modes—Program, Aperture Priority, Shutter Priority, or Manual.)

In order to choose what settings are stored for Recall Custom Hold 1, 2, and 3, you use the menu option being discussed here—Register Custom Shooting Settings. With this option, you can, if you want, assign a different group of shooting settings to each of those three slots, and then assign each of those slots to a different control button. In that way, you can press the button assigned to a given group of settings to instantly call up those settings. The settings will stay in effect while you keep the assigned button pressed down, and the camera will revert to the settings that are currently in effect once you release the button.

This feature can be useful if, say, you are photographing scenery or people at an outdoor event, but you want to be ready to take a picture of a bird in flight if you suddenly see that opportunity. When you see the bird flying, you can press the button assigned to the settings stored in the Recall Custom Hold 1 slot, and keep the button pressed while you shoot images of the flying bird. Then release the button, and you can resume your other image-making without having had to change any settings on the camera.

Here is how to use this menu option. When you highlight it and press the Center button, you will see the screen in Figure 4-35, with three options for the Recall Custom Hold slots. Highlight and select one to move to the next screen, which is shown in Figure 4-36.

Figure 4-35. Register Custom Shooting Settings - Menu Screen

Figure 4-36. Register Custom Shooting Settings - Options for Slot

This screen shows the first five of the ten settings that can be stored: Shooting mode, aperture, shutter speed, Drive Mode, exposure compensation, ISO, Metering Mode, Focus Mode, Focus Area, and AF On. Using the control wheel or the Down button, scroll through these lines. If you want to include a setting for a given item, when its line is highlighted, use the Left button or control dial to highlight the check box at the left and press the Center button to add the check mark. If you want to remove a check mark, press the Center button again.

To change the setting for a given item, highlight the line itself (rather than the check box) and press the Center button. The camera will then display a screen like that shown in Figure 4-37, which shows the options for shooting mode.

Figure 4-37. Register Custom Shooting Settings - Options for Shooting Mode

Highlight and select the item you want to set for that option, and press the Menu button to return to the list of options. Continue through the list, checking the box for each item you want to include and then selecting the setting for that item. When you have made all of your selections, move the orange highlight bar to the bottom of the list, and highlight and select the Register item, as shown in Figure 4-38.

Figure 4-38. Register Option Highlighted on Menu Screen

The listed settings will then be registered to the chosen slot, such as Recall Custom Hold 1, and that slot of settings is ready to be assigned to a control button using the Custom Key (Still Images) menu option.

If you prefer, you can make all of the desired settings on the camera itself, and then highlight and select the Import Current Setting block at the bottom of the list of settings. If you do that, the camera will display a screen showing the current settings, with a message asking if you want to import that group of settings, as shown in Figure 4-39.

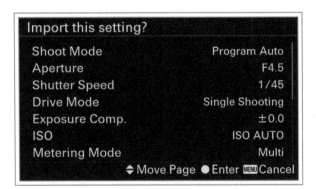

Figure 4-39. Screen to Import Current Settings

Press the Center button to confirm, and those settings will be loaded to the selected Recall Custom Hold slot. However, to store them to that slot so they can be recalled, you still need to go back to the bottom of the screen and select the Register option, as shown in Figure 4-38. Then the settings will be stored and ready to recall with a press of the assigned button.

So, if you see a quick opportunity for an action shot, you can press the button assigned to your group of settings, including, for example, Shutter Priority mode with continuous autofocus and a fast shutter speed, and be ready to shoot very quickly, without having to change a single setting.

You can store settings only for the Program, Aperture Priority, Shutter Priority, and Manual exposure modes, and, as noted earlier, you can recall them only when the camera is set to one of those modes.

The items on screen 5 of the Camera Settings1 menu are shown in Figure 4-40.

Figure 4-40. Screen 5 of Camera Settings1 Menu

Focus Mode

The Focus Mode option gives you five choices for the method the camera uses for focusing. This is one of the more important choices you can make for your photography. Following are details about each of the five selections, which are shown in Figure 4-41.

Figure 4-41. Focus Mode Menu Options Screen

Single-Shot AF

The first Focus Mode option is single-shot AF, indicated by the AF-S icon. With this option, the camera tries to focus on the scene using the focus area that is selected using the Focus Area menu option, discussed below. If the Pre-AF option on screen 6 of the Camera Settings1 menu is turned on, the camera will continuously adjust focus, even before you press the shutter button halfway down. When you do press the button halfway down, the camera will lock in the focus and keep it locked as long as you keep the button pressed halfway.

If the Pre-AF menu option is not turned on, the camera will not make any attempt to adjust focus until you press the shutter button halfway down.

Once you press the shutter button halfway down, you will see one or more green focus brackets or blocks on the screen indicating the point or points where the camera achieved sharp focus, as shown in Figure 4-42, and you will hear a beep (unless beeps have been turned off through the Setup menu, as discussed in Chapter 8).

Figure 4-42. Green Blocks Indicating Sharp Focus

In addition, a green dot in the lower left corner of the display will light up steadily indicating that focus is confirmed. If focus cannot be achieved, the green dot will blink and no focus brackets will appear on the screen.

Once you have pressed the shutter button halfway to lock focus, you can use the locked focus on a different subject that is at the same distance as the one the camera originally locked its focus on. For example, if you have focused on a person at a distance of 15 feet (4.6 m), and then you decide you want to include another person or object in the scene, once you have locked the focus on the first person by pressing the shutter button halfway down, you can move the camera to include the other person or object in the scene as long as you keep the camera at about the same distance from the subject. The focus will remain locked at that distance until you press the shutter button the rest of the way down to take the picture.

AUTOMATIC AF

The second option for Focus Mode, automatic AF, designated by the AF-A icon, is a combination of the first and third options, single-shot AF and continuous AF. With automatic AF, the camera locks focus on the subject as with single-shot AF, but, if the subject or camera then moves in a way that changes the focus point, the camera

will continue to adjust focus, as with continuous AF. I generally prefer to use either single AF or continuous AF, so I will know whether the camera is going to be adjusting focus, rather than relying on its electronic judgment as to whether focus needs to be changed. But, in a case where the subject initially is stationary but may be moving, this mode could be useful.

CONTINUOUS AF

The next option for Focus Mode, continuous AF, is designated by the AF-C icon on the menu. With this option, as with single-shot AF, the a6400 focuses continuously before you press the shutter button if the Pre-AF menu option is turned on. If that option is turned off, the camera does not adjust focus until you press the shutter button halfway.

The difference with this mode is that the camera does not lock in the focus when you press the shutter button halfway. Instead, the focus will continue to be adjusted if the subject moves or the distance to the subject changes through camera motion. You will not hear a beep or see any focus brackets to confirm focus. Instead, the green dot in the lower left corner of the display will change its appearance to show the focus status.

If the green dot is surrounded by curved lines, as shown in Figure 4-43, that means focus is currently sharp but is subject to adjustment if needed.

Figure 4-43. Curved Lines Indicating Continuous Focusing

If only the curved lines appear, that means the camera is still trying to achieve focus. If the green dot flashes, that means the camera is having trouble focusing.

This focusing mode can be useful when you are shooting a moving subject. With this option, you can get the a6400 to fix its focus on the subject, but you don't have to let up the shutter button to refocus; instead, you can hold the button down halfway until the instant when you take the picture. In this way, you may save some time, rather than having to keep starting the focus and exposure process over by pressing the shutter button halfway again.

Also, you have to use the continuous AF setting in order to take advantage of the camera's excellent tracking capability. If you set the Focus Area option to Tracking, the a6400 will keep focus locked on your subject with its moving focus frame. This capability gives you an excellent system for achieving sharp images of sporting events, of children and pets at play, and the like.

Continuous AF is the only autofocus option available for recording movies.

DMF

The next option for Focus Mode is DMF, which stands for direct manual focus. This feature lets you use a combination of autofocus and manual focus. DMF can be helpful if you are shooting an extreme closeup of a small object, when focus can be critical and hard to achieve. With the DMF option, you can start the focusing process by pressing the shutter button halfway down. The camera will make its best attempt to focus sharply using the autofocus mechanism. Then, if you continue to hold the shutter button halfway down, you can use the camera's manual focusing mechanism to fine-tune the focus, concentrating on the parts of the subject that you want to be most sharply focused.

When DMF is activated, you can turn on Peaking through screen 13 of the Camera Settings1 menu, as discussed below, and that feature will function for autofocus as well as for manual focus. You also can use the MF Assist feature from that same menu screen with DMF. That feature is discussed below in connection with manual focus.

DMF is not available with all lenses that can be used with this camera. For example, it is not available with the Sony DT 50mm f/1.8 SAM lens (SAL50F18).

Manual Focus

The final selection on the Focus Mode menu is Manual Focus. As I indicated in the discussion of DMF, there are situations in which you may achieve sharper focus by adjusting it on your own rather than by relying on the camera's autofocus system. Those situations include

shooting extreme closeups; shooting a group of objects at differing distances; or shooting through a barrier such as glass or a wire fence.

Also, manual focus gives you the freedom to use a soft focus effect purposely. As I will discuss later in this chapter, the a6400 includes a setting on the Picture Effect menu called "Soft Focus," which adds a pleasing softness to your image. If you would rather create this effect on your own by controlling the focus directly, you can set the camera for manual focus and defocus the subject in precisely the way you want.

The method for setting manual focus mode varies according to the lens you are using. If the lens has an AF/MF switch, you can move that switch to the MF position to activate manual focus mode. You also can turn on manual focus by using the Focus Mode menu, even if the AF/MF switch is at the AF position, with some lenses, including both kit lenses for the a6400. However, with some lenses, such as the Sony DT 50mm f/1.8 (used with the Mount Adaptor), you have to use the AF/MF switch on the lens to activate manual focus mode.

Once manual focus is selected, use the focusing mechanism on the lens itself, which may be a large, ridged ring like the one on the 18-135mm kit lens. There are several functions available to assist with manual focusing. I will discuss those menu options separately later in this chapter, but I will briefly describe them here so you can get started with manual focus.

The first option, MF Assist, is controlled through the fifth item on screen 13 of the Camera Settings1 menu. With MF Assist turned on, whenever you start adjusting manual focus, the image on the display is magnified 5.9 times, as shown in Figure 4-44, so you can more clearly check the focus.

Figure 4-44. Enlarged Screen with MF Assist

Once the magnified image is displayed, if you press the Center button, the image is magnified further to 11.7 times normal. Press the Center button again to return to the 5.9-times view and press the shutter button halfway to return the display to normal size. You can adjust how long the magnified display stays on the screen using the Focus Magnification Time option, also found on screen 13 of the Camera Settings1 menu. I prefer to set the time to No Limit, so the magnification does not disappear just as I am getting the focus adjusted as I want it. With the No Limit setting, the magnification remains on the screen until you dismiss it by pressing the shutter button halfway.

If you don't want the camera to enlarge the image as soon as you start focusing, you can use the Focus Magnifier option instead of MF Assist. You can find Focus Magnifier also on screen 13 of the Camera Settings1 menu, or you can assign it to a control button using the Custom Key (Still Images) option on screen 8 of the Camera Settings2 menu.

Once Focus Magnifier is activated, a small orange frame appears on the screen. You can move that frame around the screen with the control wheel, the control dial, or the direction buttons, or by dragging it with your finger if touch screen operations are turned on. The frame represents the area that will be magnified when you press the Center button. By pressing the Center button, you can switch magnification to various levels, as discussed later in this chapter.

You can use both MF Assist and Focus Magnifier, though I see no need to do so. My preference is to use only the MF Assist option. I prefer not to go through the steps to turn on the Focus Magnifier option, which does not add that much to the focusing options. However, when I am faced with a challenging task such as shooting in dim lighting, I sometimes use the Focus Magnifier option because it is easier to deal with that situation by being able to see the subject clearly at its normal size and selecting the focus point before using magnification and starting to focus. However, MF Assist is not available when shooting movies or when a Mount Adaptor is attached, for using an A-mount lens, so Focus Magnifier is the only option in those cases.

The a6400 provides one more aid to manual focusing, called Peaking, which is controlled using the Peaking Setting option on screen 13 of the Camera Settings1

menu. It has three sub-options: Peaking Display, Peaking Level, and Peaking Color. Peaking Display can be on or off, and Peaking Level can be set to Low, Mid, or High. When Peaking Level is turned on at any of those levels, then, when you are using manual focus or DMF, the camera places bright pixels around the areas of the image that it judges to be in focus, as shown in Figure 4-45 (without Peaking) and Figure 4-46 (with Peaking Level set to Mid).

Figure 4-45. Peaking Turned Off

Figure 4-46. Peaking Set to Mid

Besides setting the intensity of this display, you can set its color—white, red, yellow, or blue—using the Peaking Color option. I find Peaking to be especially useful in dark conditions because the Peaking effect contrasts with the dark display. Also, as noted above, Peaking works with both the autofocus and manual focus aspects of the DMF option. I will discuss Peaking further later in this chapter.

Finally, there is another way to customize the use of manual focus with the a6400. On screen 8 of the Camera Settings2 menu, as noted above, you can use the Custom Key (Still Images) menu option to assign a button to control any one item from a long list of functions. One of those functions, called AF/MF Control Toggle, is useful if you often need to switch back and forth between autofocus and manual focus.

When this function is assigned to a button, you can press the button to switch instantly between these two focus modes. This is so much more convenient than going back to the Shooting menu and using the Focus Mode menu option, that it may be worthwhile dedicating a button to this use. Note, though, that this function works to switch from manual focus into autofocus only when the switch on the lens (if there is such a switch) is in the AF position. If that switch is at the MF position, the AF/MF Control Toggle function cannot override the setting of that switch.

Priority Set in AF-S

This next menu option lets you determine how the camera sets its priority between releasing the shutter and making sure focus is sharp when using autofocus. This first of two similar options governs the camera's behavior when Focus Mode is set to AF-S, for single autofocus. It also applies when that option is set to AF-A, for automatic autofocus, or to DMF, for direct manual focus. The options are AF, Release, or Balanced Emphasis, as shown in Figure 4-47.

Figure 4-47. Priority Set in AF-S Menu Options Screen

If you choose AF, the camera will not release the shutter when you press the shutter button down, if the subject is not in focus. If you choose Release, the camera will release the shutter regardless of whether the subject is in focus. With the Balanced Emphasis option, the camera will attempt to achieve focus, but will still release the shutter even if focus could not be achieved.

The choice you make for this option depends on your needs in a given shooting session. If you are photographing a one-time event, you might want to choose Release, to make sure you don't miss a shot completely. If you are capturing images that need to be in focus when time is not critical, you might choose AF.

For many purposes, the Balanced Emphasis selection is a good compromise.

Priority Set in AF-C

This option is similar to the one discussed above, except that it applies only when Focus Mode is set to AF-C, for continuous autofocus. This setting can be important when you are using continuous shooting. If you are shooting bursts of shots with Focus Mode set to AF-C, the camera will focus continuously, and the setting you make for Priority Set in AF-C can have a significant impact on the speed of shooting.

If you choose AF, the shots are likely to be in focus, but the speed of shooting may slow down significantly as the camera ensures that focus is sharp before permitting the next shot to take place. To speed up shooting, you can choose Release, but focus is likely to suffer if the subject is moving. Even with Balanced Emphasis, you may find that the shots you take are not well focused. So, as with the previous menu option, the choice you make depends on how strongly you value accurate focus versus speed and the number of shots you can capture in a short period of time.

Focus Area

The next option on this menu screen, Focus Area, lets you choose the area the camera focuses on when using an autofocus setting or DMF, as selected with the Focus Mode menu option. The three autofocus modes are single, automatic, and continuous. Direct manual focus, or DMF, is a mode that lets you use both manual focus and autofocus. The Focus Area menu option sets the focus area for all four of those focus modes.

Before I discuss the various choices for the Focus Area menu option, it is important to note that these settings were originally designed for use with a camera that does not have any touch screen features. If you don't want to use the touch screen for focusing, that is fine—you can just use the Focus Area setting to control where the camera directs its focus. However, you also can use the touch screen for focusing to some extent, with any of these settings in place.

I will discuss touch screen options in more detail in Chapter 6, where I discuss the LCD screen and other physical features of the camera. Briefly, when shooting still images with an autofocus mode in effect, if Focus Area is set to Wide or Center (or the Wide or Center setting for Tracking AF), and Function of Touch Operation on screen 9 of the Camera Settings2 menu is set to Touch Focus, you can choose the focus point by touching the screen. Just put your finger on the screen at the chosen point, and the camera will place a focus frame there. You can then drag that frame around the screen if you want. Then press the shutter button to focus and take the picture.

If the conditions mentioned above are in place, but Focus Area is set to Flexible Spot or Expand Flexible Spot (or the Flexible Spot or Expand Flexible Spot setting for Tracking AF), you can drag the focus frame on the screen to move it, or tap the screen to place the frame at a new location. If Focus Area is set to Zone, you can touch the screen to move the focus zone. The situation is similar for video recording, with a few variations, as discussed in Chapters 6 and 9.

In the following discussion of Focus Area options, I will not often mention the Touch Focus feature, but remember that it is available as an alternative way to use autofocus.

The choices for Focus Area are Wide, Zone, Center, Flexible Spot, Expand Flexible Spot, and Tracking AF. Figure 4-48 shows five of these options; you have to scroll down to see the last one.

Figure 4-48. **Focus Area Menu Options Screen**

The ways these selections operate vary somewhat depending on whether you select single-shot autofocus, automatic autofocus, continuous autofocus, or DMF for Focus Mode on the menu. If you select DMF, you can use autofocus in the same way as with single autofocus, so DMF is the same as single autofocus with respect to Focus Area. I will discuss the following options assuming at first that you are using single autofocus or

DMF for Focus Mode. I will also assume that Face/Eye Priority in AF and Face Detection Frame Display are turned off through the sub-options under the Face/Eye AF Settings item on screen 6 of the Camera Settings1 menu; if those options are turned on and a face is detected, a face detection frame will be seen in addition to any Focus Area frame that may be visible

WIDE

With the Wide setting for Focus Area, the a6400 uses multiple focus zones that cover the whole screen, and tries to detect one or more items within the scene to focus on based on their locations. When it has achieved sharp focus on one or more subjects, the camera displays a green frame or a group of small green blocks indicating each focus point. The camera displays frames when focusing on a larger area, and blocks when focusing on a smaller area. You may see one or several green frames or numerous blocks, depending on how many focus points are detected at the same distance. An example with multiple blocks is shown in Figure 4-49.

Figure 4-49. **Green Focus Blocks Indicating Sharp Focus**

When you are using single-shot autofocus, the Wide option is good for shots of landscapes, buildings, and the like. In continuous autofocus mode, the a6400 does not display stationary frames or blocks as it does with the Wide setting. Instead, it displays small, moving blocks where focus is located, if Display Continuous AF Area is turned on through screen 7 of the Camera Settings1 menu. The camera tries to focus on subjects that appear to be the main ones.

ZONE

The Zone setting is similar to Wide, but the camera displays an area that uses only part of the screen. With this setting, the camera will be limited to focusing on a subject within the designated zone. When you select this option, the camera displays a set of gray frames that outline the overall focus zone, with arrows pointing to the four edges of the display, as shown in Figure 4-50.

Figure 4-50. Screen for Setting Zone Focus Area

Use the four direction buttons to move the focus zone around the display. If touch screen operations are turned on, you can drag the zone around the screen. If you press the Custom 2/Delete button while the zone is activated for moving, it will move back to the center of the display. When the zone is located where you want it, press the Center button to fix it in place. The camera will display a black frame in the chosen location. When you press the shutter button halfway to focus, the camera will display green frames or small green blocks that indicate where focus is sharp within the designated zone.

This setting is useful when you want to focus within a certain area, but the location of the actual subject is not certain. For example, if you are photographing a show in which the performers are located on the right side of the stage, you can set the zone to the right side and let the camera direct its focus to the action within that limited area.

Center

If you select Center for the Focus Area setting, the camera places a black focus frame in the center of the display, as shown in Figure 4-51, and focuses on whatever it finds within that frame.

Figure 4-51. Focus Area Set to Center

When you press the shutter button halfway, if the camera can focus it will beep and the frame will turn green. This option is useful for an object in the center of the scene.

Even if you need to focus on an off-center object, you can use this setting. To focus on an object at the right, center that object in the focus frame and press the shutter button halfway to lock focus. Keeping the button pressed halfway, move the camera so the object is on the right, and press the button to take the picture.

If you turn on continuous autofocus with the Center setting, the camera still will display a black focus frame. When you press the shutter button halfway, the frame will turn green when focus is sharp, but the camera will not beep. As the camera or subject moves, the camera will continue to re-focus as you hold the shutter button halfway down. You can use this technique to carry out your own focus tracking, by moving the camera to keep the center frame targeted on a moving subject.

Flexible Spot

The Flexible Spot option gives you more control over the Focus Area, with a frame you can move around the screen and resize. After you highlight this option on the Camera Settings1 menu, press the Right or Left button or turn the control dial to select the size of the Flexible Spot focus frame: L, M, or S, for Large, Medium, or Small.

After choosing a size, press the Center button and you will see a screen like that in Figure 4-52, with a gray focus frame of that size with arrows pointing to the four edges of the display.

Figure 4-52. Flexible Spot Focus Area Frame - Ready to Move

Use the four direction buttons to move the frame around the display. When the frame is located as you want it, press the Center button to fix it in place. The camera will display a black frame of the chosen size in the chosen location. When you press the shutter button halfway to focus, the focus frame will turn green when focus is sharp.

This frame operates the same way as the frame for the Center option, except for the ability to change the location and select a size. To return the frame quickly to the center of the screen, press the Custom 2/Delete button while the frame is activated for moving, and it will move back to the center of the display.

This option is useful for focusing on a particular point, such as an object at the far right, without having to move the camera to place a focus frame over that object. This might help if you are using a tripod, for example, and need to set up the shot with precision, focusing on an off-center subject. If the subject is small, using the smallest focus frame can make the process even easier.

If you use continuous autofocus, the Flexible Spot option works the same way as the Center option, discussed above, but with the added ability to select the size and change the location of the frame.

One problem with the Flexible Spot option is that it can be cumbersome to move the frame again once you have fixed it in place. One way to do this is to select the Focus Area menu option and repeat all of the steps discussed above. There are several quicker ways to move the frame, though.

The easiest way to do this is to have the Touch Operation and Touch Panel items turned on through screen 3 of the Setup menu. With those settings active, you can touch the LCD screen with your finger to

choose a new focus point, or drag the focus frame to a new location. (If the Touch Pad option is also activated through that menu screen, you can move the focus frame by touching the LCD screen when you are using the viewfinder to view the scene.)

Another easy way to move the focus frame, without using the touch screen, is to go to screen 8 of the Camera Settings2 menu and select the Custom Key (Still Images) option. On the next screen, select a button, such as the Center button, and assign the Focus Standard setting to that button. Then, whenever Flexible Spot is in effect, just press the assigned button when the shooting screen is displayed, and the screen for moving the focus frame will appear. You can quickly use the direction buttons to move the frame where you want it, and you can press the Custom 2/Delete button to center it on the display. Press the Center button again to fix the frame in place.

Another option for moving the focus frame is to assign Focus Area to a control button using the Custom Key (Still Images) menu option. Then, when you press the assigned button, the camera displays the Focus Area menu, from which you can choose the size and location of the Flexible Spot frame. Or, you can assign Focus Area to the Function menu, which is called up by pressing the Function button. I will discuss that menu in Chapter 6.

My preference is to use the touch screen, which is simple and does not require using a control button for the Focus Standard option. As an alternative, I recommend assigning the Focus Standard setting to the Center button. Then, to move the focus frame, just press that button and it is an easy matter to adjust the frame's location. I will discuss the Custom Key menu options further in Chapters 5 and 6.

EXPAND FLEXIBLE SPOT

This next option for Focus Area is a variation of the previous one, Flexible Spot. It operates in the same way, except that the only available frame size is small. You can move it around the display with the direction buttons.

When you use this frame to fix the focus for your shot, the camera will first try to focus on a subject within the frame. If it cannot find a focus point in that small area, it will expand its scope and try to focus on a subject within the area immediately surrounding the frame.

That area is outlined by four small brackets outside the corners of the focus frame, as shown in Figure 4-53.

Figure 4-53. Expand Flexible Spot Focus Frame

This option can be of use when you want to focus on a small area, but you don't want the focusing to fail if focus can't be achieved in that exact spot.

TRACKING

The final option for Focus Area is Tracking, which sets up the camera to track a moving object. This menu option is available for selection only when Focus Mode is set to Continuous AF. When you highlight this option on the menu, as shown in Figure 4-54, the camera gives you seven choices for the Tracking focus frame: Wide, Zone, Center, Flexible Spot Small, Flexible Spot Medium, Flexible Spot Large, or Expand Flexible Spot. These frames correspond to the other choices for Focus Area, discussed above, and they also include the Tracking frame's ability to "lock on" to a subject and track it as it moves.

Figure 4-54. Tracking Option Highlighted on Focus Area Menu

After choosing one of these seven settings, aim the camera at the subject, place the focus frame (if there is one) over it, and press the shutter button halfway. The camera will try to keep the subject in focus as the subject or camera moves. The camera will display a small focus frame that moves with the subject. When

you are ready to take the picture, press the shutter button all the way. If the autofocus system worked as expected, the image should be in focus.

When you are deciding which of the seven sub-options to choose for Tracking AF, consider the subject that you want the camera to lock on to, and choose accordingly. For example, if the subject is an automobile that is not too far away, you can probably choose Wide. If the subject is a person some distance away, you may want to choose Flexible Spot Small or Medium. Or, you can choose Center and position the central frame over the subject.

Note that this choice affects only how the camera selects the subject to lock on to. Once it has locked onto that subject, the camera will attempt to track whatever subject it has selected, as the subject moves around. So, even if you started with the Flexible Spot Small setting, if the camera locks on to a nearby face, the camera should continue to track the face, even if the face is larger than the initial focus frame.

If you select an option with a movable focus frame or zone, such as Zone, Flexible Spot, or Expand Flexible Spot, you can move that frame around the screen in the same way as described earlier for those Focus Area options.

If you assign a control button, such as the AF/MF button, to the Tracking On function through the Custom Key (Still Images) option on screen 8 of the Camera Settings2 menu, you can activate the Tracking setting for Focus Area temporarily by holding down that button.

The Tracking AF option will not give good results if the subject moves too rapidly or erratically, or moves completely out of the frame. But, for subjects that are moving moderately in stable patterns, the Tracking AF system is an excellent feature. This option is not available on the Focus Area menu when recording movies, or when the Subject Detection option under the Face/Eye AF Settings option on screen 6 of the Camera Settings1 menu is set to Animal.

Note, though, that there is another way to activate tracking autofocus with the a6400 camera, which works somewhat differently from the Tracking option on the Focus Area menu. As I will discuss in Chapter 6, you can turn on Touch Tracking through the Function of Touch

Operation option on screen 9 of the Camera Settings2 menu. With that option activated, you can touch the screen to initiate focus tracking at the selected point. This option is similar to the Tracking option on the Focus Area menu, with two significant differences. First, it works in all autofocus modes—single-shot AF, automatic AF, continuous AF, and DMF, not just continuous AF, as is the case with the Tracking option for Focus Area. Second, Touch Tracking works when recording movies, unlike the Tracking option for Focus Area. Touch Tracking, like the Focus Area Tracking option, does not work when Subject Detection is set to Animal.

The only Focus Area setting available is Wide when the camera is in Auto or Scene mode, when the Smile Shutter is in use, or when recording movies.

Focus Area Limit

This menu option gives you a way to limit the available selections on the Focus Area menu. If you know you will only be using a few (or just one) of the various options for a particular shooting session, or in general, you can use this option to hide the options you won't be needing, so it will be quicker to select a setting that you want.

Figure 4-55. Focus Area Limit Menu Options Screen

When you select this option and move to its selection screen using the Center button, the camera displays a screen like that in Figure 4-55, showing all possible settings for Focus Area represented by icons, with boxes for check marks above them. Move through the icons using the control wheel, the control dial, or the direction buttons. When a setting you want to remove from the menu is highlighted in orange, press the Center button to remove the check mark from its box. To restore it to the list, highlight it and press the Center button again. When you have finished adding or removing options,

highlight the OK block at the lower left of the screen and press the Center button to lock in your choices.

I find this menu option quite helpful. I rarely use the Zone or Expand Flexible Spot options, so I remove the check boxes from those items, and from the Tracking versions of those versions, to reduce the clutter on the menu.

This option is especially helpful if you assign the Switch Focus Area option to a control button, using the Custom Key (Still Images) menu option. That option cycles through the available Focus Area settings when you press the assigned button, so it would be cumbersome to have more than a few options assigned for Focus Area when using that control button.

Switch Vertical/Horizontal AF Area

This last option on screen 5 of the Camera Settings1 menu is designed for photographers who need to change the orientation of the camera between horizontal and vertical fairly often, and would like to have the camera automatically move the focus point and/or the focus area when that happens. For example, this feature could be useful for a person who is shooting sporting events or weddings, and often uses a focus point in the upper middle of the LCD screen when shooting horizontally. If the camera is then rotated to the left, with the side with the shutter button held up in the right hand, that focus point will have moved to the left side of the screen. To compensate for that effect, you can use this menu option, which causes the camera to memorize the focus points and sizes of focus frames that you specify for each orientation.

Figure 4-56. Switch Vertical/Horizontal AF Area Options Screen

To do this, select either AF Point Only or AF Point + AF Area, as shown in Figure 4-56, then press the Menu button to return to the shooting screen. Then, assuming you chose AF Point + AF Area, first, with the camera in its normal, horizontal orientation, select a setting for the Focus Area menu option (Wide, Center, Flexible Spot, etc.). Also, if you selected a setting with a movable focus frame, such as Flexible Spot, move the frame where you want it on the display. (Use any technique available to move the focus frame—the touch screen, the Focus Standard option assigned to a control button, or the Focus Area menu option, as discussed in connection with the Focus Area menu option.)

Then, tilt the camera to a different orientation (90 degrees to the left or right). Select the Focus Area setting you want for that orientation, and, if applicable, move the focus frame where you want it. Finally, tilt the camera to the third orientation (right or left), and again select a Focus Area setting and, if applicable, a location for the focus frame.

Then, as long as this menu option is turned on, the camera will automatically use the Focus Area setting you selected for a given orientation when you move the camera between the vertical and horizontal orientations, and it will move the focus point if that was selected as well. If you later change the setting for this menu option, the Focus Area settings and focus frame positions you selected will not be retained. However, they are retained when the camera is powered off and back on, as long as the menu option setting has not been changed.

This option does not work with the Auto modes, video recording, Digital Zoom, continuous shooting, and in several other situations.

I don't do enough shooting in different orientations that I would find this feature useful, but it is available if you need it.

The options on screen 6 of the Camera Settings1 menu are shown in Figure 4-57.

Figure 4-57. Screen 6 of Camera Settings1 Menu

AF Illuminator

The AF Illuminator item lets you disable the reddish lamp on the front of the camera for autofocusing. By default, this option is set to Auto, which means that when you are shooting a still image in a dim area, the camera will turn on the lamp briefly if needed to light the subject and assist the autofocus mechanism in gauging the distance to the subject. If you want to make sure the light never comes on for that purpose— to avoid causing distractions in a museum or other sensitive area, or to avoid alerting a subject of candid photography—set this option to Off. In that case, the lamp will never light up for focusing assistance, though it will still illuminate if the self-timer is activated.

Face/Eye AF Settings

This option has five sub-options for controlling how the camera uses its abilities to detect faces and eyes. (Two of these sub-options were added through a firmware update to version 2.00, issued by Sony on June 13, 2019. If you still have Version 1.00, you may want to upgrade the camera's firmware, as discussed in Chapter 8.)

The first sub-option, Face/Eye Priority in AF, determines whether or not the camera uses face and eye detection when using autofocus. If this option is turned on, the camera will detect any human faces, up to eight in total, and select one as the main face to concentrate its settings on.

The second sub-option, Subject Detection, determines whether the camera looks for human eyes or animal eyes. It cannot look for both at the same time. For most purposes, you will probably want to choose Human for this setting, but if you are on a safari, at the zoo, or photographing the family dog or cat, choose Animal.

Note, though, that when the Animal option is selected, the camera cannot use its tracking autofocus functions, either through the Focus Area menu option or through the Touch Tracking option on the Function of Touch Operation menu, as discussed earlier in this chapter.

The third sub-option, Right/Left Eye Select, determines whether the camera focuses on the subject's right or left eye, or, with the Auto setting, decides for itself which eye to focus on. (The subject's right eye is the eye to the left, from the photographer's point of view.) This setting is available only when face and eye detection is turned on and Subject Detection is set to Human.

The fourth sub-option, Face Detection Frame Display, determines whether the camera displays a frame when it has detected a face, even before you press the shutter button halfway down to evaluate focus.

The final sub-option, Animal Eye Display, determines whether the camera displays an eye detection frame when it has detected an animal's eye.

If you have the first four of these sub-options turned on, with the second one set to Human and the third one to Auto, the camera will display white or gray frames around any human faces it finds, as shown in Figure 4-58. When you press the shutter button halfway to lock focus and exposure, the camera will place a small block on the eye it has chosen to focus on.

Figure 4-58. Human Face and Eye Detection in Use

When using face/eye detection, you need to be aware of the setting for Focus Area on screen 5 of the Camera Settings1 menu. If Focus Area is set to Wide, the camera will find a face and focus on it. However, if Focus Area is set to an option such as Center, Flexible Spot, or Expand Flexible Spot, the camera will not focus on a face unless the face is within the area of the focus frame. So, if you want to rely on the camera to find and focus on faces,

you should set Focus Area to Wide. Of course, you can always use Touch Focus to touch a face you want the camera to focus on, no matter what Focus Area setting is in use, as long as touch operations are enabled. You also can assign a control button to Eye AF, and press that button to cause the camera to focus on a human eye.

Face detection does not work when some other settings are in use. For example, it does not work with the Landscape, Night Scene, or Sunset scene settings, when Picture Effect is set to Posterization, when Digital Zoom or Clear Image Zoom is in use, when the Sweep Panorama mode is in use, or when using the Focus Magnifier option. It also does not function when recording a video with Record Setting set to 120p (100p if the PAL system is in use), or when recording an S & Q Motion video with the 120p/100p setting for S &Q Frame Rate.

Face/Eye Priority in AF is automatically turned on in the Intelligent Auto and Superior Auto modes.

AF w/Shutter

Normally, when you press the camera's shutter button halfway down, the camera uses its autofocus system, assuming Focus Mode is set to AF-S, AF-A, AF-C, or DMF. With this menu option, you can disable that function, so that a half-press of the shutter button does not cause any autofocus activity. You may want to do this if you prefer to use "back button focus," a system by which you activate the autofocus system using a button other than the shutter button, such as the AF/MF button or one of the custom buttons. In order to use that system, you have to assign one of the control buttons to the AF On option using the Custom Key (Still Images) option on screen 8 of the Camera Settings2 menu.

With the back button focus system, you are free to compose and shoot your images without having the camera refocus every time you press the shutter button.

If you want to disable the shutter button's action of evaluating exposure when you press it halfway down, there is a separate menu option for that: AEL w/ Shutter, on screen 9 of the Camera Settings1 menu.

Pre-AF

The Pre-AF setting affects the way the a6400 uses autofocus for capturing still images. When this option is turned on and Focus Mode is set to AF-S, AF-A, AF-C, or DMF, the camera continuously tries to focus on a subject, even before you press the shutter button halfway. With this setting, the camera's battery is depleted more quickly than normal, but the final focusing operation may be speeded up because the camera can reach an approximate focus adjustment before you press the shutter button to evaluate focus and take the picture.

If this setting is turned off, the camera makes no attempt to use its autofocus mechanism until you press the shutter button halfway to check focus. I usually leave this setting off to avoid running the battery down too soon. But, if I were taking pictures of moving subjects, I might activate this setting to speed up the focusing process.

When the camera is recording movies, it always uses the equivalent of the Pre-AF setting; this menu option has no effect for movie recording. Pre-AF works only when an E-mount lens is attached to the camera.

Eye-Start AF

This option is available only when you have an A-mount lens attached to the a6400, which requires the use of an adapter, as discussed in Appendix A. If you have such a lens on the camera, and you turn this feature on while Focus Mode is set to an autofocus option, the camera will make its initial autofocus attempt when you raise the camera to your eye. In this way, the camera gets a head start on focusing. This option might be of use in situations when you need to focus quickly on a sporting event or other quickly unfolding action, without wasting time making an initial focus adjustment.

AF Area Registration

This option lets you register a location for a movable focus frame, so you can assign a button to instantly place the frame on the display at that location. This is a multi-step process. First, you have to set this menu option to On. Then, go to the shooting screen and position a movable focus frame, such as Flexible Spot, in the location you want on the display. Then, press

and hold the Function button for a second or two. The camera will display a message saying the AF area has been registered.

Next, go to the Custom Key (Still Images) option on screen 8 of the Camera Settings2 menu and assign a control button, such as the AEL button, to the option called Registered AF Area Hold. Then, when the camera is in shooting mode, you can press the assigned button (AEL in this case) and the focus frame will appear at the registered location as long as you hold down the button.

If you don't want to have to hold down the assigned button, you can choose the Registered AF Area Toggle option, in which case you only need to press and release the button. Or, you can select Registered AF Area + AF On, in which case, when you press the assigned button, the camera will place the frame at the registered location and also will use its autofocus at that point. You cannot assign the Left, Right, or Down button to the Registered AF Area Hold function, but any of those buttons can be assigned to Registered AF Area Toggle.

You cannot call up a registered AF area when the mode dial is at the Auto, Movie, Scene, Panorama, or S & Q position.

This option can be convenient if, for example, you are at a baseball game and you are focusing on the action at first base, but you occasionally need to switch quickly to focusing on third base. You can position a Flexible Spot focus frame over third base and register it there. Then, while you are focusing on first base, you can press the assigned button to instantly bring the focus point to third base and catch the action there.

The options on screen 7 of the Camera Settings1 menu are shown in Figure 4-59.

Figure 4-59. Screen 7 of Camera Settings1 Menu

Delete Registered AF Area

This option lets you delete an AF area registration that you set up using the previous menu option. Although you can always register a new location, you might want to delete the current registration, because, even if the registered AF area is not assigned to a control button, the camera causes the registered area to flash on the shooting screen, as a reminder that there is a registered AF area available for assignment to a button. The flashing can be quite distracting, so I am glad to be able to delete the registration.

AF Area Auto Clear

This option controls whether or not the camera continues to display one or more green focus frames or small green blocks after it has achieved sharp focus when Focus Mode is set to AF-S, AF-A, or DMF. By default, this option is turned off, so the autofocus area is not cleared from the display when focus is achieved; the frames or blocks remain on the display until you press the shutter button all the way down to capture an image.

If you turn this option on through the menu, then the frames or blocks will disappear from the display about one second after you press the shutter button halfway down to focus, so you can have a clear view of the subject before you press the shutter button all the way down to take the picture. If Focus Mode is set to AF-C, the focus frames or blocks will stay on the screen even if this option is turned on, because the camera continues to evaluate focus in that mode.

The setting you use for this option is a matter of personal preference. I usually don't mind seeing the green focus indicators on the display, so I leave this option turned off most of the time. There could be situations, though, when you want to confirm focus by viewing the green frames or blocks but then want to see the subject clearly without the frames or blocks, before you actually capture an image.

Display Continuous AF Area

This option can be turned either on or off. When it is turned on, it controls whether the camera displays small, green focus blocks to show what area of the scene is in focus, when Focus Mode is set to continuous autofocus and the Focus Area option is set to Wide or Zone. If this option is turned off, the camera does not display any focus frames or blocks under those conditions.

I find this option useful, because, without it, there is no obvious way to tell what part of the scene or subject is currently in focus. With continuous autofocus in effect and Focus Area set to Wide or Zone, the camera's autofocus mechanism adjusts constantly as you half-press the shutter button, and there is no frame or other indicator that shows where the focus is being set, other than judging with your eyes what parts of the image look sharper than others. When this menu option is turned on, the camera displays a constantly changing set of focus blocks, as the autofocus mechanism selects a main subject to focus on within the boundaries of the Wide or Zone Focus Area setting.

Circulation of Focus Point

With this menu option, you can control how the camera displays the focus point when you are setting up the location of a movable focus frame for the Zone, Flexible Spot, or Expand Flexible Spot setting for Focus Area. If this option is left at its default setting of Off, you can move the zone or focus frame only to the edges of the monitor or viewfinder. If you turn this option on, when you move the zone or frame to the edge of the screen, it "circulates" back through the opposite edge of the screen, as if there were a continuous wraparound effect. This setting can let you move the frame from, say, the right side of the screen back to the left side very quickly. If you need to move the focus frame fairly often, it is convenient to leave this option turned on. Remember that you also can cause the movable frame to jump back to the center of the screen by pressing the Custom 2/ Delete button.

AF Micro Adjustment

This menu option is for use when you have attached an A-mount lens to the a6400 using the Sony LA-EA2 or LA-EA4 Mount Adaptor. As discussed in Appendix A, those adapters let you attach to the a6400 Sony lenses that use the A-mount system, which are designed for cameras such as the Sony a99 and other cameras.

If you are using one of those lenses with the adapter, you can use this menu option to make fine adjustments to the autofocusing of the lens, to compensate for any differential in the lens's focusing behavior.

Figure 4-60. AF Micro Adjustment Menu Options Screen

To use this option, first set the AF Adjustment Setting option to On, then use the Amount option to make the actual adjustment, using the control wheel, the control dial, or the Up and Down buttons, as shown in Figure 4-60. The camera will register the setting for up to 30 lenses. After that point, you will have to use the Clear option to clear the value for one of the previously adjusted lenses before you can adjust and register another lens.

The options on screen 8 of the Camera Settings1 menu are shown in Figure 4-61.

Figure 4-61. Screen 8 of Camera Settings1 Menu

Exposure Compensation

This first option on screen 8 of the Camera Settings1 menu adjusts exposure compensation. Another way to adjust that setting is by using the Down button, which by default is assigned to that option. You also can use the Custom Key menu options, the My Dial menu option, or the Dial/Wheel EV Compensation menu option to assign one of the other control buttons or dials to adjust exposure compensation, as discussed in

Chapter 5, or you can use the Function menu or Quick Navi menu for that purpose, as discussed in Chapter 6.

Once you select this menu option, the EV (exposure value) scale appears on the display, as shown in Figure 4-63. Use the Left and Right buttons, the control wheel, or the control dial to set the amount of positive or negative compensation, to make the image brighter or darker than it would be otherwise.

Here is an example of the use of this setting. In Figure 4-62, I aimed the camera at a horse figurine in Program shooting mode. The horse was somewhat dark, but the background was white. The camera's autoexposure system measured the light from the overall scene, and because of the white background, it decreased the exposure setting, making the horse appear too dark.

Figure 4-62. Exposure Compensation Example - Before Adjustment

I adjusted the setting on the scale to apply 1.5 EV of positive exposure compensation, as shown in Figure 4-63, making the horse appear at a normal brightness.

Figure 4-63. Exposure Compensation Example - After Adjustment

With a negative value, the image will be darker than it otherwise would; with a positive value, it will be brighter. The camera's display will change to show the effect of the adjustment, if you have set the camera to show the effect. To see the effect as you adjust exposure compensation, go to screen 7 of the Camera Settings2 menu, select Live View Display, and choose Setting Effect On. If you choose the other possibility, Setting Effect Off, you will not see the effect of exposure compensation on the shooting screen, though it will appear in the final image.

You might consider using exposure compensation on a routine basis. Some photographers generally leave exposure compensation set at a particular amount, such as negative 0.7 EV. You could do this if you find your images often look slightly overexposed or if you see that highlights are clipping in many cases. (You can tell if highlights are clipping by checking the playback histogram, as discussed in Chapter 7. If the histogram chart is bunched to the right, with no space between the graph and the right side of the chart, the highlights are clipping, or reaching the maximum value.) It is difficult to recover details from images whose highlights have clipped, so it can be a safety measure to underexpose your images slightly to avoid that situation.

If you don't plan to leave a permanent exposure compensation setting in place, you should return the setting to the zero point when you are finished with it, so you won't inadvertently change the exposure of later images that don't need the adjustment. (The exposure compensation setting will remain in place even after the camera has been turned off and back on again.)

In Manual exposure mode, exposure compensation has no effect unless ISO is set to Auto ISO. Exposure compensation is not available in Intelligent Auto or Scene mode. In Movie mode and S & Q Motion mode, exposure compensation can be adjusted only up to 2.0 EV positive or negative, instead of the 5.0 EV available for still images. You can control whether this menu option adjusts flash output as well as exposure settings by using the Exposure Compensation Setting option on screen 10 of the Camera Settings1 menu, as discussed later in this chapter.

If you want to program the camera to use a small amount of exposure compensation for all shots taken with a particular Metering Mode setting, you can do so using the Exposure Standard Adjustment option on screen 9 of the Camera Settings1 menu, as discussed later in this chapter.

ISO Setting

ISO is a measure of the sensor's sensitivity to light. When ISO is set to higher values, the camera's sensor needs less light to capture an image and the camera can use faster shutter speeds and narrower apertures. The problem with higher values is that their use produces visual "noise" that can reduce the clarity and detail in your images, adding a grainy, textured appearance.

In practical terms, shoot with low ISO settings (around 100) when possible; shoot with high ISO settings (800 or higher) when necessary to allow a fast shutter speed to stop action and avoid motion blur, or when desired to achieve a creative effect with graininess.

With that background, here is how to set ISO on this camera. As is discussed in Chapters 5 and 6, with the a6400 you can get quick access to the ISO setting using the Right button, which is assigned by default to control ISO. You also can use the Function menu, the Quick Navi system, or you can assign a control button or dial to this function. However, you can also set ISO from the Camera Settings1 menu, and you can get access to some additional ISO settings only from this menu. So, it's important to understand how to use this menu item.

Figure 4-64. ISO Menu

ISO

The main menu option, called ISO Setting, is the gateway to the three sub-options that provide the actual settings. The first sub-option, called simply ISO, lets you choose the ISO value for your shots. After you highlight it, press the Center button to bring up the vertical ISO menu at the left of the screen, as seen in Figure 4-64. Scroll through the options by turning the control wheel or by pressing the Up and Down buttons to select a value ranging from one of the top two options—Multi Frame Noise Reduction and Auto ISO—through 100, 125, 160,

200, and other specific values, to a maximum of 102400 at the bottom of the scale. You can scroll through this menu more quickly, skipping over two values at a time, by using the control dial.

If you choose Auto ISO (the second option on the menu, highlighted in Figure 4-64), the camera will select a numerical value automatically depending on the lighting conditions and other camera settings. You can select both the minimum and maximum levels for Auto ISO. In other words, you can set the camera to choose the ISO value automatically within a defined range such as, say, ISO 200 to ISO 1600. In that way, you can be assured that the camera will not select a value outside that range, but you will still leave some flexibility for the setting.

To set minimum and maximum values, while the orange highlight is on the Auto ISO option, press the Right button to move the highlight to the right side of the screen, where there are two rectangles that are labeled (when highlighted) ISO Auto Minimum and ISO Auto Maximum, as shown in Figure 4-65.

Figure 4-65. Screen to Select Minimum and Maximum for Auto ISO

Move the highlight to each of these blocks in turn using the Right button and change the value as you wish, by pressing the Up and Down buttons or turning the control wheel, which scrolls through all values in increments of 1/3 EV, or the control dial, which skips over some values for quicker scrolling, moving in increments of 1 EV. You can set both the minimum and the maximum to values from 100 to 102400. When both values have been set, press the Center button to move to the shooting screen.

Once the minimum and maximum values are set, the camera will keep the ISO level within the range you have specified whenever you select Auto ISO or the Auto setting for Multi Frame Noise Reduction, discussed below. Of course, you can always set a specific ISO value at any other level by selecting it from the ISO menu.

Multi Frame Noise Reduction

The top item on the ISO menu, whose icon includes the ISO label and a stack of frames, as shown in Figure 4-66, is a special setting called Multi Frame Noise Reduction (MFNR). With this option, the camera uses the ISO value you select and also uses a different type of image capture to enhance the quality of the shot.

Figure 4-66. Multi Frame Noise Reduction Icon Highlighted on Menu

With this option, you can set an ISO value as high as 102400, the same as with ISO or Auto ISO. When you use MFNR, the camera takes multiple shots in a rapid burst and creates a composite image with reduced noise. The camera also attempts to select frames with minimal motion blur.

After you have highlighted MFNR on the menu, use the Right button to move the highlight to the right side of the screen, on the selection block for the ISO value to be used.

Use the Up and Down buttons or turn the control wheel or the control dial to select a value, which can be Auto or a specific value from 100 all the way up to 102400. If you choose Auto, the camera will select an ISO value within the limits set for ISO Auto Minimum and Maximum, and it will take multiple shots using that value. You cannot use the flash when MFNR is in effect. Also, you cannot use Raw quality, DRO, HDR, Picture Profile, Picture Effect, or continuous shooting with this setting. MFNR is not available in the Auto, Scene, or Sweep Panorama modes.

After selecting the ISO value for MFNR, press the Right button one more time to move the highlight to the block for NR Effect, as shown in Figure 4-67. For this value you can select Standard or High, to specify how much noise reduction is applied to the MFNR images you capture.

Figure 4-67. **Noise Reduction Effect Block Highlighted**

If you are faced with the prospect of taking pictures in a dark environment, consider using this specialized setting, which really is more akin to a shooting mode than to an ISO setting.

Figure 4-68. **Multi Frame Noise Reduction Example**

For Figure 4-68, I used this setting to capture a view of two groups of people doing whitewater rafting, shortly before sunset. The a6400 set the ISO to 2500 and used a shutter speed of 1/250 second at f/5.6 to capture the action in the fading light.

Here are some more notes on ISO. As I discussed in Chapter 3, with the a6400, you can select Auto ISO in Manual exposure mode. In that way, you can set both the shutter speed and aperture, and still have the camera set the exposure automatically by varying the ISO level. In the Auto, Scene, and Sweep Panorama modes, Auto ISO is automatically set, and you cannot adjust the ISO setting. The available ISO settings for movie recording are different from those for stills; I will discuss that point in Chapter 9. If you find you cannot select an ISO value lower than 500, check the Picture Profile setting. If you are using a setting that includes S-Log2 or S-Log3 for Gamma, the ISO must be set to at least 500.

Figure 4-69. **Non-native Values on ISO Menu**

Also, note that the settings for ISO 40000 and higher are surrounded by lines on the menu, as shown in Figure 4-69. The lines indicate that those settings are not "native" to the a6400's sensor, whose highest native ISO value is 32000. So, although using the highest settings appears to offer more sensitivity to light, in reality those settings are achieved with internal processing by the camera. However, they are certainly worth experimenting with, and they may produce the results you need.

My recommendation is to use Auto ISO for general photography when the main consideration is to have a properly exposed image. When you know you will need a fast shutter speed, select a high ISO setting as necessary. When you need to use a wide aperture to blur the background or a slow shutter speed to smooth out the appearance of flowing water, use a low ISO setting. When you are shooting in unusually dark conditions, consider using the MFNR setting with a high setting for ISO.

ISO Range Limit

The second sub-option for ISO Setting, ISO Range Limit, lets you limit the settings that the camera displays on the ISO menu. If you know you will never want to use certain settings, such as those above 32000, you can use this menu option to remove those from the ISO menu display, so you don't have to scroll through a long list that includes values you will never use. If you later decide you need to use one or more of the excluded values, return to this menu option and restore those settings to the list.

Note that this menu option does not set the limit for values the camera chooses when Auto ISO is in effect. That setting is made by pressing the Right button when Auto ISO is highlighted on the ISO menu, and then setting values for Minimum and Maximum for Auto ISO. So, for example, if you set ISO Range Limit to a range from 100 to 16000, the effect will be that you cannot set ISO manually to values above 16000. However, if you set ISO to Auto ISO, and set the maximum ISO value to, say, 64000, the camera will still be able to set ISO to values up to 64000 if the lighting conditions call for such a value.

ISO Auto Minimum Shutter Speed

This final sub-option under the ISO Setting menu item lets you set a minimum shutter speed, or shutter speed range, for the camera to use when ISO is set to ISO Auto or to MFNR with the value set to Auto. This option is available for selection only when the shooting mode is set to Program or Aperture Priority, the only two advanced shooting modes in which the camera chooses the shutter speed. The purpose of this setting is to ensure that the camera uses a shutter speed fast enough to stop the action for the scene you are shooting.

For example, if you are shooting images of children at play with the camera set to Program mode and ISO Auto in effect with a range from 200 minimum to 1600 maximum, the camera ordinarily may choose a relatively low ISO setting in order to maintain high image quality and low noise. However, using that setting may result in the use of a fairly slow shutter speed, such as 1/30 second, in order to provide enough light for the exposure. With the ISO Auto Minimum Shutter Speed setting, you can set the minimum shutter speed you want the camera to use, such as, say, 1/125 second, to avoid motion blur. You also can specify a more general range of shutter speeds, using several categories, as discussed below.

To use this option, make sure the shooting mode is set to Program or Aperture Priority and that ISO is set to Auto ISO, or to Multi Frame Noise Reduction, with Auto ISO in effect for that setting. Then, highlight this option and press the Center button. You will see a menu with numerous options as you scroll down through several screens.

All but one of the options are specific shutter speeds, ranging from 1/4000 second to 30 seconds. If you select one of those values, the camera will try to use a shutter speed at least that fast for each shot while maintaining the minimum ISO setting. Once the camera has found

it necessary to lower the shutter speed to the minimum value, it will start raising the ISO level as needed. If the camera has set the ISO value to the upper range specified for Maximum ISO and still cannot expose the image properly at the ISO Auto Minimum Shutter Speed, the camera will set a shutter speed slower than the minimum value, in order to achieve a proper exposure.

For example, in the situation discussed above, using ISO Auto with a range from 200 to 1600, if there is plenty of light, the camera may select shutter speeds such as 1/250 second or 1/500 second. It will maintain the ISO at 200 if possible, and it will never select a shutter speed slower than 1/125 second. If the lighting conditions become such that the camera needs to lower the shutter speed all the way to the minimum setting of 1/125 second, the camera will raise the ISO as needed. If the light becomes too dim, the camera may set the ISO to the top of its Auto ISO range at 1600 but still find it impossible to get a good exposure using 1/125 second for the shutter speed. In that case, the camera will use a slower setting, such as 1/60 second or 1/30 second, as needed.

The item at the top of the menu for this option lists settings that are not specific shutter speeds: Standard, Fast, Faster, Slower, and Slow. You can use one of these if you don't need to specify a particular shutter speed but just want to set general guidance for the camera to use. If you choose Standard, the camera tries to maintain a normal shutter speed based on its programming, taking into account the current focal length of the lens. So, if you use a zoom lens at a 24mm wide-angle setting, the camera will try to maintain a shutter speed faster than 1/24 second. If the lens is zoomed in to 100mm, the camera will try to use a shutter speed faster than 1/100 second. If you choose Fast or Faster, the camera attempts to maintain a faster shutter speed than with Standard; Slow or Slower has the opposite effect.

I generally leave this setting at Standard, unless I am faced with a situation in which I definitely need a particularly fast shutter speed.

Metering Mode

This option lets you choose among the five patterns of exposure metering offered by the a6400—Multi, Center, Spot, Entire Screen Average, and Highlight—as shown in Figure 4-70.

This choice tells the camera's automatic exposure system what part of the scene to consider when setting the exposure. With Multi, the camera uses the entire scene that is visible on the display, but it divides that area into segments and analyzes the pattern of the segments in order to determine the optimum exposure.

Figure 4-70. Metering Mode Menu Options Screen

With Center, the camera still measures all of the light from the scene, but it gives additional weight to the center portion of the image on the theory that your main subject is in or near the center.

With Spot, the camera evaluates only the light that is found within the spot metering zone. You can change the size of that zone between Standard and Large by pressing the Left and Right buttons or turning the control dial when the Spot icon is highlighted.

With the Spot option, particularly with the Standard setting, you can see the effects of the exposure system clearly by selecting Program exposure mode and aiming the small circle at various points, some bright and some dark, and seeing how sharply the brightness of the scene on the camera's display changes. If you try the same experiment using Multi, Center, or Entire Screen Average mode, you will see more subtle and gradual changes.

If you choose Spot metering, the circle you will see is different from the rectangular frames the camera uses to indicate the Center or Flexible Spot Focus Area mode settings. If you make either of those Focus Area settings at the same time as the Spot metering setting, you will see both a Spot metering circle and an autofocus frame in the center of the LCD screen, as in Figure 4-71, which shows the screen with the Spot metering and Center Focus Area settings in effect.

Be aware of which one of these settings is in effect, if a circle or a frame is visible in the center of the screen.

Remember that the circle is for Spot metering, and the rectangular bracket is for Center or Flexible Spot autofocus (or an equivalent Tracking AF setting). You can use the Spot Metering Point menu option, discussed later in this chapter, to set the Spot metering point to track with the Flexible Spot or Expand Flexible Spot focus frame.

Figure 4-71. Spot Metering and Flexible Spot Frames

The next choice for metering mode, Entire Screen Average, bases the exposure on the overall brightness of the entire screen, without regard to where the subject is located. This option may be useful if the scene is uniform in its brightness or if you know from past experience that basing the exposure on the average brightness will yield a good result.

The last option, Highlight, causes the camera to base the exposure on the brightest point in the scene, regardless of its location. This setting is especially useful for a situation such as a stage performance that is illuminated by one or more spotlights, to avoid overexposure.

In Auto mode and all varieties of Scene mode, the only metering method available is Multi. That method also is the only one available when Clear Image Zoom or Digital Zoom is in use. (The conflict arises only when the lens is actually zoomed beyond the limit of optical zoom; at that point, the camera will change the metering method to Multi, and will change it back when the lens is zoomed back within the optical zoom limit.)

The Multi setting is best for scenes with relatively even contrast, such as landscapes, and for action shots, when the location of the main subject may move through different parts of the frame. The Center setting is good for sunrise and sunset scenes, and other situations with a large, central subject that exhibits considerable contrast with the rest of the scene. The Spot setting is good for portraits, macro shots, and other images in which there is a relatively small part of the scene where exposure is critical. Spot metering also is useful when lighting is intense in one portion of a scene, such as when a concert performer is lit by a spotlight. However, the Highlight option may be preferable for scenes with stage lighting, because the camera will expose for the brightest part of the scene, even if it changes position.

Face Priority in Multi Metering

This option works in a way similar to the Set Face Priority in AF feature, discussed earlier in this chapter under the Face/Eye AF Settings menu option. The Face Priority in Multi Metering option lets you set whether or not the camera optimizes exposure for a detected face, when metering mode is set to Multi. If it is turned on, the camera ignores the overall exposure reading and concentrates the exposure setting based on the highest-priority face. If it is turned off, the camera ignores the faces, and uses the standard algorithm for metering based on the overall scene. In Intelligent Auto or Superior Auto mode, this option is turned on and cannot be disabled.

This feature can be quite useful if, for example, you are photographing a person against a window with bright sunshine outside. With this option turned off, with Multi metering activated, the camera would expose for the bright window, and leave the person's face too dark. With the option turned on, the camera would expose for the face, and let the window area be overexposed. So, if you are photographing people in a variety of lighting conditions, it can be a good idea to leave this option turned on.

Spot Metering Point

When Spot metering is in effect, you can use the Spot Metering Point menu option to set the Spot circle to move along with the Flexible Spot or Expand Flexible Spot focus frame, whenever either of those frames is in use for Focus Area. This menu option has two choices—Center or Focus Point Link. If you choose Center, the Spot circle will always stay in the center of the frame. If you choose Focus Point Link, the Spot Circle will move as you move the Flexible Spot or Expand Flexible Spot focus frame.

If Focus Area is set to Tracking AF with the Flexible Spot or Expand Flexible Spot sub-option, with the Focus Point Link option the Spot metering circle will be located where the focus frame is before focus tracking begins, but the metering area will not move as focus is tracked.

Exposure Step

This option lets you set the size of the exposure interval between settings when you are setting the aperture or shutter speed on the camera. The choices are either 0.3EV (exposure value) or 0.5EV. If you choose the smaller step of 0.3EV, you will have more choices for both aperture and shutter speed. For example when using the Sony 18-135mm kit lens, with the 0.3EV setting the choices for aperture include f/3.5, f/4.0, f/4.5, f/5.0, f/5.6, and f/6.3. With the 0.5EV setting, the choices include f/3.5, f/4.0, f/4.5, f/5.6, and f/6.7.

For shutter speed, with the 0.3EV setting the choices include 1/40, 1/50, 1/60, 1/80, 1/100, and 1/125. With the 0.5EV setting, the choices include 1/45, 1/60, 1/90, and 1/125.

If you don't want to limit the choices that can be made for these exposure values, choose the 0.3EV setting. If you want to make it slightly quicker to scroll through the settings, choose the 0.5EV setting. I don't find the increased speed of making settings very significant, so I leave this setting at 0.3EV.

The items on screen 9 of the Camera Settings1 menu are shown in Figure 4-72.

Figure 4-72. Screen 9 of Camera Settings1 Menu

AEL with Shutter

This menu item controls how the shutter button handles autoexposure lock. There are three possible settings for this feature: Auto, On, and Off.

With the default option, Auto, pressing the shutter button halfway locks exposure when Focus Mode is set to AF-S for single-shot autofocus or DMF for direct manual focus. When Focus Mode is set to AF-C for continuous autofocus or MF for manual focus, pressing the shutter button halfway does not lock exposure. When Focus Mode is set to AF-A for automatic autofocus, pressing the shutter button halfway locks exposure as long as the subject does not move. If the subject starts to move, the exposure will no longer be locked.

If AEL with Shutter is set to On, pressing the shutter button halfway locks exposure in all situations, regardless of what focus mode is in place. So, for example, if Focus Mode is set to the AF-C for continuous autofocus, pressing the shutter button halfway locks exposure, though the focus mechanism will continue adjusting focus. If Focus Mode is set to MF for manual focus, pressing the shutter button halfway locks exposure, even though focus is not adjusted.

If this menu option is set to Off, pressing the shutter button halfway never locks exposure, in any focus mode. You may want to use this setting when you need to press the shutter button halfway to lock focus and then move the camera to change the composition somewhat. You might want the camera to re-evaluate the exposure, even though you have already locked the focus.

Another important use for the Off setting is when you are using the continuous shooting settings of Drive Mode. As I discussed earlier in this chapter, if you want the camera to adjust its exposure for each shot in a continuous burst, you need to set AEL with Shutter to Off, or set it to Auto with Focus Mode set to continuous AF or automatic AF. Otherwise, the camera will lock exposure with the first shot, and will not adjust it if the lighting changes during the burst.

Of course, you may not want to use the Off or Auto setting in that scenario, because it can slow down the burst of shots, and, depending on the situation, it may not be likely that the lighting will change during a brief burst of shots. But this option is available for those times when you want the camera to keep evaluating and adjusting exposure while you take a burst of shots.

Exposure Standard Adjustment

This second and final item on screen 9 of the Camera Settings1 menu is provided so you can fine-tune the exposure settings for the various metering modes. You can use this option to program in an adjustment of up to one stop of EV (exposure value) adjustment for each of the camera's five metering modes: Multi, Center, Spot, Entire Screen Average, and Highlight.

This adjustment ordinarily should not be necessary, but it is included for photographers who know that, when they use a particular metering mode, their exposure generally needs a particular adjustment. For example, a photojournalist who covers rock concerts may have found that her shots need to be adjusted upward by 0.5 EV so the non-highlighted areas on the stage are not lost in shadows when she is using the Highlight setting for metering mode. She can use this menu option to set a positive adjustment in that amount.

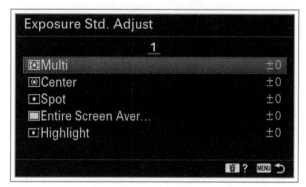

Figure 4-73. Exposure Standard Adjustment Option - List of Metering Modes

To make this adjustment, select this menu option and press the Center button to move to a screen with a message saying this adjustment is usually not necessary; then select the OK block to move to the screen listing the metering modes, shown in Figure 4-73. On that screen, select the metering mode you want to adjust, and move to the adjustment screen, shown in Figure 4-74, where you can select the adjustment you want. Then press the Menu button repeatedly, or just press the shutter button halfway, to return to the shooting screen.

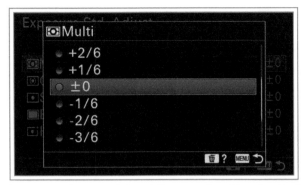

Figure 4-74. Screen to Select Adjustment for a Metering Mode

I consider this option to be a somewhat esoteric one, which I don't recommend using unless you have a definite need for it.

The items on screen 10 of the Camera Settings1 menu are shown in Figure 4-75.

Figure 4-75. Screen 10 of Camera Settings1 Menu

Flash Mode

This menu option controls the behavior of the camera's built-in flash as well as that of any compatible flash that is attached to the Multi Interface Shoe. There are five choices for this setting—Flash Off, Autoflash, Fill-flash, Slow Sync, and Rear Sync, as shown in Figure 4-76. Flash Off and Autoflash are dimmed on this screen, because those settings are not available for selection in the Program shooting mode, illustrated here. There is no shooting mode in which all five options are available.

FLASH OFF

To make sure the flash will not fire, choose Flash Off. This is a good choice when you are in a museum or other place where you don't want the flash to fire, or if you know you will not be using flash. It also can be helpful to avoid depleting a battery that is running low. This option is available for selection in Auto mode and

with the Portrait, Sports Action, Macro, Landscape, and Sunset settings of Scene mode. Of course, with the a6400 you also have the option of just not raising the flash with the flash pop-up button, or not turning on a flash attached to the Multi Interface Shoe, which will have the same effect as using this Flash Mode option.

Figure 4-76. Flash Mode Menu

With any of the flash modes discussed below, the camera will synchronize with the flash at shutter speeds up to 1/160 second, provided you are using either the built-in flash or a compatible external unit.

AUTOFLASH

With Autoflash, you leave it up to the camera to decide whether to fire the flash. The camera will analyze the lighting and other aspects of the scene and decide whether to use flash without further input from you. This selection is available only in Auto mode and the Portrait and Macro settings of Scene mode.

FILL-FLASH

With Fill-flash, you are making a decision to use flash no matter what the lighting conditions are. If you choose this option, the flash will fire every time you press the shutter button, if the flash is popped up. This is the setting to use when the sun is shining and you need to soften shadows on a subject's face, or when you need to correct the lighting when a subject is backlit.

For example, for Figures 4-77 and 4-78 I took two shots of a mannequin outdoors on a sunny day: one without flash and one using Fill-flash. In Figure 4-78, for which flash was used, the harsh shadows are largely eliminated, providing more even lighting for the face.

Fill-flash is available with all shooting modes except Movie, S and Q Motion, and Sweep Panorama, and these Scene mode settings: Night Scene, Hand-held Twilight, Night Portrait, and Anti Motion Blur.

Figure 4-77. Image Captured Without Flash

Figure 4-78. Image Captured with Fill-flash

SLOW SYNC

The Slow Sync option is designed for use when you are taking a flash photograph of a subject at night or in dim lighting, when there is some natural light in the background.

With this setting, the camera uses a relatively slow shutter speed so the ambient (natural) lighting will have time to register on the image. In other words, if you're in a fairly dark environment and fire the flash normally, it will likely light up the subject (such as a person), but because the exposure time is short, the surrounding scene may be black. If you use the Slow Sync setting, the slower shutter speed allows the surrounding scene to be visible also.

I took the images in Figures 4-79 and 4-80 with identical lighting and camera settings, except that I took the first image with the flash set to Fill-flash and shutter speed at 1/60 second, and I took the second image with the flash set to Slow Sync, resulting in a longer shutter speed of 1/4 second.

Figure 4-79. Image Captured with Normal Flash

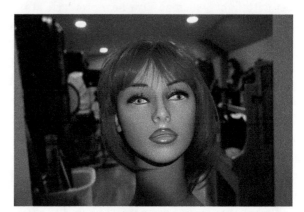

Figure 4-80. Image Captured with Slow Sync Flash

In Figure 4-79, the flash illuminated the mannequin head in the foreground, but the background is dark. In Figure 4-80, the room behind the mannequin is illuminated by ambient light because of the slower shutter speed.

When you use Slow Sync, you should use a tripod, because the camera may choose a very slow shutter speed, such as three seconds or longer. Note that you can choose Slow Sync even in Shutter Priority mode. If you do so, you should select a slow shutter speed because the point is to use a long exposure to light the background with ambient light. With Shutter Priority mode you can choose any shutter speed, but it would not make sense to select a relatively fast one, such as, say, 1/30 second. The same considerations apply for Manual exposure mode, in which you also can select Slow Sync.

Slow Sync can be selected only in the Program, Aperture Priority, Shutter Priority, and Manual exposure modes. With the Night Portrait setting of Scene mode, Slow Sync is set by the camera and cannot be changed.

REAR SYNC

The next setting for Flash Mode is Rear Sync. You should not need this option unless you encounter the special situation it is designed for. If you don't activate this setting (that is, if you select any other flash mode in which the flash fires), the camera uses the unnamed default setting, which could be called "Front Sync." In that case, the flash fires very soon after the shutter opens to expose the image. If you choose the Rear Sync setting instead, the flash fires later—just before the shutter closes.

Rear Sync helps avoid a strange-looking result in some situations. This issue arises, for example, with a relatively long exposure, say one-half second, of a subject with lights, such as a car or motorcycle at night, moving across your field of view. With normal (Front) sync, the flash will fire early in the process, freezing the vehicle in a clear image. However, as the shutter remains open while the vehicle keeps going, the camera will capture the moving lights in a stream extending in front of the vehicle. If, instead, you use Rear Sync, the initial part of the exposure will capture the lights in a trail that appears behind the vehicle, while the vehicle itself is not frozen by the flash until later in the exposure. With Rear Sync in this particular situation, if the lights in question are taillights that look more natural behind the vehicle, the final image is likely to look more natural than with the Front Sync (default) setting.

The images in Figures 4-81 and 4-82 illustrate this concept using a flashlight. I took both pictures using the built-in flash, with a shutter speed of 1/2 second. For each shot, I waved the flashlight from right to left. In Figure 4-81, using the normal (Fill-flash) setting, the flash fired quickly, making a clear image of the flashlight at the right of the image, and the light beam continued on to the left during the long exposure to make a light trail in front of the flashlight's path of movement.

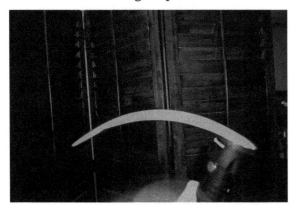

Figure 4-81. Image Captured Using Normal Flash

Figure 4-82. Image Captured Using Rear Sync Flash

In Figure 4-82, using Rear Sync, the flash did not fire until the flashlight had traveled all the way to the left, and the trail of light from its beam appeared behind the flashlight's path of motion. If you are trying to convey a sense of natural movement, the Rear Sync setting, as seen here, is likely to give you better results than the default setting.

A good general rule is to use Rear Sync only when you have a definite need for it. Using this option makes it harder to compose and set up the shot, because you have to anticipate where the main subject will be when the flash finally fires late in the exposure process. But, in the relatively rare situations when it is useful, Rear Sync can make a dramatic difference. Rear Sync is available only in the more advanced shooting modes: Program, Aperture Priority, Shutter Priority, and Manual exposure.

Flash Compensation

This menu item lets you control the output of the camera's built-in flash unit, or of an external unit if a compatible one is attached to the flash shoe. This function works similarly to exposure compensation, discussed earlier in this chapter, which is available in the more advanced shooting modes. The difference between the two options is that flash compensation varies only the brightness of the light emitted by the flash, while exposure compensation varies the overall exposure of a given shot, whether or not flash is used. (You can control whether the exposure compensation setting adjusts flash output as well as camera settings by using the Camera Settings1 menu's Exposure Compensation Setting option, discussed immediately below.)

Flash compensation is useful when you don't want the subject overwhelmed with light from the flash.

I sometimes use this setting when I am shooting a portrait outdoors with the Fill-flash setting to reduce shadows on the subject. With a bit of negative flash compensation, I can keep the flash from overexposing the image or casting a harsh light on the subject's face.

To use this option, highlight it on the menu screen and press the Center button. On the next screen, press the Left and Right buttons or turn the control dial or the control wheel to set the amount of positive or negative compensation you want.

When the flash is popped up or an external flash unit is in use, an icon in the upper right corner of the shooting screen shows the amount of flash compensation in effect, even if it is zero. Be careful to set the value back to zero when you are done with the setting, because any setting you make will stay in place even after the camera has been powered off and back on again.

The Flash Compensation option is not available in the Auto, Scene, or Sweep Panorama modes.

Exposure Compensation Setting

This next option has two possible settings: Ambient & Flash, or Ambient Only.

With Ambient & Flash, the default setting, when you adjust exposure compensation, the camera will adjust not only its exposure settings, but also the intensity of the flash. If you choose Ambient Only, then adjusting exposure compensation will control only the exposure settings, and not the flash.

To give the a6400 flexibility in adjusting exposure compensation, leave the setting at Ambient & Flash. However, results can be different using the Ambient Only setting, so you may want to experiment with both options to see which one you prefer in a given situation. Remember that the camera has a separate adjustment for Flash Compensation on the Camera Settings1 menu, and you can set that value separately if you need to adjust the output of the flash. I recommend using the Ambient & Flash setting unless you have a particular reason for using the Ambient Only option.

Wireless Flash

The next option on screen 10 of the Camera Settings1 menu, Wireless Flash, gives you the ability to control one or more off-camera flash units using Sony flash equipment. Because this option is separate from the Flash Mode menu option, you can turn on wireless flash capability and also use one of the other settings for Flash Mode, such as Slow Sync or Rear Sync.

Sony offers two different types of wireless flash. One system, which is built into some Sony flash units, uses pulses of light to communicate between a flash attached to the camera and one or more remote flashes. The other system, which is available in the form of a transmitter unit and a receiver unit, and also is built into at least one Sony flash unit, uses radio signals to transmit information from the camera to one or more off-camera flash units. I will provide information about both of these systems here, with more emphasis on the light-based process.

USING SONY'S LIGHT-BASED WIRELESS PROTOCOL

In order to use the light-based flash system, you need to have at least two flash units that are compatible with this Sony wireless system—one attached to the camera's accessory shoe and another one (or multiple units) positioned off the camera.

The flash on the camera acts as the controller. The built-in flash on the a6400 camera cannot act as a wireless controller using this protocol, so you need to use an external unit. One option for this purpose is the Sony HVL-F20M, a small and relatively inexpensive unit, which I discuss in Appendix A. One negative point about this unit is that it cannot act as a remote unit using the Sony wireless protocol, only as the controller. That is not much of a problem, though; you can just dedicate this unit as your controller and use other, larger units as the remote flash units. Another option I have used as a controller is the Sony HVL-F32M.

One remote unit I have used is the Sony HVL-F43M, also discussed in Appendix A. This full-sized flash has features such as a rotating head and a built-in video light. For wireless purposes, it can serve as either the controller or the remote unit for the Sony protocol.

I will describe how to set up a shot using the Sony optical wireless flash protocol in Aperture Priority mode using the HVL-F20M flash as the controller and the HVL-F43M flash as the remote unit; the procedure would be similar with other compatible Sony flash units.

1. Attach the HVL-F43M to the a6400, turn the camera and flash on, and set the camera to Aperture Priority mode, which is one of the modes that permit the use of the Wireless Flash option. On the Camera Settings1 menu, set the Wireless Flash menu option to On and press the shutter button halfway. Make sure the flash's display shows that it is now set to Wireless mode, on Channel 1. If necessary, press the Mode button on the flash to set the flash to RMT (remote) mode.

2. Remove the HVL-F43M flash from the camera and set it up aiming at your subject, on a light stand, on its own plastic stand, or handheld by the subject or other person. The red AF Illuminator light on the flash unit should now be flashing, indicating that the remote unit is ready to receive a signal from the controller unit.

3. Attach the HVL-F20M to the a6400 and turn the flash on by pulling it up into a vertical position. On the a6400, set up your shot using Aperture Priority mode.

4. On the camera, make sure the Wireless Flash option is still turned on. When the camera is aimed at the subject, make sure that the flash from the HVL-F20M can be seen by the remote flash. (The line of sight can be indirect, from bouncing off a wall or ceiling.) To test the setup, press the AEL button on the camera to fire a test flash, which should trigger the remote flash.

5. When the shot is set up as you want it, press the shutter button to take the picture.

The flash unit on the camera sends a coded signal to the remote flash telling it to fire a pre-flash. The camera then evaluates that pre-flash and sets the remote flash to fire the flash at the proper intensity for the actual exposure. You will see the pre-flash, followed fairly quickly by the actual flash for the exposure.

Figure 4-83 shows an image taken with a setup similar to this one, using flash from the HVL-F43M.

Figure 4-83. Image Captured Using Wireless Flash

This image was taken with a single remote flash. I used Aperture Priority mode with the 18-135mm kit lens, and the camera exposed the image for 1/60 second at f/9.5 with ISO set to 250. I experienced difficulty using this system with ISO set to Auto ISO. With that setting, in a darkened room, the camera overexposed the shots, setting ISO to the very high level of 25600. Setting the ISO to a specific value of 250 solved this problem for me.

There are other Sony flash units that work with the optical wireless protocol, including the HVL-F32M and the HVL-F60M. You can use multiple external flash units if you want.

USING SONY'S RADIO-BASED FLASH SYSTEM

The other system offered by Sony for remote flash control with the a6400 involves sending radio signals from a transmitter attached to the a6400 to a remote receiver with a compatible flash unit attached to it. I will set forth the basic steps for using this system with the Sony transmitter and receiver. (You also can use certain Sony flash units as the transmitter or receiver.) These units are discussed further in Appendix A.

1. Attach the Sony Wireless Radio Commander, model number FA-WRC1M, to the accessory shoe on top of the a6400, and attach the Sony Wireless Radio Receiver, model number FA-WRR1, to a light stand or other support. Attach a compatible flash, such as the Sony HVL-32M, to the flash shoe on top of the receiver.

2. Turn on the Wireless Radio Commander, press its Menu button, select Pairing from the menu, then scroll to Add, and press the center button in the device's controller.

3. Make sure the Wireless Radio Receiver is turned off. Then, after selecting Add on the Commander, press and hold the on/off button on the Receiver for about seven seconds. The Commander should display a message saying Added: 1.

4. At this point, the Commander and Receiver should be paired, and two green lights should illuminate on the back of the Receiver. Press the center button on the Commander's controller to exit from the pairing process. Make sure the Commander is set to TTL, with the TTL indicator on the screen. If it is not, press the Fn button on the Commander to highlight the current setting, such as Release, Group, or Manual, then press the center button on the controller, and select TTL from the menu that appears by highlighting it and pressing the center button.

5. Turn on the a6400 and set the Wireless Flash menu option to On. Turn on the Flash that is attached to the Receiver, and put that flash into TTL mode. You can now shoot images with the a6400, and the remote flash should fire each time you press the shutter button. As with the optical-based wireless system, I have found that it is advisable to set ISO to a specific value, such as 200, rather than to Auto ISO, to avoid overexposure.

Red Eye Reduction

This final option on screen 10 of the Camera Settings1 menu is designed to combat "red-eye"—the eerie red glow in human eyes that appears in images when on-camera flash lights up the blood vessels on the retinas. This menu item can be set to either On or Off. If it is turned on, then, whenever the flash is used, it fires a few times before the actual flash that illuminates the image. The pre-flashes cause the subject's pupils to narrow, reducing the ability of the later, full flash to enter the pupils, bounce off the retinas, and produce the unwanted red glow in the eyes.

I prefer to leave this option turned off and deal with any red-eye effects using editing software. However, if you will be taking flash photos at a party, you may want to use this menu option to minimize the occurrence of red-eye effects in the first place.

Figure 4-84 shows screen 11 of the Camera Settings1 menu.

Figure 4-84. Screen 11 of Camera Settings1 Menu

White Balance

The White Balance menu option is needed because cameras record colors of objects differently according to the color temperature of the light illuminating those objects. Color temperature is a value expressed in Kelvin (K) units. A light source with a lower K rating produces a "warmer," or more reddish light. A source with a higher rating produces a "cooler," or more bluish light. Candlelight is rated about 1,800 K, indoor tungsten light (ordinary light bulb) is rated about 3,000 K, outdoor sunlight and electronic flash are rated about 5,500 K, and outdoor shade is rated about 7,000 K. If the camera is using a White Balance setting that is not designed for the light source that illuminates the scene, the colors of the recorded image are likely to be inaccurate.

The a6400, like most cameras, has an Auto White Balance setting that chooses the proper color correction for any given light source. The Auto White Balance setting works well, and it will produce good results in many situations, especially if you are taking snapshots whose colors are not critical.

If you need more precision in the white balance of your shots, the a6400 has settings for common light sources, as well as options for setting White Balance by color temperature and for setting a custom white balance based on the existing light source.

Once you have highlighted this menu option, press the Center button to bring up the vertical menu at the left of the screen, as shown in Figure 4-85.

Figure 4-85. **White Balance Menu**

Press the Up and Down buttons or turn the control wheel to scroll through the choices: Auto White Balance (AWB); Daylight (sun icon); Shade (house icon); Cloudy (cloud icon); Incandescent (round light bulb icon); Fluorescent Warm White (bulb icon with -1); Fluorescent Cool White (same, with 0); Fluorescent Day White (same, with +1); Fluorescent Daylight (same, with +2); Flash (WB with lightning icon); Underwater Auto (AWB with fish icon); Color Temperature/Filter (K and filter icon); and three numbered Custom choices. It takes several screens to scroll through all of these choices.

To select a setting without making any further adjustments, highlight it and press the Center button. Most of the settings describe a light source in common use. There are four settings for fluorescent bulbs, so you should be able to find a good setting for any fluorescent light, though you may need to experiment to find the best setting for a given bulb. For settings such as Daylight, Shade, Cloudy, and Incandescent, select the setting that matches the dominant light in your location. If you are indoors and using only incandescent lights, this decision will be easy. If you have a variety of lights turned on and sunlight coming in the windows, you may want to use either the Color Temperature/Filter setting or the Custom option.

The Color Temperature/Filter option lets you set the camera's white balance according to the color temperature of the light source. One way to determine that value is with a color meter like the Sekonic C-700.

Those devices work well when you need accuracy in white balance settings. If you don't want to use a meter, you can still use the Color Temperature/Filter option, but you will have to do some guesswork or use your own sense of color. For example, if you are shooting under lighting that is largely incandescent, you can use the value of 3,000 K as a starting point, because, as

noted earlier in this discussion, that is an approximate value for the color temperature of that light source. Then you can try setting the color temperature figure higher or lower, and watch the camera's display to see how natural the colors look.

As you lower the color temperature setting, the image will become more "cool," or bluish; as you raise it, the image will appear more "warm," or reddish. Once you find the best setting, leave it in place and take your shots. (The Live View Display option on screen 7 of the Camera Settings2 menu must be set to Setting Effect On for these changes to appear on the display, as discussed in Chapter 5.)

To make this setting, after you highlight the icon for Color Temperature/Filter, press the Right button to move the orange highlight to the right side of the camera's screen so that it highlights the color temperature value bar, as shown in Figure 4-86.

Figure 4-86. **Scale to Set White Balance by Color Temperature**

Raise or lower that number by pressing the Up and Down buttons or by turning the control wheel or control dial, and press the Center button to select that value. Or, when the icon for Color Temperature/Filter is highlighted, you can just start turning the control dial to adjust the color temperature value.

If you don't want to use the Color Temperature/Filter option, you can set a Custom White Balance. The three Custom icons, just below the Color Temperature/Filter icon, are used to set the camera to one of three currently stored Custom White Balance settings. Before you can use any of the three Custom icons, you need to set the Custom White Balance value as you want it and store it to one of those icons.

To set and store a Custom White Balance, highlight any one of the three Custom icons and press the Right button to move the highlight to the Set icon. Press the Center button to select this option, and the camera will display a message saying "Press the [Center] button to capture data of central area of screen," as shown in Figure 4-87. Aim the camera at a gray or white surface, lit by the light source you are measuring, that fills the circle on the screen. Press the Center button, and the camera will set the white balance.

Figure 4-87. Screen to Set Custom White Balance

The lower area of the screen will show the measured color temperature along with letters and numbers indicating variations along two color axes. If there is some variation, you will see an indication such as G-M: G1, meaning one unit of variation toward green along the green-magenta axis. If there is no variation, it will say A-B: 0 and G-M: 0.

Press the Center button to return to the shooting screen. To use the Custom White Balance setting you saved, select the 1, 2, or 3 Custom icon on the White Balance menu, depending on the slot you used to save the setting. You can change any of the Custom settings whenever you want to, if you are shooting under different lighting conditions.

There is one more way to adjust the White Balance setting by taking advantage of the two color axes discussed above. If you want to tweak the White Balance setting to the nth degree, when you have highlighted your desired setting on the White Balance menu (whether a preset, Auto, or a Custom setting), press the Right button, and you will see a screen for fine adjustments, as shown in Figure 4-88.

This screen has a pair of axes that intersect at a zero point marked by an orange dot. The axes are labeled G, B, M, and A for green, blue, magenta, and amber.

Figure 4-88. Screen to Make Fine Adjustments to White Balance

You can now use all four direction buttons to move the orange dot along any of the axes to adjust these four values until you have the color balance exactly how you want it. You also can use the control wheel to adjust the G-M axis and the control dial to adjust the B-A axis. Press the Center button to confirm the setting.

Be careful to undo any adjustments using these axes when they are no longer needed; otherwise, the adjustments will alter the colors of all of your images that are shot with this White Balance setting in a shooting mode for which White Balance can be adjusted, even after the camera has been powered off and then back on.

Some final notes about White Balance: First, if you shoot using Raw quality, you can always correct the white balance after the fact in your Raw software. So, if you are using Raw, you don't have to worry so much about what setting you are using for White Balance. Still, it's a good idea always to check the setting before shooting to avoid getting caught with incorrect White Balance when you are not using the Raw format, and to avoid having to adjust white balance unnecessarily for Raw images.

Second, before you decide to use the "correct" white balance in every situation, consider whether that is the best course of action to get the results you want. For example, I know of one photographer who generally keeps his camera set for Daylight white balance even when shooting indoors because he likes the "warmer" appearance that comes from using that setting. I don't necessarily recommend that approach, but it's not a bad idea to give some thought to straying from a strict approach to white balance, at least on occasion.

The White Balance setting is fixed to Auto White Balance in the Auto and Scene modes.

Before I leave this topic, I am including a chart in Figure 4-89 that shows how White Balance settings affect images taken by the a6400. I took the photos in the chart under daylight-balanced light using each available White Balance setting, as indicated on the chart.

White Balance Chart for Sony a6400

Auto White Balance	Fluorescent Cool White
Daylight	Fluorescent Day White
Shade	Fluorescent Daylight
Cloudy	Flash
Incandescent	AWB Underwater
Fluorescent Warm White	Color Temp: 5500K

Custom

Figure 4-89. White Balance Comparison Chart

Most of the settings yielded acceptable results. The only ones that clearly look incorrect for this light source are the Incandescent, Fluorescent Warm White, and Fluorescent Cool White settings. The other settings produced variations that might be appropriate, depending on how you plan to use the images.

Priority Set in Auto White Balance

This option gives you a way to tweak the white balance of shots taken using the Auto White Balance setting. You can leave it set to its default setting of Standard, or set it to Ambient or White. It is intended for use when you are shooting a scene illuminated by incandescent lighting. If you set this option to Standard, the camera makes no change to its normal Auto White Balance setting.

With Ambient, the camera adjusts white balance to the warmer side, making the shot a bit more yellowish than it would otherwise be. With the White setting, the camera adjusts to the cooler side, producing a more ice-tinged white. I generally leave this option at the Standard setting, but if you are doing extensive shooting under incandescent lighting using the Auto White Balance setting, this menu item gives you a way to make a mild adjustment to the color balance of your images.

DRO/Auto HDR

The next option on the Camera Settings1 menu lets you control the dynamic range of your shots using the DRO/HDR processing of the a6400. These settings can help correct problems with excessive contrast in your images. Such issues arise because digital cameras cannot easily process a wide range of dark and light areas in the same image—that is, their "dynamic range" is limited. So, if you are taking a picture in an area that is partly lit by bright sunlight and partly in deep shade, the resulting image is likely to have some dark areas in which details are lost in the shadows, or some areas in which highlights, or bright areas, are excessively bright, or "blown out," so, again, the details of the image are lost.

One way to deal with this situation is to use high dynamic range (HDR) techniques, in which multiple photographs of the same scene with different exposures are combined into a composite image that has clear details throughout the entire scene. The a6400 can take HDR shots on its own, or you can take separate exposures yourself and combine them in software on a computer into a composite HDR image. I will discuss those HDR techniques later in this chapter.

The a6400's DRO (dynamic range optimizer) setting gives you another way to deal with the problem of uneven lighting, with special processing in the camera that can boost details in dark areas and reduce overexposure in bright areas at the same time, resulting in a single image with better-balanced exposure than would be possible otherwise. To do this, the DRO setting uses digital processing to reduce highlight blowout and pull details out of the shadows.

To use the DRO feature, press the Menu button and highlight this option, then press the Center button to bring the DRO/Auto HDR menu up on the camera's display, as shown in Figure 4-90. Scroll through the options on that menu using the Up and Down buttons or by turning the control wheel.

Figure 4-90. DRO/Auto HDR Menu Options Screen

With DRO Off, no special processing is used. With the second choice, press the Right and Left buttons or turn the control dial to move through the DRO choices: Auto, or Level 1 through Level 5. With the Auto setting, the camera analyzes the scene to pick an appropriate amount of DRO processing. Otherwise, you can pick the level; the higher the number, the greater the processing to even out contrast between light and dark areas.

Figures 4-91 through 4-93 are examples of images captured using various levels of DRO processing, ranging from Off to Level 5.

As you can see, the greater the level of DRO used, the more evenly the a6400 processed lighting in the scene, primarily by enhancing details in the shadowy areas.

Figure 4-91. DRO Off

Figure 4-92. DRO Set to Level 3

Figure 4-93. DRO Set to Level 5

There is some risk of increasing visual noise in the dark areas with this sort of processing, but the a6400 does not seem to do badly in this respect; I have not seen increased noise levels in images processed with the DRO feature.

The final option for this menu item, HDR, involves in-camera HDR processing. With traditional HDR processing, the photographer takes two or more shots of a scene with contrasting lighting, some underexposed and others overexposed, and merges them using Photoshop or HDR software to blend differently exposed portions from all of the images. The end result is a composite HDR image with clear details throughout all parts of the photograph.

Because of the popularity of HDR, many makers have incorporated some degree of HDR processing into their cameras in an attempt to help the cameras even out areas of excessive brightness and darkness to preserve details. With the a6400, Sony has provided an automatic method for taking multiple shots that the camera combines internally to achieve one HDR composite image. To use this feature, highlight the bottom option on the DRO/Auto HDR menu.

Press the Right and Left buttons or turn the control dial to scroll through the various options for the HDR setting until you have highlighted the one you want, then press the Center button to select that option and exit to the shooting screen. The available options are Auto HDR and HDR with EV settings from 1.0 through 6.0.

If you select Auto HDR, the camera will analyze the scene and the lighting conditions and select a level of exposure difference on its own. If you select a specific level from 1.0 to 6.0, the camera will use that level as the overall difference among the three shots it takes.

For example, if you select 1.0 EV for the exposure difference, the camera will take three shots, each 0.5 EV level (f-stop) different in exposure from the next— one shot at the metered EV level, one shot at 0.5 EV lower, and one shot at 0.5 EV higher. If you choose the maximum exposure difference of 6.0 EV, then the shots will be 3.0 EV apart in their brightness levels.

When you press the shutter button, the camera will take three shots in a quick burst; you should either use a tripod or hold the camera very steady. When it has finished processing the shots, the camera will save the composite image as well as the single image that was taken at the metered exposure.

For Figure 4-94 through Figure 4-97, I took shots of a red watering can in conditions of mixed sunlight and shadow, to illustrate the effectiveness of the HDR settings. For Figure 4-94, HDR was turned off; for Figure 4-95, it was set at 3.0EV; for Figure 4-96, HDR was set to its highest value, 6.0EV. The image using HDR at 6.0EV gave the best results in terms of pulling details out of the shadows.

For comparison, I took several shots of the subject using a range of exposure levels in Manual exposure mode. I merged those images together in Photoshop and tweaked the result until I got what seemed to be the optimal dynamic range.

Figure 4-94. HDR Off

Figure 4-95. HDR Set to 3.0 EV

Figure 4-96. HDR Set to 6.0 EV

Figure 4-97. Image Processed in Photoshop

In my opinion, the HDR image done in software, shown in Figure 4-97, did a better job of evening out the contrast than the Auto HDR images processed in the camera. However, these images were taken under fairly extreme conditions. The in-camera HDR option is an excellent option for subjects that are partly shaded and partly in sunlight, when you don't have the time or inclination to take multiple pictures and combine them later with HDR software into a composite image.

My recommendation is to leave the DRO Auto setting turned on for general shooting, especially if you don't plan to do post-processing. If the contrast in lighting for a given scene is extreme, then try at least some shots using the Auto HDR feature.

If you are planning to do post-processing, you may want to use the Raw setting for file Format, so you can work with the shots later using software to achieve evenly exposed final images. You also could use Manual exposure mode or exposure bracketing to take shots at different exposures and merge them with Photoshop, Photomatix, or other HDR software. The a6400 provides high levels of dynamic range in its Raw files, particularly if you shoot with low ISO settings. Therefore, you very well may be able to bring details out of the shadows and reduce overexposure in highlighted areas using your Raw processing software.

Note that the Auto HDR setting cannot be used if you are using the Raw format for your images. The other DRO settings do work with Raw images, but they will have no effect on the Raw images unless you process them with Sony's Imaging Edge software or some other software that has been programmed to recognize the DRO settings embedded in the Raw files. When I used Adobe Camera Raw to open a Raw file taken with by the a6400 with DRO set to LV5, the image did not show

any effects of the DRO processing, although the effects were apparent in Imaging Edge.

You cannot adjust DRO and Auto HDR settings in the Auto, Scene, and Sweep Panorama modes. With the Sunset, Night Scene, Night Portrait, Hand-held Twilight, and Anti Motion Blur settings, and in Sweep Panorama mode, DRO/Auto HDR is turned off. With other scene types and in Auto mode, DRO is turned on. DRO/HDR cannot be used when Multi Frame NR, Picture Effect, or Picture Profile is active. You can use flash with the DRO/HDR settings, but it will fire only for the first HDR shot, and it defeats the purpose of the settings to use flash, so you probably should not do so.

Creative Style

The Creative Style setting provides options for altering the appearance of your images with in-camera adjustments to their contrast, saturation (color intensity), and sharpness. Using these settings, you can add or subtract intensity of color or make subtle changes to the look of your images, as well as shoot in monochrome. Of course, if you plan to edit your images on a computer using software such as Photoshop, you can duplicate these effects readily at that stage. But, if you don't want to spend time processing your images in that way, having the ability to alter the look of your shots using this menu option can add a good deal to the enjoyment of your photos.

Figure 4-98. Creative Style Menu

To use this feature, highlight Creative Style on screen 11 of the Camera Settings1 menu and press the Center button to go to the next screen, as shown in Figure 4-98. Using the Up and Down buttons or turning the control wheel, scroll through the 13 main settings: Standard, Vivid, Neutral, Clear, Deep, Light, Portrait, Landscape, Sunset, Night Scene, Autumn Leaves, Black and White, and Sepia. If you want to choose one of these settings with no further adjustment, just press the Center button when your chosen option is highlighted.

If you use an option other than Standard, you may see a change on the display in shooting mode. For example, if you choose Sepia or Black and White, the screen will have that coloration.

This effect will be visible, though, only if the Live View Display option on screen 7 of the Camera Settings2 menu is set to Setting Effect On. If that menu option is set to Setting Effect Off, the display will not show any change from the Creative Style setting. You will still see an icon showing which setting is in effect, in the lower right of the screen. For example, Figure 4-99 shows the display when the Sepia setting is active but Setting Effect is off. (The VIEW indicator in the upper middle of the display indicates that Setting Effect is turned off.)

Figure 4-99. Shooting Screen with Setting Effect Off

ADJUSTING CONTRAST, SATURATION, AND SHARPNESS

To adjust contrast, saturation, or sharpness for a Creative Style setting, move the highlight bar to the setting, such as Portrait, and press the Right button or turn the control dial to put a new highlight bar on the right of the screen. You will see a label above a line of icons at the bottom of the screen, as shown in Figure 4-100.

As you move the highlight bar over each icon with the Left and Right buttons or the control dial, the label will change to show which value is active and ready to be adjusted. When the chosen value (contrast, saturation, or sharpness) is highlighted, use the Up and Down buttons or turn the control wheel to adjust the value upward or downward by up to three units. When the Black and White or Sepia setting is active, there are only two adjustments available—contrast and

sharpness. Saturation is not available because it adjusts the intensity of colors and there are no colors to adjust for those two settings.

Figure 4-100. Screen to Adjust Creative Style Parameters

By varying the amounts of these three parameters, you can achieve a range of different appearances for your images. For example, by increasing saturation, you can add punch and make colors stand out. By adding contrast and/or sharpness, you can impose a "harder" appearance on your images, making them look grittier and more realistic.

Figure 4-101. Image with All Parameters at Minimums

Figure 4-102. Image with All Parameters at Maximums

Figure 4-101 was taken with the Standard setting with all three parameters adjusted to their minimums, and

Figure 4-102 was taken with the same setting, but with the contrast, sharpness, and saturation all adjusted to their maximum levels of +3 units. As you can see, Figure 4-102 is noticeably brighter, with a crisper look than that in Figure 4-101.

If you want to save the adjusted settings for future use, you can create and save six different custom versions, using any of the 13 basic settings with whatever adjustments you want. To do this, scroll down on the Creative Style menu to the numbered items, starting just below the Sepia item, as shown in Figure 4-103.

Figure 4-103. Numbered Icons for Custom Creative Style Settings

There are six numbered icons, of which the first four are visible on the screen shown here. They all work in the same way. Highlight a numbered icon, then, using the Right button or the control dial, move the highlight to the right side of the screen, on the name of the setting (Vivid, Neutral, Deep, etc.). Use the control wheel or the Up and Down buttons to select any one of the 13 basic Creative Style settings. Then, scroll to the right and adjust contrast, saturation, and sharpness as you want them. When all the adjustments are made, press the Center button to accept them. Whenever you want to recall that customized setting for use, call up the Creative Style menu and scroll to the numbered icon for the style you adjusted.

The Creative Style option works with all shooting modes except Auto mode and Scene mode. You can use it with the Raw format, but the results will vary depending on the Raw-conversion software you use. For example, when I shot a Raw image in Program mode using the Black and White setting, the image showed up in black and white on the camera's screen. However, when I opened the image in Adobe Camera Raw software, the image was in color; that software ignored the information in the image's data about Creative Style setting.

When I opened the image using Sony's Imaging Edge software, though, the image appeared in black and white, because Sony's software recognized the Creative Style information. So, if you want to use this menu option with Raw files, be aware that not all software will use that data when processing the images.

The Creative Style menu option cannot be used when the Picture Effect or Picture Profile option is in use.

Sony a6400 Creative Styles Chart - Part 1

Figure 4-104. Creative Style Comparison Chart - Part 1

Figures 4-104 and 4-105 include comparison photos showing each Creative Style setting as applied to the same subject under the same lighting conditions to illustrate the different effects you can achieve with each variation. General descriptions of these effects are provided after the comparison charts.

Sony a6400 Creative Styles Chart - Part 2

Portrait

Night Scene

Landscape

Autumn Leaves

Sunset

Black and White

Sepia

Figure 4-105. **Creative Style Comparison Chart - Part 2**

STANDARD

The Standard setting uses what Sony considers to be appropriate processing to give a pleasing overall appearance for everyday photographs, with some enhancements to make color photographs appear bright and sharp. This option is intended to be a good default setting for general purposes.

VIVID

The Vivid setting increases the saturation, or intensity, of all colors in the image, as well as the contrast. As you can see from the samples, it calls attention to the scene, though it does not produce dramatic effects. The

Vivid setting might work well to emphasize the colors in images taken at a birthday party or at a carnival.

NEUTRAL

With the Neutral setting, the a6400 leaves images with reduced saturation and sharpness, so you can process them to your own taste using software.

CLEAR

The Clear option emphasizes the highlighted areas in an image, giving them added intensity. Some users feel this setting yields images with more intensity than the Vivid setting.

DEEP

Sony says that this setting is intended to show the "solid presence" of the subject. In effect, it emphasizes the shadow tones and lowers the overall brightness of the image.

LIGHT

This setting is the opposite of Deep; it emphasizes the highlight tones and results in a brighter, lighter appearance.

PORTRAIT

The main feature of the Portrait setting is a reduction in the saturation and sharpness of colors to soften the appearance of skin tones. You might want to use this setting to take portraits that are flattering rather than harsh and realistic. Because this setting provides midrange values for the colors and contrast, some photographers find this to be their favored Creative Style setting for general photography.

LANDSCAPE

With the Landscape setting, the a6400 increases all three values—contrast, saturation, and sharpness—to make the features of a landscape, such as trees and mountains, stand out with clear, sharp outlines. It is similar to Portrait in its processing of colors, but the sharper outlines and contrast might be too strong for portraits.

Sunset

With the Sunset option, the camera increases the saturation to emphasize the red hues of the sunset. In my opinion, this setting produces more changes in color images than any of the others.

Night Scene

Night Scene lowers contrast in an attempt to soften the harsh effect that may result from shots taken in dark surroundings, without affecting the saturation or hues of the colors.

Autumn Leaves

This setting, designed for enhancing shots of fall foliage, increases the intensity of existing red and yellow tones in the image, but does not alter the color balance or introduce new reddish shades, as the Sunset setting does.

B/W

This setting removes all color, converting the scene to black and white. Some photographers use this setting to achieve a realistic look for their street photography.

Sepia

This second monochrome setting also removes the color from the image, but adds a sepia tone that gives an old-fashioned appearance to the shot.

The a6400 also has settings for Portrait, Landscape, Sunset, and Night Scene in Scene mode, discussed in Chapter 3. However, the similar settings of the Creative Style option are available in the more advanced shooting modes, including Program, Aperture Priority, Shutter Priority, and Manual exposure, so you have access to settings such as ISO, metering mode, and others. And, as noted above, you can tweak Creative Style settings by fine-tuning contrast, saturation, and sharpness.

I don't often use the Creative Style settings, because I prefer to shoot with the Raw format and process my images in software such as Photoshop. I occasionally use the Sunset setting to enhance an evening view. The Creative Style settings are of value to a photographer who needs to take numerous photographs with a certain appearance and process them quickly. For example, a wedding or sports photographer may not have time to process images in software; he or she may need to capture hundreds of images in a particular visual style and have them ready for a client or a publication without delay. For this type of application, the Creative Style settings are invaluable. The settings also are useful for any photographer who wants to maintain a consistent appearance of his or her images and is not satisfied with how the JPEG files look when captured with the factory-standard settings.

Picture Effect

The Picture Effect menu option includes a rich array of settings for shooting images with in-camera special effects. The Sony a6400 gives you a variety of ways to add creative touches to your shots, and the Picture Effect settings can produce excellent results.

The Picture Effect settings are not available in the Auto, Scene, or Sweep Panorama modes and do not work with Raw images. If you set a Picture Effect option and then select Raw (or Raw & JPEG) for Quality, the Picture Effect setting will be canceled. However, with a Picture Effect setting turned on, you still have control over many of the most important settings, including JPEG Image Size, White Balance, ISO, and even, in most cases, Drive Mode. So, unlike the situation with the Scene mode settings, when you select a Picture Effect option, you are still free to control the means of taking your images as well as other aspects of their appearance.

To use these effects, select the Picture Effect menu option as seen in Figure 4-106, and scroll through the choices at the left using the control wheel or the Up and Down buttons.

Figure 4-106. Picture Effect Menu

Some selections have no other options, and some have sub-settings that you can make by pressing the Left and

Right buttons or by turning the control dial when their icon is highlighted on the menu.

I will discuss each option in turn and include sample images taken with each of the effects.

OFF

The top setting on the Picture Effect menu is used to cancel all Picture Effect settings. When you are engaged in ordinary picture-taking or video shooting, you should make sure the Off setting is selected so that no unwanted special effects interfere with your images.

TOY CAMERA

The Toy Camera option is an alternative to using one of the "toy" film cameras such as the Holga, Diana, or Lomo, which are popular with hobbyists and artists who use them to take photos with grainy, low-resolution appearances. With all of the Toy Camera settings, the a6400 processes the image so it looks as if it were taken by a camera with a cheap lens: The image is dark at the corners and somewhat blurry.

The several sub-settings for Toy Camera, reached by pressing the Right and Left buttons or turning the control dial, act as follows:

Normal: No additional processing.

Cool: Adjusts color to the "cool" side, resulting in a bluish tint.

Warm: Uses a "warm" white balance, giving a reddish hue.

Green: Adds a green tint, similar to dialing in an adjustment on the green axis for white balance.

Magenta: Similar to the Green setting, but adjustment is along the magenta axis.

I took Figure 4-107 with the Toy Camera option using its Green setting. This setting seemed appropriate to add vignetting and an old-fashioned appearance to this fountain.

Figure 4-107. **Toy Camera - Green Example**

POP COLOR

This setting, according to Sony, is meant to give a "vivid look" through emphasis on bright colors. As you can see in Figure 4-108, which shows a colorful truck parked in a riverfront recreation area, this setting is another way to add "punch" and intensity, along with added brightness, to color images.

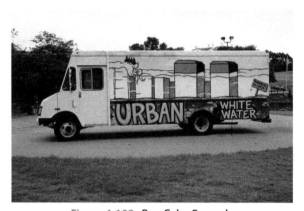

Figure 4-108. **Pop Color Example**

POSTERIZATION

This is a dramatic effect. Using the Right and Left buttons or the control dial when its icon is highlighted, you can choose to apply this effect in color or in black and white. In either case, the camera places extra emphasis on colors (or dark and light areas if you select black and white) and uses a high-contrast, pastel-like look. It is somewhat like an exotic type of HDR processing. The number of different colors (or shades of gray) used in the image is decreased to make it look as if the image were created from just a few poster paints; the result has an unrealistic but dramatic effect, as you can see in Figure 4-109, with its view of the city skyline.

Figure 4-109. Posterization Example

Remember that with all Picture Effect options, you can adjust other settings, including White Balance, exposure compensation, and others. With Posterization, you might use exposure compensation, which can change the appearance of this effect dramatically. I have found the results with this setting often are improved by using negative exposure compensation to avoid excessive brightness. I recommend using Posterization to achieve a striking effect, perhaps for a distinctive-looking poster or greeting card.

RETRO PHOTO

With this setting, the a6400 uses sepia tint and reduced contrast to mimic the appearance of an aging photo. This effect is not as pronounced as the sepia effects I have seen on other cameras; with the a6400, a good deal of the image's original color still shows up, but there is subtle softening of the image with the sepia coloration.

Figure 4-110. Retro Photo Example

In Figure 4-110 I used this effect for a shot of a bridge across the river, to give it an air of days gone by.

SOFT HIGH-KEY

"High key" is a technique that uses bright lighting throughout a scene for an overall look with light colors and few shadows. With the a6400, Sony has added softness to give the image a light appearance without the harshness that might otherwise result from the unusually bright exposure. In Figure 4-111 I used this setting for a photo of a fountain in the downtown area, to give it a somewhat lighter appearance.

Figure 4-111. Soft High-key Example

PARTIAL COLOR

The Partial Color effect lets you choose a single color to retain in an image; the camera reduces the saturation of all other colors to monochrome, so that only objects of that single hue remain in color in the image. I really enjoy this setting, which can be used to isolate a particular object with dramatic effect. In Figure 4-112, I used this setting for a photo of a mannequin with red hair, to set it off from its surroundings.

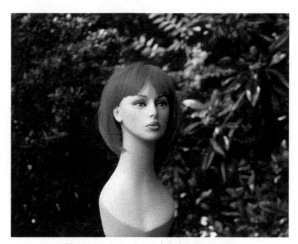

Figure 4-112. Partial Color Example

The choices for the color to be retained are red, green, blue, and yellow; use the Left and Right buttons or the control dial to select one of those colors. When you aim the camera at your subject, you will see on the display what objects will show up in color, if the Live View Display menu option is set to Setting Effect On.

There is no direct way to adjust the color tolerance of this setting, so you cannot, for example, set the camera to accept a broad range of reds to be retained in the image. However, if you change the White Balance setting, the camera will perceive colors differently.

So, if there is a particular object that you want to depict in color, but the camera does not "see" it as red, green, blue, or yellow, you can try selecting a different White Balance setting and see if the color will be retained. You also can fine-tune the white balance using the color axes to add or subtract these hues if you want to bring a particular object within the range of the color that will be retained.

By choosing a color that does not appear in the scene at all, you can take a straight monochrome photograph.

High Contrast Monochrome

This setting lets you take black and white photographs with a stark, high-contrast appearance. You might want to consider this setting for street photography or any other situation in which you are not looking for a soft or flattering appearance.

Figure 4-113. High Contrast Monochrome Example

I used this setting for Figure 4-113, another view of the city skyline shown with the Posterization setting in Figure 4-109.

Soft Focus

The Soft Focus effect is another setting that is variable; you can select either Low, Mid, or High by pressing the

Right and Left buttons or turning the control dial. This effect is straightforward; the camera blurs the focus to achieve a dreamlike aura. This is the first of several Picture Effect settings that cannot be previewed on the screen; you have to take the picture and then play it back to see the results of the Soft Focus setting. (As an alternative to using this setting, you can set Focus Mode to manual focus and defocus the image to your own taste to achieve a similar effect.)

Figure 4-114. Soft Focus Mid Example

For Figure 4-114, I used this option for an image of a person walking beside a canal among the trees and green bushes. I find that this effect is often good for adding a feeling of peacefulness to a scene.

HDR Painting

The HDR Painting setting is similar to the HDR setting of the DRO/Auto HDR menu option. With this option, the camera takes a burst of three shots at different exposure settings and combines them internally into a single image to achieve even exposure over a range of areas with differing brightness. Unlike the more standard HDR setting, this one does not let you select the specific exposure differential for the three shots, but it lets you choose Low, Mid, or High for the intensity of the effect. Also, it adds stylized processing to give the final image a painterly appearance.

I often have good results with this setting when I shoot from an indoor area through a window on a sunny day, especially when there is a variety of colorful items outside. For Figure 4-115, though, I chose a view of the river from under a bridge and through a variety of trees and bushes. I chose the Low setting for this image, to avoid having an overly unrealistic effect.

Figure 4-115. HDR Painting Low Example

Because the camera takes multiple images with this option, you can't preview the results on the screen before taking the picture. Using a tripod is advisable to avoid blur from camera motion while the three shots are being taken.

Rich-Tone Monochrome

I consider the Rich-tone Monochrome setting to be a black and white version of the HDR Painting setting. With this option, like that one, the a6400 takes a triple burst of shots at different exposures and combines them digitally into a single composite photo with a broader dynamic range than would otherwise be possible. Unlike the color setting, though, this one does not let you select the intensity of the effect. I used it in Figure 4-116 for another view of the city skyline seen previously with other effects. This setting is good for producing traditional, postcard-like views of scenic subjects.

Figure 4-116. Rich-tone Monochrome Example

Miniature Effect

With the Miniature Effect option, the camera adds blurring at one or more sides or the top or bottom of an image to simulate the look of a photograph of a tabletop model or miniature. Such images often appear hazy in

one or more areas, either because of the narrow depth of field of these closeup photos, or because of the use of a tilt-and-shift lens, which causes blurring at the edges.

For this feature to work well, you need an appropriate subject. I have found that this effect looks interesting when applied to something like a street scene or a train, which might actually be reproduced in a tabletop model. For example, if you are able to get a high vantage point above a road intersection or a railroad, you may be able to use this processing to make it look as if you had photographed a high-quality tabletop display.

After highlighting this option on the Camera Settings1 menu, press the Right and Left buttons or turn the control dial to choose Top, Middle (Horizontal), Bottom, Right, Middle (Vertical), Left, or Auto for the configuration of the effect. If you choose a specific area, that area will remain sharp.

For example, if you choose Top, then, after you take the picture, the top area (roughly one-third) will remain sharp, and the rest of the image below that area will appear blurred. If you choose Auto, the camera will select the area to remain sharp based on the area that was focused on by the autofocus system and by the camera's sensing how you are holding the camera.

Figure 4-117. Miniature Effect Example

You will not see how the effect will alter the image while viewing the scene, though the camera will place gray areas on the parts of the image that will ultimately be blurred to give an idea of how the final product will look. In Figure 4-117, I used this setting for a view of a city street with parked cars. I was able to capture it from a high vantage point, which added to the effectiveness of the setting. This effect can provide a lot of fun if you experiment with it; it can take some work to find the right subject and the best arrangement of sharp and blurry areas to achieve a satisfying result.

WATERCOLOR

The Watercolor effect blurs the colors of an image to make it look as if it were painted with watercolors that are bleeding together. You need to choose a subject that lends itself to this sort of distortion. For example, I have found that the faces of dolls and other figures can be pleasantly altered to have an impressionistic appearance. I have also had some pleasing results with plants and trees. In Figure 4-118, I used this setting for an image of the canal seen earlier in Figure 4-114.

Figure 4-118. Watercolor Example

ILLUSTRATION

The Illustration effect finds edges of objects in the scene and adds contrast, making the image seem like a pen-and-ink illustration that has been colored in. You can set the intensity of the effect to Low, Mid, or High using the Right and Left buttons or the control dial. If you choose a subject with edges that can be outlined and a repeating pattern, you can achieve a pleasing result. This is another effect whose final result you cannot judge while viewing the live scene; you need to see the recorded image to know what the actual effect will look like.

As you can see in Figure 4-119, taken with Illustration set to Mid, this effect can transform an ordinary view into a stylized image while leaving the scene recognizable. The images produced with this effect may be more suited as decorative items than as depictions of

actual objects or locations, but their appearance can be very striking and unusual. This setting often produces good results when people are included in the scene, especially if they are wearing clothes with bright colors.

Figure 4-119. Illustration Mid Example

Here are some more notes about the Picture Effect settings. Several of the options are not available for shooting movies. Those settings are Soft Focus, HDR Painting, Rich-tone Monochrome, Miniature Effect, Watercolor, and Illustration. If one of those effects is turned on when you press the Movie button, the camera will turn off the effect while the movie is being recorded, and turn it back on after the recording has ended. You also cannot use continuous shooting or any type of bracketing with any of those six effects.

Picture Profile

Picture Profile, the final item on the eleventh screen of the Camera Settings1 menu, provides powerful tools for adjusting the appearance of your files, particularly video footage. This option is similar in some ways to the Creative Style option, which provides a separate set of preset adjustments that affect image processing, as discussed earlier in this chapter. Like Creative Style, the Picture Profile option includes several presets from which you can easily choose the one that best suits your current needs and instantly apply it to all of the videos and images you record using that setting. You also can make adjustments to several parameters within any of the Picture Profile settings, just as you can with the Creative Style settings, and you can save the adjusted settings for future use.

However, apart from those similarities, the Picture Profile option is considerably different from the Creative Style feature. Creative Style is straightforward in the adjustments it provides, both in its 13 preset options (Standard, Vivid, Neutral, etc.) and in the adjustments you can make to those settings (contrast, saturation, and sharpness). It is easy to understand what is being adjusted for the presets and to see the resulting differences in the appearance of your images and videos.

The Picture Profile option does not provide such easily categorized adjustments. These adjustments are technical ones intended for use by experienced videographers, to produce footage that is ready for post-processing, or that matches footage from other cameras using the same profile.

In this section, I will explain how to apply a Picture Profile setting and how to adjust one, and I will discuss parameters that can be tweaked for each profile. I will not try to give a detailed explanation of all possible adjustments for the various settings involved, such as gamma, knee, and detail.

To use this setting, highlight Picture Profile on the menu screen and press the Center button to display the vertical menu of settings, as shown in Figure 4-120.

Figure 4-120. Picture Profile Menu

Use the control wheel, the control dial, or the Up and Down buttons to scroll through the eleven settings, including PP Off and PP1 through PP10.

If you don't need or want to bother with setting a profile, just leave this item set to PP Off and you won't have to deal with it further. To use one of the ten preset profiles, scroll to that setting and press the Center button to choose it. That profile will then be displayed in an icon in the lower left corner of the detailed shooting screen.

The basic characteristics of the ten preset profiles that come with the camera are as follows:

PP1   Uses the standard gamma curve for movies.

PP2   Uses the standard gamma curve for still images.

PP3   Uses ITU709 gamma curve for natural color tone. The ITU709 standard is the normal set of specifications for HD television. This is a good profile to use for shooting that won't need extensive post-processing. This is also good for matching footage with that of other cameras.

PP4   Uses the ITU709 standard for color tone. Should not need much post-processing for color tone.

PP5   Uses Cine1 gamma curve to reduce contrast in dark areas and modify bright areas to produce a "relaxed" color effect. Good for sunny days and conditions with high contrast.

PP6   Uses Cine2 gamma curve, optimized for editing with up to 100% video signal; generally similar to Cine1, for use with less need for post-processing to avoid clipping highlights.

PP7   Uses S-Log2 gamma curve, designed to yield increased dynamic range, for footage that will be adjusted with post-processing software.

PP8   Uses S-Log3 gamma curve, which is similar to S-Log2 but has some technical differences. See the links in Appendix C for a discussion of the differences between those two settings. This profile has Color Mode set to S-Gamut3.Cine, as opposed to PP9, which has a different setting for Color Mode.

PP9   Uses S-Log3 gamma curve with Color Mode set to S-Gamut3.

PP10   Uses HLG2 gamma curve, which can be used as the basis for recording HDR footage or images.

You should be able to get good results for general footage with any of the first four Picture Profile settings. On a particularly bright day or in contrasty conditions, you might try PP5, which uses the Cine1 gamma, designed to compress the dynamic range to avoid clipping highlights, or PP6, which uses the Cine2 gamma, which compresses the range even more.

If you will be doing post-processing to correct the color of your footage, you may want to use PP7, PP8, or PP9, which use the S-Log2 or S-Log3 gamma curve settings. With any of these options, your footage will look dull and somewhat dark as shot, but its dynamic range will be considerably greater than normal, so you will have excellent options for producing good-looking footage with your post-processing software. However, because of the way these settings expand dynamic range, they require the use of an ISO setting of 500 or greater. So, if you use PP7, PP8, PP9, or any profile that includes S-Log2 or S-Log 3 gamma, the camera will not set the ISO any lower than 500, and will reset a lower ISO value to 500. (There also are some limits on ISO settings available with various other gamma settings, but most of those limits are not as severe as for the S-Log settings.)

If you want to record HDR video footage, you can use PP10, which includes a gamma setting of HLG2. For HDR recording, the Picture Profile setting has to include a gamma setting of HLG, HLG1, HLG2, or HLG3. PP10 is provided as a preset option that is ready to use for HDR recording. Or, you can modify it to use one of the other HLG settings for gamma.

The chart in Figure 4-121 shows the effects of the ten preset Picture Profile settings, as well as the same image with no Picture Profile in place, to give a general idea of how these settings affect an image.

As you can see, PP7, PP8, and PP9, which use S-Log2 or S-Log 3 gamma, and PP10, which uses HLG2 gamma, produce a dark image on the camera's display. When you are using any of those four settings, you can activate the Gamma Display Assist feature, which sets the display to a higher level of contrast, so you can compose your shot accurately. That feature is found on screen 1 of the Setup menu. You also can assign it to a control button using the Custom Key (Still Images) or Custom Key (Movies) option on screen 9 of the Camera Settings2 menu, as discussed in Chapter 5.

If you are serious about video production, you may not be content with any of the ten preset Picture Profile settings. You can easily modify any of them in the camera. I don't recommend that you do this unless you are knowledgeable about video production, but the option is available. I will discuss the mechanics of how to adjust the various parameters for the Picture Profile settings, but I will not engage in a technical discussion of when and why to adjust them. (Appendix C has links to resources with further information.)

Picture Profiles Comparison

Figure 4-121. Picture Profile Comparison Chart

To adjust a Picture Profile setting, first highlight the Picture Profile menu option and press the Center button to display the menu of Picture Profile options, as shown in Figure 4-120. Scroll to the one you want to adjust and press the Right button. You will then see a screen like that in Figure 4-122, listing the first six parameters that can be adjusted: black level, gamma, black gamma, knee, color mode, and saturation.

Figure 4-122. Adjustment Screen for Picture Profile Parameters

Turn the control wheel or dial, or press the Up and Down buttons, to scroll through this list and on to the remaining parameters: color phase, color depth, and detail. The last two options, copy and reset, are for copying the settings or restoring the default settings.

When you have highlighted a parameter to adjust, such as gamma, press the Right button or the Center button to bring up the adjustment screen, as shown in Figure 4-123.

Figure 4-123. Screen to Adjust Gamma for Picture Profile

Use the control wheel or dial or the Up and Down buttons to choose the value to set, and press the Center button to set the value and return to the previous screen. Continue scrolling through the parameters to set each as you want it. Once you have made the adjustments, the Picture Profile number you adjusted will retain those changes, even if the camera is turned off and back on. If you want to copy the settings from one Picture Profile slot to another, use the copy item near the bottom of the list of parameters. Use the reset option to restore the Picture Profile setting to its default values.

Following are general descriptions of the nine parameters that you can adjust for each Picture Profile setting:

Black Level. Default 0; adjustment from -15 to +15. Adjusting in the negative direction strengthens the black color in the image; adjusting in the positive direction fades or weakens it.

Gamma. No default. Choices are Movie, Still, Cine1, Cine2, Cine3, Cine4, ITU709, ITU709 (800%), S-Log2, S-Log3, HLG, HLG1, HLG2, or HLG3. The gamma curve is an adjustment to the video signal to account for the difference between recorded video and the output characteristics of various display devices, such as cathode ray tubes, HDTVs, etc. The first two choices are self-explanatory. Cine1 has the signal compressed to avoid clipping of highlights; Cine2 is compressed further for the same purpose. Cine3 increases contrast between light and dark areas. Cine4 is similar to Cine3, but increases contrast more intensely. The ITU709 setting is a standard one for HDTV. The ITU709 (800%) option provides greater dynamic range than ITU709. It applies standard contrast and color levels to the video signal and turns off the knee circuit. It can be used as the finished product for video production. You may need to use this standard or S-Log2 when recording to certain external recorders. The S-Log2 standard, which provides greater-than-normal dynamic range, produces a flat, somewhat dark signal. This standard is for use when you will adjust the appearance of the video file with post-processing software. S-Log3 is similar to S-Log2 with some technical differences; see Appendix C for further information. The HLG options are variations of an industry standard setting known as Hybrid Log-Gamma. These settings are designed to provide a wider dynamic range than other settings, in a way similar to the function of the HDR setting for still images. HLG is the basic setting. Each of the other three options provides additional dynamic range, but also introduces more possibility of visual noise in the scene because of the use of lesser amounts of noise reduction. As noted earlier, PP10 includes the HLG2 setting by default.

Black Gamma. Range default is Middle; can be set to Wide or Narrow. Level default is 0; can be set from -7 to +7. Increasing Level brightens the image and decreasing Level darkens it. Adjusting Range determines whether the Level adjustment affects only blacks (Narrow) or a wider range of grays. The black gamma value is fixed at 0 when gamma is set to HLG, HLG1, HLG2, or HLG3.

Knee. The knee adjustment sets a curve for compressing the signal in the brightest parts of the video image to avoid clipping or washing out of highlights. The Mode can be set to Auto or Manual. If you select Auto, then you need to use the Auto Set option to choose the Max Point and Sensitivity. If you choose Manual, you need to use the Manual Set option to set the Point and Slope.

Color Mode. No default. Can be set to Movie, Still, Cinema, Pro, ITU709 Matrix, Black & White, S-Gamut, S-Gamut3.Cine, S-Gamut3, BT.2020, or 709. Movie is designed for use with the Movie setting for Gamma; Still for the Still setting; Cinema for the Cine1 or Cine2 setting; Pro for the gamma curve of Sony professional video cameras; ITU709 Matrix for use with the ITU709 gamma curve; Black & White for shooting in monochrome; S-Gamut for shooting with the S-Log2 gamma curve; S-Gamut3.Cine and S-Gamut3 for use with the S-Log3 gamma curve. BT.2020 and 709 are the only color mode settings available when gamma is set to HLG, HLG1, HLG2, or HLG3. If you select the Black & White setting, the video will be shot in black and white.

Saturation. Default 0. Can be set from -32 to +32. This adjustment is similar to the saturation adjustment available with the Creative Style menu option. A negative setting lowers the intensity of colors, reducing them almost completely to black and white at the -32 level, while a positive value increases their intensity.

Color Phase. Default 0. Can be set from -7 to +7. Adjusting in the negative or positive direction makes the colors shift their hues. You can use this setting to match the color output of the a6400 to that of another camera you are using for video production.

Color Depth. Default 0. Can be set from -7 to +7 for each of six colors: red, green, blue, cyan, magenta, and yellow. A higher number makes the color darker and richer; a lower number makes it brighter and paler.

Detail. There are two main settings: Level and Adjust. Level has a default of 0 and can be adjusted from -7 to +7. This setting affects the sharpness of edges in the image. A lower number softens the image and a higher number gives it sharper contrast. The other main setting, Adjust, has several settings, starting with Mode, which can be set to Auto or Manual. If you set Mode to Auto, you can ignore the other settings. If you set it to Manual, you can adjust V/H Balance, B/W Balance, Limit, Crispening (misspelled on the camera's menu), and Hi-Light Detail. Sony's user's guide recommends changing only the Level setting, at least at first, but the guide provides details

on the other settings. You can see those details at Sony's website, http://helpguide.sony.net/di/pp/v1/en/index.html. If you are planning to use software to process your video, you may want to reduce Level to -7 so you can determine the proper amount of sharpening on your own.

The good news about the Picture Profile setting is that you do not need to worry about it if you don't want to. If you are shooting primarily still images or videos for your own use, you don't have to select any Picture Profile setting. However, if you are using the a6400 for professional video production, perhaps as a second camera, you may need to set the Picture Profile so the camera's output will match that of your other cameras.

Picture Profile cannot be used when DRO/HDR, Creative Style (other than Standard), Multi Frame Noise Reduction setting for ISO, or Picture Effect is in use. Picture Profile settings affect Raw files, but the black level, black gamma, knee, and color depth settings are not reflected in Raw images.

As indicated earlier, some settings for gamma restrict the ability to use the lower ISO settings. With ITU709 (800%), S-Log2, and S-Log3, the lowest ISO available is 500. With Cine4, the lowest ISO available is 200. With HLG and HLG3, the lowest setting available is 125.

If you want to explore Picture Profile in greater detail, check out the resources listed in Appendix C.

The items on screen 12 of the Camera Settings1 menu are shown in Figure 4-124.

Figure 4-124. Screen 12 of Camera Settings1 Menu

Soft Skin Effect

This setting softens skin tones in the faces of subjects for still images. The option is dimmed and unavailable in some situations, such as when one of the continuous shooting options or the Raw setting for File Format is selected. After you select this option and turn it on, you can use the Right and Left buttons or the control dial to set the level at Lo, Mid, or Hi. However, even if you turn the Soft Skin Effect option on, it will not affect your images unless you also have Face/Eye Priority in AF turned on through the Face/Eye AF Settings option on screen 6 of the Camera Settings1 menu, and the a6400 has detected a human face. (The Soft Skin Effect setting is not available if Subject Detection under the Face/Eye Priority AF option is set to Animal. That option was discussed earlier in this chapter.)

When it works, this setting reduces sharpness and contrast in areas that the camera perceives as skin tones. It can do a good job of smoothing out wrinkles. Figures 4-125 and 4-126 show the results of a test I made. Figure 4-125 was taken with the effect turned off; Figure 4-126 had the setting at its Hi level.

Figure 4-125. Soft Skin Effect Off

Figure 4-126. Soft Skin Effect Set to High

This can be a useful option for doing some basic retouching of your JPEG portraits in the camera.

Shutter Auto White Balance Lock

This option lets you control whether or not the camera locks white balance while the shutter is pressed halfway down, or during continuous shooting, when White Balance is set to Auto White Balance or Underwater Auto White Balance. The reason for using this option is to avoid having the camera alter the White Balance setting during a series of shots because of flickering of the lights, a cloud passing over the sun, or some other unexpected circumstance.

The available settings are Shutter Halfway Down, Continuous Shooting, or Off. If you choose the first option, the camera locks white balance when you press the shutter halfway down, and keeps it locked as long as the shutter stays in that position. In addition, the camera locks white balance during continuous shooting.

With the second setting, the camera locks white balance only during continuous shooting.

With the third setting, the camera does not lock white balance, and may adjust it at any time.

Another way to lock white balance using Auto White Balance is to assign AWB Lock Hold or AWB Lock Toggle to a control button, using the Custom Key (Still Images) option on screen 8 of the Camera Settings2 menu. If you use that approach, you can keep white balance locked for as long as you hold down the assigned button, or, if you use the AWB Lock Toggle option, until you press the assigned button a second time to release the lock.

The items on screen 13 of the Camera Settings1 menu are shown in Figure 4-127.

Figure 4-127. Screen 13 of Camera Settings1 Menu

Focus Magnifier

The Focus Magnifier option gives you a way to enlarge a small portion of the display so you can check the focus of that area. It is useful primarily when using manual focus or direct manual focus (DMF), but it can also be used when Focus Mode is set to AF-S or AF-A. It cannot be used when Focus Mode is set to AF-C. This option works somewhat differently when recording movies, as discussed later in this section. For this discussion, I'm assuming the Initial Focus Magnification menu option, discussed later in this section, is set to x1.0.

When you select this menu option, the camera places an orange frame on the display, as seen in Figure 4-128.

Figure 4-128. Focus Magnifier Frame on Shooting Screen

You can move the frame to any position on the display using the direction buttons, the control wheel, or the control dial. When the frame is over the area where you want to check focus, press the Center button. The camera will then enlarge the area within the frame to 5.9 times normal, as shown in Figure 4-129. (The enlargement factor is different when shooting movies; see discussion below.)

Figure 4-129. Focus Magnifier at 5.9 Times Enlargement

An inset square will show the position of the Focus Magnifier frame. You can move the frame around the

display while the display is enlarged and recall the frame to the center of the display by pressing the Custom 2/ Delete button. Press the Center button again, and the focus area will be magnified to 11.7 times normal. A final press will restore the display to normal size and dismiss the magnifier frame.

When you have activated the Focus Magnifier frame, you can also move it around the screen by dragging it with your finger, if the Touch Operation features are turned on through screen 3 of the Setup menu. The dragging action works in any focus mode, including autofocus. When the camera is set to manual focus mode, you can activate Focus Magnifier at the x5.9 magnification factor just by tapping twice quickly on the screen. Then you can drag the magnified area around the screen; tap twice quickly again to dismiss the magnification.

The Focus Magnifier option can be a bit confusing because it acts in a similar way to another option, which is activated from an item further down on the same menu screen, called MF Assist. As I will discuss later in this chapter, when you turn on MF Assist with manual focus in effect, the focus area is enlarged to 5.9 times normal as soon as you start turning the focus ring to adjust the focus. Then, once the focus area is enlarged with that option, pressing the Center button will magnify the focus area to 11.7 times normal. You can toggle between the 5.9 and 11.7 magnifications using the Center button, and exit to the shooting screen by half-pressing the shutter button.

In other words, if the MF Assist menu option is active, pressing the Center button magnifies the focus area once you have started to adjust focus in manual focus mode. If you select the Focus Magnifier menu option, the difference is that pressing the Center button will magnify the display before you start focusing.

The advantage of using the Focus Magnifier menu option is that you can select the position of the enlarged focus area before you start adjusting focus. If you use the MF Assist option, the camera will enlarge the display as soon as you start turning the lens ring to adjust focus, and you will not be able to choose the location of the enlarged focus area until the display is already enlarged.

The MF Assist option works well for me, because it operates as soon as I start adjusting focus. However, if you prefer to be able to adjust the location of the frame for the enlarged focus area before starting to adjust focus, the Focus Magnifier option is useful.

In addition, as noted earlier, you can use Focus Magnifier even with autofocus (though not with continuous autofocus). The way Focus Magnifier operates in autofocus modes depends on the setting for the AF in Focus Magnifier menu option, three items below Focus Magnifier on the same menu screen. If that option is set to On, when you activate Focus Magnifier in an autofocus mode, the screen stays magnified so you can evaluate the focus and, if necessary, move the focus point around and continue to re-focus until you have the scene focused exactly how you want it. The screen will remain magnified until you press the shutter button all the way down to take the picture.

If, on the other hand, you set AF in Focus Magnifier to Off, when you use Focus Magnifier in an autofocus mode, the magnification stops as soon as you press the shutter button halfway down to evaluate focus.

The Focus Magnifier feature is easier to use if you assign it to one of the control buttons. For example, you can use the Custom Key (Still Images) option on screen 8 of the Camera Settings2 menu to assign Focus Magnifier to the Left button. Then, you can just press that button to bring the enlargement frame up on the display. You can quickly adjust the position of the frame, press the Center button once or twice to enlarge that area, and then adjust the focus and take the picture.

You can adjust the length of time the screen stays enlarged with this feature by using the Focus Magnification Time option, discussed immediately below. I prefer to set the time to No Limit so the magnification lasts as long as I need it. You also can set the Focus Magnifier option to use an initial magnification factor of x1.0 or x5.9 using the Initial Focus Magnification item, discussed below.

As noted above, Focus Magnifier works slightly differently for movies than for still images. If you assign this option to a control button, you can call it up while recording a movie to check the focus of the area within the frame. The only magnification factor when shooting movies is x4.0, rather than x5.9 and x11.7, the factors when shooting still images.

Focus Magnification Time

This option lets you select how long the display stays magnified when you use either the Focus Magnifier option, discussed above, or the MF Assist option, discussed later in this chapter. The choices are two or five seconds or No Limit. The default option is two seconds. With No Limit, the image will stay magnified until you press the shutter button all the way to take the picture, or press it halfway to dismiss the enlarged view. When using MF Assist, the time limit of two or five seconds starts once you stop adjusting focus with the focus ring. My preference is to use the No Limit option, so I can take my time in adjusting manual focus precisely, even if I stop turning the ring.

Initial Focus Magnification

This menu option lets you select either x1.0 or x5.9 as the initial magnification factor for the Focus Magnifier frame when it first appears on the screen. If you select the default of x1.0 for this menu option, the Focus Magnifier frame will appear on the display with no magnification until you press the Center button. The first press magnifies the area within the frame to 5.9 times, and a second press magnifies it to 11.7 times; a third press removes the frame from the display. If you select x5.9 for this option, the frame will appear with the 5.9 times magnification already in effect.

Note: If you use the In-Camera Guide help system, which can be assigned to a control button using the Custom Key (Still Images) option, and press that button when this menu item is highlighted, the help system says that this option controls the initial magnification for the Focus Magnifier option and for the MF Assist option. However, this option controls the initial magnification only for the Focus Magnifier option. The MF Assist screen always displays initially at the x5.9 magnification, regardless of the setting for this option.

AF in Focus Magnifier

I discussed this option in connection with the Focus Magnifier option, above. This option lets you determine whether the Focus Magnifier screen remains magnified while you use autofocus to adjust focus, or not. If this option is turned off, the screen reverts to its non-magnified display as soon as you press the shutter button halfway down to evaluate focus. If the option is turned on, you can adjust autofocus multiple times by pressing the shutter button halfway, even while the Focus Magnifier screen retains its magnification. When this option is in effect, the camera places a black plus sign in the center of the screen, to indicate the point where autofocus will be directed.

MF Assist

The MF Assist option is available to assist with focusing when manual focus or DMF is in use. When MF Assist is turned on in manual focus mode, the a6400 enlarges the image on the display screen to 5.9 times normal size as soon as you start turning the focusing ring on the lens, as shown in Figure 4-130. To increase magnification to 11.7 times, press the Center button; press that button again to return to the 5.9 times enlargement factor. Press the shutter button halfway down to return the image to normal size. This feature is helpful in judging whether a particular area is in sharp focus. If you turn this option off, you can use another focusing aid, such as Focus Magnifier, discussed above, or Peaking, discussed immediately below.

Figure 4-130. MF Assist Screen at 5.9 Times Enlargement

Or, you can use this option and Peaking at the same time, to provide even more assistance.

When DMF is in effect, you have to keep the shutter button pressed halfway down while turning the focusing ring to use the MF Assist enlargement feature.

Note that, as discussed above in connection with the Focus Magnifier option, when the camera is in manual focus mode, you can tap twice on the screen to magnify the image to 5.9 times normal, and drag the magnified area around the screen with your finger; tap twice again to return the size to normal.

I find MF Assist helpful, especially when I set the camera to leave the enlarged screen in place indefinitely using the Focus Magnification Time option, discussed immediately below. However, the Focus Magnifier option also is helpful, and may be preferable in one way because the screen does not become magnified until you select the area to be magnified using the orange frame and press the Center button to magnify the screen. (You can change that behavior with the Initial Focus Magnification menu option, discussed above.)

In some cases, where a subject (like the moon) does not have clear edges or other features to focus on, enlarging the view may not be that much help. In those situations, Peaking may be more useful. Or, you may find that using Peaking in conjunction with MF Assist is the most useful approach of all. You should experiment with the various options to find what works best for you.

MF Assist is not available when recording movies or when using a lens with a Mount Adaptor. You can use Focus Magnifier in those situations. While recording movies, Focus Magnifier would have to be assigned to a control button, because you cannot get access to the menu system during the recording process.

Peaking Setting

The Peaking Setting menu option controls the use of the Peaking display to assist with manual focus. When Peaking is turned on with Focus Mode set to manual focus or DMF, the camera displays bright pixels at areas where focus is sharp, to help you adjust focus. The Peaking Display option controls whether the Peaking feature is activated or not; the Peaking Level option controls the intensity of the display; and Peaking Color determines the color of the pixels that are displayed.

You can set the level to Low, Mid, or High and the color to red, yellow, blue, or white. Figures 4-45 and 4-46 illustrated this feature earlier in this chapter.

The idea is that these areas of bright pixels provide a more definite indication that the focus is sharp than just relying on your judgment of sharpness. Some photographers set Creative Style to black and white while focusing so the Peaking color will stand out, and some set Peaking Level to Low so the color is not overwhelming, letting them see when the color just starts to appear. Some turn on MF Assist to enlarge the screen when using Peaking. You should experiment to find what approach works best for you.

Note that Peaking also works with DMF, even if you are using the autofocus function of that setting.

The items on screen 14 of the Camera Settings1 menu are shown in Figure 4-131.

Figure 4-131. Screen 14 of Camera Settings1 Menu

Face Registration

This first option on screen 14 of the Camera Settings1 menu lets you register human faces so the a6400 can give those faces priority when it uses face detection. You can register up to eight faces and assign each one a priority from one to eight, with one being the highest. The camera will try to detect the registered faces in the order you have assigned them, if you have turned on the Face Priority in AF option under the Face/Eye AF Settings item on screen 6 of the Camera Settings1 menu, and you have turned on the Registered Faces Priority option, which is directly below Face Registration on screen 14 of the menu. This feature could be useful if, for example, you take pictures at school functions and you want to make sure the camera focuses on your own children rather than on other kids.

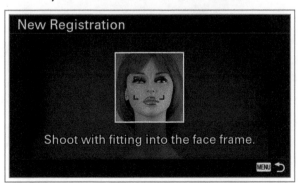

Figure 4-132. Screen to Register New Face

To use this setting, select this menu option, and on the next screen, select New Registration. Press the Center button, and the camera will place a square on the screen. Compose a shot with the face to be registered in that frame, as shown in Figure 4-132, and press the shutter button to take a picture of the face. If the process succeeds, the camera will display the face with the message "Register face?" Highlight the Enter bar on that screen and press the Center button to complete the registration process.

Later, you can use the Order Exchanging option to change the priorities of the registered faces, and you can delete registered faces using other menu options.

Registered Faces Priority

When you activate this menu option, the camera searches for faces that you have previously registered using the Face Registration option, discussed above. If the camera detects a registered face, it should consider that face to have priority, in which case it will place a white frame on the face and adjust the focus for that face. If there are multiple faces, some of which are registered, the camera should place a white frame over the one with the highest priority and purple frames over registered faces with lower priorities.

Smile Shutter

The next option on this menu screen is Smile Shutter, a sort of self-timer that is activated when the subject smiles. After selecting this option and highlighting its On icon, use the Left and Right buttons or the control dial to choose the level of smile that is needed to trigger the camera—Slight Smile, Normal Smile, or Big Smile. Then press the Center button to exit back to the shooting screen, and aim the camera at the subject or subjects. (You can, of course, put the camera on a tripod and aim it at yourself, if you want.)

Figure 4-133. Smile Shutter Meter at Left of Screen

As shown in Figure 4-133, the camera will show a meter at the left of the screen with a pointer to indicate how large a smile is needed to trigger a shot.

As soon as the camera detects a big enough smile from any person, the shutter will fire. If a person smiles again, the camera will be triggered again, with no limit on the number of shots that can be taken. If there are multiple faces in the scene and Touch Tracking is enabled through the Function of Touch Operation item on screen 9 of the Camera Settings2 menu, you can touch the screen to designate a face, and that face will be the only one the camera checks for smiles.

In effect, this feature acts as a limited kind of remote control with one specific function. I consider this option to be something of a novelty, which can be entertaining but is not necessary for everyday photography.

Smile Shutter does not work in Sweep Panorama mode, the Landscape, Night Scene, Sunset, Hand-held Twilight, or Anti Motion Blur settings for Scene mode, with the Picture Effect option turned on, or when recording movies or S & Q Motion sequences.

Auto Object Framing

This option provides a somewhat unusual function: It rearranges the composition of your shot based on the camera's electronic judgment. To activate it, set it to Auto on the menu. Then, after you capture your image, the camera will display a white cropping frame around what it believes to be the subject if it finds that the image can benefit by being trimmed to fit the subject better. For this feature to work with faces, you need to have Face/Eye Priority in AF turned on under the Eye/AF Settings option on screen 6 of the Camera Settings1 menu. Besides faces, Sony says that the feature will work with macro shots and objects tracked with Tracking AF.

When you take a picture of the face or other subject, the camera may, if it finds it possible, crop the image and produce a new version of the image with the frame trimmed and resized to emphasize the subject in a more pleasing way.

An example is shown in Figure 4-134 and Figure 4-135, which show the uncropped and cropped versions, respectively, of a mannequin head I photographed with face detection activated. The camera's cropping looks appropriate, but I would rather do the cropping myself in Photoshop or just compose the image in this way to begin with.

The camera saves both versions, so there is no harm in using this feature. It could be useful if you are pressed for time or are unable to get into position to take the shot you want. If you need a more nicely cropped version of the image quickly for a slide show, perhaps, this could be a good way to fill that need.

Figure 4-134. Auto Object Framing - Original Image

Figure 4-135. Auto Object Framing - After Cropping

This feature is available for selection only if the camera is set for autofocus with File Format set to JPEG. This option does not work with Raw images or when the lens is zoomed beyond the full optical zoom range. It also does not work when the camera is set for a feature that involves multiple shots, such as continuous shooting, HDR, or Multi Frame Noise Reduction, or certain Picture Effect settings. It does not work in Sweep Panorama, Movie, or S & Q mode, or with some Scene mode settings.

Self-portrait Timer

This last option on the Camera Settings1 menu can be turned either on or off. If it is turned on, then, when you rotate the LCD screen so it faces forward, the camera will display a large three-step countdown timer when you press the shutter button, so you can get ready for a self-portrait. You also can touch your image on the monitor to initiate the countdown. The timer screen, shown in Figure 4-136, includes a three-second self-timer icon in the lower right corner. If this menu option is turned off, you can still take a self-portrait, but without the on-screen timer.

Figure 4-136. Self-portrait Timer Countdown Screen

When you use this option, the camera locks focus when you press the shutter button or touch the monitor at the location of your face, and, if your position changes during the countdown, the focus may be incorrect.

To avoid this problem, you can turn off this option and take the picture with no delay. Another approach is to control the camera from a smartphone via Wi-Fi as discussed in Chapter 10, or to use a wired remote control as discussed in Appendix A. Or, you can just make sure your face does not change its distance from the camera after you press the shutter button to start the self-portrait timer.

CHAPTER 5: THE CAMERA SETTINGS2 MENU

The second menu that is represented by a camera icon deserves a separate chapter, because its settings are not just a continuation of those on the Camera Settings1 menu. The Camera Settings2 menu contains all of the camera's settings that directly affect video recording, such as file formats, audio recording options, and the like. This menu also includes a number of settings that affect still photography as well as video recording, such as options for Digital Zoom and switching between the LCD screen and viewfinder. Each of these items is discussed below. However, I do not discuss in this chapter the details of options that are strictly used for video recording. I will mention those items below, but I will discuss them in detail in Chapter 9, where I discuss movie making. Screen 1 of this menu is shown in Figure 5-1.

Figure 5-1. Screen 1 of Camera Settings2 Menu

Exposure Mode (Movies)

This first menu item on this screen is available for selection only when the mode dial is set to Movie mode (the position marked by a movie-film icon). It lets you select one of the four available exposure settings for recording movies in that mode: Program Auto, Aperture Priority, Shutter Priority, or Manual Exposure. The Movie mode is for recording movies at normal speeds, as opposed to the different frame rates used for slow-motion and fast-motion movies recorded in the S & Q mode. I will discuss this option in Chapter 9.

Exposure Mode (S & Q)

This second item on the Camera Settings2 menu is another mode-specific one. It is available for selection only when the mode dial is set to S & Q, for slow and quick motion movie recording. This option lets you choose one of the four exposure modes for recording slow-motion or fast-motion movies, which are similar to the modes mentioned above for Movie mode. I will discuss those settings, as well as other aspects of S & Q Motion recording, in Chapter 9.

File Format (Movies)

This next option applies only for normal-speed movies. I will discuss the details of this setting in Chapter 9. For now, you should know that XAVC S (either 4K or HD) gives the highest quality but is available only if you are using an SDHC or SDXC card rated in Speed Class 10 or UHS Speed Class 1 (UHS Speed Class 3 for some settings). The AVCHD option yields high quality also and does not require a special memory card.

Record Setting

This option is related to the File Format option, discussed above. I will discuss the details of this option in Chapter 9. The available settings will be different depending on whether you choose XAVC S 4K, XAVC S HD, or AVCHD for File Format. They also will be different if you have set the NTSC/PAL selector, on screen 2 of the Setup menu, to PAL, the TV system used in much of Europe and some other locations. In this book, I will discuss the video options that are applicable for the NTSC system, as used in the United States, Japan, and elsewhere.

S & Q Settings

This menu option controls the settings for S & Q Motion mode, which enables slow and quick video recording, when the mode dial is set to the S & Q position. I will discuss this option and other aspects of S & Q Motion recording in Chapter 9.

Proxy Recording

This option can be used to set the camera to record a smaller-sized video file at the same time as a high-quality version, so you can share the smaller file quickly or use it for proxy editing. I will discuss this option in Chapter 9.

The items on screen 2 of the Camera Settings2 menu are shown in Figure 5-2.

Figure 5-2. Screen 2 of Camera Settings2 Menu

AF Drive Speed

This option controls the speed at which the camera's autofocus system changes focus when recording video. I will discuss it in Chapter 9.

AF Tracking Sensitivity

This option, located after AF Drive Speed on the menu, controls how quickly the autofocus system tracks a moving subject when recording video. I will discuss it in Chapter 9.

Auto Slow Shutter

This option lets the camera automatically set a slower shutter speed than normal when shooting a movie, in order to compensate for dim lighting. I will discuss this option in Chapter 9.

Initial Focus Magnification (Movies)

This option is similar to the Initial Focus Magnification item for still images, which was discussed in Chapter 4. This option sets the magnification factor to either x1.0 or x4.0 when you are using the Focus Magnifier option for recording movies. As discussed in Chapter 4, the magnification factor for movies is different from that for still images, so this separate menu option is needed in order to set the initial magnification for movies.

Audio Recording

The Audio Recording item on the Camera Settings2 menu can be set either on or off. If you are certain you won't need the sound recorded by the camera, then you can turn this option off. I never turn it off, because I can always turn down the volume of the recorded sound when playing the video. Or, if I am editing the video on a computer, I can delete the sound and replace it as needed—but there is no way to recapture the original audio from the camera after the fact if this option was turned off during the recording.

Audio Recording Level

This option is available for selection only when the mode dial is set to Movie mode. If you record movies by pressing the Movie button in any other shooting mode, the camera will set the level for recording sound, and you cannot control it. If the mode dial is set to Movie mode, you can control the sound level using this menu option. I will discuss its use in Chapter 9.

The items on screen 3 of the Camera Settings2 menu are shown in Figure 5-3.

Figure 5-3. Screen 3 of Camera Settings2 Menu

Audio Level Display

This option controls whether audio level meters appear during movie recording in any shooting mode and before recording a video when the camera is set to Movie mode. The meters have green indicators that extend to the right to indicate increases in the volume of audio, as shown in Figure 5-4.

Figure 5-4. Audio Level Display Meters on Shooting Screen

The meters appear on detailed information screens; if this option is on and you don't see the meters when recording a video, press the Display button to call up one of the other screens. Also, check to see if the Audio Recording option, discussed above, is turned on; if that option is turned off, the meters will not be displayed. I generally leave this option turned on; seeing the movement of the audio levels on the meters reassures me that the audio is being recorded successfully.

Wind Noise Reduction

This option also is one that applies only to movies. I will discuss it in Chapter 9.

Marker Display

This option, which can be turned either on or off, determines whether or not various informative guidelines, called "markers," are displayed on the camera's screen for movie recording. I will discuss the details of this option in Chapter 9.

Marker Settings

This menu option works together with the Marker Display option, discussed above. This option lets you activate any or all of the four available markers—Center, Aspect, Safety Zone, and Guideframe. I will

discuss this setting in Chapter 9.

Movie w/Shutter

This final option on screen 3 of the Camera Settings2 menu can be turned either on or off. If it is turned on, you can start and stop movie recording by pressing the shutter button when the camera is set to Movie mode, or to S & Q Motion mode, for slow and quick motion movies. I will discuss this option in Chapter 9.

The items on screen 4 of the Camera Settings2 menu are shown in Figure 5-5.

Figure 5-5. Screen 4 of Camera Settings2 Menu

Silent Shooting (Still Images)

This option gives you a convenient way to silence the sounds of the camera's operation when capturing still images. It is available only in the four PASM modes. This option turns off the sound of the shutter operating, but it does not silence the beep that is emitted when the camera achieves sharp autofocus. If you want to silence that sound also, go to the Audio Signals option on screen 9 of the Camera Settings2 menu.

When you activate Silent Shooting, you cannot use the flash, Auto HDR, Picture Effect, Picture Profile, Long Exposure NR, e-Front Curtain Shutter, Superior Auto Image Extraction, the Bulb setting for shutter speed, or the Multi Frame NR setting for ISO.

This feature is very useful for continuous shooting in an environment where the steady clicking of the shutter might attract attention or startle your subject, such as when capturing images of birds or pets.

E-Front Curtain Shutter

The Sony a6400 camera is equipped with the electronic front curtain shutter feature, which reduces the time lag between shutter operations. In many situations, this feature is useful because of this time saving effect. However, in some cases, according to Sony, the feature can cause unwanted effects, such as interfering with the circles of blur that are produced when using a lens with a wide aperture setting, when shooting with a high shutter speed. You also might see dark banding across the image.

If you notice either of those issues, you can turn the E-Front Curtain Shutter option off, and see if that helps. For a very detailed explanation of this issue by a Sony expert, check out the video at https://youtu.be/xhFhTDnIvO0. This menu option cannot be used if Silent Shooting is turned on.

Release without Lens

This menu option lets you enable the camera to release its shutter when no lens is attached. This feature is needed, for example, if you are shooting images or video with the camera attached to a telescope or other device other than a lens. A standard lens has metal contacts through which it communicates with the camera. If you are using a device that does not have those contacts, the camera will not sense that any lens is attached, and ordinarily will not allow the shutter to be operated. In that case, set this option to On, so the shutter will operate even without a standard lens attached.

Release without Card

This option can be set to either Enable or Disable. If it is set to Enable, you can operate the camera's shutter release button even if there is no memory card inserted in the camera. In that case, the camera will display a NO CARD warning message, but it will let you operate the shutter and an image will be saved temporarily. This setting is useful if the camera is on display in a retail store, so customers can operate the controls and see how a saved image would look, without having to have an expensive memory card left in the camera. As I noted in Chapter 1, there is no easy way to save an image taken when this setting is active, although in an emergency you may be able to send the image through the HDMI port to a video capture device.

If you select Disable for this item, the NO CARD warning is still displayed. In addition, if you try to press the shutter button, the camera will display a warning message advising that the shutter cannot be operated with no memory card inserted, as shown in Figure 5-6. This setting is the safest one to use, because it protects you against operating the camera when there is no card inserted to save images or videos.

Figure 5-6. Warning Message for Shooting with No Memory Card

Note, though, that if you have the camera connected to a computer using the PC Remote feature with Sony's Imaging Edge software, you can capture images with the camera through the software controls, even if there is no card in the camera and Release without Card is set to Disable. In that situation, you have to go to the PC Remote Settings option on screen 5 of the Setup menu and set the Still Image Save Destination to PC Only. If that option is set to PC + Camera, you cannot capture images using Sony's Imaging Edge software with no memory card installed in the camera. The PC Remote feature is discussed in Chapter 8, in connection with the USB Connection item on the Setup menu.

SteadyShot

SteadyShot is Sony's optical image stabilization system, which compensates for small movements of the camera to avoid motion blur, especially during exposures of longer than about 1/30 second. It is important to note that SteadyShot is not incorporated into the a6400 camera's body; instead, it is included as a feature in many of Sony's lenses. If it is included for a given lens, the lens will have the designation OSS, for optical steadyshot, included in its name. This menu option allows you to control whether SteadyShot is activated within the attached lens or not.

This setting is turned on by default, and I recommend leaving it on at all times, except when the camera is on a tripod. In that case, SteadyShot is not needed, and there is some chance it can "fool" the camera and cause it to try to correct for motion that does not exist, resulting in image blur.

The items on screen 5 of the Camera Settings2 menu are shown in Figure 5-7.

Figure 5-7. Screen 5 of Camera Settings2 Menu

Zoom

The Zoom menu option is provided to give you a way to zoom the lens beyond the normal optical focal length range, when the lens attached to the camera is not a PZ (power zoom) lens. For example, if you have a prime (non-zoom) lens attached, such as a Sony DT 50mm f/1.8 SAM A-mount lens (attached using the Mount Adaptor LA-EA4), there is no way to zoom the lens itself. However, the camera has the ability to zoom the lens electronically to focal lengths beyond the normal focal length of the lens, using the Smart Zoom, Clear Image Zoom, and Digital Zoom features.

So, if you are using a lens of that sort, you can use the Zoom menu option to "zoom" the lens electronically, but only if one or more of those three non-optical zoom settings is enabled. (The three non-optical zoom types are discussed below, in connection with the Zoom Setting menu option.) The Zoom menu option also can be used when you are using a zoom lens that is not a PZ lens, such as the Sony E 18-135mm OSS kit lens. That lens can be zoomed manually using its zoom ring, but the zoom ring will not zoom it beyond its optical zoom limit of 135mm.

If you are using a PZ lens, you can use the zoom lever on the lens to zoom the lens beyond the optical zoom range. With that sort of lens, the Zoom menu option is dimmed and unavailable for selection.

Assuming one or more of the non-optical zoom settings is active and you are using a prime lens or a non-PZ zoom lens, you can use the Zoom menu option to carry out the actual zooming of the lens beyond the optical zoom range. There are several ways to do this. First, you can highlight this menu option and select it by pressing the Center button. You will then see the screen shown in Figure 5-8, with a zoom scale in the lower right corner.

Figure 5-8. Zoom Scale for Zoom Menu Option

The initial view will show a magnifying glass icon at the left and a zoom factor of 1.0 at the right. To enlarge the view through the lens, press the Right button or turn the control wheel or control dial to the right. To reduce the zoom factor, use the Left button or turn the wheel or dial to the left.

As soon as you start to zoom the lens, the icon at the left of the scale will change. If you are using Smart Zoom (based on the Image Size setting), the letter S will appear. If you are using Clear Image Zoom, a C will appear. If you are using Digital Zoom, a D will appear. In addition, the zoom factor will change at the right of the scale as the zoom level increases or decreases. If you are using S for Image Size and have Digital Zoom turned on, the maximum zoom level available is 8.0 times normal.

An easier way to use the Zoom option is to assign it to a control button. As discussed later in this chapter, using the Custom Key (Still Images) option on screen 8 of the Camera Settings2 menu, you can assign this option any one of several buttons. If you do that, then, when you press the assigned button, the zoom screen appears and you can proceed to zoom the lens using the Right and Left buttons or the control wheel or control dial. (The Left or Right button will still change the zoom factor of the lens, even if it has been assigned to activate the Zoom function.)

Another way to use the Zoom option is to attach a

wired remote control to the Multi port on the left side of the camera. If you do that, and the remote has a zoom control, such as the Sony RM-VPR1, just press that control to zoom the lens, assuming the non-optical zoom function is currently available because of the Zoom Setting option or the Image Size setting. You then do not have to use any controls on the camera, such as the Left and Right buttons or the control wheel or dial; just use the zoom control on the remote. You also can use the Sony RMT-P1BT, a Bluetooth remote, or the RMT-DSLR2, an infrared remote, both of which have zoom buttons among their controls. All of the remotes mentioned here are discussed in Appendix C.

It's important to remember that the Zoom menu option is useful only for zooming the lens in its non-optical zoom range. If you are using a zoom lens, you need to use the lens's normal zooming control to zoom it within its optical zoom range.

Zoom Setting

The next option on screen 5 of the Camera Settings2 menu, Zoom Setting, provides two ways to give the a6400 extra zoom range, using features called Clear Image Zoom and Digital Zoom. To explain these features in context, I will discuss all three zoom methods the camera can use, depending on the lens that is attached—optical zoom, Clear Image Zoom, and Digital Zoom. (I will also discuss a fourth feature related to these, called Smart Zoom.)

Optical zoom is the camera's "natural" zoom capability—moving the lens elements so they magnify the image, just as binoculars do. You can call optical zoom a "real" zoom because it increases the amount of information that the lens gathers. The optical zoom of the a6400 depends on what lens is attached. If a prime lens, with only a single focal length such as 50mm, is attached, then the lens has no optical zoom ability. If a zoom lens is attached, the optical zoom capability is stated in the model designation of the lens. For example, my camera came with a kit lens, the Sony 18-135mm zoom lens; it has an optical zoom capability of 135mm.

You should note that the optical zoom range of a lens is always stated in terms of "35mm-equivalent." That is, the stated range gives the focal lengths of the lens if it were attached to a camera that uses 35mm film, which is an industry standard for reporting the focal lengths of lenses. Because the a6400 camera uses an APS-C sensor, whose image size is smaller than the image made on 35mm film, you need to multiply the focal length(s) of the lens by a factor of 1.5 to determine the effective focal length(s) of the lens. So, the 18-135mm kit lens has an effective optical zoom range of 27-202.5mm. Similarly, the Sony FE 100-400mm f/4.5-5.6 GM OSS lens, which can zoom optically up to 400mm when used with a full-frame camera like the Sony a7 III, has an optical zoom range of 150mm to 600mm with the a6400.

The Digital Zoom feature on the a6400 magnifies the image electronically without any special processing to improve the quality. This type of zoom does not really increase the information gathered by the lens; rather, it just increases the apparent size of the image by enlarging the pixels within the area captured by the lens.

The other option on the a6400, Clear Image Zoom, is a special type of digital zoom developed by Sony. With this feature, the a6400 does not just magnify the area of the image; rather, the camera uses an algorithm based on analysis of the image to add pixels through interpolation, so the pixels are not just multiplied. The enlargement is performed in a way that produces a smoother, more realistic enlargement than the Digital Zoom feature. Therefore, with Clear Image Zoom, the camera achieves greater quality than with Digital Zoom, though not as much as with the "pure" optical zoom.

Finally, there is another way the a6400 can have a zoom range greater than the normal range of an attached zoom lens, with no reduction in image quality. The standard optical zoom range is available when Image Size is set to Large. However, if Image Size is set to Medium or Small, the camera needs only a portion of the pixels on the image sensor to create the image at the reduced size. It can use the "extra" pixels to enlarge the view of the scene. This process, which Sony calls Smart Zoom, is similar to what you can do using editing software such as Photoshop. If the final image does not need to be at the Large size, you can crop out some pixels from the center (or other area) of the image and enlarge them, thereby retaining the same final image size with a magnified view of the scene.

So, with Smart Zoom, if you set Image Size to M or S, the camera can zoom to a greater range than with Image Size set to L and still retain the full quality of the optical zoom. You will, of course, end up with lower-resolution images, but that may not be a problem if you are going to post them on a website or share them via e-mail.

In short, optical zoom provides the best quality for magnifying the scene; Clear Image Zoom gives excellent quality; and Digital Zoom produces magnification accompanied by deterioration of the image. Smart Zoom lets you get greater zoom range with no image deterioration, but at the expense of resolution.

Here is how to use these settings. I will assume for now that you are leaving Image Size set to L, because that is the best setting for excellent results in printing and editing your images. I also will assume that you are using a lens with some optical zoom capability.

As I discussed in connection with the Zoom menu option, above, the a6400 uses the non-optical zoom range of a lens differently for different types of lenses. With a PZ (power zoom) lens, you can press the zoom lever on the lens to get access to all parts of the zoom range, both optical and non-optical. With any other type of lens, you have to use the Zoom menu option or a compatible remote control device to get access to the non-optical areas of zoom.

Figure 5-9. Zoom Setting Menu Options Screen

When you select the Zoom Setting menu option and press the Center button, the camera displays the screen shown in Figure 5-9, giving you the choice of Optical Zoom Only; On: Clear Image Zoom; or On: Digital Zoom. If you turn on Digital Zoom, Clear Image Zoom will automatically be activated also. Optical Zoom is always available, no matter what settings are used, if you are using a lens that has an optical zoom range.

If you turn on only Clear Image Zoom, you will have greater zoom range than normal, as discussed above, with minimal quality loss. If you also turn on Digital Zoom, you will get even greater zoom range, but quality will suffer as the lens is zoomed past the Clear

Image Zoom range. When these various settings are in effect, you will see different indications on the camera's display, though the types of indications you see will vary according to the type of lens you are using.

Figure 5-10. Optical Zoom Only, with Power Zoom Lens

Figure 5-11. Zoom Scale with Clear Image Zoom in Use, with Power Zoom Lens

In Figure 5-10, for which I used the 16-50mm kit lens with power zoom, Image Size is set to L with Clear Image Zoom and Digital Zoom turned off. The zoom indicator at the top of the screen goes only as far as 50mm, the limit of the optical zoom range.

In Figure 5-11, Clear Image Zoom is turned on, using the same lens with power zoom. The lens can be zoomed up to two times the normal range, as seen in this example. There is a small vertical line in the center of the zoom scale marking the point where the zoom changes from optical-only to expanded (either Clear Image Zoom or Digital Zoom, depending on the settings). The magnifying glass icon with the "C" beneath the scale means Clear Image Zoom is turned on. Also, once the lens zooms past the optical zoom range, the sound of the zoom mechanism stops, so you can tell by listening when the camera has entered the range of Clear Image Zoom and Digital Zoom, when using a lens with power zoom.

Figure 5-12. Zoom Scale with Digital Zoom in Use, with Non-Power Zoom Lens

In Figure 5-12, both Clear Image Zoom and Digital Zoom are turned on. For this image, though, I was using the 18-135mm kit lens, which does not have power zoom. In this situation, the camera places a zoom scale in the bottom right corner of the display, showing the degree of non-optical zoom in use. The magnifying glass icon beneath the scale has a "D" beside it, indicating that Digital Zoom is now in effect. Lenses without power zoom do not display any zoom scale for optical zoom; they display a scale only for non-optical zoom that is activated through the Zoom menu option.

With an Image Size setting smaller than Large, the camera will display an S to show that it is using Smart Zoom, as the zoom range extends beyond the standard optical zoom range (if you are using a lens that has an optical zoom capability).

Figure 5-13. Display When Smart Zoom is in Use, with Non-Power Zoom Lens

For example, in Figure 5-13, using the 18-135mm kit lens (with no power zoom) with Image Size set to Small, the lens is zoomed in to 1.7 times the optical range, and the zoom indicator displays an S to indicate that Smart Zoom is in effect. With smaller image sizes, the ranges of Clear Image Zoom and Digital Zoom also are expanded.

My preference is to limit the camera to optical zoom (when using a zoom lens) and thereby avoid any deterioration. However, many photographers have found that Clear Image Zoom yields good results, and it is worth using when you cannot get close to your subject. I do not like to use Digital Zoom to take a picture. However, it can be useful to zoom in to meter a specific area of a distant subject, or to check the composition of your shot before zooming back out and taking the shot using Clear Image Zoom or optical zoom.

Clear Image Zoom and Digital Zoom are not available in connection with some other settings, including Raw images, Sweep Panorama mode, Face/Eye AF settings, the AEL Hold and AEL Toggle functions, and Scene Recognition in the Auto modes. Smart Zoom is not available for recording movies.

When the lens is zoomed in to the range of Clear Image Zoom or Digital Zoom and autofocus is in use, the Focus Area menu option is disabled and the camera uses a broad focus frame, which is represented by a dotted area like that seen in Figure 5-14.

Figure 5-14. Dotted Focus Area Frame when Non-optical Zoom in Use

Zoom Ring Rotate

This menu option is available for use only when the attached lens has power zoom capability and supports this function. If it is available, it lets you reverse the direction of rotation for zooming in and out. Sony lenses with power zoom capability have PZ in their model names, such as the E PZ 18-105mm f/4 G OSS. However, not all PZ lenses are compatible with this menu option. For example, it is not possible to use the Zoom Ring Rotate feature with the E PZ 16-50mm f/3.5-5.6 OSS lens, which is a standard kit lens for the a6400.

The items on screen 6 of the Camera Settings2 menu are shown in Figure 5-15.

Figure 5-15. Screen 6 of Camera Settings2 Menu

Display Button

This option lets you choose what screens appear in shooting mode as you press the Display button. There are sub-options for the monitor (LCD) and viewfinder, as seen in Figure 5-16.

Figure 5-16. Display Button Menu Options Screen

You can make different choices for the LCD screen and viewfinder, so pressing the Display button when you are using the monitor may bring up different screens than when you are using the viewfinder. After you decide to choose screens for the monitor or the viewfinder, you will see a screen like that shown in Figure 5-17.

This screen shows the six display screens you can select for the monitor, as well as a seventh choice, Monitor Off. The selection screen for the viewfinder is similar to this one, except that the sixth and seventh choices, For Viewfinder and Monitor Off, are not available. The For Viewfinder screen is designed to appear on the monitor to provide shooting information when you are viewing the live view through the viewfinder, and it would not be useful when you are using the viewfinder. The Monitor Off setting also is intended for use when

you are using the viewfinder and don't need to see additional shooting information on the monitor.

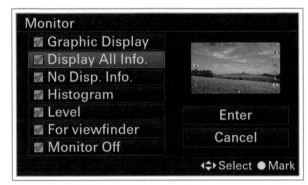

Figure 5-17. Display Screens Available for LCD Monitor

Five of the six display screens available for the monitor are shown in Figure 5-18 through Figure 5-22. The screen displaying just the image with no information is not shown here, nor is the screen with the monitor turned off.

Figure 5-18 shows the version of the screen with the Graphic Display in the lower right corner; that display is supposed to illustrate the use of faster shutter speeds to stop action and the use of wider apertures to blur backgrounds. I find it distracting and not especially helpful, but if it is useful to you, by all means select it. This display screen does not appear when the camera is set to Sweep Panorama mode.

Figure 5-18. Graphic Display Screen

I find the Display All Information screen, shown in Figure 5-19, to be cluttered, but it has useful information. You can always move away from this screen by pressing the Display button (if there is at least one other display screen available), and I like to have it available for times when I need to see what settings are in effect.

The third option, displaying only the image, is not shown here. That display is useful for focusing and composing your shots. I always include it in the cycle of screens.

Figure 5-19. **Display All Information Screen**

The fourth screen, shown in Figure 5-20, displays the histogram. This shooting-mode histogram, unlike the one displayed in playback mode, shows only basic exposure information with no color data. However, it gives you an idea of whether your image will be well exposed, letting you adjust exposure compensation and other settings as appropriate while watching the live histogram on the screen. If you can make the histogram display look like a triangular mountain centered in the box, you are likely to have a good result.

Figure 5-20. **Histogram Screen**

You should try to keep the body of the histogram away from the right and left edges of the graph, in most cases. If the histogram runs into the left edge, that means shadow areas are clipping and details in those areas are being lost. If it hits the right edge, you are losing details in highlights. If you have to choose, it is best to keep the graph away from the right edge because it is harder to recover details from clipped highlights than from clipped shadows. The histogram screen does not appear when the camera is in Sweep Panorama mode.

The fifth available display screen, shown in Figure 5-21, includes the a6400's level, which is a useful tool for leveling the camera both side-to-side and front-to-back.

Watch the small orange lines on the screen; when the

outer two ones have turned green, the camera is level side-to-side; when the inner two lines are green, the camera is level front-to-back.

Figure 5-21. **Level Screen**

The sixth choice, shown in Figure 5-22, which is available only for the monitor, is called For Viewfinder. This option does not include the live view in shooting mode. Instead, it displays a black screen with detailed information about the camera's settings, so you can check your settings after (or before) you look at the live view in the viewfinder.

In addition, as I will discuss in Chapter 6, this screen includes the Quick Navi system. When you press the Function button, the settings on the screen become active. You can navigate through the settings using the direction buttons and adjust them using the control wheel and the control dial.

The For Viewfinder screen does not display when the camera is set to Movie mode or S & Q Motion mode.

Figure 5-22. **For Viewfinder Screen**

The seventh choice, Monitor Off, is available only for the monitor. It produces a completely blank screen.

Once you select the Display Button option and choose whether to select screens for the monitor or viewfinder, you can scroll through the seven (monitor) or five (viewfinder) choices using the control wheel, control dial, or direction buttons. When a screen you want to have displayed is highlighted, press the Center button to put an orange check mark in the box to the left of the screen's label, as seen earlier in Figure 5-17.

You can also press that button to unmark a box. The camera will let you uncheck all seven of the items (or all five for the viewfinder), but if you do that, you will see an error message as you try to exit the menu screen. You have to check at least one box so that some screen will display when the camera is in shooting mode. (Though you can select only the Monitor Off option, and the camera will not display any error message.)

After you select from one to seven screens for the monitor and from one to five for the viewfinder, highlight the Enter block and press the Center button. Then, whenever the camera is in shooting mode, the selected screens will be displayed; you cycle through them by pressing the Display button (Up button). If you have selected only one screen, pressing the Display button will have no effect in shooting mode when the live view is displayed.

If you select only the one screen that includes the live view but no shooting information, the camera will still always display the shutter speed, aperture, exposure compensation, and ISO; all of those values are displayed on a line at the bottom of the screen. In Movie mode and S & Q Motion mode, the camera will also display the counter or other video tracking indicator, as well as the REC/STBY indicator.

Finder/Monitor

This next option, shown in Figure 5-23, lets you choose whether to view shooting, menu, and playback displays on the a6400's LCD screen or in the viewfinder.

Figure 5-23. Finder/Monitor Menu Options Screen

The viewfinder provides the same information as the LCD screen, but its display is viewed inside an eye-level window that is shaded from daylight, giving you a clear view of the shooting, playback, and menu screens.

By default, this menu option is set to Auto, which means the camera switches to the viewfinder automatically when you move your head near the eye sensor to the right of the viewfinder. The camera turns on the viewfinder display and blacks out the LCD.

If you prefer to use either the viewfinder or the LCD screen at all times, set this menu option to Viewfinder (Manual) or Monitor (Manual), according to your preference. With either of those settings, the camera will not switch to the other method of viewing unless you go back to this menu option and change the setting.

For me, the Auto option works well, and I rarely change that setting. But if you will be using the LCD while working with your head (or another object) very close to the camera's viewfinder, you might want to use the Monitor (Manual) option so the screen does not blank out unexpectedly.

Finder Frame Rate

This option lets you set the rate at which the electronic viewfinder's screen refreshes when you are shooting still images. If you set this option to High, the motion of subjects in the viewfinder may appear smoother, but the resolution (number of megapixels in the display) is lowered to compensate for the increased frequency of the refreshing. The Standard setting is the normal choice, and it provides sufficient speed for most purposes. The value is fixed at Standard during playback, when an HDMI cable is connected to the camera, and when the camera's temperature has risen to a certain point.

Zebra Setting

This next Camera Settings2 menu option gives you a tool for measuring the exposure level of an image or video when you are composing your shots. This menu item has two sub-options, Zebra Display and Zebra Level, as shown in Figure 5-24.

Figure 5-24. Zebra Setting Menu Options Screen

Zebra Display can be turned either on or off, to determine whether the Zebra stripes are displayed on the shooting screen. The Zebra Level option can be set to a value from 70 to 100 IRE in five-unit increments, or 100+ for values greater than 100. The IRE units are a measure of relative brightness or exposure, with 0 representing black and 100 representing white.

You also can save and later use two custom values, C1 and C2, as discussed below. Figure 5-25 shows the screen for selecting values up to 90.

When you turn Zebra Display on at any level, you very likely will see, in some parts of the display, the black-and-white "zebra" stripes that give this feature its name.

Zebra stripes originally were created as a feature for professional video cameras, so the videographer could see whether the scene would be properly exposed. This tool often is used in the context of recording an interview, when proper exposure of a human face is the main concern.

Figure 5-25. Zebra Level Adjustment Screen

There are various approaches to using these stripes. Some videographers like to set the zebra function to 90 IRE and adjust the exposure so the stripes barely appear in the brightest parts of the image. Another

recommendation is to set the option to 75 IRE for a scene with Caucasian skin, and expose so that the stripes barely appear in the area of the skin.

Figure 5-26. Zebra Level Set to 75 IRE

In Figure 5-26, I set IRE to 75 and exposed to have the stripes appear clearly on the mannequin's face and neck.

As the brightness of the lighting increases for a subject, there may be no stripes at first, then they will gradually appear until they cover the subject, then they will seem to disappear, because the exposure is so bright that the subject is surrounded by an outline of "marching ants" rather than having stripes in its interior.

If you want to save customized values for Zebra, you can save settings to the C1 and C2 slots. A standard way to use these two values is to set C1 to a value for exposure confirmation and C2 to a value for flare confirmation.

To set C1 for exposure confirmation, select Zebra Level, scroll down to the C1 block and press the Right button. You will see a screen like that in Figure 5-27, with the Std+Range block highlighted in orange. (Press the Up or Down button or turn the control wheel or control dial if necessary to bring that label into the block.)

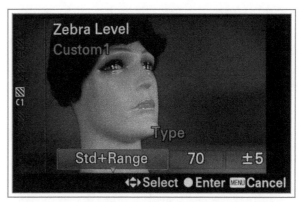

Figure 5-27. Screen to Set C1 Value for Zebra

With the Std+Range block highlighted, press the Right button to move to the next block, and use the Up and Down buttons or the control wheel or dial to set a value, which can be from zero to 109, in one-unit increments. Then press the Right button to move to the next block and select a range, which can be from ±1 to ±10.

For example, you might set the first block to 77 and the second block to ±5, so the Zebra pattern would appear when the brightness of the scene was within five units of 77, plus or minus. You could then set Zebra to C1 to confirm that the scene's exposure is within that range.

To set the C2 value for flare confirmation, scroll down to that block and press the Right button. Make sure the highlighted block contains the Lower Limit label, as shown in Figure 5-28.

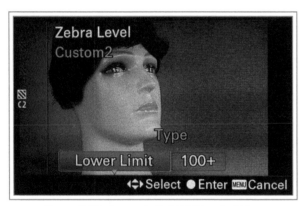

Figure 5-28. **Screen to Set C2 Value for Zebra**

Then press the Right button to move to the second block and select a setting from 50+ to 109+ in one-unit increments. That value represents the brightness level that you don't want to exceed. You can then set Zebra to the C2 block and check the scene to make sure the lighting stays within that limit, to avoid flare. The Zebra pattern will appear if that limit is exceeded.

Zebra is a feature to consider, especially for video recording, but the a6400 has an excellent metering system, including both live and playback histograms, so you can manage without this option if you don't want to deal with its learning curve.

Grid Line

With this option, you can select one of four settings for a grid to be superimposed on the shooting screen. By default, there is no grid. If you choose one of the grid options, the lines will appear in your chosen configuration whenever the camera is showing the live view in shooting mode, whether the detailed display screen is selected or not. Of course, the grid does not appear when the For Viewfinder display, with its black screen full of shooting information, is displayed. The four options are seen in Figure 5-29.

Figure 5-29. **Grid Line Menu Options Screen**

Here are descriptions of these choices, other than Off, which leaves the screen with no grid.

RULE OF THIRDS GRID

This arrangement has two vertical lines and two horizontal lines, dividing the screen into nine blocks, as shown in Figure 5-30.

Figure 5-30. **Rule of Thirds Grid in Use**

This grid follows a rule of composition that calls for locating an important subject at an intersection of these lines, which will place the subject one-third of the way from the edge of the image. This arrangement can add interest and asymmetry to an image.

SQUARE GRID

With this setting, the grid has five vertical lines and three horizontal lines, dividing the display into 24 blocks. In this way, you can still use the Rule of Thirds, but you have additional lines available for lining up items, such as the horizon or the edge of a building, that need to be straight.

DIAGONAL PLUS SQUARE GRID

The last option gives you a square grid of four blocks in each direction and adds two diagonal lines.

The idea is that placing a subject or, more likely, a string of subjects along one of the diagonals can add interest to the image by drawing the viewer's eye into the image along the diagonal line.

Exposure Settings Guide

This option places a display on the screen to simulate one or two sliding bands showing the settings for aperture, shutter speed, or both. The display varies according to the shooting mode.

In Program mode, the bands move to display the current aperture and shutter speed when you activate Program Shift. In Shutter Priority, Aperture Priority, and Manual exposure modes, and in Movie mode or S & Q Motion mode when the exposure mode is set to Shutter Priority, Aperture Priority or Manual Exposure, a single band displays the shutter speed or aperture as you adjust it. In other shooting modes, this menu option has no effect. Figure 5-31 shows the display when shutter speed is being adjusted.

Figure 5-31. Exposure Settings Guide for Shutter Speed

I find this display distracting so I leave it turned off, but it might be useful to see this large display to let you know what value is being set, in some circumstances.

The items on screen 7 of the Camera Settings2 menu are shown in Figure 5-32.

Figure 5-32. Screen 7 of Camera Settings2 Menu

Live View Display

This menu option can be important for getting results that match your expectations. It lets you choose whether or not the camera displays the effects that certain settings will have on your final image, while you are composing the image.

When you select this option, you will see two sub-options on the next screen: Setting Effect On and Setting Effect Off, as shown in Figure 5-33.

If you select Setting Effect On, then, when you are using Program, Aperture Priority, Shutter Priority, or Manual exposure mode, the camera's display in shooting mode will show the effects of exposure compensation, White Balance, Creative Style, and Picture Effect, with some limitations. In addition, it will show the effects of exposure changes in Manual exposure mode and other advanced modes, to some extent.

Figure 5-33. Live View Display Menu Options Screen

In some cases, it may be helpful to see what effect a particular setting will have on the final image, and in other cases that feature might be distracting or might even make it difficult to take the shot.

For example, when you are setting White Balance, it can

be helpful to see how the various options will alter the appearance of your final images. If you have selected Setting Effect On, then, as you scroll through the White Balance menu options, you will instantly see the effect of each setting, such as Daylight, Cloudy, Shade, and Incandescent. That change in the display is not distracting; it is actually very informative.

However, if you are using the Picture Effect option and experimenting with a setting such as Posterization, which drastically alters the appearance of your images, you might find it difficult to compose the image with Setting Effect On selected.

There is one particular use for the Live View Display menu option that I find very useful. On occasion, I use the a6400 to trigger external, non-Sony flash units, with the camera set to Manual exposure mode. For some of these shots, I use settings such as f/16.0, 1/200 second, and ISO 100. This shot will be exposed properly with the flash units I am using, but, with Setting Effect On selected, the camera's screen is quite dark as I compose the shot. That is because the camera's programming does not account for the fact that flash units will be fired.

If I use the Setting Effect Off setting, then the camera displays the scene using the available ambient light, ignoring the exposure settings I have made. In this way, I can see the scene on the camera's display in order to compose the shot properly.

The Setting Effect On option, though, can be useful when using Aperture Priority, Shutter Priority, or Manual exposure mode when you are shooting in unusually dark or bright conditions, because the camera's display screen will change its brightness to alert you that a normal exposure may not be possible with the current settings. (You should see the aperture, shutter speed, M.M., ISO, or exposure compensation value flashing to alert you to this situation, also.)

With the Picture Effect setting, some of the options will not change the appearance of the display, even with Setting Effect On activated. Those options are Soft Focus, HDR Painting, Rich-tone Monochrome, Miniature, Watercolor, and Illustration. (With Rich-tone Monochrome, the live view will be in black and white, but it will not show the full effect of the setting.) You can see the effects of those settings in playback mode, after you have captured an image using one of the settings.

When Setting Effect Off is selected, the camera will display a VIEW icon on the screen, as shown in Figure 5-34, to remind you that the camera's display is not showing the effects of all your settings.

Figure 5-34. VIEW Icon on Display for Setting Effect Off

My recommendation is to leave this option at Setting Effect On unless you are faced with a situation in which it is difficult to compose a shot, either because the display is too dark or light, or because a setting such as Picture Effect interferes with your ability to view the subject clearly.

In the Intelligent Auto, Scene, Sweep Panorama, S & Q Motion, and Movie modes, this option is forced to Setting Effect On and cannot be changed.

Auto Review

The Auto Review option, shown in Figure 5-35, sets the length of time that an image appears on the display screen immediately after you take a still picture.

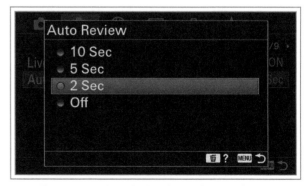

Figure 5-35. Auto Review Menu Options Screen

The default is two seconds, but you can set the time to five or ten seconds, or you can turn the function off. If you turn it off, the camera will return to shooting mode as soon as it has saved a new image to the memory card. When this option is in use, you can always return to the live view by pressing the shutter button halfway. The Auto Review option does not apply to movies; the camera does not display the beginning frame of a movie that was just recorded until you press the Playback button.

While the new image is being displayed, you can use the various functions of playback mode, such as enlarging the image, bringing up index screens, moving to other images, or pressing the Delete button to delete the image. If you start one of these actions before the camera has reverted to shooting mode, the camera will stay in playback mode.

The items on screen 8 of the Camera Settings2 menu are shown in Figure 5-36.

Figure 5-36. Screen 8 of Camera Settings2 Menu

Custom Key (Still Images)

As I will discuss in Chapter 6, several of the camera's control buttons and dials can have their functions changed through menu options. In particular, nine buttons can each be assigned to carry out one operation when the button is pressed in shooting mode. The Custom Key (Still Images) menu option is the mechanism for assigning these operations to buttons for shooting still images; there are other options for movies and playback, discussed later in this chapter.

Figure 5-37. Custom Key (Still Images) Main Options Screen

When you select this option, you will see the screen shown in Figure 5-37, which shows the first three buttons that can be assigned; the other controls are listed on later screens of this menu option. One of the buttons, the Focus Hold button, is located on a lens, not on the camera, so it may or not be available, depending on what lens you have attached to the camera.

Move through the four screens of this menu item using the control dial or the Right and Left buttons. When you have reached the screen that shows the button you want to assign to a function, use the Up and Down buttons or the control wheel to navigate to the line for that button. For example, Figure 5-37 shows the first screen, with the line for the AF/MF button highlighted. (Note that the AF/MF button is physically the same as the AEL button; you switch between those two controls using the AF/MF/AEL switch lever, which surrounds the button.) The current assignment for the highlighted control, in this case, AF/MF Control Hold, is listed on that line.

With the line for the AF/MF button highlighted, press the Center Button. You will see one of several screens (for this button, 25 screens) that list all the options that can be assigned to that button. You can scroll quickly from screen to screen using the Left and Right buttons or the control dial; once you have located the screen with the feature you want to assign, you can scroll within that screen using the Up and Down buttons or the control wheel. Scroll to the feature you want to assign to the selected button and press the Center button. An orange dot will appear to the left of the assignment and the button will now control that operation in shooting mode when the camera is set to a mode for shooting still images..

In most cases, the available assignments are self-explanatory. When you assign an option, such as ISO, to a button, pressing the button calls up the menu screen for ISO, which lets you set the ISO just as if you had selected ISO (under ISO Setting) on the Camera Settings1 menu. However, there are differences for some options, and there are some items that can be assigned through this menu option that are not available for selection on any other menu. I will discuss these details below, as I provide information about each of the items for this menu option.

AF/MF BUTTON

If you select AF/MF Button from the Custom Key (Still Images) menu screen, the camera will display a screen like that shown in Figure 5-38, one of 25 screens of options that can be assigned to this button.

Figure 5-38. One of 25 Screens of Options for AF/MF Button

The complete list includes the following choices:

- File Format
- JPEG Quality
- JPEG Image Size
- Aspect Ratio
- Drive Mode
- Self-timer During Bracket
- Interval Shooting
- Memory
- Recall Custom Hold 1
- Recall Custom Hold 2
- Recall Custom Hold 3
- Focus Mode
- AF/MF Control Hold
- AF/MF Control Toggle
- Focus Standard
- Focus Area
- Switch Focus Area
- Register AF Area Hold

- Register AF Area Toggle
- Register AF Area + AF On
- Tracking On
- Face/Eye Priority in AF
- Eye AF
- Subject Detection
- Switch Right/Left Eye
- AF On
- Focus Hold
- Exposure Compensation
- ISO
- ISO Auto Minimum Shutter Speed
- Metering Mode
- Face Priority in Multi Metering
- AEL Hold
- AEL Toggle
- Spot AEL Hold
- Spot AEL Toggle
- Flash Mode
- Flash Compensation
- Wireless Flash
- FEL Lock Hold
- FEL Lock Toggle
- FEL Lock/AEL Hold
- FEL Lock/AEL Toggle
- White Balance
- Priority Set in Auto White Balance
- AWB Lock Hold
- AWB Lock Toggle
- DRO/Auto HDR

- Creative Style
- Picture Effect
- Picture Profile
- Soft Skin Effect
- Focus Magnifier
- Peaking Display Select
- Peaking Level
- Peaking Color
- Smile Shutter
- Auto Object Framing
- In-Camera Guide
- Movie [acts as Movie button to start or stop recording]
- Frame Rate (S & Q Motion)
- Audio Recording Level
- Audio Level Display
- Marker Display Select
- Silent Shooting
- SteadyShot
- Zoom
- Aperture Preview
- Shot Result Preview
- Finder/Monitor Select
- Finder Frame Rate
- Zebra Display Select
- Zebra Level
- Grid Line
- Live View Display Select
- Bright Monitoring
- My Dial 1 During Hold

- My Dial 2 During Hold
- My Dial 3 During Hold
- My Dial 1—2—3
- Toggle My Dial 1
- Toggle My Dial 2
- Toggle My Dial 3
- Audio Signals
- Send to Smartphone
- Playback
- Monitor Brightness
- Gamma Display Assist
- Touch Operation Select
- TC/UB Display Switch
- Not Set

Scroll through this list and press the Center button to make your selection. The dot next to the chosen option will turn orange to mark the choice.

Many of these options are self-explanatory because, when the button has the option assigned, pressing the button simply calls up the menu screen for that option, if the option is available in the current shooting mode. For example, if the Custom 1 button is assigned to Drive Mode, then, when you press the button, the camera displays the Drive Mode menu, just as if you had used the Menu button to get access to that option. I will not discuss those options here; see Chapter 4 for discussion of the Camera Settings1 menu, Chapter 5 for discussion of the Camera Settings2 menu, Chapter 8 for discussion of the Setup menu, and Chapter 10 for discussion of the Network menu.

In a few cases, the assigned button switches between menu options without first calling up a menu screen. For example, this is the case with the Switch Focus Area, Marker Display Select, Finder/Monitor Select, and TC/UB Display Switch options. (I will discuss Switch Right/Left Eye separately below, because it is somewhat more involved than the other options listed here.)

There are some other selections for the AF/MF button (and the other buttons) that do not call up a menu screen or switch between menu items. Instead, they perform a function that does not come from any menu option. I will discuss those selections below.

Recall Custom Hold 1, 2, and 3

These options work together with the Register Custom Shooting Settings option on screen 4 of the Camera Settings1 menu, which I discussed in Chapter 4. In order to use that option, you first select a set of shooting settings, including items such as shooting mode, shutter speed, Drive Mode, exposure compensation, ISO, and others. You then store them to slots called Custom Hold 1, 2, and 3. When you assign the Recall Custom Hold 1, 2, or 3 option to a control button, that button will call up that complete set of shooting settings instantly when it is pressed in shooting mode. You have to hold down the button while you are using those settings. When you release the button, the camera reverts to the settings that were in effect before you pressed the button.

AF/MF Control Hold

If you select AF/MF Control Hold for the assigned button's function, pressing the button switches the camera between autofocus and manual focus, but only while you hold down the button. If the camera is set to any autofocus mode, pressing and holding the button will switch the camera into manual focus mode. Releasing it will switch to the autofocus mode that was originally set.

If the camera is set to manual focus mode, pressing and holding the button will switch to single-shot AF mode. However, if you are using a lens with an AF/MF switch, that switch must remain in the AF position for this option to work. If the physical switch on the lens is in the MF position, the AF/MF Control Hold option will not override the MF setting. This option will override the camera's Focus Mode setting to MF, but not the physical setting of the switch on the lens to MF.

In this situation, with the camera set to MF through the menu system, when you press the assigned button, the camera will also evaluate the focus and lock focus, if possible. With this option, the assigned button can be used for "back button focus," letting you focus the camera without having to half-press the shutter button. Releasing the button will switch back to manual focus

mode. If the camera is set to DMF mode, the button will toggle between DMF and manual focus.

This function is useful in situations when it is difficult to use autofocus, such as dark areas, extreme close-ups, or areas where you have to shoot through obstructions such as glass or wire cages. You can switch very quickly into manual focus mode and back again, as conditions warrant.

Also, this capability is helpful if you want to set "zone" focusing, so you can shoot quickly without having to wait for the autofocus mechanism to operate. For example, if you are doing street photography, you can set the camera to single-shot autofocus mode and focus on a subject at about the distance you expect to be shooting from—say, 25 feet (7.6 meters). Then, once focus is locked on that subject, press and hold the button to switch the camera to manual focus mode, and the focus will be locked at that distance in manual focus mode. You can then take shots of subjects at that distance without having to refocus. If you need to set another focus distance, just release the button to go back to autofocus mode and repeat the process.

Finally, it is convenient to be able to quickly get the camera to use autofocus when it is set to manual focus mode. With this function, as noted above, when you press and release the button, the camera will quickly focus using autofocus, and then go back to manual focus mode for any further adjustments you want to make.

AF/MF Control Toggle

If you select AF/MF Control Toggle for the setting of the assigned button's function, pressing the button switches the camera between autofocus and manual focus. This option works the same as AF/MF Control Hold, except that you do not hold down the control button; you just press it and release it. The switched focus mode then stays in effect until you press the button again. However, when the camera is set to manual focus mode, pressing the assigned button does not cause the camera to evaluate focus. To get that capability, you have to use AF/MF Control Hold, discussed above.

Focus Standard

The Focus Standard option can be assigned to any one of several buttons. That button can then be used to perform focus-related functions in two situations when autofocus is in use. First, when Focus Area is set to

Zone, Flexible Spot, Expand Flexible Spot, or Tracking AF with either of the Flexible Spot options, pressing the button assigned to Focus Standard instantly makes the focus area active, ready to be moved by pressing the direction buttons.

Second, when autofocus is in effect and Focus Area is set to Wide or Center, or to the Wide or Center option for Tracking, pressing the button assigned to Focus Standard causes the camera to focus in the center of the screen.

Registered AF Area Hold/Registered AF Area Toggle/Registered AF Area + AF On

These three options work in conjunction with the AF Area Registration option on screen 6 of the Camera Settings1 menu, which I discussed in Chapter 4. With that option, you can register a particular point on the camera's display as the point where you want the camera to use its autofocus. Once that area is registered, you can assign the Register AF Area Hold option to a control button. When you press that button in shooting mode, the camera will place the autofocus frame at the registered area on the display. Then, while you hold down the assigned button, you can cause the camera to focus at that area.

If you assign the button to the Registered AF Area Toggle option, you don't have to hold down the assigned button; just press it and release it, and the autofocus area will be placed at the registered point. You then have to press the assigned button again to remove the autofocus area frame from the display.

If you assign the button to the Registered AF Area + AF On option, when you press the button, the camera places the autofocus frame at the registered location and immediately focuses at that position also, so you don't have to use the shutter button (or some other button assigned to AF-On) to cause the camera to autofocus.

It's useful to remember that the registered AF Area will be flashing on the screen in shooting mode, to remind you of its location, so you can compose the shot with that frame at the proper position.

This function works only in the Program, Aperture Priority, Shutter Priority, and Manual shooting modes.

Tracking On

This option lets you turn on the Tracking setting for Focus Area temporarily by pressing the assigned button. When you press the button assigned to Tracking On, Focus Area switches from the current setting to the corresponding Tracking setting. For example, if Focus Area is set to Center, pressing the assigned button will temporarily switch the setting to Tracking (Center). You have to hold down the button to keep tracking turned on. It is probably best to assign Tracking On to a button on the back of the camera so you can press it with your thumb and use your index finger to press the shutter button halfway down to lock tracking on your subject.

If you press the shutter button halfway before pressing the Tracking On button, the tracking will lock on to the currently focused subject as soon as the assigned button is pressed.

This feature works only in continuous autofocus mode, because that is the only mode in which tracking focus works.

Eye AF

If you assign Eye AF to a control button, then, if the camera is set to an autofocus mode, when you press this button the camera will look for human eyes and focus on them if possible. If the camera detects an eye, it will display a small green frame to show that it has focused on the eye, as shown in Figure 5-39.

Figure 5-39. Eye AF in Use

Continue to hold down the assigned button to lock focus on the eye while you press the shutter button to take the picture. The camera does not have to have Face/Eye Priority in AF turned on for this option to work, and it functions with all focus modes (S, A, C, and DMF) other than manual focus, and with all settings for Focus Area. However, Subject Detection, an option under Face/Eye AF Settings, should be set to Human rather than

Animal. If there are multiple faces in the scene, move the focus frame (if any) over the face you want to focus on before pressing the button assigned to Eye AF; the camera will then use that face for the Eye AF focus.

Eye AF can be especially useful when depth of field is shallow, such as when the lens is zoomed in to a long focal length or you are shooting a closeup, to make sure the focus is sharpest on the subject's eyes rather than on the nose or some other feature. A portrait generally looks best when the eyes are in sharp focus.

This option also is useful to give you an instant way to focus on a face when you were not expecting to take a portrait and do not have the camera set up for face and eye detection. You can just press and hold the assigned button to focus on the nearest eye, which should result in a well-focused portrait. Eye AF is not available when recording movies.

Subject Detection

This item actually does duplicate a menu option, but I will list it here because it might not be obvious what it involves. This option lets you choose between humans and pets for purposes of face and eye detection. The camera cannot recognize both types of eyes and faces, so you must tell it which kind to look for. This capability was added through a firmware update (to version 2.00) in June 2019, so it is possible your camera does not have this option in its list of choices for assignment to a button. The Subject Detection menu option is found under Face/Eye AF Settings on screen 6 of the Camera Settings1 menu.

Switch Right/Left Eye

This option works in conjunction with the Right/Left Eye Select option, which is found under the Face/Eye AF Settings option on screen 6 of the Camera Settings1 menu. That option, which can be set to Auto, Right, or Left, determines how the camera chooses a human eye to focus on. (That option is not available if Subject Detection is set to Animal.) If that option is set to Right or Left, pressing a button assigned to the Switch Right/Left Eye option changes to the opposite eye, left or right. If that option is set to Auto, pressing the assigned button temporarily switches to the eye other than the one the camera has chosen to focus on. If you press the button again, the camera will switch back to the other eye.

AF On

If you assign the AF On option to a control button, when you press the button in shooting mode the camera will use its autofocus immediately, without your having to press the shutter button halfway. The camera will use the current focus settings, including the settings for Focus Mode and Focus Area. However, if manual focus is in effect, pressing the assigned button will have no effect.

You can use this button assignment to set up the camera for "back button focus." To do that, assign a button to AF On, and then go to screen 6 of the Camera Settings1 menu and set AF w/Shutter to Off, so the camera will not focus when you press the shutter button halfway down. In addition, you may want to turn off the Pre-AF option on that same menu screen, so the camera does not use its autofocus automatically, before you press the button to cause it to autofocus.

Focus Hold

Some lenses have one or more Focus Hold buttons, and the diagram within the a6400's menu system shows a Focus Hold button on the fourth page of diagrams of button locations. But you can assign the Focus Hold feature to any one of several buttons, regardless of whether the lens you are using has a Focus Hold button.

Once you have used the camera's autofocus system to achieve sharp focus, press the button assigned to Focus Hold and hold the button down. As long as the button is held down, the camera will not adjust focus again. So, if you need to adjust the angle of your shot or re-frame the composition, you can then press the shutter button while holding down the assigned button, to take the picture without disturbing the original focus setting.

This is not a function you may need often, but it can be useful if you have focused the camera on a particular subject and are waiting for that subject to appear in the frame again. If you hold the focus with the assigned button, that subject will be in focus when it appears again. If you didn't hold focus, the camera might refocus on some other subject when you pressed the shutter button to take the picture. In addition, you can use this feature for a pull-focus effect when recording movies, by holding the focus on a subject in the distance, for example, with the button assigned to Focus Hold, and then releasing the button so the camera will change its focus to a closer subject.

AEL Hold

If you set a control button (presumably the AEL button in this case) to the AEL (autoexposure lock) Hold option, then, when the camera is in shooting mode, pressing the button will lock exposure at the current setting as metered by the camera, as long as you hold down the button.

If the camera is set to Manual exposure mode with ISO set to ISO Auto, pressing the button to activate AEL Hold will lock the ISO setting. If you press the button in Manual exposure mode with ISO set to a specific value, you can use the Manual Shift feature by adjusting the aperture to a different value; the camera will then select a new shutter speed to match the new aperture value.

When exposure is locked in this way, a large asterisk will appear in the lower right corner of the display and remain there until the assigned button is released.

For example, you might want to use AEL Hold to make sure your exposure is calibrated for an object that is part of a larger scene, such as a dark painting on a light wall. You could lock exposure while holding the camera close to the painting, then move back to take a picture of the wall with the locked exposure ensuring the painting will be properly exposed.

To do this, assuming the camera is in Program mode, hold the camera close to the painting until the metered aperture and shutter speed appear on the screen. Press and hold the AEL button and an asterisk (*) will appear on the screen, as shown in Figure 5-40, indicating that exposure lock is in effect.

Figure 5-40. Asterisk Indicating AEL in Use

Now you can move back (or anywhere else) and take your photograph using the exposure setting that you locked in. Once you have finished using the locked exposure setting, release the AEL button to make the

asterisk disappear. The camera is now ready to measure a new exposure reading.

AEL Toggle

If you set a control button to the AEL Toggle option, then, in shooting mode, pressing the button will lock exposure just as with AEL Hold. The difference with this setting is that you just press and release the AEL button; the exposure will remain locked until you press the button again to cancel the exposure lock.

Spot AEL Hold

The next option for assignment to a control button is listed on the menu as AEL Hold with a spot icon before the name. The icon means that, with this setting, when you press the button and hold it, the camera will lock exposure as metered by the spot-metering area in the center of the display, no matter what metering method is currently in effect. It will use whichever size for the metering spot was last set with the metering mode menu option, either Standard or Large.

This option can be useful if you think you will want to switch to spot metering just for one or two shots. You can press the assigned button to make sure the center of the display covers the area that you want to use for evaluating the exposure, and take the shot with the exposure adjusted for that spot.

Spot AEL Toggle

The Spot AEL Toggle option is similar to the AEL Toggle option, except that the camera meters in the spot area in the very center of the display. As with the previous option, the camera uses the size of the spot as it was last set through the metering mode menu option.

FEL Lock Hold/FEL Lock Toggle/FEL Lock/AEL Hold/FEL Lock/AEL Toggle

These next four possible button assignments can be discussed together. They all involve FEL Lock, or flash exposure lock. FEL functions in a way similar to AEL, or autoexposure lock, discussed earlier, except that it locks the output of the flash, rather than the exposure settings. To use it, assign it to a button, pop up the flash (or attach a compatible flash) and take a picture with the main subject filling the frame as much as possible, so the camera will evaluate the light for that subject. Then press the assigned button, and the camera will fire a pre-flash from the flash unit, and record the amount of light that was needed for the exposure. Then, while still holding down the assigned button, recompose the shot with the subject off to the side, or however you need it, and shoot using the locked flash exposure.

As with AEL Lock, there are multiple versions of this setting. If you choose the Hold option, you have to hold the assigned button down to keep the flash value locked; with Toggle, you just press and release the button, and the value will stay locked until the picture is taken. If you choose FEL Lock/AEL Hold or FEL Lock/ AEL Toggle, the camera will evaluate the light whether or not the flash fires. So, if, for example, you turn off the flash for some shots, the camera will still measure the exposure and lock it for you.

It appears that the FEL Lock feature works best when the camera's ISO is set to a specific value rather than to Auto ISO.

AWB Lock Hold/AWB Lock Toggle

These two related functions are similar in function to the Shutter AWB Lock option on screen 12 of the Camera Settings1 menu, discussed in Chapter 4. If you assign AWB Lock Hold to a control button while Auto White Balance or Underwater Auto White Balance is selected, the camera will stop adjusting White Balance while the button is held down. With the Toggle option, the adjustments will stop until the button is pressed a second time. As with the menu option, you can use this feature to ensure that the Auto White Balance setting will not change during continuous shooting or during any series of shots for which you want the color balance of the shots to remain consistent.

In-Camera Guide

If you assign In-Camera Guide to a control button, the camera provides a convenient help system for explaining menu options. Once this assignment is made, whenever the camera is displaying a menu screen, including a Function menu or Quick Navi screen, you can press the assigned button to bring up a brief message with guidance or tips about the use of the option that is currently highlighted. For example, if you go to screen 7 of the Camera Settings2 menu and highlight the Live View Display item, then press the button assigned to In-Camera Guide, the camera displays the message shown in Figure 5-41.

Figure 5-41. In-Camera Guide Text for Live View Display

If you select a sub-option for a menu item and then press the In-Camera Guide button, the camera will display a different message providing details about that sub-option. For example, Figure 5-42 shows the screen that was displayed when I pressed the assigned button after highlighting the Toy Camera-Magenta option for the Picture Effect item.

Figure 5-42. In-Camera Guide Text for Toy Camera - Magenta

This help system is quite detailed; for example, it has guidance for different ISO settings such as ISO 100, 160, and 6400, with tips about what shooting conditions might call for a given setting. The system operates with all of the menu systems, including Camera Settings 2, Playback, Setup, and the others, not just the Camera Settings1 menu.

Movie

The Movie setting does not call up a menu option. Instead, when you assign a button to this setting, the button takes on the same role as the camera's red Movie button. This option gives you another way to start and stop the recording of a video. If you set the Movie Button option on screen 9 of the Camera Settings2 menu to Movie Mode Only, this button will start recording a video only if the mode dial is set to Movie mode or S & Q Motion mode. However, the Custom Key (Still Images) button assignment works only when the mode dial is set for a still-shooting mode. Therefore, an assignment to the Movie option for Custom Key (Still Images) works only if the Movie Button menu option is set to Always.

Aperture Preview

When using an A-mount lens with a Sony Mount Adaptor, the a6400 does not stop down its aperture to the value that has been set until the image is captured. However, if you assign a button to the Aperture Preview option, you can press and hold the assigned button to see a preview of how the current aperture setting will affect the final image, before the image is captured. In this way, you can judge the depth of field, which is likely to be affected by the aperture setting when the set aperture is a narrow one, such as f/16 or higher. (This function is not needed if you are using an E-mount lens, because that type of lens provides a view of the scene with the aperture stopped down at all times.)

Shot Result Preview

This next option is similar to the Aperture Preview option, discussed above, but this one is supposed to let you preview the DRO setting, shutter speed, and ISO setting, as well as the aperture setting, to see how the final shot will look with all of those settings applied. I tried it with various combinations of settings, with both an A-mount and an E-mount lens, and found that it did not give a reliable view of the final shot.

Some photographers have found this function to be useful when using a Sony flash in the camera's flash shoe, because the Setting Effect On option for Live View Display does not show the view under the ambient light conditions. They use Shot Result Preview instead in that situation. Overall, I have not found a use for this option.

Bright Monitoring

This option is intended for a specific situation: when you are shooting in one of the PASM shooting modes, using manual focus in dark conditions that make it difficult to evaluate the focus on the LCD screen or in the viewfinder. In that situation, when you press the button assigned to the Bright Monitoring option, the camera changes the display to increase its brightness and sets the Live View Display option to Setting Effect Off, if it was not already set that way. With Setting Effect Off, the display does not darken or brighten to show the effects of exposure settings; instead, it maintains a normal brightness if possible.

If you have Focus Mode set to any option other than manual focus, this key assignment will have no effect. It works only with manual focus, and it does not work if either MF Assist or Focus Magnifier is turned on and in use. When you have finished using this feature, press the assigned button again to turn it off.

This setting is designed for use when you can't see well enough to compose your shot on the LCD screen or in the viewfinder, such as when you are trying to make a long exposure outdoors at night or you need to take a portrait in very dim light.

My Dial 1/2/3 During Hold

These three settings are used in conjunction with the My Dial Settings option on screen 8 of the Camera Settings2 menu, discussed later in this chapter. With that menu option, you can assign any one of several settings, such as aperture, shutter speed, exposure compensation, ISO, White Balance, moving the autofocus point, and others, to the control wheel and the control dial, to be used temporarily when you activate them with the assigned control button.

You can store three different combinations of settings in slots labeled My Dial 1, My Dial 2, and My Dial 3. So, for example, you might use the My Dial Settings menu option to set up the My Dial 1 slot with exposure compensation adjusted by the control wheel and ISO adjusted by the control dial. Next, you can assign My Dial 1 During Hold to the C1 button. Then, when shooting images, if you press and hold down the C1 button, you can adjust exposure compensation and ISO using the wheel and the dial.

Figure 5-43. Icons on Display for My Dial Settings

The shooting screen's icons will change to show the current assignments of the wheel and dial, as shown in Figure 5-43. You can store different sets of settings to the My Dial 2 and My Dial 3 slots, and assign each of those to a different control button if you want. Or, you can use the My Dial 1—2—3 option, discussed immediately below.

Because the My Dial assignments are only temporary, the control wheel and control dial will still retain their default assignments of adjusting shutter speed and aperture in Aperture Priority, Shutter Priority, and Manual exposure modes.

My Dial 1—2—3

This next option is similar to the My Dial 1/2/3 During Hold options, discussed above, but it permits you to assign all three of the My Dial slots of settings to a single control button. So, for example, if you have assigned three sets of options for the control wheel and control dial to the My Dial 1, My Dial 2, and My Dial 3 slots using the My Dial Settings menu option, instead of assigning each of those sets to a different control button, you can assign the My Dial 1—2—3 option to, say, the C1 button.

Then, when you press that button in shooting mode, the wheel and dial assignments for My Dial 1 are called up. Press the button a second time to call up the My Dial 2 assignments, a third time for the My Dial 3 assignments, and a fourth time to return to the default assignments. With this option, you do not need to hold down the control button; the My Dial settings remain active until you press the assigned button again.

Toggle My Dial 1/2/3

With these next three options, you can assign Toggle My Dial 1, 2, or 3 to a control button. This option is similar to the My Dial 1/2/3 During Hold options, except that you do not have to hold down the assigned button for the My Dial assignments to stay active. Just press and release the assigned button, and the My Dial settings will remain in effect until you press the assigned button again.

Playback

With this option, you can assign a control button to act like the Playback button, which places the camera into playback mode. I'm not sure why you would want to use a control button for this purpose, since the camera has a dedicated Playback button that cannot be reassigned to any other purpose. But this possibility exists, and you can do this if you want.

Not Set

The last option that can be assigned to a control button is called Not Set. If you choose this option, the button will not be assigned any special function. I cannot think of any reason to use this option, unless you will be using a limited number of settings and don't want to risk activating a different setting by pressing the button accidentally.

AEL Button

The next button that appears on the first page of control assignments is the AEL button, which, as noted earlier, is physically the same as the AF/MF button. You switch the button's functions between those two options using the AF/MF/AEL switch lever. This button can be assigned to any of the same options as the AF/MF button.

Custom Button 2

This button can be assigned to any of the same functions as the AF/MF and AEL buttons.

Center Button

You can assign the Center button to any of the same options as for the AF/MF and AEL buttons, except for In-Camera Guide.

Left Button

For the Left button, the choices of assignment are the same as for the AF/MF and AEL buttons, except that several of the choices are not available: Recall Custom Hold 1, 2, and 3; AF/MF Control Hold; Focus Standard; Switch Focus Area; Register AF Area Hold; Register AF Area + AF On; Tracking On; Eye AF; AF On; Focus Hold; AEL Hold, Spot AEL Hold; FEL Lock Hold; FEL Lock/ AEL Hold; In-Camera Guide; Aperture Preview; Shot Result Preview; and My Dial 1/2/3 During Hold.

So, if you want to set the Left button to lock exposure or to switch between autofocus and manual focus, the button will act only as a toggle, not as one that you have to hold down. Presumably, Sony made this choice because it would be awkward to hold down the Left button while pressing the shutter button. (Eye AF also requires that you hold down the button while pressing the shutter button.)

RIGHT BUTTON

The choices of assignment for the Right button are the same as those for the Left button.

DOWN BUTTON

The assignment choices for the Down button are the same as those for the Left and Right buttons.

CUSTOM BUTTON 1

The C1 button can have any function assigned to it from the complete list available for the AF/MF, AEL, and C2 buttons.

FOCUS HOLD BUTTON

Finally, the Focus Hold button is assigned by default to the Focus Hold option, but you can assign it to any of the functions listed above for the other buttons. Of course, this button is located on a lens and not on the camera, so you will not have this button available if you are using a lens that does not have it. Some lenses have multiple Focus Hold buttons. In that case, any assignment for the Focus Hold button will be active with all of those buttons.

Custom Key (Movies)

This next option on screen 8 of the Camera Settings2 menu lets you assign a function to any of the same control buttons as for the Custom Key (Still Images) option, discussed above. The choices are similar to those for that menu option, but there are some differences. First, the assignment will take effect only if the mode dial is set to the Movie mode or the S & Q Motion mode position. So, if you shoot a movie in a still-shooting mode, pressing a control button may call up an assignment to that button made with the Custom Key (Still Images) option, but it will not call up an assignment made with the Custom Key (Movies) option.

Next, for each of the buttons, the last option in the list of choices for assignment to the control is called Follow Custom (Still Images). If you assign that option to a control, the control will have the same function as was assigned to that control using the Custom Key (Still Images) menu option.

That assignment will be in place even if it cannot take effect. For example, if the Left button is assigned to the JPEG Image Size option with the Custom Key (Still Images) option, and you then choose Follow Custom (Still Images) for the assignment of the Left Button with the Custom Key (Movies) option, that assignment will be in place, even though the JPEG Image Size option is not compatible with movie recording.

The other difference from the Custom Key (Still Images) option is that the lists of possible assignments for the various controls are in most cases shorter for the Custom Key (Movies) option. The lists are as follows:

AF/MF, AEL, CUSTOM 1 AND 2, AND FOCUS HOLD BUTTON:

The list of possible assignments for these buttons for Movie mode are as follows:

- Memory
- Focus Mode
- AF/MF Control Hold
- AF/MF Control Toggle
- Focus Standard
- Focus Area
- Switch Focus Area
- Face/Eye Priority in AF
- AF On
- Focus Hold
- Exposure Compensation
- ISO
- Metering Mode
- Face Priority in Multi Metering
- AEL Hold
- AEL Toggle
- Spot AEL Hold
- Spot AEL Toggle
- White Balance
- Priority Set in Auto White Balance

- AWB Lock Hold

- AWB Lock Toggle

- DRO/Auto HDR

- Creative Style

- Picture Effect

- Picture Profile

- Focus Magnifier

- Peaking Display Select

- Peaking Level

- Peaking Color

- In-Camera Guide

- MOVIE

- Frame Rate (S & Q)

- Audio Recording Level

- Audio Level Display

- Marker Display Select

- SteadyShot

- Zoom

- Finder/Monitor Select

- Zebra Display Select

- Zebra Level

- Grid Line

- My Dial 1/2/3 During Hold

- My Dial 1—2—3

- Toggle My Dial 1/2/3

- Audio Signals

- Send to Smartphone

- Playback

- Monitor Brightness

- Gamma Display Assist

- Touch Operation Select

- TC/UB Display Switch

- Not Set

- Follow Custom (Still Images)

CENTER BUTTON

The Center button can be assigned any of the same options as the other buttons, except for In-Camera Guide.

LEFT, RIGHT, AND DOWN BUTTONS

The Left, Right, and Down buttons can be assigned any of the same options as the other buttons, except for AF/MF Control Hold, Focus Standard, Switch Focus Area, AF On, Focus Hold, AEL Hold, Spot AEL Hold, AWB Lock Hold, In-Camera Guide, and My Dial 1/2/3 During Hold.

Custom Key (Playback)

This next menu option lets you assign two of the camera's control buttons to each handle a single function when the camera is in playback mode. The main screen for this option is shown in Figure 5-44.

Figure 5-44. Custom Key (Playback) Main Options Screen

As shown on the two screens of this menu option, the buttons that can be assigned a function for playback mode are the Function (Fn) button and the Custom 1 button (C1).

The options that can be assigned to the Function button are the following:

- Finder/Monitor Select

- Send to Smartphone

- Protect

- Rotate

- Delete

- Rating

- Photo Capture

- Enlarge Image

- Image Index

- Touch Operation Select

- TC/UB Display Switch

- Not Set

The C1 button can be assigned to any option from the same list, and, in addition, it can be assigned to Follow Custom (Still Images or Movie). With that last setting, the C1 button will switch into shooting mode and carry out either the assignment for Still Images or Movie, depending on the current position of the mode dial.

For example, suppose you have assigned the C1 button as follows, using the Custom Key options: Picture Effect for Still images, Audio Signals for Movies, and Follow Custom (Still Images or Movie) for Playback. Then, with the mode dial at P for Program mode and the camera in playback mode, when you press the C1 button, the Picture Effect menu will appear. If you then turn the mode dial to the Movie position and put the camera into playback mode, when you press the C1 button the Audio Signals menu will appear.

Function Menu Settings

As I will discuss in Chapter 6, when you press the Function button in shooting mode, the camera displays up to 12 options in blocks at the bottom of the display.

Move through those options with the direction buttons. Adjust the main settings with the control wheel and secondary settings with the control dial. Use the Function Menu Settings menu item to assign options to the 12 blocks of the Function menu. When you select this menu option, the camera displays the screen shown in Figure 5-45, showing the assignments for all 12 blocks of the Function menu.

Figure 5-45. Function Menu Settings Options Screen

When you press the Center button on any one of those blocks, you will see a screen like that in Figure 5-46, listing the options that can be assigned to that block.

Figure 5-46. Function Menu Settings - List of Options for Each Block

For each block, the options that can be assigned are:

- File Format

- JPEG Quality

- JPEG Image Size

- Aspect Ratio

- Shooting Mode

- Drive Mode

- Self-timer During Bracket

- Interval Shooting

- Focus Mode

- Focus Area

- Face/Eye Priority in AF

- Subject Detection

- Right/Left Eye Select

- Exposure compensation
- ISO
- ISO Auto Minimum Shutter Speed
- Metering Mode
- Face Priority in Multi Metering
- Flash Mode
- Flash Compensation
- Wireless Flash
- White Balance
- Priority Set in Auto White Balance
- DRO/Auto HDR
- Creative Style
- Picture Effect
- Picture Profile
- Soft Skin Effect
- Peaking Display
- Peaking Level
- Peaking Color
- Smile Shutter
- Auto Object Framing
- Frame Rate (S & Q Motion)
- Audio Recording Level
- Audio Level Display
- Marker Display
- Silent Shooting
- SteadyShot
- Finder Frame Rate
- Zebra Display
- Zebra Level
- Grid Line

- Live View Display
- Audio Signals
- Gamma Display Assist
- Touch Operation
- Not Set

Press the Center button when the option you want to assign to a given block is highlighted, and the camera will place an orange dot on that line to indicate that that feature is assigned to that block.

I recommend you assign a function to each of the 12 blocks and experiment to find the best setup. Remember that you can use the control buttons for your most important settings, such as, perhaps, ISO, exposure compensation, and White Balance, so you can reserve these 12 blocks for other options.

My Dial Settings

As I discussed earlier in connection with the Custom Key (Still Images) menu option, there are various My Dial settings that can be assigned to control buttons, including My Dial 1/2/3 Hold and several others. With each of those options, the assigned button calls up one of three possible slots that are available for storing settings for the control wheel and control dial. The My Dial Settings menu option is the mechanism you use for storing wheel and dial settings to those three slots.

Figure 5-47. My Dial Settings Menu Options Screen

When you highlight this option and press the Center button, the camera displays the screen shown in Figure 5-47, which has two lines—one for the control wheel and one for the control dial, with the settings for the slots numbered 1, 2, and 3 in three columns at the right side of the display. Use the control wheel or the Up and

Down buttons to move between the two lines, and use the control dial or the Left and Right buttons to move among the three columns.

Figure 5-48. One of Five Screens of Options for My Dial Control

When the highlight is on the slot you want to change for the wheel or dial, press the Center button and the camera will display a screen like that shown in Figure 5-48, which is one of five screens of options for that slot. Scroll through that list and select the option you want to assign to that slot. Once all of the slots are assigned as you want (with Not Set selected for any that you don't want to assign), move the highlight down to the OK block at the bottom of the initial options screen and select it, to lock in your choices. Then you can use the various My Dial options under the Custom Key menu items, as discussed earlier.

Dial/Wheel Setup

This menu item lets you change the assignments of the control wheel and control dial for adjusting aperture and shutter speed in Manual exposure mode, and in the Movie and S & Q Motion modes when the Exposure Mode setting is Manual Exposure.

By default, the control wheel adjusts shutter speed and the control dial adjusts aperture, as indicated on the top line of the choices for this option. If you choose the second option, the roles are reversed, so the control wheel adjusts aperture and the control dial adjusts shutter speed. This is strictly a matter of personal preference. Note that this option has no effect on the controls for the Aperture Priority and Shutter Priority modes. In those modes, either the control wheel or the control dial can be used to adjust the one value that can be adjusted in that mode—either aperture or shutter speed.

The options on screen 9 of the Camera Settings2 menu

are shown in Figure 5-49.

Figure 5-49. Screen 9 of Camera Settings2 Menu

Av/Tv Rotate

This menu item lets you change the direction of rotation when you use the control wheel or control wheel to adjust aperture or shutter speed in Aperture Priority, Shutter Priority, or Manual exposure mode, or in Movie mode or S & Q Motion mode with Exposure Mode set to A, S, or M. The choices are normal or reverse. This is strictly a matter of personal preference, which I have never found a need to use.

Dial/Wheel EV Compensation

This menu item gives you the option of setting either the control dial or the control wheel to adjust exposure compensation, when the camera is set to a mode in which exposure compensation can be adjusted, except for Manual exposure mode. This feature, in effect, adds one more control to those that can be assigned an option for shooting mode.

If you use this option in Aperture Priority Mode or Shutter Priority mode, in which either the control dial or the control wheel adjusts aperture or shutter speed, using one of those dials to adjust exposure compensation will not be a problem, because there will still be one dial left to adjust aperture or shutter speed. In Manual exposure mode, where you need both the control wheel and control dial to adjust aperture and shutter speed, the Dial/Wheel EV Compensation option does not operate, although it will still be accessible and can be set through the menu system.

Function of Touch Operation

This menu option has three sub-options—Touch Shutter, Touch Focus, and Touch Tracking—which control how the camera uses the touch screen for focusing and for capturing still images. For all three of these features, Touch Operation must be turned on through screen 3 of the Setup menu. You can select only one of the three options, because only one of them can be in effect at any given time.

TOUCH SHUTTER

This first sub-option lets you turn on the Touch Shutter function, which is available for capturing images in still image shooting modes. When Touch Shutter is turned on, you will see a special icon with a finger in the upper right corner of the monitor, as shown in Figure 5-50.

When you touch that icon with your finger, the camera will add a small orange bar at the icon's left side, indicating that the Touch Shutter option is active. Then, the next time you touch the screen, the camera will focus on the spot you touched and take a picture at the same time. You can then keep touching the screen to take more pictures. To cancel the Touch Shutter function, touch the Touch Shutter icon again. If burst shooting or bracketing is turned on, you can press the icon to activate those operations. For burst shooting or continuous bracketing, keep your finger pressed on the icon for as long as you want the burst to continue, or as long as the bracketing requires.

Figure 5-50. Touch Shutter Icon on Shooting Screen

The Touch Shutter option is not available when using the viewfinder or in the Movie, S & Q Motion, or Panorama modes. It also is not available when Smile Shutter is turned on, with manual focus, Digital Zoom, Clear Image Zoom, or when Focus Area is set to Flexible Spot or Expand Flexible Spot.

TOUCH FOCUS

This option is similar to the previous one, except that it sets the camera only to focus at the spot where you touch the monitor, not to take a picture also. For still images, touch the subject on the monitor where you want the camera to focus. The camera will place a focus frame there. When you press the shutter button halfway down, the camera will focus on the subject within that frame. If you are using the viewfinder, you can move the focus area around by dragging your finger on the monitor.

In its user guide, Sony says you need to select a setting other than Flexible Spot or Expand Flexible Spot for Focus Area. However, if you have Focus Area set to one of those options, you can still focus by touching the monitor where you want the camera to focus. In that case, though, Sony does not consider this action to amount to Touch Focus; instead, it amounts to moving the existing focus frame. So, in effect, if Touch Focus is turned on, you can touch the screen to focus where you want, regardless of the Focus Area setting.

If you are recording a movie, touch the monitor where you want focus to be directed. The camera will focus at the spot you touched and will activate manual focus temporarily to let you make a further adjustment using the focusing ring on the lens. (Sony calls this function "spot focus.") You can cancel the spot focus operation by pressing the hand icon with an X, or by pressing the Center button. (If Focus Area is set to Flexible Spot or Expand Flexible Spot, spot focus does not work; instead, the camera lets you move the focus frame.)

Touch Focus is not available in Sweep Panorama mode or when actually using Clear Image Zoom or Digital Zoom. It also is not available if you are using an A-mount lens with the Sony LA-EA2 or LA-EA4 Mount Adaptor.

TOUCH TRACKING

The third and final setting for the Function of Touch Operation option sets the camera up to track a subject when you touch the image of that subject on the monitor, for still images or movies. When you touch the screen, the camera places a tracking frame on the subject, and will attempt to keep that subject in focus while the subject or camera moves. The camera displays a message advising you to press the Center button to cancel tracking.

Touch Tracking is not available in the same situations as Touch Focus, and also when Scene mode is set to Hand-held Twilight or Anti Motion Blur, or when the Record Setting option on screen 1 of the Camera Settings2 menu is set to any of the 120p settings (100p for cameras using the PAL video system).

Note that Touch Tracking is available for recording movies, even though tracking AF is not available as a selection for Focus Area for recording movies. So, if you want to track a moving subject when recording a movie, you can use the Touch Tracking feature to do so.

Movie Button

This option, shown in Figure 5-51, lets you lock out the operation of the Movie button to avoid accidentally starting a video recording. The two choices are Always and Movie Mode Only. If you want to be able to start recording a video at any time without delay, you should leave the Movie Button option set to Always. With that setting, you can start recording a movie by pressing this button, no matter what shooting mode is set on the mode dial. This is a convenient setting, because you can start shooting a video at a moment's notice without having to turn the mode dial to the Movie or S & Q Motion position.

If you choose Movie Mode Only, pressing the Movie button starts recording a movie only when the mode dial is set to the Movie or S & Q Motion position. (A movie recorded in S & Q Motion mode is not a normal-speed movie, but it is a movie, and can be recorded by pressing the Movie button.)

The main reason to choose the Movie Mode Only option is if you are afraid you may press the Movie button by mistake.

Figure 5-51. **Movie Button Menu Options Screen**

With the a6400, I have never pressed the Movie button by mistake, because the button does not come within range of my thumb unless I intend to press it. So, with this camera I leave this option set to Always, to avoid missing video opportunities. But you should consider whether you want to use this option to protect against unwanted footage. Of course, if you have no interest in video recording, you can set this option to Movie Mode Only to avoid unwanted uses of the button.

As discussed earlier, if you assign a control button to have the Movie function, which gives that button the same function as the red Movie button, this menu option affects the operation of that button also. If you turn on the Movie w/Shutter option on screen 3 of the Camera Settings2 menu, which lets you start a movie recording in Movie mode with the shutter button, you can still use the Movie button for that purpose.

Dial/Wheel Lock

This next option on screen 9 of the Camera Settings2 menu has two possible settings, Lock and Unlock. If you select Lock, you can lock the functioning of the control wheel and control dial. To engage the actual lock, after this menu item is set to Lock, press and hold the Function button for several seconds when the shooting screen is displayed, until a Locked message appears on the screen.

After that, you will see an icon in the lower right corner of the display indicating that the lock is in effect, as shown in Figure 5-52. Once the lock is in effect, turning the control wheel or control dial will not have any effect on the camera's settings.

Figure 5-52. **Lock Icon on Screen for Dial/Wheel Lock**

For example, if the control wheel has been set to adjust exposure compensation using the Dial/Wheel EV Compensation menu option, turning the dial will not adjust exposure compensation while the lock is in effect. Similarly, when the camera is in Shutter Priority or Manual exposure mode, turning the control dial will not change the shutter speed, as it normally would. However, the dial and wheel will still carry out their functions of navigating through menu screens, even with the lock in effect.

This option can prevent these dials from accidentally changing your settings. If you make an important adjustment to your settings, you can lock the dials so the settings will stay in place. If you need to change settings, press and hold the Function button again to remove the lock.

I have not had occasion to use this feature myself, but I can see its value for situations in which you need to keep a setting locked in and want to guard against accidental slipping of the wheel or dial.

Even when the Lock option is turned on, the Function button can be used to call up the Function menu. A quick press of the button will call up that menu, and a longer press-and-hold will lock or unlock the wheel and dial.

Audio Signals

This last option on the Camera Settings2 menu lets you choose whether to activate the sounds the a6400 makes when operations take place, such as pressing the shutter button halfway down to focus, pressing the Movie button to start a recording, or using the self-timer. By default, these sounds are turned on, but it can be helpful to silence them in a quiet area, during a religious ceremony, or when you want to avoid alerting your subjects that a camera is being used.

To silence the shutter operation sound for shooting still images, use the Silent Shooting option on screen 4 of the Camera Settings2 menu.

CHAPTER 6: PHYSICAL CONTROLS

The Sony a6400, like other compact cameras, does not have as many physical controls as an advanced DSLR camera. But the a6400 has more controls than most compact cameras, and the ones it has provide many options for customizing. You can assign the most-used functions to buttons and dials.

In this chapter, I'll discuss each of the camera's physical controls and how they can be used to best advantage, starting with the controls on the top of the camera, shown in Figure 6-1.

Figure 6-1. Controls on Top of Camera

Shutter Button

The shutter button is the single most important control on the camera. When you press it halfway, the camera evaluates exposure and focus (unless you're using manual exposure or manual focus or have disabled either of those functions, as discussed below). Once you are satisfied with the settings, press the button all the way to take the picture. When the camera is set for continuous shooting, you hold this button down while the camera fires repeatedly. You also can press this button halfway to exit from playback mode, menu screens, and help screens to get the camera set to take its next picture. You can half-press this button to wake the camera up after it has powered down because of the Power Save Start Time option on the Setup menu.

You can disable the use of the shutter button to cause the camera to use autofocus by turning off the AF w/ Shutter option on screen 6 of the Camera Settings1 menu. You can disable the use of this button to evaluate exposure by turning off the AEL w/Shutter option on screen 9 of that menu.

When the mode dial is set to Movie mode or S & Q Motion mode, the behavior of this button depends on the setting of the Movie w/Shutter option on screen 3 of the Camera Settings2 menu. If that option is turned off, pressing the shutter button in either of those modes has no effect. If the Movie w/Shutter option is turned on, pressing the shutter button in Movie mode or S & Q Motion mode will start or stop the recording of a movie.

On/Off Switch

This switch surrounding the shutter button is used to turn the camera on and off.

Mode Dial

The mode dial, at the right side of the camera's top, has just one function—to set the shooting mode for capturing still images or videos. I discussed those modes in Chapter 3. To take a quick still picture, turn this dial to the green AUTO label and fire away. To take a quick video sequence, turn the dial to that position and then press the red Movie button, at the extreme right edge of the camera's back. You can record a normal-speed movie with the mode dial set to any position except S & Q, which is used for slow-motion or speeded-up movies. There is a Movie mode on this dial, marked by a movie film icon, but you do not have to select that icon to record movies.

Note, though, that screen 9 of the Camera Settings2 menu has an option called Movie Button that can lock out the use of the Movie button unless the camera is set to Movie mode or S & Q Motion mode. If the mode dial is set to Auto, Program, or any setting other than Movie or S & Q Motion mode, the Movie button will not work if that menu option is set to Movie Mode Only.

If the mode dial is set to Movie mode or S & Q Motion mode, the camera cannot take still images. In those modes, you can only record videos.

Control Dial

The control dial is the unmarked black dial directly to the right of the mode dial. One important function of this dial is to adjust the camera's aperture or shutter speed in the shooting modes in which those values can be adjusted. The dial also can be set to control other settings through certain menu options, such as Dial/ Wheel EV Compensation and the various My Dial settings, discussed in Chapter 5.

This dial also is used for selecting sub-options in some cases. For example, when you choose Picture Effect from the shooting menu or the Function menu, some settings, such as Toy Camera, have sub-settings that can be selected by turning the control dial. In Program mode, turning the dial activates Program Shift, which causes the camera to pick a new pair of shutter speed and aperture settings to match the current exposure. In Sweep Panorama mode, turning this dial changes the panorama direction. In Scene mode, turning the dial changes the scene setting, such as Portrait, Landscape, and the others.

Figure 6-2. Icon Showing Control Dial Adjusts Shutter Speed

When the control dial is set to control a particular setting, the camera displays an icon for the dial next to a label or icon for that setting. For example, in Figure 6-2, the display shows that the dial controls shutter speed (indicated by Tv, which stands for time value).

In playback mode, you can turn the control dial to navigate through the images and videos stored on the camera's memory card. Turning the dial will move to

another image at the same enlargement factor when an image has been enlarged using the AEL button, the Enlarge Image menu option, or the touch screen. The dial also will move through movies slowly when paused or rapidly when they are playing.

Custom Button 1

This small button labeled C1, for Custom 1, is a powerful control. Using the Custom Key (Still Images) or Custom Key (Movies) option on screen 8 of the Camera Settings2 menu, you can assign any one of numerous settings to this button, including Drive Mode, Flash Mode, ISO, and many others. I discussed all of the options in Chapter 5, where I discussed the Camera Settings2 menu. Because of the convenient location of this button, in easy range of the index finger of your right hand, it is a good idea to choose an often-used option to be operated by the Custom 1 button.

In addition, Custom Button 1 is one of the two buttons on the camera that also can be assigned a function to be used when the camera is in playback mode using the Custom Key (Playback) menu option. I also discussed that option in Chapter 5.

Multi Interface Shoe

The shoe on top of the a6400 comes with a protective cap; slide that cap out, and the shoe is ready to accept several accessories. The most obvious accessory for this shoe is an external flash. I will discuss some available flash units, as well as a radio flash trigger, in Appendix A, where I discuss accessories.

This shoe has special circuitry built into it so it can accept certain other accessories that are designed to interact with the camera. Sony makes microphones that can work with the shoe, including model ECM-XYST1M and model ECM-W1M. Sony also offers an accessory kit, model XLR-K2M, that lets you use professional-level, balanced microphones with XLR connections. I will discuss those items in Appendix A. Sony undoubtedly will release other accessories that can take advantage of this interface as time goes by.

Sensor Plane Indicator

This small symbol located to the left of the Multi

Interface Shoe shows the position of the digital sensor within the a6400. This indicator is provided in case you need to measure the exact distance from the sensor plane to your subject for macro photography.

Built-in Flash

The camera's built-in flash unit is normally retracted and hidden in the center of the camera's top. The camera cannot use it until you pop it up manually using the flash pop-up button located on the back of the camera, to the left of the Menu button. To put the flash back down, press it gently into the camera until it clicks into place.

The controls on the back of the camera are shown in Figure 6-3.

Figure 6-3. **Controls on Back of Camera**

Viewfinder and Eye Sensor

The viewfinder window lets you view the live scene and shooting information displays in shooting mode, as well as the playback of images and videos in playback mode, the same as on the LCD monitor. You can control what display screens are available in the viewfinder in shooting mode with the Display Button option on screen 6 of the Camera Settings2 menu.

The eye sensor is a small window in the viewfinder eyepiece to the right of the main viewfinder window. When your head approaches this small slot and blocks the light that reaches it, the camera automatically switches from using the LCD screen to using the viewfinder, if a menu option is set for that behavior. To enable this automatic switching, go to screen 6 of the Camera Settings2 menu, select the Finder/Monitor item, and choose Auto. If you don't want the automatic switching, choose Viewfinder (Manual) or Monitor (Manual), to keep either one of those viewing options

as the permanent setting.

The camera comes with a separate eyepiece cup, which you can slide down over the basic viewfinder if you want to have a well-shaded view through the viewfinder. However, the cup may interfere slightly with the operation of the diopter adjustment wheel and with the self-portrait position for the LCD monitor, so you may need to remove it at times.

Diopter Adjustment Wheel

The diopter adjustment wheel is a small, ridged wheel to the right of the viewfinder. You can turn this wheel to adjust the viewfinder according to your vision. If you wear eyeglasses, you may find that you can adjust the setting of the viewfinder so you can see it clearly without your glasses.

Flash Pop-up Button

This button at the center of the camera's back above the LCD screen, marked with a lightning bolt, has one function—to release the flash and let it pop up. The flash on this camera will not operate until you use this button to pop it up. If you think you may have a need for the flash, be sure to press this button to pop it up. On the other hand, if you definitely do not want the flash to fire, such as when you are in a museum or other setting where flash is not permitted, don't press this button, and the flash will not pop up.

Menu Button

The Menu button, to the right of the flash pop-up button, has a straightforward function. Press it to enter the menu system and press it again to exit to the mode the camera was in previously (shooting or playback). The button also cancels out of sub-menus, taking you to the previous menu screen. You can press the Menu button to wake the camera up into the menu system when it has powered down from the Power Save Start Time option. It also is used to confirm some operations, such as the Protect and Delete options on the Playback menu. You can press this button to return an image to normal size when it has been enlarged in playback mode.

AF/MF/AEL Button and AF/MF/AEL Switch Lever

Located to the right of the Menu button is the AF/MF/AEL button, which is surrounded by the AF/MF/AEL switch lever. When that lever is pointed at the AF/MF label, the button is known as the AF/MF button. When the lever is moved downward to point at the AEL label, the button is known as the AEL button.

As discussed in Chapter 5, the AF/MF button and the AEL button are considered to be two separate controls, each of which can be assigned to one of numerous possible functions using the Custom Key (Still Images) or Custom Key (Movies) menu options on screen 8 of the Camera Settings2 menu. It is natural to assign the AF/MF button to one of the AF/MF operations, such as AF/MF Control Hold, but that is not required; you can assign it instead to call up the White Balance menu, the Focus Mode menu, or any one of the many other choices. Similarly, the AEL button can be assigned to control the AEL (autoexposure lock) function, but that assignment is not the only one possible.

This button also has another specific assignment for use with the Wireless Flash setting. When you have the camera set up with a control flash unit and a remote flash unit, you can press the AEL button to fire a test flash that will verify that the flash units are communicating properly with the camera.

When the camera is set to playback mode, the AEL button serves to enlarge a still image that is displayed on the camera's screen, as indicated by the magnifying glass icon with a plus sign next to the button on the camera's back. This function remains assigned to the button for playback mode, even if you change the button's assignment for shooting mode.

Function Button

The button marked Fn, for Function, located to the right of the top of the LCD monitor, has several roles, depending on whether the camera is in shooting mode or playback mode.

FUNCTION MENU

When the camera is set to shooting mode, the Function button gives you quick access to menu options.

When you press the button the camera displays the Function menu, from which you can select a setting for immediate adjustment. Using the Function Menu Settings option on screen 8 of the Camera Settings2 menu (discussed in Chapter 5), you can assign up to 12 functions to this menu, from among 48 possibilities. The items that can be assigned include settings such as ISO, Drive Mode, White Balance, Flash Mode, Focus Area, and Picture Effect. You also can choose Not Set, which leaves a blank slot on the Function menu.

Once you have assigned up to 12 options to this menu, it is ready for action. To use it, press the Function button when the camera is in shooting mode, and a menu will appear along the bottom of the display in two rows with six choices in each, as shown in Figure 6-4.

Figure 6-4. Function Menu on Shooting Screen

Use the direction buttons to move the highlight block at the bottom of the display over the item you want to select. With that setting highlighted, turn the control wheel to cycle through the possible settings. As you do so, a moving line of options will appear near the top of the display, showing the range of settings. When the one you want to select is highlighted, press the Function button to select it and exit back to the shooting screen. If there are sub-settings, use the control dial to scroll through those before exiting the menu.

For example, if you have moved the orange highlight block to the JPEG Quality item, turn the control wheel until the setting you want to make appears, as shown in Figure 6-5, where Fine is selected. Then press the Function button to confirm the setting and exit from the Function menu screen. Or, if you want to make multiple settings from the Function menu options, after changing one setting you can press the Center button to go back to the Function menu and make more settings before you press the Function button to exit to the shooting screen.

Figure 6-5. Fine Selected for JPEG Quality on Function Menu

To take an example with a sub-setting, call up the Function menu and scroll to Focus Area, then use the control wheel to select the Flexible Spot setting. At that point, an additional line of icons will appear below the main options, with choices for the size of the focus frame, as seen in Figure 6-6.

Figure 6-6. Flexible Spot Setting for Focus Area on Function Menu

Use the control dial to scroll through the choices and select small, medium, or large. With your selection highlighted, press the Function button to confirm it and exit to the shooting screen. (Or, press the Center button to make more choices from the Function menu.)

Note that there may be some items at the bottom of the screen whose icons are dimmed because the item is unavailable for selection in the current context. If you move the orange highlight block to one of those items and then try to change the setting, the camera will display an error message.

Also, the selections I discussed above may not be available because they have not been assigned to the Function menu. If that is the case, you can use the Function Menu Settings menu option to assign them if you want to follow the examples.

QUICK NAVI SYSTEM

In shooting mode, the Function button also gives you access to the Quick Navi system for changing settings rapidly. This system is similar to the Function menu system I just discussed, but there are significant differences.

The Quick Navi system comes into play only in one situation—when you have called up the special display screen shown in Figure 6-7, which Sony calls the "For Viewfinder" display.

Figure 6-7. For Viewfinder Display Screen

This is the only shooting-mode display screen that includes shooting information but does not include the live view. It is called "For Viewfinder" because the idea is that you will select this display when using the viewfinder, so you can have an unobstructed live view through the viewfinder and see details of your settings on this display, which appears only on the LCD screen.

The For Viewfinder display screen is summoned by pressing the Display button, but only if you have selected it for inclusion in the cycle of display screens. You select it using the Display Button option on screen 6 of the Camera Settings2 menu. From that option, select the sub-option for Monitor, then check the box for the For Viewfinder item on the next screen, as discussed in Chapter 5.

As seen in Figure 6-7, the For Viewfinder screen displays a lot of information at the right, including Drive Mode, White Balance, Focus Area, DRO, Picture Effect, Picture Profile, Creative Style, and several others.

Normally, these items are displayed only for your information; you cannot adjust them. But, if you press the Function button, an orange highlight appears at the right, as shown in Figure 6-8. You can then use the direction buttons to navigate through the settings;

this screen then becomes what Sony calls the Quick Navi screen, which permits adjustments. You also can move the orange highlight block to the left, to the settings for options such as ISO, SteadyShot, exposure compensation, and JPEG Image Size.

Figure 6-8. Orange Highlight on Quick Navi Screen

When you have highlighted a setting to adjust, turn the control wheel to scroll through the available values and make the adjustment quickly. When you adjust certain settings, such as Aspect Ratio, a secondary window opens in the top part of the display, as shown in Figure 6-9, showing the various options available for the setting.

Figure 6-9. Secondary Window for Aspect Ratio on Quick Navi Screen

For sub-settings, make the main setting with the control wheel and the sub-setting with the control dial. For example, move the highlight to Picture Effect, turn the control wheel to highlight Partial Color, and turn the control dial to highlight Yellow, as shown in Figure 6-10. Or, if you prefer, you can press the Center button when the main setting is highlighted to get access to a menu with the sub-options for that setting.

After changing a setting, you can move to other settings using the direction buttons. Once you have made all of your changes, press the Function button again to exit to the static For Viewfinder display, which will now show the new settings in place.

Figure 6-10. Partial Color Setting on Quick Navi Screen

Dial/Wheel Lock

The Function button can carry out one other operation in shooting mode, depending on how a Camera Settings2 menu option is set. The next-to-last item on screen 9 of that menu is the Dial/Wheel Lock option, which I discussed in Chapter 5. If that option is set to Lock, then, when you press and hold the Function button for several seconds when the shooting screen is displayed, the shooting-related operations of the control wheel and control dial are locked. The wheel and dial will still operate to navigate through menu screens and menu settings, but they will not set items such as exposure compensation, aperture, and shutter speed.

Send to Smartphone

When the camera is in playback mode, by default, pressing the Function button brings up a screen allowing you to send the current image or multiple images to a smartphone or tablet, if that function is available. I will discuss this option in Chapter 10, where I discuss the camera's Wi-Fi functions.

You can change the assignment of the Function button, for playback mode only, using the Custom Key (Playback) option on screen 8 of the Camera Settings2 menu, as discussed in Chapter 5.

Playback Button

This button to the lower left of the control wheel, marked with a small triangle, is used to put the camera into playback mode, which allows you to view recorded images and videos on the LCD screen or in the viewfinder. When the camera is in playback mode, pressing this button will switch the camera to shooting mode. When the camera has powered down because of the Power Save Start Time menu option, you can press this button to wake the camera up into playback mode.

Custom Button 2/Delete Button

The C2/Delete button, located at the extreme lower right of the camera's back, can be assigned to one of many functions for use in shooting mode using the Custom Key (Still Images) or Custom Key (Movies) menu option.

Figure 6-11. Delete Screen from Pressing C2 Button

In playback mode, when an image or video is displayed, this button acts as the Delete button, as indicated by the trash can icon on the button. If you press the button, the camera displays the message shown in Figure 6-11, prompting you to select Delete or Cancel. If you highlight Delete and press the Center button, the camera will delete the image or video that was displayed. If you choose Cancel, the camera will return to the playback mode screen.

This button also has a specialized function that is not obvious. When you have used a Focus Area menu option such as Zone or Flexible Spot to activate a movable focus zone or frame, and have moved that zone or frame to a new position on the camera's display, you can press the C2/Delete button to return the zone or frame immediately to the center of the display.

Movie Button

The red button at the extreme right edge of the camera has just one function—to start and stop the recording of movie sequences. As I noted in discussing the mode dial earlier in this chapter, you can control how the Movie button operates. If you want to be able to start recording a movie in any shooting mode, go to the Camera Settings2 menu and select the Movie Button option on screen 9. If you set that menu option to

Always (the default setting), then the Movie button will operate in any shooting mode. If you set that option to Movie Mode Only, then the Movie button will not operate unless the camera is set to Movie mode or S & Q Motion mode using the mode dial. (Movie mode is the mode marked by the movie film icon.)

This is a fairly important decision to make, and it depends on your preferences and likely uses of the camera. If you want to be able to start recording a video at any time without delay, you should leave the Movie Button option set to Always. The reason you might not want to do this is if you believe you may press the Movie button by mistake. When you press the button by mistake, you have to press it again to stop the recording, and then wait for the camera to finish processing the movie before you can use any other controls. And, of course, the camera will have an unwanted file cluttering the memory card.

With the a6400, I never press the Movie button by mistake, because the button does not come within range of my thumb unless I want to press it. So, with this camera I leave the option set to Always, to avoid missing video opportunities. But you should consider whether you want to use that menu option as a precaution against unwanted footage.

There are differences in how the camera operates for video recording in different shooting modes. I will discuss movie-making in detail in Chapter 9.

Control Wheel and Its Buttons

Several important controls are within the perimeter of the control wheel, the ridged wheel with a large button in its center. The four edges of the wheel (Up, Down, Left, and Right) function as buttons. That is, if you press the wheel's rim at any of those four points, you are, in effect, pressing a button.

On the a6400, the Up button is permanently assigned as the Display button, which you can press to cycle through the various display screens for the LCD monitor or the viewfinder. The Right, Down, and Left buttons all have default assignments, but each of them also can be programmed to handle a different function through the Custom Key menu options, as discussed in Chapter 5. Following are details about the control wheel and each of its buttons.

Control Wheel

In many cases, to choose a menu item or a setting, you can turn this wheel, which is centrally located on the camera's back. In some cases, you have the choice of using this wheel or pressing the direction buttons. In others, you can turn this wheel or the control dial, located at the upper right of the camera's back.

When the camera is in Shutter Priority mode, this wheel adjusts shutter speed; in Aperture Priority mode, it adjusts aperture. In Manual exposure mode, by default it adjusts shutter speed; you can change that setting so it adjusts aperture using the Dial/Wheel Setup option on screen 8 of the Camera Settings2 menu. (The same settings apply when Exposure Mode is set to A, S, or M in Movie or S &Q Motion mode.)

You can set this wheel to adjust exposure compensation using the Dial/Wheel EV Compensation option on screen 9 of the Camera Settings2 menu. (That setting does not work in Manual exposure mode or in modes in which exposure compensation is not available.)

You also can set this wheel to operate a chosen function temporarily when you press an assigned control button to call up a set of My Dial settings that are assigned to this wheel and the control dial using the My Dial Settings option on screen 8 of the Camera Settings2 menu.

When you are viewing a menu screen, you can navigate up and down through the lists of options by turning the wheel. When you are adjusting items using the Function menu or the Quick Navi menu, you can change the value for the highlighted setting by turning the control wheel. When you are using manual focus and you have the Focus Magnifier or MF Assist option turned on, you can turn the control wheel to choose the area of the scene that is being magnified.

In playback mode, you can turn the control wheel to navigate from one image to the next on the LCD screen. When a video is being played on the screen and has been paused, you can turn the control wheel to move the video either forward or in reverse. While a movie is playing, you can use the wheel to fast-forward or fast-reverse the footage.

Center Button

The large button in the center of the control wheel has many uses. On menu screens that have additional options, such as the JPEG Image Size screen, this button takes you to the next screen to view the other options. It also acts as a selection button when you choose certain options. For example, after you select Flash Mode from screen 10 of the Camera Settings1 menu and then navigate to your desired option, you can press the Center button to confirm your selection and exit from the menu screen back to the shooting screen.

When the camera is set to manual focus and the MF Assist option is turned on, once you turn the focusing ring on the lens to start focusing, pressing the Center button roughly doubles the magnification of the display: from 5.9 times to 11.7 times. Pressing the button again toggles the display back to the 5.9 times magnification level. When the Focus Magnifier menu option is turned on, pressing the Center button magnifies the screen when the orange magnifier frame is on the display.

The Center button also has several other possible uses, depending on how it is set up in the menu system. The Custom Key (Still Images) and Custom Key (Movies) options on Screen 8 of the Camera Settings2 menu let you assign a function to the Center Button for either still-shooting or movies, or both.

If you select the Focus Standard option, if Focus Area is set to a movable setting such as Flexible Spot, pressing the Center button re-activates the screen to adjust the location of the focus frame. Also, when autofocus is in effect and Focus Area is set to Wide or Center, or to the Wide or Center option for Tracking, pressing the button assigned to Focus Standard causes the camera to focus in the center of the screen.

If you prefer not to use the Focus Standard option, you can assign this button to carry out any one of numerous functions. I discussed those functions in Chapter 5, in connection with the Camera Settings2 menu.

The button also has several miscellaneous functions. For example, in playback mode, you press the Center button to start playing a video whose first frame is displayed on the camera's screen. Once the video is playing, press the Center button to pause the playback and then to toggle between play and pause. When a panoramic image is displayed, press the Center button to make it scroll on the screen at a larger size using the full height of the display screen. When you have enlarged an image in playback mode, you can return it immediately to its normal size by pressing the Center button. When you are selecting images for deletion or protection using the appropriate Playback menu option, you use the Center button to mark or unmark an image for that purpose. When you are setting a custom white balance, you press this button to evaluate the lighting and lock in a new White Balance setting.

DIRECTION BUTTONS

Each of the four edges of the control wheel—Up, Down, Left, and Right—is also a "button" you can press to get access to a setting or operation, if the button has had one assigned to it. Sometimes it can be tricky to press in exactly the right spot, but these four buttons are important to control of the camera. You use them to navigate through menus and through screens for settings, whether moving left and right or up and down.

You also can use them in playback mode to move through your images and, when you have enlarged an image, to scroll around within the magnified image.

In addition to the above duties, the direction buttons have functions in connection with various settings. For example, when a movie is being played, pressing the Down button opens the control panel for controlling playback of the movie. In playback mode, pressing this button brings up an index screen showing thumbnails of images and videos. And, as with the Center button, the Right, Left, and Down buttons (but not the Up button) can be assigned to carry out other functions through the Custom Key options on the Camera Settings2 menu, as discussed in Chapter 5.

Finally, one of the direction buttons, the Up button, comes pre-assigned as the Display button, as discussed below.

Up Button: Display

The Up button, marked "DISP," is used to switch among the displays of information on the camera's LCD screen and in the viewfinder, in both shooting and playback modes. As discussed in Chapter 5, you can change the contents of the shooting mode screens using the Display Button option on screen 6 of the Camera Settings2 menu. The display screens that are available in playback mode are discussed in Chapter 7. Because it is dedicated to display duties, the Up button cannot be programmed to perform any other functions.

Left Button

The Left button is assigned by default to bring up the Drive Mode menu, but it can be assigned to carry out any one or two out of a number of functions for both still shooting and movies, using the Custom Key (Still Images) and Custom Key (Movies) options on screen 8 of the Camera Settings2 menu, as discussed in Chapter 5.

Right Button

The Right button is assigned to adjust ISO by default, but it can be re-assigned to other duties using the Custom Key menu options.

Down Button

The Down button is assigned by default to control exposure compensation, but it also has the same options as the Left button for having other functions assigned to it.

LCD Monitor

Tilting Features

The camera's LCD monitor is not really a "control," but it does allow some physical adjustment. This screen, even without its tilting ability, is a notable feature of the camera. It has a diagonal span of 2.95 inches (7.5 cm) and provides a resolution of 921,600 dots.

The screen can tilt downward as much as 74 degrees, as shown in Figure 6-12. When the LCD is tilted in this way, you can hold the camera high above your head and view the scene as if you were an arm's length taller or were standing on a small ladder. If you attach the camera to a monopod or other support and hold it up in the air, you can extend the camera's height even farther and still view the screen quite well. You can activate the self-timer before raising the camera up in the air.

Figure 6-12. LCD Monitor Tilted Down for Overhead Shots

You also can use a smartphone or tablet connected to

the camera by Wi-Fi to trigger the camera by remote control while it is raised overhead, as discussed in Chapter 10, or you can use one of Sony's remote controls, as discussed in Appendix A.

Figure 6-13. LCD Monitor Rotated for Self-portraits

The screen can also rotate upward and forward about 180 degrees, as shown in Figure 6-13, so you can take a self-portrait. You can use the Self-portrait/Self-timer option on screen 14 of the Camera Settings1 menu to display a countdown timer on the LCD for use with self-portraits.

If you need to take images from near ground level, you can rotate the screen so it tilts upward, as shown in Figure 6-14, and hold the camera down as far as you need to get a low-angle view of the scene.

It can be helpful to shoot upward like this when your subject is in an area with a busy, distracting background. You can hold the camera down low and shoot with the sky as your background to reduce or eliminate the distractions. (Similarly, you may be able to shoot from a high angle to frame your subject against the ground or floor to have a less-cluttered background.)

Figure 6-14. LCD Tilted Up for Low-angle Shots

The tilting display also can be useful for street photography: You can fold the screen upward and look down at the camera while taking photos of people on the street without drawing undue attention to yourself, especially if you are using a lens with a long telephoto reach.

Touch Screen Features

The second category of special features of the LCD screen is its limited functionality as a touch screen. I have discussed these features to some extent in earlier chapters, and I will provide a summary of these features here.

For any touch screen features to work, you first have to make sure the Touch Operation item on screen 3 of the Setup menu is set to activate them. To have all touch functions working, choose Touch Panel + Pad for the Touch Panel/Pad menu option on the same screen. In addition, the discussion below assumes that you have set Function of Touch Operation to Touch Focus on screen 9 of the Camera Settings2 menu.

The camera's Touch Focus capability when shooting still images works in any shooting mode for stills other than Sweep Panorama, and it works with all focus modes except manual focus. The way it works depends on the Focus Area setting on screen 5 of the Camera Settings1 menu. If that option is set to Wide or Center, or to the Wide or Center setting for Tracking AF, you can touch the screen where you want the camera to focus, and it will place a small focus frame at that point. You can then proceed to focus and shoot as you would normally, with the focus point at that location. The camera also places a pointing-finger icon and an X on the screen, as shown in Figure 6-15; you can touch that icon, or press the Center button, to cancel the Touch Focus operation.

Figure 6-15. Icon to Cancel touch Focus

At that point, the camera will resume its focusing operations as it would with no touch screen in use, though you can always touch the screen again to set a new focus point. You also can drag the focus frame around the screen with your finger.

If Focus Area is set to Flexible Spot or Expand Flexible Spot (or the Flexible Spot or Expand Flexible Spot setting for Tracking AF), if you touch the screen, you can drag the focus frame to a new location or set a new focus point outside of the existing frame. In this situation, the camera does not place a cancel icon on the screen.

With Tracking AF in effect, you can touch a point on the screen to lock the tracking frame at that point, or move the existing frame to a new position, depending on which sub-option for Tracking AF is in effect.

With Face/Eye Priority in AF turned on, you can touch the screen to move the focus point to a different face, or to a point that is not on any face.

When the camera is shooting movies, the touch screen operation works somewhat differently than it does with stills. With Focus Area set to a setting other than Flexible Spot or Expand Flexible Spot, when you touch the screen the camera uses what Sony calls "spot focus." The camera will direct its focus to that point, and it will also switch the camera into manual focus mode; you will see the MF icon appear on the screen. That happens so you can fine-tune the focus if you want.

The camera will stay in manual focus mode until you touch the screen again to choose a new focus point, or you touch the finger icon with the X (or press the Center button) to cancel the spot focus feature and let the camera continue with its normal autofocus system. The camera does not display any focus frame at the point where it directs its focus, but you should be able to see that the focus has become sharp at the selected point.

If you want to create a nice "pull focus" effect, touch one subject to focus on it. Then, when you are ready to switch the focus to the other subject, touch it, and the camera will change its focus point to the new subject. You can control the speed of the pull-focus transition using the AF Drive Speed option on screen 2 of the Camera Settings2 menu. There is a considerable difference in the effects produced by using the Slow, Normal, or Fast setting for that option. If you want a quick, possibly startling focus change, choose Fast; for a leisurely, relaxed transition, choose Slow.

If Focus Area is set to Flexible Spot or Expand Flexible Spot when recording video, the Touch Focus operation is somewhat different. In that case, you can still touch a point on the screen to cause the camera to focus at that point, but the camera does not switch into manual focus mode. You can also drag the focus frame to a new position, and the camera will focus at that new location. You can use this dragging action to carry out a "pull focus" effect, as discussed above for the spot focus feature.

If you find the Touch Focus features do not work as described above for recording movies, check to make sure Function of Touch Operation is set to Touch Focus on screen 9 of the Camera Settings2 menu. If it is set to Touch Tracking, the camera will use tracking focus rather than spot focus when you touch the screen.

You also can use the LCD screen as a touch pad to control focus operations when you are viewing the scene through the viewfinder. The Touch Focus features can work as described above in that case, but you can change their behavior to some extent with a menu option, Touch Pad Settings, on screen 3 of the Setup menu. If you set the Touch Position Mode option of that menu item to Absolute, then you can touch any point on the operational area of the screen and the focus will be set there. You also can drag the focus frame, depending on the Focus Area setting. However, if you set Touch Position Mode to Relative, then you cannot select a new focus point just by touching the screen; you can only drag an existing focus frame to a new point.

Besides focusing, the a6400 offers a couple of other touch screen features. First, when the camera is in playback mode, you can tap the screen twice to enlarge an individual still image. You can then scroll the enlarged image around with your finger, and tap twice again to return it to normal size. Sometimes it can be difficult to tap at the right speed to get this function to work, but it does work fairly well.

Also, when the camera is in shooting mode with manual focus in use, you can tap the screen twice to call up the Focus Magnifier feature, which enlarges the screen so you can judge the focus. You can scroll the screen around with a finger, and tap twice again to reduce it to normal size.

Ports for Audio, HDMI, and Other Functions

Several important jacks and ports are located on the left side of the camera. Figure 6-16 shows this side of the camera with the protective doors closed. When those doors are opened, the jacks and ports are readily accessible, as seen in Figure 6-17.

Figure 6-16. **Left Side of Camera with Door Over Ports Closed**

The top item is the Multi port. This is where you plug in the USB cable for charging the battery, powering the camera with the AC adapter, uploading images and videos to your computer, or connecting the camera to a computer to control the camera through tethering. You also can plug in other accessories that are compatible with this special terminal, including various Sony remote controls, which I discuss in Appendix A.

The next item in this area is the HDMI port, where you plug in an optional micro HDMI cable to connect the camera to an HDTV for viewing images and videos. You also can view the shooting display from the camera through this connection, so you can connect the camera to an HDTV to act as a monitor for your shooting of still images or videos. In addition, you can use this port to output a "clean" HDMI video signal for video production. For example, you can output the video signal to an external video recorder. I discuss that process in Chapter 9. The bottom jack is for an external microphone with a 3.5mm stereo plug. I will discuss external microphones in Appendix A.

Figure 6-17. **Ports on Left Side of Camera**

Speaker

The speaker where the camera plays audio from movies is located above the door that covers the ports. Be sure not to block the speaker's openings if you want to hear that audio.

Figure 6-18. **Right Side of Camera**

NFC Active Area

On the right of the camera is a decorative letter N, which marks the NFC active area for the a6400. This is where you touch the camera against the similar area on a compatible smartphone or tablet that uses the near field communication protocol. As discussed in Chapter 10, when the two devices are touched together at their NFC active areas, they should automatically connect through a Wi-Fi connection. Once the connection is established, they can share images and the phone or tablet can control the camera remotely in some ways.

The items on the front of the camera are seen in Figure 6-19.

Figure 6-19. **Items on Front of Camera**

Lens Mount and Lens Release Button

The metallic area around the opening in the front of the camera's body is the lens mount, where you attach a compatible lens. To do this, remove the rear cap from the lens and the body cap from the camera, and, taking care not to let any dust or debris get inside the camera, line up the mounting index on the camera with the similar mark on the lens. Gently push the lens flat against the mount and turn the lens clockwise until it clicks definitely into place.

To remove the lens, press and hold the lens release button and rotate the lens counterclockwise until it comes free from the camera's body. Either attach another lens to the camera or cover the lens mount with the camera's body cap, and place caps on the front and rear of the lens to protect it.

AF Illuminator/Self-Timer Lamp

The lamp on the front of the camera next to the lens has two uses. Its reddish light blinks to signal use of the self-timer and it turns on in dark conditions to assist with autofocusing for still images. You can control the lamp's autofocus function with the AF Illuminator item on screen 6 of the Camera Settings1 menu, as discussed in Chapter 4. If you set that menu item to Auto, the lamp will light as needed for autofocus; if you set it to Off, the lamp will never light for that purpose, though it will still illuminate for the self-timer.

Infrared Remote Sensor

The infrared remote sensor receives signals from a compatible remote control to operate the camera's shutter and to start and stop movie recording. Remote controls are discussed in Appendix A.

Microphone

The two openings for the camera's built-in stereo microphone are located above the area where the lens sits on the front of the camera. This microphone provides excellent quality for everyday video recording. However, if you need greater quality, there are several options available for using higher-quality external microphones, as discussed in Appendix A.

Bottom of Camera

The final items are on the bottom of the a6400, seen in Figure 6-20.

Figure 6-20. **Items on Bottom of Camera**

The major items here are the tripod socket and the battery/memory card compartment. The battery compartment door has a small flap located at its edge. That flap is provided so you can insert an AC adapter or other power source into the battery compartment and run its cord through the flap, so the compartment's door can be latched securely shut. I will discuss the AC adapter and other power sources in Appendix A. The access lamp, located near the hinge of the battery/memory card compartment door, lights up red when the camera is writing data to a memory card, indicating that you should not remove the battery or memory card while that process is underway.

CHAPTER 7: PLAYBACK

Normal Playback

First, you should be aware of the Auto Review option on screen 7 of the Camera Settings2 menu. This setting determines whether and for how long the image stays on the screen for review when you take a new picture. If your major interest for viewing images in the camera is to check them right after they are taken, this setting is all you need to be concerned with. As discussed in Chapter 5, you can leave Auto Review turned off or set it to two, five, or ten seconds.

To control how your images are viewed later on, you need to work with the options that are available in playback mode. For plain review of images, the process is simple. Once you press the Playback button (marked with a triangle icon), the camera is in playback mode, and you will see an image or video saved to the camera's memory card. (Which item is displayed depends on the setting for View Mode, discussed later, as well as on which one was viewed last.)

To move back through older items, press the Left button or turn the control wheel or control dial to the left. To see more recent ones, use the Right button or turn the control wheel or control dial to the right. To speed through the images, hold down the Left or Right button.

Index View and Enlarging Images

In normal playback mode, you can press the Down button to view an index screen of your images and videos or to enlarge a single image. When you are viewing an individual image, press that button, and you will see a screen showing either 12 or 30 images, one of which is outlined by an orange frame, as shown in Figure 7-1.

Figure 7-1. Playback Index Screen

(You can choose whether this screen shows 12 or 30 images and videos using the Image Index option on the Playback menu, discussed later in this chapter.)

You can press the Center button to bring up the outlined image or video on the screen, or you can move through the items on the index screen by pressing the Left and Right buttons or by turning the control wheel. If you move the orange highlight to the vertical bar at the far left of the display, as seen in Figure 7-2, you can use the Up and Down buttons to move through the images a screen at a time.

Figure 7-2. Highlight on Playback Navigation Bar at Left

If you press the Center button while that bar is highlighted, the camera displays the Calendar screen, as seen in Figure 7-3. On that screen, you can move the orange frame to any date and press the Center button to bring up a view with images and videos from that date. If you move the orange highlight to the narrow strip to the left of the calendar, as seen in Figure 7-4, you can move through the items by months with the Up and Down buttons.

Figure 7-3. Calendar Index Screen

Figure 7-4. Highlight on Month Navigation Bar at Left

If you move the highlight to the bar at the extreme left of the calendar screen, you can use the Up and Down buttons to move through the five icons that are arranged vertically in that bar, as shown in Figure 7-5. From the top, those icons represent the date view, still-images view, AVCHD videos view, XAVC S HD videos view, or XAVC S 4K videos view. I will discuss those options later in this chapter, in connection with the View Mode item on the Playback menu.

Figure 7-5. Highlight on Bar with View Mode Icons at Left

At any time when you are viewing the thumbnails in the index screen, you can turn the control dial to move

through the images and videos a screen at a time.

When you are viewing a single still image, a press of the AF/MF/AEL button enlarges the image, with the enlargement centered on the point where the camera used autofocus, if it did so. If the camera did not use autofocus, the camera will zoom in on the center of the image. (You can change this behavior with the Enlarge Initial Magnification and Enlarge Initial Position menu options, discussed later in this chapter.) You will see a display in the lower left corner of the image showing a thumbnail with an inset orange frame that represents the portion of the image that is now filling the screen in enlarged view, as shown in Figure 7-6. This feature is useful for quickly checking the focus of the image.

Figure 7-6. Enlarged Image in Playback Mode

If you keep pressing the AF/MF/AEL button, the image will be enlarged to increasing levels. While it is magnified, you can scroll in it with the four direction buttons; you will see the orange frame move around within the thumbnail image. To increase or decrease the magnification level, turn the control wheel. Press the Center button or the Menu button to revert immediately to normal size. You can press the Custom 2/Delete button to bring up the Delete screen for the image while it is enlarged. To move to other images while the display is magnified, turn the control dial.

You also can enlarge an image in Playback mode by tapping twice on the LCD screen, if the Touch Operation option on screen 3 of the Setup menu has been set to turn on the touch features of the screen. You can then drag the enlarged image around with a finger, and tap twice again to reduce the image to normal size.

Playback Display Screens

When you are viewing an image in single-image

display mode, pressing the Display button (Up button) repeatedly cycles through three playback screens: (1) the full image with no information; (2) the full image with basic information, including date and time it was taken, image number, Aspect Ratio, aperture, shutter speed, ISO, and Image Size and Quality, as shown in Figure 7-7; and (3) a thumbnail image with detailed recording information, including aperture, shutter speed, ISO, shooting mode, White Balance, focal length, DRO setting, and other data, plus a histogram, as shown in Figure 7-8.

Figure 7-7. Playback Display Screen with Basic Information

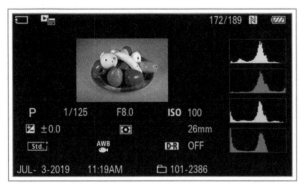

Figure 7-8. Playback Display Screen with Full Information

A histogram is a graph showing distribution of dark and bright areas in the image. Dark blacks are represented by peaks on the left and bright whites by peaks on the right, with continuous gradations in between. With the a6400, the graph's top box gives information about the overall brightness of the image. The three lower boxes contain information about the brightness of the basic colors that make up the image: red, green, and blue.

If a histogram has brightness values bunched at the left side, there is an excessive amount of black and dark areas (high points on the left side of the histogram) and very few bright and white areas (no high points on the right). If the graph runs into the left side of the chart,

it means the shadow areas are "clipped"; that is, the image is so dark that some details have been lost in the dark areas. The histogram in Figure 7-9 illustrates this degree of underexposure.

Figure 7-9. Histogram for Underexposed Image

A histogram with its high points bunched on the right means the image is too bright, as shown in Figure 7-10.

Figure 7-10. Histogram for Overexposed Image

If the lines of the graph run into the right side of the chart, that means the highlights are clipped and the image has lost some details in the bright areas.

A histogram for a normally exposed image has high points arranged evenly in the middle. That pattern, illustrated by Figure 7-11, indicates a good balance of light, dark, and medium tones.

Figure 7-11. Histogram for Normally Exposed Image

When the playback histogram is on the screen, any areas containing highlights that are excessively bright will flash to indicate possible overexposure, alerting you that you might need to take another shot with the exposure adjusted to avoid that situation.

The histogram is an approximation and should not be relied on too heavily. It can give you helpful feedback as to how evenly exposed your image is. There may be times when it is appropriate to have a histogram skewed to the left or right for intentionally "low-key" (dark) or "high-key" (brightly lit) scenes.

If you want to see the histogram when the camera is in shooting mode, you can turn on that option for the monitor, the viewfinder, or both, using the Display Button option on screen 6 of the Camera Settings2 menu, as discussed in Chapter 5.

Deleting Images with the Delete Button

As I mentioned in Chapter 6, you can delete individual images by pressing the Delete button, also known as the Custom 2 or C2 button, at the bottom right of the camera's back. If you press this button when a still image or a video is displayed, whether individually or highlighted on an index screen, the camera will display the Delete/Cancel box shown in Figure 7-12.

Figure 7-12. Delete Screen from Pressing C2 Button

Highlight your choice and press the Center button to confirm. You can delete only single images or videos in this way, except for bursts of continuous shots. If you press the C2 button while a set of continuous shots is displayed as a group, you can delete all shots in the group at once, as discussed later in this chapter. If you want to delete multiple items that are not part of the same group, you can use the Delete option on the Playback menu, discussed below in this chapter.

Playback Menu

The other options that are available for controlling playback on the a6400 appear as items on the Playback menu, whose first screen is shown in Figure 7-13.

Figure 7-13. Screen 1 of Playback Menu

You get access to this menu by pressing the Menu button and navigating to the menu marked by a triangle icon. Following is information about each item on this menu.

PROTECT

With the Protect feature, you can "lock" selected images or videos so they cannot be erased with the normal erase functions, including using the Delete button and using the Delete option on the Playback menu, discussed above. However, if you format the memory card using the Format command, all data on the card will be erased, including protected images.

When you select the Protect command, the menu offers you various choices, as shown in Figure 7-14.

Figure 7-14. Protect Menu Options Screen

These choices may include Multiple Images, All in this Folder, or All with this Date, depending on the current view that has been selected with the View Mode option, discussed below. If you choose Multiple Images, the camera will display the still images or videos with a check box at the left side of each item, as shown in Figure 7-15.

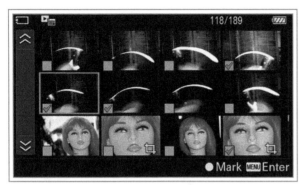

Figure 7-15. Selection Screen for Delete Option

The images and videos may be shown individually or on an index screen, depending on whether you started from an individual image or an index screen. You can change from the full-screen view to the index view by pressing the Down button, even after choosing the Protect option.

Scroll through the images and videos with the control wheel, the control dial, or the Left and Right buttons. When you reach an item you want to protect, press the Center button to place a check mark in the box for that item. To unmark an image or video, press the Center button again. Continue with this process until you have marked all items you want to protect. Then, press the Menu button to move to the next screen, where the camera will prompt you to highlight OK or Cancel, and press the Center button to confirm. If you select OK, all of the marked items will be protected. If you want to cancel before you have marked any items, press the Playback button to return to normal playback mode.

If, instead of Multiple Images, you choose All in this Folder or All with this Date, the camera will display a screen asking you to confirm protection of all of those files. Any image that is protected will have a key icon in the upper right corner to the left of the battery icon, as shown in Figure 7-16. The key icon will be visible when the image is viewed with the detailed information screen or the basic information screen, but it will not appear in the image-only view.

Figure 7-16. Key Icon on Protected Image

To unprotect all images or videos in one operation, select the appropriate Cancel option from the Protect item on the Playback menu. That option will prompt you to Cancel All with this Date or to Cancel All in this Folder, depending on the View Mode setting.

ROTATE

The Rotate menu option gives you a way to rotate an image. Select this menu item, and you will see a screen like that in Figure 7-17, prompting you to press the Center button to rotate the image. Each time you press the button, the image will rotate 90 degrees counter-clockwise. You can use this option for images taken vertically, when the Display Rotation option, discussed later in this chapter, is off. This option will be dimmed if View Mode is set to a view for videos only.

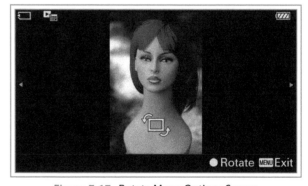

Figure 7-17. Rotate Menu Options Screen

DELETE

The Delete command lets you erase multiple images and videos from your memory card in one operation. (If you just want to delete one or two items, it's usually easier to display each one on the screen, then press the Delete button and confirm the erasure.)

The procedure for using this option is similar to the one for protecting images, discussed earlier. The menu screen offers you two choices, as shown in Figure 7-18. If you select Multiple Images, the camera will present you with either index screens or individual images. As with the Protect option, you can scroll through your images and videos and mark any item's check box for deletion by pressing the Center button. When you have finished marking them, press the Menu button and the camera will display a confirmation screen. If you select OK to confirm, the marked items will be deleted.

Figure 7-18. Delete Menu Options Screen

If, instead of Multiple Images, you choose All in this Folder or All with this Date, the camera will display a screen asking you to confirm deletion of all of those files. If any images have a key icon displayed at the top, those images are protected, and cannot be deleted using this option unless you first unprotect them, as discussed earlier in this chapter.

RATING

This option lets you assign a rating of from one to five stars to any individual still image. (This option does not work for movies or for images displayed as a group, taken in burst mode.) After you select this item, the camera will display a rating selection screen, as shown in Figure 7-19.

Figure 7-19. Rating Menu Option - Initial Selection Screen

Use the Left and Right buttons or turn the control wheel to display an image to be rated. When it is displayed, press the Center button and the camera will display a screen like that in Figure 7-20.

Figure 7-20. Screen to Select Stars for Rating

On that screen, use the Left and Right buttons or the control wheel to select a rating. The camera will change the number of orange stars at the top of the image.

Figure 7-21. Screen Showing Stars for Final Rating

When the star rating is changed as you want, press the Center button to confirm, and the stars at the top of the image will turn white, indicating the final rating, as shown in Figure 7-21. The rating you assigned will show up in software that reads such metadata, such as Adobe Bridge and Sony's Imaging Edge.

RATING SET (CUSTOM KEY)

This menu option works in conjunction with the ability to assign a control button to the Rating option using the Custom Key (Playback) option on screen 8 of the Camera Settings2 menu. If you assign a button to the Rating option, you can use the Rating Set (Custom Key) menu option to choose the number of stars to be assigned by that button. So, for example, if you choose three stars, then, in playback mode, if you press the assigned control button when an image is displayed, that image will be assigned a rating of three stars. If you choose more than one number of stars, you can use successive presses of the assigned button to cycle through those settings. For example, if you select one, three, and five stars as the available ratings for the assigned button, then, when you first press the button in playback mode, the camera will display one star on the image. If you press the button a second time, it will display three stars, and a third press will produce a rating of five stars.

SPECIFY PRINTING

This option lets you use the DPOF (Digital Print Order Format) function, a standard printing protocol that is built into the camera. The DPOF system lets you mark various images on your memory card to be added to a print list, which can then be sent to a printer. Or, you can take the memory card to a commercial printing company to print out the selected images.

To add images to the DPOF print list, select the Specify Printing option from the Playback menu. On the next screen, shown in Figure 7-22, select Multiple Images.

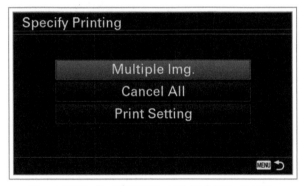

Figure 7-22. Specify Printing Menu Options Screen

The camera will display the first image with a check box at the left, or an index screen with an orange frame around the currently selected image and a check box in the lower-left corner of each image thumbnail, as shown in Figure 7-23.

Figure 7-23. Screen to Select Images to Print

You can choose to display individual images or index screens using the Down button. There will be a small printer icon in the lower left of the display with a zero beside it at first, meaning no copies of any images have been set for printing yet. Use the control wheel, control dial, or direction buttons to move through the images.

When an image you want to have printed is displayed, press the Center button to mark it for printing or to unmark it. If you want to mark all images in a folder or for a date, scroll until you find and highlight with an orange line the box for that folder or date, and press the Center button to mark it. However, if the number of images to be marked exceeds the allowable limit of 100 images, that operation will not succeed.

You can then keep browsing through your images and adding (or subtracting) them from the print list. As you add images to the list, the DPOF counter in the lower left corner of the display will show the total number of images selected for printing. You cannot use this function to print more than one copy of any given image. You cannot specify printing for images in a group of continuous-shooting images while the group is expanded or displayed as a group. If you want to print images from such a group, you have to set the Display as Group option to Off on screen 3 of the Playback menu, or set View Mode to Folder View (Still).

When you have finished selecting images to be printed, press the Menu button to move to a screen where you can confirm your choices by selecting OK.

Figure 7-24. Print Setting Options Screen

You also can turn the Date Imprint option on or off to specify whether or not the pictures will be printed with the dates they were taken. To do this, go to the first screen of the Specify Printing menu option and select Print Setting. On the next screen, shown in Figure 7-24, set Date Imprint to On and then select Enter, to specify that the date should be printed on each image.

You can take the memory card with the DPOF list to a service that prints photos using this system. If you want to cancel a DPOF order, select the Specify Printing menu item, and choose the Cancel All option on the next screen.

The items on screen 2 of the Playback menu are shown in Figure 7-25.

Figure 7-25. Screen 2 of Playback Menu

Photo Capture

This next option on the Playback menu gives you tools for saving one or more frames from a movie that was recorded with the camera. To use this option, first find the movie that you want to save a still image from. You can use the View Mode option discussed earlier in this chapter to find movies of various formats, to help narrow the search. If View Mode is set to Folder View (Still), this option will not be available for selection.

When you have the chosen movie displayed on the screen in playback mode, select the Photo Capture menu option, and the camera will display the movie again, but this time with a circular area with several icons at the right side of the display that represent the camera's direction buttons and Center button, as shown in Figure 7-26.

Figure 7-26. Photo Capture Control Icons on Screen

The top icon represents slow playback; the right one is for single-frame forward; the left one is for single-frame reverse; the center one is for play or pause; and the bottom one is for photo capture.

Using the four direction buttons and the Center button according to that scheme, play the movie to the exact frame you want to save, then press the Down button to capture the frame as a still image. The camera will display a Processing message briefly, and then will save the image to the memory card. The image will have the same resolution as the movie from which it was saved. For example, if you save a frame from a 4K movie, it will have a resolution of 3840 x 2160 pixels, or about eight megapixels. Images captured from standard HD movies will be 1920 x 1080 pixels in resolution.

If you prefer, you can start the Photo Capture process without using the menu system. To do that, start a movie playing, and press the Center button to pause it. Then press the Down button, and you will see a control panel at the bottom of the screen, as shown in Figure 7-27.

Figure 7-27. Movie Control Panel Icons

The Photo Capture icon is the third one from the right. Use the direction buttons to navigate to that icon and select it, to start using the Photo Capture feature. Figure 7-28 is a frame that was saved from a 4K video using this feature.

Figure 7-28. Image Saved Using Photo Capture Feature

ENLARGE IMAGE

This option performs the same image magnification discussed earlier, which you can also do by pressing the AF/MF/AEL button or by tapping on the screen twice, if the touch screen features are enabled. When you select this option, the enlarged image will appear on the screen; you can then use the control wheel to change the enlargement factor. When the image is enlarged, you can press the Center button or the Menu button, or tap twice on the screen, to return the image to normal size. You can move the enlarged image around the screen with your finger, if the touch screen is turned on, or with the direction buttons. You can turn the control dial to move to other images at the current magnification level.

ENLARGE INITIAL MAGNIFICATION

This option lets you choose either Standard Magnification or Previous Magnification, as shown in Figure 7-29. With the Standard Magnification option, when you use any of the techniques mentioned above to enlarge an image in playback mode, the camera uses the standard magnification factor.

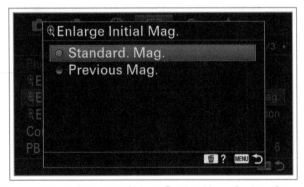

Figure 7-29. Enlarge Initial Magnification Menu Options Screen

If you choose Previous Magnification, the camera will use whatever magnification level was used for the last image that was viewed. So, if you like to zoom your images in with three presses of the AF/MF/AEL button, you can choose Previous Magnification for this option, and, once you have enlarged one image to that degree, other images will be enlarged to that degree when you first press the button or use another method to enlarge them.

ENLARGE INITIAL POSITION

This option lets you choose whether, when an image is enlarged, the camera centers it on the point where focus was achieved (if any), or on the center of the image. The menu options screen is shown in Figure 7-30.

Figure 7-30. Enlarge Initial Position Menu Options Screen

To check focus in playback mode, it can be convenient to have the enlarged image automatically centered on the focus point. For that option, choose Focused Position from this menu screen.

CONTINUOUS PLAYBACK FOR INTERVAL SHOOTING/PLAYBACK SPEED FOR INTERVAL SHOOTING

These two options work together to control the playback of a group of shots taken using the Interval Shooting option on screen 3 of the Camera Settings1 menu, also known as the time-lapse option.

To use these options, first, highlight Continuous Playback for Interval on the menu and press the Center button to activate it. Then, navigate to a group of shots taken with the Interval Shooting option. When you have located the group of shots, leave one of them on the camera's monitor in playback mode. If the Display as Group option on screen 3 of the Playback menu is turned on, the images in the group will be displayed as a single image that looks like a stack of frames.

Then, with a single image or group of images displayed, press the Center button, and the images should play back quickly in a continuous stream. Press the Down button when the camera displays the screen shown in Figure 7-31, to play the images again. You can change speed of playback with the control wheel or control dial, or by using the Playback Speed for Interval Shooting option on screen 3 of the Playback menu.

This feature also provides continuous playback of images shot with the continuous shooting option of Drive Mode.

Figure 7-31. Screen with Prompt - Press Down Button for Continuous Playback

The items on screen 3 of the Playback menu are shown in Figure 7-32.

Figure 7-32. Screen 3 of Playback Menu

SLIDE SHOW

This feature lets you play your still images and videos in sequence at an interval you specify. This menu option will be dimmed and unavailable if the View Mode option on the Playback menu is set to AVCHD View or either of the two XAVC S View settings. If that is the case, use the View Mode menu option to select either Date View or Folder View (Still). If you select Date View, the Slide Show option will display all of your movies, in all formats, along with your still images. Each movie will play in full before the show advances to the next item, unless you interrupt it with one of the controls. If you select Folder View (Still), the Slide Show option will display only the still images from the folder you selected.

When you select the Slide Show option and press the Center button, the next screen has two options you can set: Repeat and Interval, as seen in Figure 7-33. If Repeat is turned on, the show will keep repeating; otherwise, it will play only once.

The camera will not power off automatically in this mode, so be sure to stop the show when you are done

with it. The Interval setting, which controls how long each still image stays on the screen, can be set to one, three, five, ten, or 30 seconds. (The Interval setting does not apply to movies, each of which plays to its end.)

Figure 7-33. Slide Show Menu Options Screen

With the options set, navigate to the Enter box at the bottom of the screen using the control wheel, the control dial, or the Down button, and press the Center button to start the show. You can move forward or back through the images (and videos, if included) using the Right and Left buttons. Hold the buttons down to move quickly through the images and videos.

You can stop the show by pressing the Menu button or the Playback button. There is no way to pause the show and resume it. You can control the volume for movies at any time by pressing the Down button and adjusting the level with the Left and Right buttons or with the control wheel or control dial. Each movie plays fully before the next movie or image is displayed, but you can skip to the next movie or image using the Right button.

The Slide Show option does not provide settings such as transitions, effects, or music. You cannot select which images to play; this option just plays all still images from the selected folder, if you are using Folder View, or all still images and videos starting from the selected date, if you are using Date View.

VIEW MODE

This second option on screen 3 of the Playback menu lets you choose which images or videos are currently viewed in playback mode. The options are Date View, Folder View (Still), AVCHD View, XAVC S HD View, and XAVC S 4K View, as shown in Figure 7-34.

Figure 7-34. **View Mode Menu Options Screen**

If you select Date View, the camera will display the calendar screen shown earlier in Figure 7-3. You can navigate through the dates for a given month using the control wheel or the direction buttons. Highlight a date and press the Center button; the camera will display all images and videos starting from that date. You can move to other screens of images using the control dial.

If you select Folder View (Still), the camera will display the screen shown in Figure 7-35, which shows the folders available for selection.

Figure 7-35. **Folder View (Still) Display Screen**

Highlight the folder you want (there may be only one) and press the Center button; the camera will display all still images in that folder. You can navigate through the index screens for those images and select the image or images you want to view.

If you select AVCHD View, the camera will display a calendar screen with thumbnail images indicating which dates have AVCHD files associated with them. You can then highlight any date with a thumbnail image and press the Center button to move to an AVCHD video from that date.

If you select XAVC S HD View or XAVC S 4K View, the camera will display a calendar screen showing the dates on which videos in the selected format were recorded.

My preference is to use the Date View option, because then I can view both images and videos from any date. However, if I want to locate a particular video, it can be quicker to choose one of the video views so I can limit my search to videos only.

You can select a view option from an index screen without using the Playback menu. When you are viewing the calendar display or the folder display, you can move the highlight to the line of five icons at the left of the screen that represent these five view modes, and select one of the modes from that display by highlighting its icon and pressing the Center button.

IMAGE INDEX

This menu option, shown in Figure 7-36, gives you the choice of having the camera include either 12 images and videos or 30 images and videos when it displays an index screen.

Figure 7-36. **Image Index Menu Options Screen**

When you make this selection, the camera displays the index screen you chose, and it will display that screen whenever you call up the index screen using the Down button, as discussed earlier.

Whether you choose the 12-image screen or the 30-image screen depends on your personal preference as well as some other factors, including how many images and videos you have altogether and how easy it is to distinguish one from another by looking at the small thumbnail images.

The thumbnails on the 12-image screen are considerably larger than those on the 30-image screen, and it may make sense to choose the 12-image screen unless you have so many images that it would be burdensome to scroll through them 12 at a time.

The Image Index menu option will be dimmed and

unavailable for selection if there are no items available to view for the currently selected View Mode option. For example, if you have not recorded any 4K videos but View Mode is set to XAVC S 4K View, the Image Index item will not be available for selection.

DISPLAY AS GROUP

This option controls how the camera displays still images that were captured using the continuous shooting setting for Drive Mode or the Interval Shooting option on screen 3 of the Camera Settings1 menu. If this option is turned on, those images are displayed as a group that behaves like a single image.

Figure 7-37. Continuous Shooting Images Displayed as Single Item

For example, Figure 7-37 shows the playback screen when a group of continuous shots is displayed in the camera. The group is displayed in a stack, as indicated by the edges of the image frames at the right side of the screen. This group of images acts as a single image when scrolling through the images on the memory card. If you press the C2/Delete button when this group is displayed, the camera displays the message shown in Figure 7-38, announcing that deleting this item will delete all images in the group.

Figure 7-38. Message that All Images in Group Will Be Deleted

The message at the lower right of the screen in Figure 7-37 indicates that you can press the Center button to

expand the group.

Figure 7-39. Continuous Shooting Image Displayed as Individual Shots

If you press that button, the display changes to one like that shown in Figure 7-39, which shows a single image in the group, and indicates by the numbers in the upper right corner that this is the fourth of 140 images in the group. Now you can scroll through all of those images individually and delete any one of them or otherwise manipulate it as needed. When you are finished viewing the images individually, you can press the Center button again to end the expansion, and view the images as a single group again.

If you turn off the Display as Group menu option, the images always display individually, rather than as a group. Also, it is important to note that this option works only when View Mode is set to Date View. With any other setting for View Mode, continuous-shooting and interval-shooting images will display individually regardless of the setting for this menu item.

DISPLAY ROTATION

This next item on the Playback menu controls whether images shot with the camera held vertically appear that way when you play them back on the camera's screen. By default, this option is set to Auto, meaning images taken vertically are automatically rotated so that the vertical shot appears in portrait orientation on the horizontal display, as shown in Figure 7-40. What is unusual about this setting is that, if you tilt the camera sideways so one side is up, a vertical image will rotate to fill the screen. In this way, you get the best of both worlds: Vertical images display in proper orientation (but smaller than normal) within the horizontal display, and, when you tilt the camera, they display at full size.

Figure 7-40. Vertical Image Displayed on Horizontal Screen

If you change the setting to Manual, a vertical image will appear vertically on the horizontal screen, in the same way as shown in Figure 7-40. The difference with this setting from Auto is that, if you tilt the camera, the image will not change its orientation.

If you set this option to Off, then a vertical image will display in landscape orientation on the display, as shown in Figure 7-41, so you would have to tilt the camera to see it in its proper orientation.

Figure 7-41. Vertical Image Displayed at Full Size

With all of these settings, you can use the Rotate option on the Playback menu, discussed earlier in this chapter, to rotate an image manually to a different orientation.

IMAGE JUMP SETTING

This final option on the Playback menu gives you a way to set one of the camera's dials to "jump" only to a certain category of images in playback mode, to help you locate a particular image more quickly than you can by scrolling through every image.

When you select this option and press the Center button, the camera displays the screen shown in Figure 7-42, with options for Select Dial/Wheel and Image Jump Method. With the first option, you can select either the control dial (on top of the camera) or the

control wheel (on the back of the camera) as the control that will jump only to certain images. The control you do not select will continue to scroll through all of the images and videos one by one.

Figure 7-42. Image Jump Setting Menu Options Screen

Next, go to the Image Jump Method option and select it to bring up the screen shown in Figure 7-43, with several options for the jump method. You can set the selected wheel or dial to move through images one by one; to jump only to images protected using the Protect option, discussed earlier in this chapter; to jump only to images with some rating; to jump to images with a specific rating; or to jump to images with no rating.

Figure 7-43. Image Jump Method Options Screen

After you have made your selection, you can use the selected control to jump as you chose. That control will jump only to still images; it will always skip over videos. (If you want to view only videos, you can use the View Mode menu option, discussed earlier.) The Image Jump Setting feature works only when View Mode is set to Date View. With any other setting, the selected control will scroll through all images and videos one by one, in the normal way.

Chapter 8: The Setup Menu and My Menu

In earlier chapters, I discussed the options available in the Shooting and Playback menu systems. The Sony a6400 has one other menu system that helps you set up the camera and customize its operation—the Setup menu. In addition, the camera includes the My Menu feature, which you can use to create your own shortened menu with up to 30 of your most-used options, for quick access. In this chapter, I will discuss the use of the Setup and My Menu options. I'll discuss details of menu options for Movie mode in Chapter 9 and I'll discuss the options on the Network menu in Chapter 10.

Setup Menu

The Setup menu, represented by the toolbox icon, has its tab to the right of the tab for the Playback icon on the list of menu icons. The first screen of the Setup menu is shown in Figure 8-1.

Figure 8-1. Screen 1 of Setup Menu

This seven-screen menu contains options that control technical matters such as USB connections, display brightness, audio volume, file numbering, formatting a memory card, and others. I will discuss each menu item below.

Monitor Brightness

When you highlight and select this menu option, the camera first displays a screen that shows the current setting, as seen in Figure 8-2.

Figure 8-2. Monitor Brightness Menu Options Screen

If you press the Center button on that screen, you will see a screen for choosing one of two available settings for controlling the brightness of the LCD display: Manual or Sunny Weather, as shown in Figure 8-3.

Figure 8-3. Monitor Brightness Adjustment Screen

If you choose Manual, the camera displays the screen shown earlier in Figure 8-2. Using the controls on that screen, you can adjust brightness to one or two units above or below normal. After pressing the Down button or turning the control wheel to highlight the brightness scale, press the Left or Right button or turn the control dial to make the adjustment.

If your battery is running low and you don't have a spare, you may want to set the monitor to its minimum brightness to conserve power. Conversely, you can increase brightness if you're finding it difficult to compose the image on the screen.

If you are shooting outdoors in bright conditions, you can choose Sunny Weather, which sets the display to a very bright level. Of course, you can switch to using the viewfinder in bright conditions, but there may be times when you want to hold the camera away from your head as you compose the shot, even in bright sunlight. Or, you may want to play back your images for friends while outdoors. The Sunny Weather setting drains the camera's battery fairly rapidly, so you should turn it off when it is no longer needed.

VIEWFINDER BRIGHTNESS

This second option on the Setup menu is similar to the Monitor Brightness selection, discussed above, but it has some differences. With this option, you have to be looking into the viewfinder to make adjustments. There is no Sunny Weather setting, because the viewfinder is shaded from the sun and there is no need for a super-bright setting. You can set the brightness to Auto or Manual. If you select Manual, you can make the same adjustments as with the LCD screen. Again, there is not much need for brightness adjustments because the view is always shielded from outside light.

This option can only be set to Manual when Finder Frame Rate on screen 6 of the Camera Settings2 menu is set to High.

FINDER COLOR TEMPERATURE

This option lets you adjust the color temperature of the view through the viewfinder. As with the Viewfinder Brightness setting, you have to look into the viewfinder to make the adjustments. You can use the camera's controls to adjust the color temperature downward by one or two units, which will make the view appear slightly more reddish, or "warmer," or you can adjust upward by one or two units to make it more bluish, or "cooler."

I have not found a reason to take advantage of this adjustment, but, if it is helpful to you, it is easy to use.

GAMMA DISPLAY ASSIST

This option is a specialized one intended for use only if you are using a Picture Profile setting that includes the S-Log2, S-Log3, HLG, HLG1, HLG2, or HLG3 setting for gamma. As I discussed in Chapter 4, those gamma

options are special settings that enable the camera to record video with an extended dynamic range, so it can record scenes clearly even if there is considerable contrast between shadowed areas and bright ones. One characteristic of the S-Log and HLG settings is that the image on the camera's display screen will appear quite dark and low in contrast. In order to take advantage of the high dynamic range available with the S-Log settings, the footage needs to be processed with video software that can deal with the video files properly. For the HLG settings, the footage needs to be viewed on an HDR-compatible monitor to be appreciated fully.

Therefore, Sony has provided the Gamma Display Assist option so you can clearly view a scene being recorded or played back with one of the listed gamma settings in effect. When Gamma Display Assist is activated, the images on the camera's display will be boosted in contrast to a level that makes it appear as if a more standard setting was used—specifically, the ITU709(800%) setting, the HLG(BT.2020) setting, or the HLG(709) setting.

This option has five settings: Off, Auto, S-Log2, S-Log3, HLG 2020, and HLG 709, as shown in Figure 8-4.

Figure 8-4. Gamma Display Assist Menu Options Screen

If you choose Off, the option is not activated in any situation, and video shot with an S-Log or HLG gamma setting will appear rather dark and low in contrast, as it normally would. If you choose Auto, then the camera will boost the contrast of the display if the Picture Profile setting in use includes an S-Log or HLG gamma setting. (The PP7 setting for Picture Profile includes the S-Log2 setting by default; the PP8 and PP9 settings include S-Log3; and PP10 includes HLG2. You can change any Picture Profile setting to include any of the S-Log or HLG settings, as discussed in Chapter 4.)

If you choose either of the other settings for Gamma

Display Assist, labeled as S-Log2, S-Log3, HLG 2020, and HLG 709, the camera always boosts the contrast of the video (or still image) on the display, regardless of the Picture Profile setting.

My preference is to leave this option turned off. I do not have difficulty viewing the display when an S-Log or HLG gamma setting is in use. However, if you are having a problem viewing the scene on the display screen when using one of those settings, this menu option might be useful. It also can be useful to provide a preview of how the footage will look when properly processed or when viewed on the proper type of monitor.

VOLUME SETTINGS

This option lets you set the volume for video playback at a level anywhere from 0 to 15. You can also set this level when a movie is playing by pressing the Down button to get access to the detailed controls, which include a volume setting option.

TILE MENU

If you turn this option on, the camera displays a screen with six tiles representing the various menu systems, as shown in Figure 8-5, when you press the Menu button.

Figure 8-5. Tile Menu Option in Use

This screen is helpful because it gives you a graphic representation of which menu is which, and lets you choose a menu and get quick access to it. You navigate through the six tiles using the direction buttons, the control wheel, or the control dial.

I prefer to leave this option turned off, because, without it, pressing the Menu button takes me right into the last menu option I was using. From there, I can navigate quickly to any other menu system. But for those who are new to this camera or who like having a large display to show the menu choices clearly, the Tile

Menu option may be worth using.

Screen 2 of the Setup menu is shown in Figure 8-6.

Figure 8-6. Screen 2 of Setup Menu

MODE DIAL GUIDE

This menu item gives you a way to turn on or off the Mode Dial Guide, a graphic display that appears on the camera's screen when you turn the mode dial to select a shooting mode, as shown in Figure 8-7.

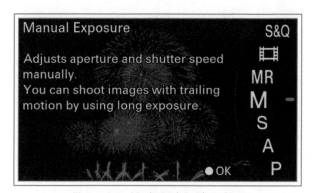

Figure 8-7. Mode Dial Guide in Use

This guide can be helpful when you first get the camera, but it can be annoying if you don't need reminders, because you have to press a button to dismiss the screen. (You can press the Center button or Menu button or press the shutter button halfway; you also can press the Playback button, which puts the camera into playback mode.) I leave this option turned off to speed up my shooting.

DELETE CONFIRMATION

This menu item has two options as shown in Figure 8-8: "Delete" First or "Cancel" First. This option lets you fine-tune the way the menu system operates for deleting images. Whenever you press the Delete button to delete an image or video in playback mode, the camera displays a confirmation screen, as shown in

Figure 8-9, with two choices: Delete or Cancel.

Figure 8-8. Delete Confirmation Menu Options Screen

Figure 8-9. Delete Screen from Pressing C2 Button

One of those choices will be highlighted when the screen appears; you can then just press the Center button to accept that choice and the operation will be done. Of course, you also can use the control wheel, control dial, or Up or Down button to highlight the other choice before you press the Center button to carry out your choice.

Which option you choose for this menu item depends on your habits, and how careful you want to be to guard against the accidental deletion of an item. If you like to move quickly in deleting images and videos, choose "Delete" first. Then, as soon as the confirmation screen appears, you can press the Center button to carry out the deletion. If you prefer to have some assurance against an accidental deletion, choose "Cancel" first, so that, if you press the Center button too quickly when the confirmation screen appears, you will only cancel the operation, rather than deleting an image.

Unless you use this process often and need to save time, I recommend you leave this menu item set at the "Cancel" First setting to be safe.

DISPLAY QUALITY

This menu item lets you choose Standard or High for the quality of the display. According to Sony, with the High setting the camera displays the live view on the LCD screen or in the viewfinder at a higher resolution than with the Standard setting, at the expense of additional drain on the battery.

I have tried experiments with these settings, viewing small print from a catalog using both the viewfinder and the LCD display with both Display Quality settings, and I have not found a noticeable difference. There may be situations in which this option has a more obvious impact on the display, but my recommendation is to leave it at Standard to conserve battery life.

POWER SAVE START TIME

This menu option lets you set the amount of time before the camera turns off automatically to save power, when no controls have been operated. The default setting is one minute; with this option you can also choose two, five, or thirty minutes, or ten seconds, as shown in Figure 8-10.

Figure 8-10. Power Save Start Time Menu Options Screen

When the camera goes to sleep with this option, you can wake it up by half-pressing the shutter button, or by pressing the Menu button or the Playback button. These presses will place the camera into shooting mode, the menu system, and playback mode, respectively.

You cannot turn the power-saving function off. However, the camera will not power off automatically when you are recording movies, when a slide show is playing, when the camera is connected to a computer, when it is being powered through the USB port, or when IR Remote Control on screen 4 of the Setup menu is turned on.

The setting you use depends on your habits and needs. In

my case, I am usually well aware of the camera's status, and I like to use the maximum thirty-minute period for this option so the camera does not power down just when I am about to use it again. I always have extra batteries available and I'm not too concerned if I have to replace the battery. If you are out in the field and running low on battery power, you might want to choose a shorter time for this option to conserve battery life.

Auto Power Off Temperature

This option lets you set the temperature at which the camera powers off automatically to keep it from overheating. The choices are Standard or High. I generally leave this option set to Standard. However, in an unusual case, such as if you are recording 4K video of a one-time event and you don't want the camera to power off in the middle of the event, you might want to set this menu item to High, to avoid a premature shutdown of the camera. In that case, Sony warns that the camera may become hot enough to cause "low temperature burns" of your hands.

NTSC/PAL Selector

This menu option controls which television system the camera uses for recording videos—NTSC or PAL. The NTSC system is used in the United States and other parts of North America, as well as Japan, South Korea, and some other countries. The PAL system is used in many parts of Asia, Africa, and Europe.

For purposes of using the a6400 camera, the difference between the two settings is that the NTSC system uses multiples of 30 for video frame rates (such as 30, 60, or 120 frames per second), while the PAL system generally uses multiples of 25, such as 25, 50, or 100 frames per second. You will see these differences in the options for the Record Setting item on screen 1 of the Camera Settings2 menu. If you choose NTSC, the options will be mostly in multiples of 30, although there will be some entries for 24 fps, another NTSC standard. If you choose PAL, the options will be in multiples of 25.

In general, you should use the setting that is standard for the area where you will be using the camera. I live in the United States, so I set the camera to NTSC, where the frame rates are in multiples of 30 (except for the few 24p options).

It is important to choose this setting before you start

recording files on your memory card. Once you have started using a card under one of these systems, you cannot change to the other system without re-formatting the card. When you select this menu option, you will see the message shown in Figure 8-11, warning that you will have to re-format the card to continue.

Figure 8-11. Warning Message for NTSC/PAL Selector Option

If you then select Enter and press the Center button, the camera will proceed to format the card for the other video system.

Screen 3 of the Setup menu is shown in Figure 8-12.

Figure 8-12. Screen 3 of Setup Menu

Cleaning Mode

The image sensor is the shiny area immediately behind the lens, which is visible when the lens is removed. This menu option is provided to help you keep the sensor clean. If specks of dust accumulate on the sensor, they can cause dark spots to appear on images.

To use this option, with a lens attached, select this menu item and press the Center button to confirm. The camera will shake the sensor slightly to dislodge any dust. The camera will then prompt you to turn the power off. If you want to go further with the cleaning operation, you can then remove the lens and clean the sensor manually with an air blower or other tools.

Sony provides information on this process at http://support.d-imaging.sony.co.jp/www/support/ilc/sensor/index.php.

TOUCH OPERATION

As discussed in earlier chapters, you can control some operations of the a6400 by touching the LCD screen on the back of the camera. As discussed in Chapter 6, with these functions activated, by touching the LCD screen you can select a focus point for a still photo, and you can "pull" the focus from one point to another while recording video. You can set the camera to take a picture when you touch the monitor. In addition, you can use the LCD screen as a touch pad while you are viewing the scene through the camera's viewfinder.

You can enlarge an image in playback mode by tapping twice on the LCD screen and return it to normal size by tapping twice again, and you can enlarge the shooting screen by tapping twice when the camera is using manual focus mode. When the manual focus screen is enlarged, you can drag on the screen to move the area that is magnified. When the Focus Magnifier frame is on the shooting screen, you can drag it around with your finger.

This menu option has only two choices—to turn all touch operations on or off. If you are certain you don't want to use any of the touch operations for a shooting session, it's easy to use this menu setting to disable all touch operations. Otherwise, leave this option turned on, and adjust which operations are active through other menu options, discussed below.

TOUCH PANEL/PAD

This next option lets you determine which touch panel operations are turned on to enable various focusing actions, assuming you have set the Touch Operation option, discussed above, to On. The choices for this option are Touch Panel + Pad; Touch Panel Only; and Touch Pad Only, as shown in Figure 8-13. In order to activate the ability to enlarge the screen by tapping, both in playback mode and in shooting mode, select either Touch Panel + Pad or Touch Panel Only. If you select Touch Pad Only, the enlargement features will not work.

Figure 8-13. Touch Panel/Pad Menu Options Screen

TOUCH PAD SETTINGS

As noted above, using the Touch Operation menu option, you can turn on the camera's ability to use the LCD screen on the back of the a6400 as a touch pad to select a focus point when you are viewing the scene through the viewfinder. The Touch Pad Settings menu option gives you several ways to control how this capability works in practice. It provides three options: Operation in Vertical Orientation; Touch Position Mode; and Operation Area, as shown in Figure 8-14.

Figure 8-14. Touch Pad Settings Menu Options Screen

The first sub-option, Operation in Vertical Orientation, can be turned either on or off. If it is turned on, then the LCD screen can be used as a touch pad even when the camera is rotated to one side to capture vertically oriented images or videos. You may want to disable this option if you feel that your nose may accidentally touch the screen in that orientation, causing an unwanted movement of the focus point.

The second sub-option, Touch Position Mode, can be set to Absolute Position or Relative Position. With Absolute Position, the camera will set the focus point in the viewfinder at the same point you have touched on the LCD screen, and you can also drag a focus frame to a new location. With Relative Position, the camera will move the focus point to a new location based only on the direction and distance of your dragging an existing frame with a finger on the LCD screen, without regard to the actual location that you touch on the screen. If Focus Area is set to Wide with this setting, the camera will place a focus frame in the center of the screen if you tap; you can then drag that frame to a new location. (You may have to tap firmly and leave your finger for a moment on the screen to make the focus frame appear.)

The final sub-option, Operation Area, comes into play only if you chose Relative Position for Touch Position Mode. In that case, you can restrict the area of the screen that can be used for re-positioning the focus point, in order to make it easier to move the focus point with a short movement of your finger. When you select this sub-option, the camera displays numerous options, which take more than a full screen to display. The first screen of options is shown in Figure 8-15. The whole list is as follows: Whole Screen; Right Half; Right Quarter; Upper Right; Lower Right; Left Half; Left Quarter; Upper Left; and Lower Left.

Figure 8-15. **Operation Area Menu Options Screen**

As you can see in Figure 8-15, each selection has a small diagram next to it to indicate where the operational area on the screen would be. This choice is a matter of personal preference. You may want a small area so you don't have to move your finger very far to carry out a movement, but the choice is yours.

DEMO MODE

The Demo Mode menu item automatically plays a movie if the camera has not had any controls operated for about one minute. This feature is designed for use by retail stores, so they can leave the camera turned on with a continuous demonstration on its screen. But you can use it for your own purposes, if you want to create a movie that demonstrates the camera's features for friends, for

example, or if you just like the idea of having the camera play a movie when it's not otherwise occupied.

For this feature to be available for selection on the menu screen, the camera has to be plugged into AC power using an AC adapter, such as the one supplied with the camera. Otherwise, this line on the menu will be dimmed.

When Demo Mode is turned on and the camera is in shooting mode, with View Mode on the Playback menu set to AVCHD View, after one minute of inactivity the camera enters Demo Mode. At that point, the camera will automatically play a movie, which you have to provide. It cannot be just any movie.

The movie the camera will play in Demo Mode must be recorded in the AVCHD format, it must be protected using the Protect option on the Playback menu, and it must be the oldest AVCHD movie on the memory card. So, if you have a reason to use this option, you may want to use a fresh memory card and record a single AVCHD movie on the card, and then use the Protect function to protect it. When the movie plays, it plays audio as well as video, and it will keep repeating in a loop. To exit from Demo Mode, you can press the Center button or just turn the camera off.

TC/UB (TIME CODE/USER BIT) SETTINGS

This menu item provides several sub-options that are helpful if you use the a6400 for advanced video production. For example, because of its ability to shoot 4K video (discussed in Chapter 9), the a6400 camera can be used as part of a multi-camera setup for a professional production. In such a setup, it can be useful to control whether and how the camera outputs time code, a type of metadata that is used when editing video sequences. The user bit is another form of metadata that also can be used as an organizing aid.

This option will have all but one of the sub-options dimmed and unavailable for selection unless the mode dial is at the Movie or S & Q position. If it is in any other position, you can get access only to the first sub-option, TC/UB Display Setting. For this discussion, I will assume the mode dial is at the Movie position.

I won't discuss the use of time code in detail in this book, but I will give a brief overview. Time code for video files includes numbers in a format like the following: 02:12:23:19, which stands for hours, minutes, seconds, and frames. In this example, the time code would mark the point in the video clip at 2 hours, 12 minutes, 23 seconds, and 19 frames into the next second.

Because video (in the NTSC system) is normally played back at 30 fps or 24 fps, the number in the final position is based on those values, even if the video is recorded in a format such as XAVC S HD with Record Setting set to 120p 100M. With a Record Setting value of 120p, 60p, 60i, or 30p, the number of frames can be set from 00 to 29. When Record Setting is set to 24p, the number of frames can be set only to 00, 04, 08, 12, 16, or 20. For PAL devices, the number of frames can go from 00 to 24, because the video is played back at 25 fps.

When you see a time code like the one in this example, you know what frame of the video is being identified, so you can make an edit at that point or synchronize this video clip with another video clip, as long as both clips are using the same time code format and had the time code recorded in synchronization.

If you are not going to use your camera for that sort of video production, you can largely ignore this menu option, though it is helpful to know what settings you can control. The sub-options are discussed below.

TC/UB Display Setting

This first option controls what figures display in the lower left corner of the camera's screen during video recording. There are three choices—Counter, TC, or U-Bit, for user bit, as shown in Figure 8-16.

Figure 8-16. TC/UB Display Setting Menu Options Screen

No matter which you choose, the display appears on the screen during recording in all shooting modes and before recording in Movie or S & Q mode. The characters are not recorded visibly with the video and will not appear during playback, although they can be used as reference points in appropriate video-editing software.

The first choice, Counter, places a simple display of minutes and seconds of elapsed recording time, as shown in Figure 8-17. This is the default choice, and it is what you probably will want to leave in place for general use. As I noted above, the only reason to use time code (or user bit) is for advanced-level video production.

Figure 8-17. Counter in Use on Recording Screen

The second choice places time code on the screen, as shown in Figure 8-18.

Figure 8-18. Time Code in Use on Recording Screen

You may want to use this setting for advanced video production, not just to display on the screen but to output to another device, such as a video recorder, through the camera's HDMI port, as I will discuss later in this chapter.

The third choice, user bit, lets you set the camera to display a set of four figures in hexadecimal notation, in the format 0B 76 11 F8. This amounts to a string of four numbers, each of which, in hexadecimal notation, can range from 00 (0 in decimal notation) to FF (255 in decimal notation).

In actual practice, I have never used the user bit for video production. Some videographers use this capability to place notes in the video file, using the few available letters (A through F) and the numbers to make notations like C1 for camera 1.

If you don't need to include a customized notation using the user bit option, the a6400 gives you a way to have the user bit provide a running display of the current time. To do that, go to the last sub-option under TC/UB Settings, UB Time Record, and set it to On. That option sets the user bit to display the current time in the lower left corner of the display. To make that display appear, you also have to set the TC/UB Display Setting option to U-Bit.

TC Preset

This next option lets you set the initial time code for your video recording. You can set the code anywhere from all zeroes, the default, to 23:59:59:29 for some NTSC formats. As I noted earlier, the final figure can go as high as 29 for most NTSC settings and 20 for the 24p settings. For PAL systems, the highest value for that figure is 24.

You might want to use this option if you need to start with a particular time code for a technical reason, in order to synchronize your footage with existing footage or that from another camera. In addition, in some production environments the practice is to set the hours position to a particular value, such as 01, to designate some item, such as the reel number. Unless you have a need to make a setting of that nature, you can leave these values all at zero.

UB Preset

This option lets you set the user bit, as discussed above. Each of the four positions can be set anywhere from 00 to FF, using the hexadecimal system.

TC Format

This option lets you select either DF (drop-frame) or NDF (non-drop-frame) format for the time code, assuming you are using time code and are using the NTSC video system with a Record Setting option other than 24p. (Drop-frame time code is not used for PAL video.)

This is a technical setting that you may need to use in order to make sure the time code you use is compatible with that of other cameras and with your editing facilities. Drop-frame time code is used because the NTSC standard of 30 frames per second does not record exactly 30 frames every second. For technical reasons, the actual rate is 29.97 frames per second. To count the frames accurately, video editors use the drop-frame system, which drops a few frames from the counting

process at specified intervals, so the actual number of frames is counted accurately.

You can leave this option set to DF if you are using the NTSC system, unless you know of a specific reason to use NDF.

TC Run

This option lets you choose either Rec Run or Free Run for the time code. With Rec Run, the time code increases only while the camera is actually recording. With Free Run, the time code continues to run all the time. Which system to choose is a matter of preference, depending on how you will use the time code for editing. With Rec Run, there should be no gaps in the time code, which can be an advantage. With Free Run, you can set up the time code to match the time of day, which can be useful if you need to find a clip that corresponds to a particular time during the day's video recording.

Free Run time code continues to run even when the camera is powered off. When you turn the camera on again and set it to Movie mode, the current time should be displaying in the lower left corner of the display, assuming you set the initial value for the time code to the current time.

TC Make

This setting is what you use to set the camera to record the time code option you have selected. The two choices are Preset or Regenerate. If you choose Preset, the camera starts recording time code using the value you entered for TC Preset, discussed earlier. If you choose Regenerate, the camera starts the time code recording based on the last value recorded previously.

UB Time Record

This last option, found on the second screen of the TC/UB Settings menu item, lets you choose whether or not to set the user bit option to display and record the time of day instead of a user bit formula that you set yourself. If you select On for this option and set the TC/UB Display Setting option to U-Bit, the camera will display the current time in the lower left corner of the screen as the video is recorded, as shown in Figure 8-19. The display shows the hour (in the 24-hour format), minute, and second; the last set of digits is left at zeroes. In this case, the time was 56 seconds after 9:43 a.m.

Figure 8-19. Time Displayed on Screen with UB Time Record Option

Screen 4 of the Setup menu is shown in Figure 8-20.

Figure 8-20. Screen 4 of Setup Menu

IR REMOTE CONTROL

This first option on screen 4 of the Setup menu enables operation of the a6400 with a Sony infrared remote control device, which communicates with the camera through the small window in the top area of the grip on the front of the camera. The two devices that Sony says are compatible are the RMT-DSLR1 and the RMT-DSLR2, which are discussed in Appendix A. This option cannot be used if the Bluetooth Remote Control option is turned on through screen 2 of the Network menu. When this option is turned on, the camera will not shut down through the setting of the Power Save Start Time option on screen 2 of the Setup menu.

HDMI SETTINGS

The HDMI Settings menu option has six sub-options on its single screen.

HDMI Resolution

The HDMI Resolution option can be set to Auto, 2160p/1080p, 1080p, or 1080i. This setting controls how the camera displays images and videos on an HDTV in playback mode. Ordinarily, the Auto setting

will work best; the camera will set itself for the optimum display according to the resolution of the HDTV it is connected to. If you experience difficulties with that connection, you may be able to improve the image on the HDTV's screen by trying one of the other settings. The 2160p/1080p setting is designed for connection to 4K-capable TV sets, which often have a resolution of 3840 x 2160 pixels.

24p/60p Output

This menu option is present only on cameras sold in NTSC areas. It is labeled with a movie-film icon, meaning it is for use when the camera is set to Movie mode, and it has a specific, limited use. It is applicable only when you have recorded video with Record Setting set to 24p 50M, 24p 60M, or 24p 100M using the XAVC S HD File Format setting, and you have set the HDMI Resolution item, discussed above, to 1080p or 2160p/1080p.

If those conditions are met, that means you have some video footage recorded at 24 frames per second. That setting is slower than the standard NTSC setting of 30 frames per second, and produces what some people consider to be a more "cinematic" look for the footage.

When you send your 24p video footage out through an HDMI cable to an HDTV set, you may prefer to send it in a way that looks more like standard TV video, using the 60p setting. That is the function of this menu option. If the conditions described above are met, you can select 60p for the 24p/60p Output option, and your 24p footage will be sent out through the HDMI cable to the HDTV in a way that simulates 60p video.

This option also may be of use when you are sending this one variety of 24p video footage out through the HDMI cable to an external video recorder, if 60p footage is a better option for use by the recorder.

HDMI Information Display

This feature also controls the behavior of the camera when you connect it to an HDTV set or other external device using an optional micro HDMI cable. However, unlike the HDMI Resolution option discussed above, which controls what happens when the camera is in playback mode, playing your images and videos on an HDTV set, this menu option controls what happens in shooting mode when the HDMI connection is active.

If this menu option is set to On, which is the default setting, then, when the camera is connected to an

HDTV or external recorder in shooting mode, the screen of the external device displays exactly what you would see on the camera's display in that mode if the camera were not connected to the device, including icons and figures showing camera settings.

With the On setting, the HDTV acts as a large, external monitor for the a6400, and the screen of the a6400 itself is blank. I use this setting a great deal myself, because this is how I capture screen shots for this book. Once the camera is connected, I can capture all of the information and settings that appear on the shooting screens and menu screens of the camera, with a few exceptions for special settings that are not output through the HDMI port, such as the Zebra stripes.

If this menu option is set to Off, then, when the camera is connected to an HDTV or other external device in shooting mode, the external device's screen displays only the image that is being viewed by the camera, with no shooting information displayed at all. If you press the Display button, nothing will happen on the external screen; the view will not switch to another display with more information on it. However, at the same time, the camera's screen continues to display all of the shooting information it normally would, including the image and whatever information is chosen by presses of the Display button. You can even use the menu system on the camera while the external device is receiving the live image.

You might use the Off setting when you want to display images from the camera's shooting mode on a large HDTV screen, possibly at a wedding or other gathering, and not have the images cluttered or marred by any shooting information at all. For example, a camera may focus on an unsuspecting person in the audience at the event, and that person's image suddenly appears on the large screen for everyone to see.

Also, this option is useful for video production when you need to output a "clean" video signal that does not include any shooting information from the camera. That signal can be sent through an HDMI cable to a video recorder for recording to another medium, or for display on a large monitor being viewed by the production team. For example, you can record video directly from the camera to a computer by outputting the clean HDMI signal to a device such as the Intensity Pro by Blackmagic Design. There are similar devices available from companies such as AverMedia,

Hauppage, and Elgato. You also can send the clean signal to an external 4K video recorder such as the Atomos Shogun, as I will discuss in Chapter 9.

With the On setting, you can press the Display button to show a screen with very minimal shooting information, but that screen still shows the basic information of aperture, shutter speed, exposure compensation, and ISO value at the very bottom of the screen. If you don't want even that minimal level of information to interfere with the video display, choose the Off setting.

This setting does not change the behavior of the camera for playback of images; its only effect is on the display of information in shooting mode through an HDMI connection.

TC Output

This option works together with the TC/UB Settings option discussed earlier. If you have set up the camera to record time code, you can use this option to have the time code output through the HDMI cable to an external recorder, so the time code will be available in the recorded footage for use in editing. The choices are On or Off.

Rec Control

This next sub-option for HDMI Settings is another one that applies only when recording to an external device by sending a clean signal through the HDMI cable. In this case, the option controls whether the camera sends a start-recording or stop-recording signal through the cable. If you turn this option on, you can control the external recorder using the camera's controls, if the external recorder is compatible with this camera.

For example, you can connect the Atomos Shogun 4K recorder with an HDMI cable and control the recorder's starting and stopping using the camera's Movie button, if the Rec Control option is turned on. (You also can use the shutter button to control movie recording, if the Movie w/Shutter option is turned on through screen 3 of the Camera Settings2 menu.) The Rec Control option can be turned on only if the TC Output option, discussed above, also is turned on.

CTRL for HDMI

This final sub-option is of use only when you have connected the camera to an HDTV and you want to control the camera with the TV's remote control, which is possible in some situations. If you want to do that, set this option to On and follow the instructions for the TV and its remote control. This option is intended to be used when you connect the camera to a Sony Bravia model HDTV.

4K OUTPUT SELECT

This next option on the Setup menu is for use only when the camera is connected to a 4K-capable external video recorder, such as the Atomos Shogun. Unless that connection is active, this option will be dimmed and unavailable for selection. Once the connection to the external recorder is made, the following sub-options are available:

Memory Card + HDMI

With this option, the camera will record video to the memory card in the camera and also output the signal to the external recorder through the HDMI cable. This option gives you an immediate backup copy of your footage.

HDMI Only (30p)

With this option, the camera sends a 4K video signal in 30p format to the external recorder but does not record the video to the camera's memory card. This option lets you record 4K video without having a memory card that meets the specifications for that format, and, in fact, it lets you record with no memory card in the camera at all.

If you choose this option or the next one, for 4K/24p video with no card in the camera, the File Format and Record Setting items on the Camera Settings2 menu become unavailable, because the recording format has already been selected by choosing this option or the next one.

I tested this option with the a6400 connected by an HDMI cable to an Atomos Shogun external 4K recorder. The camera sent a clean 4K signal through the HDMI cable and the Shogun recorded the video with no problems. If you turn on the Rec Control menu option on the camera, you can control the operation of the Shogun recorder by pressing the Movie button on the camera to start and stop the recording.

HDMI Only (24p)

This option is the same as the previous one, apart from the use of the 24p frame rate instead of 30p.

HDMI Only (25p)

This setting is available only when the NTSC/PAL Selector option is set to PAL.

USB CONNECTION

This option sets the technical standard that the camera uses for connecting to a computer using the USB cable. This menu item has four choices, as shown in Figure 8-21: Auto; Mass Storage; MTP, which stands for Media Transfer Protocol; and PC Remote.

Figure 8-21. USB Connection Menu Options Screen

You ordinarily should select Auto, and the a6400 should detect which standard is used by the computer you are connecting the camera to. If the camera does not automatically select a standard and start transferring images, you can try one of the other settings to see if it works better than the Auto setting.

The fourth setting, PC Remote, adds an important function to the camera. If you select this option, you can then connect ("tether") the camera to a computer with the camera's USB cable, and control the camera from the computer using Sony's Imaging Edge software. Imaging Edge can be downloaded at no charge from http://support.d-imaging.sony.co.jp/app/imagingedge/en/download/. Imaging Edge comes as part of a software suite that includes image viewing and editing in addition to remote control of the camera. You use the Remote module of the software for remote control through tethering.

Figure 8-22. Remote Window on Computer when Tethered

comes with the camera), and turn the camera on. Then start the software application. You will see on the computer a window like that in Figure 8-22, showing the various items you can control from the computer. The view on the computer may also include a large window at the left with a live view of the subject, but I have cropped that out of Figure 8-22 so I can show the remote control icons at a legible size.

You will have to turn the camera's mode dial to select the shooting mode, but you can control quite a few items from the software, depending on what mode is selected. These include Drive Mode, including all settings for continuous shooting, bracketing, and the self-timer; White Balance; Picture Effect; DRO/Auto HDR; Quality; Image Size; and Aspect Ratio.

You can set autoexposure lock by clicking on the AEL icon near the top of the window. To control exposure compensation, click on the arrows next to the exposure compensation value, below the EV label. The same technique works for flash exposure compensation to the right of exposure compensation. You also can control ISO by clicking on the arrows next to the ISO reading.

When the mode dial is set to Shutter Priority or Manual exposure, you can control the shutter speed by clicking on the arrows next to that setting. When Aperture Priority or Manual exposure mode is selected, you can control the aperture from this software. You can click on the button with the AF label in the upper left of the window to simulate a half-press of the shutter button, locking focus and exposure, if autofocus is in effect.

Click on the red button at the top of the window to start or stop a video recording. Click on the camera icon to the left of that button to capture a still image. Click and hold down on the camera icon to fire a burst of shots when continuous shooting is selected for Drive Mode. You also can make focus-related settings and control several menu options using other icons on the screen.

If you want to use this tethered-shooting capability to save images to your computer, use the Save In . . . dialog box at the bottom of the remote control window and select a folder; the images captured using this feature will be stored in that folder. You can set the camera to store images only to the computer, or to both the computer and the camera, using the PC Remote Settings option on screen 5 of the Setup menu. That option also lets you set the storage destinations for files taken with

Once the remote control software is installed on your computer, set this menu option to PC Remote, connect the camera to the computer with the Sony micro USB cable (or, preferably, a longer cable than the one that the Raw & JPEG setting for File Format.

If you click on the small button with a timer dial, to the right of the red video recording button, a new window will open up with options for interval shooting. In that window, you can set the interval between shots to a value from ten seconds to 180 minutes and the number of shots from two to 1000, or leave the number of shots unspecified.

The program also gives you the option of setting up interval shooting on the camera. In that case, you can select interval-shooting options using the camera's menu system, and activate the shooting session remotely by pressing the camera icon in the remote window. Interval shooting cannot be started if there are any files currently saved in the destination folder designated in the remote window. If interval shooting will not start, be sure all files have been deleted or moved out of that folder, or designate a new folder with no files in it. For further information about remote shooting, see http://support.d-imaging.sony.co.jp/app/imagingedge/en/instruction/4_5_remote.php.

USB LUN SETTING

This next item on screen 4 of the Setup menu is a technical option that should not often be needed. LUN stands for logical unit number. This item has two possible settings—Multi or Single. Ordinarily, it should be set to Multi, the default. In particular, it should be set to Multi when the a6400 is connected to a Windows-based computer and you are using Sony's PlayMemories Home software to manage images. If you have a problem with a USB connection to a computer, you can try the Single setting to see if it solves the problem.

USB POWER SUPPLY

The USB Power Supply option, which can be turned either on or off, controls whether or not the camera's battery will be charged or the camera will be powered through the USB cable when the camera is connected by its USB cable to a computer.

If you use the AC adapter provided with the camera or an external USB power source, as discussed in Appendix A, to provide power to the camera, you do not need to have this menu option turned on. When the USB cable is connected to an external power supply, power will be provided to the camera even with this option turned off.

Turning this option on gives you another avenue for keeping the a6400's battery charged. The only problem is that if your computer is running on its battery, then that battery will be discharged more rapidly than usual. If you are connecting the camera to a computer that is plugged into a wall power outlet, there should be no problem in using this option.

As I will discuss in Appendix A, it's a good idea to get an external battery charger and at least one extra battery for the a6400 because even if you can charge the battery in the camera using the USB cable, you don't have the ability to insert a fully charged battery into the camera when the first battery is exhausted.

I recommend leaving this option at its default setting of On, unless you will be connecting the camera to a battery-powered computer or other device and you don't want to run down the battery on that device.

Screen 5 of the Setup menu is shown in Figure 8-23.

Figure 8-23. Screen 5 of Setup Menu

PC REMOTE SETTINGS

This option provides a couple of ways to control how the camera saves images when you set it up for tethered shooting by connecting it to a computer using a micro USB cable. (Tethered shooting is discussed above in this chapter, under the USB Connection menu option.)

The two sub-options are Still Image Save Destination and Raw+JPEG PC Save Image, as shown in Figure 8-24. The Still Image Save Destination sub-option has two choices: PC Only or PC+Camera. If you choose PC Only, the images you capture during tethered shooting are saved only to the computer that the camera is connected to. If you choose PC + Camera, the images are saved to both the computer and the memory card in the camera. With this setting, you have to have a suitable memory card in the camera, or else the camera will not release the shutter, even if the Release w/o Card menu option is set to Enable on screen 4 of the Camera Settings2 menu.

Figure 8-24. PC Remote Settings Menu Options Screen

The setting you choose for this option depends on your workflow. If you can see the computer's screen while you operate the camera, you may not need to save the images to a card in the camera. However, if that screen is not readily visible, you may want to have the images saved to a card in the camera so you can view them on the camera's LCD screen as they are captured.

The other sub-option for PC Remote Settings, Raw+JPEG PC Save Image, is available for selection only when the Quality option on screen 1 of the Camera Settings1 menu is set to Raw & JPEG. In that case, you can use this sub-option to decide whether, during tethered shooting, the camera sends both the Raw and JPEG images to the computer, just the Raw image, or just the JPEG image. You might want to limit which versions are transferred in order to speed up the transfer of images to the computer, because they cannot be viewed on the computer's screen until they have been transferred.

LANGUAGE

This option gives you the choice of language for information on the camera's menus and display screens. Once you have selected this menu item, scroll through the language choices using the control wheel or the direction buttons and press the Center button when your chosen language is highlighted.

DATE/TIME SETUP

I discussed this item in Chapter 1. When the camera is new or has not been used for a long time, it will prompt you to set the date and time and will display this menu option. If you want to call up these settings on your own, you can do so at any time.

When you press the Center button on this menu line, you will see a screen like that in Figure 8-25, which gives you the choice of adjusting Daylight Savings Time (On or Off), Date/Time, or Date Format. To adjust Date/Time, select that option and press the Center button. The camera will display a screen like that shown in Figure 8-26.

Figure 8-25. Date/Time Setup Menu Options Screen

Figure 8-26. Date and Time Settings Screen

Scroll through the options for setting month, day, year, and time by turning the control wheel or pressing the Left and Right buttons. As you reach each item, adjust its value by using the Up and Down buttons or by turning the control dial. When all of the settings are correct, press the Center button to confirm them and exit from this screen.

You can also go back to the first menu screen and turn Daylight Savings Time on or off depending on the time of year, and you can choose a date format according to your preference.

AREA SETTING

The next option on screen 5 of the Setup menu, Area Setting, lets you select your current location so you can adjust the date and time for a different time zone when you are traveling. When you highlight this item and press the Center button, the camera displays the map shown in Figure 8-27.

Figure 8-27. **Area Setting Map Screen**

Turn the control wheel or press the Left and Right buttons to move the light-colored highlight over the map until it covers the area of your current location, then press the Center button. The date and time will be adjusted for that location until you change the location again using this menu item. You also can press the Up or Down button or turn the control dial when this screen is displayed to turn the Daylight Savings Time setting on or off.

COPYRIGHT INFO

This next item on screen 5 of the Setup menu gives you a way to add information about the photographer and copyright holder to the metadata for images taken with the camera.

The first sub-option, Write Copyright Info, determines whether the copyright information entered for this item will be written to still images that you take. If you turn this option on, then the copyright information (names of photographer and copyright holder) will be added to the metadata for any still images captured after the option is turned on. The information will not appear on the images themselves, but can be read by any program that reads EXIF data for images, such as Adobe Bridge.

The second option, Set Photographer, lets you enter the name of the photographer. When you select this option, you will see a screen with a window for entering the name. Press the Center button when the window is highlighted and you will see the data-entry screen. Use that screen to enter any name you want. Use the control wheel and the control dial or the direction buttons to move the orange highlight bar to the first block on the left under the name window. When that

block is highlighted, press the Center button to toggle between letters, numbers and symbols. Then move the highlight bar to the block for the letter you want. Move to the up arrow to shift to uppercase letters. Press the Center button repeatedly to choose the letter you want from each group of letters.

For example, to type the letter "e," move the highlight bar to the "def" block and press the Center button quickly two times to select e. After a second or two, the blinking white cursor will move to the right, and you can repeat this process. You can move the cursor forward or back using the left and right arrows at the upper right in the blocks of characters.

When you have finished entering the name, highlight OK and press the Center button to accept the name.

The third option, Set Copyright, lets you set the name of the company or person who holds the copyright for the images to be taken with the camera.

Finally, the Display Copyright Info option lets you see what names are currently entered in the camera for these items.

FORMAT

The last option on the fifth screen—Format—is an important one. This command is used to prepare a new memory card with the appropriate data structure to store images and videos. The Format command also is useful when you want to wipe all the data off a card that has become full or when you have copied a card's images to your computer or other device. Choose this process only when you want or need to completely wipe all of the data from a memory card.

Figure 8-28. **Format Confirmation Screen**

When you select the Format option, as shown in Figure 8-28, the camera will warn you that all data currently on the card will be deleted if you proceed. If you reply by highlighting Enter and pressing the Center button to confirm, the camera will format the card that is in the camera and the result will be a card that is empty and properly formatted to store new images and videos recorded by the camera.

With this procedure, the camera will erase all images, including those that have been protected from accidental erasure with the Protect function on the Playback menu.

It's a good idea to periodically save your images and videos to your computer or other device and re-format your memory card to keep it properly set up for recording new images and videos. It's also a good idea to use the Format command on any new memory card when you first insert it into the camera. Even though it likely will work without that procedure, it's best to make sure the card is set up with Sony's method of formatting for the a6400.

Screen 6 of the Setup menu is shown in Figure 8-29.

Figure 8-29. Screen 6 of Setup Menu

FILE NUMBER

This option controls the way the camera assigns numbers to your images and videos. There are two choices: Series and Reset, as shown in Figure 8-30.

Figure 8-30. File Number Menu Options Screen

With Series, the camera continues numbering where it left off, even if you put a new memory card in the camera. For example, if you have 112 images on your first memory card, the last image likely will be numbered 100-0112: 100 for the folder number and 0112 for the image number.

If you then switch to a new memory card with no images on it, the first image on that card will be numbered 100-0113 because the numbering scheme continues in the same sequence. If you choose Reset instead, the first image on the new card will be numbered 100-0001 because the camera resets the numbering to the first number.

SET FILE NAME

This menu option lets you specify the first three characters for file names of your images. By default, those characters are DSC, so a typical image might be DSC00150.jpg. You can choose any other characters by using the data-entry screen for this option, shown in Figure 8-31. Those three characters will then appear at the beginning of the file name for any images captured after you change this setting, if the images use the sRGB color space. If the images use the Adobe RGB color space, the camera will add an underscore character before the file name, as shown in Figure 8-31.

Figure 8-31. Set File Name Menu Options Screen

SELECT REC FOLDER

When you select this item, the camera displays an orange bar with the name of the current folder, as shown in Figure 8-32. You can use the Up and Down buttons or turn the control wheel to scroll to the name of another folder if one exists, so you can store future images and videos in that folder. It might be worthwhile to use this function if you are taking photos or movies for different purposes during the same outing.

Figure 8-32. Select REC Folder Menu Options Screen

For example, if you are taking some photos for business and some for pleasure, you can create a new folder for the business-related shots (see the next menu item, below). The camera will then use that folder. Afterward, you can use the Select REC Folder option to select the folder where your personal images are stored and take more personal images that will be stored in that folder. This menu option is dimmed and unavailable for selection if Folder Name, discussed below, is set to Date Form.

NEW FOLDER

This menu item lets you create a new folder on your memory card for storing images and videos. Highlight this item on the menu screen and press the Center button; you will then see a message announcing that a new folder has been created, as shown in Figure 8-33.

Figure 8-33. New Folder Creation Message Screen

Creating a new folder can be a good way to organize images and videos from a particular shooting session. If you are going to view and process the files on your computer, it can be useful to have images from different locations arranged in different folders, for example.

FOLDER NAME

This menu option gives you a choice of two methods for naming the folders used for storing still images on

your memory card, as shown in Figure 8-34: Standard Form or Date Form. The Standard Form option uses the folder number, such as 100, 101, or higher, followed by the letters MSDCF. An example is 100MSDCF. If you choose Date Form, folder names will have the same 100 or higher number followed by the date, in a form such as 10091028 for a folder created on October 28, 2019, using only one digit to designate the year.

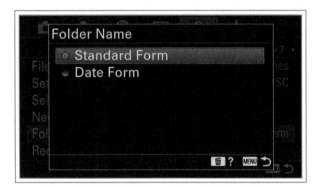

Figure 8-34. Folder Name Menu Options Screen

I find the date format confusing and hard to read, and I am used to the MSDCF format. If you use the date format, you will end up having a folder for every date on which you record still images. You may prefer having your image folders organized in that way so you can quickly locate images from a particular date. I prefer having fewer folders and organizing images on my computer according to my own preferences.

RECOVER IMAGE DATABASE

This menu item activates the Recover Image Database function. If you select this option and press the Center button to confirm it on the next screen, as shown in Figure 8-35, the camera runs a check to test the integrity of the file system on the memory card. I have never used this menu option, but if the camera is having difficulty reading the images on a card, using this option might recover the data.

Figure 8-35. Recover Image Database Confirmation Screen

Screen 7 of the Setup menu is shown in Figure 8-36.

Figure 8-36. Screen 7 of Setup Menu

DISPLAY MEDIA INFORMATION

This first item on the final Setup menu screen gives you another way to see how much storage space is remaining on the memory card that is currently in the camera. When you select Display Media Info and press the Center button, the camera displays a screen like that in Figure 8-37, with information about the number of still images and the hours and minutes of video that can be recorded using the current settings for File Format, JPEG Image Size, JPEG Quality, and video format. If the mode dial is at the Movie or S & Q position, the Still Images line will not include a number, because still images cannot be captured in those shooting modes.

Figure 8-37. Display Media Info Screen

It is nice to have this option available, although the number of images that can be recorded is also displayed on the detailed shooting screen, and the available video recording time appears on the video recording screen once a recording has been started or when the mode dial is at the Movie or S &Q position.

VERSION

This option tells you the current version of the firmware in your camera. The a6400, like other cameras, is

programmed at the factory with firmware, which is a set of electronically implanted computer instructions. These instructions control all aspects of the camera's operation, including the menu system, functioning of the controls, and in-camera image processing.

You may want to see what version is installed because the manufacturer may release an updated version of the firmware to fix problems or bugs in the system, provide minor enhancements, or, in some cases, provide major improvements, such as adding new shooting modes or menu options.

In fact, Sony released a significant firmware upgrade for the a6400 in June 2019. That upgrade, version 2.00, added real-time Eye AF for detecting the eyes of pets such as dogs and cats; added support for the RMT-P1BT wireless remote device; and "improve[d] the overall stability of the camera." This upgrade is definitely worth getting if you don't already have this version installed in your camera.

To determine the firmware version installed in your camera, highlight this menu option, then press the Center button, and the camera will display the version number, as shown in Figure 8-38. As you can see, my camera had Version 2.00 installed when this image was captured.

Figure 8-38. Version Screen

To see if firmware upgrades have been released, I recommend you visit Sony's support website, whose Internet address is http://esupport.sony.com. Enter the model name, which is ILCE-6400, and find the link for Downloads. The site will provide instructions for downloading and installing the new firmware.

SETTING RESET

This final option on the Setup menu is useful when you want to reset some or all of the camera's settings to their original (default, or factory) values. This action can be helpful if you have been experimenting with different settings and you find that something is not working as expected.

When you select this item, the camera displays two choices: Camera Settings Reset and Initialize, as shown in Figure 8-39.

Figure 8-39. Setting Reset Menu Options Screen

With Initialize, the camera resets all major settings to their original values and deletes registered data, such as faces. With Camera Settings Reset, only the values that affect shooting of images and videos are reset.

My Menu

Another menu system for the a6400, marked by a star icon at the far right of the main menu screen, is the My Menu system. This menu does not contain any options of its own, other than options for adding and organizing items from other menu systems. My Menu is a blank system that is provided for you to add your most-used options from the main menu systems, for quick access.

You can include up to 30 items from any of the menus except the Playback menu. You also cannot add the View on TV item from the Network menu. That leaves a large number of useful options that can be selected from the Camera Settings1, Camera Settings2, Network, and Setup menus.

To add an item, first, navigate to the screen shown in Figure 8-40, with choices for adding, sorting, and deleting menu items. If no items have been added to My Menu yet, this will be the only screen available. If items have been added, you may have to navigate to a higher-numbered screen. The highest-numbered screen is the one where you can add, sort, and delete items.

You will see numbers in the upper right corner, such as 2/4, 4/4, or 2/2, as shown in Figure 8-40. Those numbers indicate which screen is being displayed out of the total number of screens available.

Figure 8-40. My Menu Screen to Add, Sort, Delete Items

Once you have reached the screen shown in Figure 8-40, highlight and select Add Item. The camera will display a screen like that shown in Figure 8-41, which is one of 32 screens of menu options you can choose from to add to your personalized menus. Scroll through these screens by a full screen at a time using the Left and Right buttons or the control dial; scroll through the items on a given screen using the Up and Down buttons or the control wheel.

Figure 8-41. One of Screens of Items that Can Be Added to My Menu

When you have highlighted a menu item you want to add to My Menu, press the Center button to select it. The camera will then prompt you to select a location for the selected item. For the first item you add, there is only one location possible. For later selections, you will see an orange line, as shown in Figure 8-42. Position the orange line below an item that is already added to the My Menu items, and the new item will be added in that location, below that existing item. When you have finished adding items, press the Menu button to return to the My Menu screen. From there you can navigate to another menu system or press the Menu button again to return to the shooting screen.

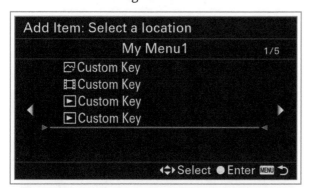

Figure 8-42. Orange Line Marking Location of Item to Add

After you have added all of the items you have chosen for My Menu, you can later move them around to get the most convenient arrangement. To move an item, while My Menu is displayed, press the Right button enough times to get to the last screen of My Menu, which holds the options for managing the menu.

Choose Sort Item from the My Menu screen. Then navigate to the item to move and select it by pressing the Center button. You can then move it to the new location you select. You also can delete an item, a whole page of items, or all items, by using the Delete Item, Delete Page, or Delete All option. Figure 8-43 shows the My Menu screen after several items have been added.

Figure 8-43. My Menu with Several Items Added

CHAPTER 9: MOTION PICTURES

Movie-Making Overview

In one sense, the basics of making movies with the a6400 can be stated in four words: "Push the red button." (That is, the red Movie button at the right edge of the camera's back.) In most situations, you can press and release that button while aiming at your subject, and get results that are quite usable. You do not need to worry about special settings, particularly if you set the camera to one of the more automatic modes, such as Auto or Scene. (You can record a normal-speed movie with the mode dial at any position except S & Q Motion, as discussed later in this chapter.)

To stop recording, press the red button again. If you prefer not to run the risk of recording unwanted movies by pressing the Movie button accidentally, you can change the button's operation so it activates movie recording only when the camera is in Movie or S & Q Motion mode, as discussed in Chapter 5.

If you're mainly a still photographer with little interest in movie making, you don't need to read further. Be aware that the red button exists, and if an interesting event starts to happen, you can turn the mode dial to Auto, press the Movie button, and capture footage to post on YouTube or elsewhere with a minimum of effort. But for those a6400 users who want to use this camera's strong motion picture capabilities, there is more information to discuss.

First, there is a requirement that may decide what memory card you get for your camera. To record movies using the high-quality XAVC S 4K or XAVC S HD format, you have to use an SDHC or SDXC memory card with a speed of at least Class 10 or UHS Speed Class 1. (You also can use a Sony Memory Stick PRO-HG Duo.) If you want to record XAVC S 4K or XAVC S HD video using a Record Setting value of 100M, meaning 100 megabits per second, you have to use an SDHC or SDXC card rated in UHS Speed Class 3.

These are not just recommendations. If you do not use a card with the listed specifications, the camera will display an error message and will not record video using the format in question. (As I will discuss later in this chapter, 4K is a designation for video files that have higher resolution than high-definition video.)

Figure 9-1. SD Cards Rated in UHS Speed Class 3

I have used the SD cards shown in Figure 9-1, all of which are rated in UHS Speed Class 3, for recording the highest-level formats on the a6400 with no problems, and there are other choices available.

Of course, if you are not going to use the highest-level formats, you can use a less-powerful card. And, as I'll discuss later in this chapter, you can actually record 4K video with no card at all, if you connect the a6400 to an external video recorder.

The a6400, unlike many smaller cameras, does not have a built-in limitation on recording time. However, the camera can overheat, causing it to shut down, if you record high-quality video, such as 4K files, for an extended period of time. You should be able to record for more than 30 minutes in one session, in most cases.

If you plan on recording a large amount of HD video, you should get a high-capacity and high-speed card. For example, a 64 GB card can hold about 75 minutes of the highest quality of 4K video, or about 8 hours and 15 minutes of the lowest-quality AVCHD video. (I will discuss these video formats later in this chapter.)

Details of Settings for Shooting Movies

As I noted above, the one necessary step for recording a movie with the a6400 is to press the Movie button. However, there are numerous settings that affect the way the camera records a movie when that button is pressed.

I will discuss four categories of settings: (1) movie-related options on the Camera Settings2 menu; (2) the position of the mode dial on top of the camera; (3) options on the Camera Settings1 menu and other menus; and (4) settings made with the camera's physical controls.

MOVIE-RELATED MENU OPTIONS

First, I will discuss the movie-related options on the Camera Settings2 menu, because those options control the format and several other settings for movies you record with the a6400. I discussed this menu in Chapter 5, but I did not provide details about all of the movie-oriented options in that chapter.

As noted above, you can press the Movie button to start a normal-speed video recording at any time and in any shooting mode (except for S & Q Motion), as long as the Movie Button option on screen 9 of the Camera Settings2 menu is set to Always. Because of this ability to shoot movies in almost any shooting mode, you can always change the settings for movie recording using the Camera Settings2 menu, no matter what shooting mode the camera is set to. I will discuss each item on the Camera Settings2 menu that has an effect on your shooting of videos.

At this point, I will discuss the Camera Settings2 menu options that apply only to movies; later in this chapter, I will discuss options on other menus that affect movies as well as still images, such as White Balance, ISO, Creative Style, Picture Effect, Picture Profile, and others.

Exposure Mode (Movies)

This menu item, the first option on screen 1 of the Camera Settings2 menu, can be selected only when the camera's mode dial is set to Movie mode, as shown in Figure 9-2. In other shooting modes, this menu option is dimmed and unavailable.

Figure 9-2. Mode Dial at Movie Position

When the camera is in Movie mode, this option lets you select an exposure mode for shooting movies. If you have the Mode Dial Guide option turned on through screen 2 of the Setup menu, you won't need to use the Exposure Mode option when you first select the Movie mode. When you turn the mode dial to the Movie position and then press the Center button, the screen with choices for the Exposure Mode item will appear automatically. If the Mode Dial Guide option is not active or if the mode dial is already set to Movie mode, you get to this screen by selecting Exposure Mode from the Camera Settings2 menu.

Figure 9-3. Exposure Mode (Movies) Menu Options Screen

With the mode dial set to Movie mode, highlight and select this menu option and a screen will appear with four options: Program Auto, Aperture Priority, Shutter Priority, and Manual Exposure, as shown in Figure 9-3. Move through these choices by turning the control wheel or control dial, or by pressing the Up and Down buttons.

You also can call up this screen of options by assigning Shoot Mode to the Function menu using the Function Menu Settings option on screen 8 of the Camera Settings2 menu. If you do that, then, with the mode dial set to Movie, you can press the Function button to activate the Function menu, scroll to the Shoot Mode item, and select your choice of movie exposure mode. (The Shoot Mode item will be labeled Exposure Mode in the Function menu when the mode dial is at the Movie position.)

Following are details about the behavior of the a6400 when shooting movies with each of these settings.

Program Auto

With the Program Auto setting, which is highlighted in Figure 9-3, the a6400 sets aperture and shutter speed according to its metering, and it uses settings from the Camera Settings1 menu that carry over to video recording, including ISO, White Balance, Metering Mode, Face/Eye AF Settings, and DRO.

In this mode, the camera can use a shutter speed as fast as 1/4000 second. The camera will normally not use a shutter speed slower than 1/25 second, 1/30 second, 1/50 second, 1/60 second, or 1/125 second, depending on the settings for File Format and Record Setting. It can use a slightly slower speed if you turn on the Auto Slow Shutter option, discussed later in this chapter.

Aperture Priority

With the Aperture Priority setting, highlighted on the menu in Figure 9-4, you set the aperture, just as in the similar mode for still images, and the camera will set the shutter speed based on its metering. As with the Program Auto exposure mode for movies, discussed above, the camera will not use shutter speeds slower than those listed for that mode, unless you turn on the Auto Slow Shutter menu option.

Figure 9-4. Aperture Priority Highlighted for Exposure Mode

With this setting, you can adjust the aperture during a video recording. This may not be something you need to do often, but it can be useful in some situations. For example, you may be recording at a garden show, and at some point you may want to open the aperture wide to blur the background as you focus on a small plant. Afterward, you may want to close the aperture down to

a narrow value to achieve a broad depth of field to keep a large area in focus.

Also, you can use the aperture setting to accomplish an in-camera fadeout. For example, in normal indoor conditions, if you are using a lens with a fairly wide maximum aperture, you may start with the aperture set to f/2.8 and ISO set to 640, with Auto Slow Shutter turned off. Press the Movie button to start recording. When you're ready, adjust the aperture value smoothly to the f/16.0 setting. You should get a nice fade to black. In brighter conditions, you may need to reduce ISO to its minimum setting for movies, which is 100.

Shutter Priority

With the Shutter Priority mode for movies, shown in Figure 9-5, you set the shutter speed, and the camera will set the aperture.

Figure 9-5. Shutter Priority Highlighted for Exposure Mode

Unlike the situation with the Aperture Priority exposure mode for movies, in which the camera normally will not set the shutter speed slower than 1/25 second (or a higher value for some formats), you are able to set the shutter speed as slow as 1/4 second in this mode in most cases, even if Auto Slow Shutter is turned off. (If Record Setting is set to 120p for XAVC S HD video, the slowest shutter speed available is 1/125 second.) You can select a shutter speed from 1/4 second to 1/4000 second.

To expose your video normally at a shutter speed of 1/4000 second or other fast settings, you must have bright lighting, a high ISO setting, or both. Using a fast shutter speed for video can yield a crisper appearance, especially when there is considerable movement, as when shooting sports or other fast-moving events. In addition, having these very fast shutter speeds gives the camera flexibility for achieving a normal exposure when recording video in bright conditions.

With slower shutter speeds, particularly below the normal video speed of 1/30 second (equivalent to 30 fps), footage can become blurry with the appearance of smearing, especially with panning motions. If you are shooting a scene in which you want to have a drifting, dreamy appearance that looks like motion underwater, this option may be appropriate. You will not be able to achieve good lip sync at the slower shutter speeds, so this technique would not work well for realistic recordings of people talking or singing.

One interesting point is that you can preview this effect on the camera's display even before you press the Movie button to start recording. If you have the shutter speed set to 1/4 second in Movie mode, you will see any action on the screen looking blurry and jerky as if it had already been recorded with this slow shutter speed. (The Live View Display option on screen 7 of the Camera Settings2 menu is forced to the Setting Effect On option in Movie mode, and you cannot change it.)

With the Shutter Priority exposure mode for movies, you also can achieve a fadeout effect, as with Aperture Priority mode, discussed above. Just turn the control dial or wheel smoothly to increase the shutter speed to its fastest speed of 1/4000 second, and the scene may go black, depending on the lighting conditions. You may need to use a low ISO setting to achieve full darkness.

Manual Exposure

The last setting for the Exposure Mode item, shown in Figure 9-6, Manual Exposure, gives you more complete control over the exposure of your videos.

Figure 9-6. Manual Exposure Highlighted for Exposure Mode

As with Manual exposure mode for stills, with this setting you can adjust both the aperture and the shutter speed to achieve a desired effect. With video shooting, you can adjust the shutter speed from 1/4000 second to 1/4 second. (If Record Setting is set to 120p for XAVC S

HD video, the slowest shutter speed available is 1/125 second.) Using these settings, you can create effects such as fades to and from black as well as similar fades to and from white.

For example, if you begin a recording in normal indoor lighting using settings of 1/60 second at f/3.5 with ISO set to 800, you can start recording the scene, and, when you want to fade out, start turning the control wheel slowly, increasing the shutter speed smoothly until it reaches 1/4000 second. Depending on how bright the lighting is, the result may be complete blackness. Of course, you can reverse this process to fade in from black.

If you want to fade to white, here is one possible scenario. Suppose you are recording video with shutter speed set to 1/400 second and aperture set to f/3.5 at ISO 6400. When you want to start a fade to white, turn the control wheel smoothly until the shutter speed decreases all the way to 1/4 second. In fairly normal lighting conditions, as in my office as I write this, the result will be a fade to a bright white screen.

There are, of course, other uses for Manual Exposure mode when recording videos, such as shooting "day for night" footage, in which you underexpose the scene by using a fast shutter speed, narrow aperture, low ISO, or all three of those settings, to turn day into night for creative purposes. Also, you might want to use Manual Exposure mode when you are recording a scene in which the lighting may change, but you do not want the exposure to change. In other words, you may want some areas to remain dark and some to be unusually bright, rather than have the camera automatically adjust the exposure. In some cases, having a constant exposure setting can be preferable to having the scene's brightness change as the metering system adjusts the exposure.

Note that you can set ISO to Auto ISO with the Manual Exposure setting. With the Auto ISO setting, you can maintain a constant aperture and shutter speed, but the camera will adjust exposure using the ISO setting to the extent that it can. You might want to use that setup if you need to maintain a narrow aperture to have a broad depth of field.

Exposure Mode (S & Q)

This second option on screen 1 of the Camera Settings2 menu lets you select an exposure mode when the mode dial is at the S & Q position, for recording slow and quick motion video. I will discuss the process for that mode of recording later in this chapter.

File Format (Movies)

The third item on screen 1 of the Camera Settings2 menu, File Format, gives you a choice of the three available movie recording formats on the a6400—XAVC S 4K, XAVC S HD, and AVCHD, as shown in Figure 9-7. This setting determines the format the camera will use to record movies when you press the Movie button.

Figure 9-7. File Format Menu Options Screen

XAVC S 4K

The XAVC S format is a consumer version of the XAVC format, developed for use with 4K video recording, sometimes known as Ultra HD. The term "4K" refers to a horizontal resolution of roughly 4,000 pixels, instead of the 1920 pixels in standard HD video (sometimes called "2K" video). On the a6400, video recorded with the 4K format has a pixel count of 3840 x 2160. Because of its high resolution, this option provides excellent quality for your videos. To enjoy the full benefit of the format, you should view the videos on a TV set that is equipped for 4K viewing.

However, even without that type of TV, you can edit 4K videos with appropriate software, such as Adobe Premiere Pro, Sony Vegas Pro, and others. Sony provides a list of such programs at the following website: http://support.d-imaging.sony.co.jp/www/support/application/nle/en.html. In the editing process, you can downsample the 4K video clips to a standard HD format, such as 1920 x 1080 pixels, and they will have greater quality than videos originally recorded in an HD format.

As noted earlier, if you use this format, you have to use a memory card rated at least in Speed Class 10 or UHS Speed Class 1. If you use the highest-quality Record Setting option, the card must be rated in UHS Speed

Class 3.

However, as I will discuss later in this chapter, you can avoid this restriction if you connect the a6400 to an external video recorder, such as the Atomos Shogun, using an HDMI cable, and record to the Shogun recorder without recording to the camera's memory card. I'm not suggesting that that system is simple or inexpensive, but it is available if you need to use the a6400 for 4K video recording without having to use a particular type of memory card.

XAVC S HD

This second option for File Format uses the high-quality XAVC S format, but records using an HD resolution of 1920 x 1080 pixels rather than the higher 4K resolution. This option will give you excellent quality without requiring the use of a 4K-capable TV set. However, it carries with it the same requirement for a high-speed memory card as the 4K format.

AVCHD

If you don't want to purchase the high-speed memory card required for the XAVC S format but you still want very high quality for your movies, you can choose AVCHD. This format, developed jointly by Sony and Panasonic, has become increasingly common in advanced digital cameras.

Record Setting

The Record Setting item on screen 1 of the Camera Settings2 menu is another quality-related option for recording video. (The accent is on the second syllable of "Record.") The choices for this item are different depending on whether you choose XAVC S 4K, XAVC S HD, or AVCHD for File Format. I will discuss these options assuming you have your camera set for NTSC, the video standard used in the United States, using the NTSC/PAL Selector option on screen 2 of the Setup menu, as discussed in Chapter 8. If your camera is set for PAL, the choices for Record Setting will include numbers such as 50p and 25p instead of 60p, 30p, and 24p.

XAVC S 4K

If you choose XAVC S 4K for File Format, the four options for Record Setting are 30p 100M, 30p 60M, 24p 100M, and 24p 60M, as shown in Figure 9-8.

Figure 9-8. Record Setting Options for XAVC S 4K

Figure 9-9. Record Setting Options for XAVC S HD

For these choices, the letter "p" stands for progressive, which means the camera records 30 or 24 full video frames per second. (The other option, used with some AVCHD formats, as discussed below, is designated by the letter "i," standing for interlaced. With those options, such as 60i, the camera records 60 fields, or half-frames, per second, which yields lower quality and fewer possibilities for editing.)

The standard speed for recording video in the United States is 30 frames per second, and using either of the 30p settings will yield excellent quality.

If you select 24p 100M or 24p 60M, your video will be recorded and played back at 24 fps. The 24p rate is considered by some people to be more "cinematic" than the 30p format. This may be because 24 fps is a standard speed for movie cameras that shoot with film. My preference is to use the 30p format, but if you find that 24p suits your purposes better, you have that option with the a6400.

The 60M or 100M designation means that these formats record video with a bit rate up to a maximum of 60 or 100 megabits per second, which are high rates that yield excellent quality. As noted earlier, when you record using the 100M setting, you have to use a memory card rated in UHS Speed Class 3.

My recommendation for this setting is to use 30p 60M unless you have a definite need for the super-high quality of the 30p 100M setting.

XAVC S HD

If you choose XAVC S HD, the seven choices for Record Setting are 60p 50M, 60p 25M, 30p 50M, 30p 16M, 24p 50M, 120p 100M, and 120p 60M, as shown in Figure 9-9. (The last of these settings is not visible in this figure; you have to scroll down to see it.)

If you use a 60p or 120p option, the camera will record at two or four times the normal speed, and therefore will record two or four times as much video information as with the 30p choice. If you use one of those higher speeds, you will be able to produce a slow-motion version of your footage at very high quality. For example, 60p footage is recorded with twice the number of full frames as 30p footage, so the quality of the video does not suffer if it is played back at one-half speed.

If you think you may want to slow down your footage significantly for playback, you should choose the 60p setting, or, for even slower motion, the 120p setting.

Video taken with the 60p or 120p setting will play back at normal speed in the camera. To play it back in slow motion, you can use a program such as iMovie for the Mac or Movie Maker for Windows. Just set the playback speed to a factor such as 0.5x or 0.25x to play the footage at the slower speed.

The 24p option is not a substantially slower rate than the 60p format or the 120p format, because the video playback rate in the United States is 30 fps, and the 60p and 120p formats are converted to 30 fps for playback in the camera.

All of these options are recorded in full HD, meaning the pixel count for each video frame is 1920 x 1080. The 120p selections (100p for cameras using the PAL system) are not available with the Auto and Scene shooting modes. With either of the 120p options, the camera cannot use face detection, non-optical zoom, Touch Tracking, Proxy Recording, or Auto Slow Shutter.

Here again, as with the 4K settings, you have to use a memory card rated in UHS Speed Class 3 card if you use the 100M setting, and at least a Speed Class 10 or UHS Speed Class 1 card for the other settings.

AVCHD

If you choose AVCHD for File Format, the two choices for Record Setting are 60i 24M(FX) and 60i 17M(FH), as shown in Figure 9-10. Both of these are recorded with a pixel count of 1920 x 1080, which is full HD. As noted earlier, the letter "i" stands for interlaced. With 60i interlaced video, the camera records 60 fields per second; a field is equal to one-half of a frame, and the two halves are interlaced to form 30 full frames. The video frame rate of 30 frames per second (fps) is the standard video playback rate in the United States.

Figure 9-10. **Record Setting Options for AVCHD**

The 24M or 17M figure states the maximum "bit rate," or volume, of video information that is recorded—either 24 or 17 megabits per second. The higher rate provides greater quality at the cost of using more storage capacity on the memory card and requiring greater computer resources to edit. The final designations, FX and FH, are proprietary labels used by Sony for two qualities of video. They have no particular meanings; they are just labels for these levels of video quality.

Choose 60i 24M for excellent quality, or 60i 17M for excellent quality that takes up fewer resources.

S & Q Settings

This menu option lets you set up the camera for slow-motion or speeded-up video, which you can record when you turn the mode dial to the S & Q position, for slow and quick motion shooting. I will discuss these options later in this chapter, in a section on S & Q shooting.

Proxy Recording

This option is somewhat like a video version of the Raw & JPEG setting for still images. When it is turned on and File Format is set to XAVC S 4K or XAVC S HD, the camera also saves a copy of the video in a smaller file format (XAVC S HD, 1280 x 720 pixels, at 9 Mbps bit rate), giving you a second video file that is easier to edit and share through social media and other means.

Because the copy is equivalent to the original in terms of frame rate and other attributes, it also can be used as a proxy file in video editing software that uses proxy editing. With that system, you can edit the smaller proxy file easily without having to wait for the computer to process effects and handle large files that can strain the memory and processor. Then, at the final editing stage, you can substitute the original, larger file for the final rendering of the video.

Proxy recording is not available when File Format is set to AVCHD, or when Record Setting is set to 120p (100p with PAL systems).

I recommend leaving this option turned off unless you have a specific reason to use it.

AF Drive Speed

This option controls the speed at which the camera's autofocus system changes focus when recording video. The choices are Fast, Normal, or Slow. The Fast option is suitable for sports or other activities when the most important goal is to keep the subject in focus, and quick focus shifts are not a problem. The slower options are for use when you are shooting static or slow-moving subjects, and it may be preferable for focus to adjust gradually, to avoid jarring the audience with abrupt focus changes.

This option is particularly useful when you are using the touch screen features of the camera to carry out a "pull focus" action. As discussed in Chapter 6 in connection with the LCD screen, you can touch one spot on the screen, and then another, to shift the focus point, or you can drag the focus frame to a new location, depending on the Focus Area setting. The choice you make for AF Drive Speed will have a clear impact on the nature of the pull focus effect.

The setting you choose for this menu option depends on your preference and what you are trying to accomplish; you may want to experiment with all three and see which one suits your taste best for a given situation.

AF Tracking Sensitivity

This option, located after AF Drive Speed on the menu, controls how quickly the autofocus system tracks a moving subject when recording video. The choices are Responsive and Standard. With Responsive, the focus will shift quickly, to track a fast-moving subject. With Normal, the focus shifts at a moderate pace. With the Standard setting, there is less risk that the camera will shift focus when an unwanted subject comes between the camera and the actual subject.

For example, if a person walks in front of the camera while you are recording a scene in the distance, with the Standard setting the camera is likely to maintain focus on your actual subject, rather than quickly shifting focus to the person who is temporarily in the way. I recommend using the Standard setting unless you need to track a fast-moving subject, such as a runner in a track meet or a moving vehicle.

Auto Slow Shutter

This menu option can be set either on or off. When it is turned on and the a6400 is recording a movie with autoexposure, the camera will automatically use a slower shutter speed than normal if the lighting is too dim to achieve proper exposure otherwise. The details of this option depend on the setting for Record Setting on screen 1 of the Camera Settings2 menu. (The File Format setting does not matter; the rules stated here apply for all File Format settings.)

If Record Setting is at a 60p or 60i setting, the camera normally will not use a shutter speed slower than 1/60 second. (In order to record 60 fields or frames per second with good quality, a shutter speed of 1/60 second is needed.) If Auto Slow Shutter is on, the camera can use a shutter speed as slow as 1/30 second.

If Record Setting is at one of the 30p settings, the camera ordinarily will use a shutter speed no slower than 1/30 second, but it will go down to 1/15 second with Auto Slow Shutter turned on.

If Record Setting is at a 24p setting, the camera ordinarily will use a shutter speed no slower than 1/50 second, but it will go down to 1/25 second with Auto Slow Shutter turned on. However, if Record setting is at one of the 120p settings (available only when File Format is set to XAVC S HD), the slowest shutter speed available is 1/125 second, and the Auto Slow Shutter option is not available.

Auto Slow Shutter cannot operate unless ISO is set to Auto ISO. In addition, it will not operate if Exposure Mode (Movies) is set to Shutter Priority or Manual Exposure, even though you can turn it on through the menu, and it will appear to be on.

The use of an unusually slow shutter speed can produce a slurred or blurry appearance because the shutter speed may not be fast enough to keep up with the motion in the scene. But, if you are recording in a dark area, this option can help you achieve properly exposed footage, so it is worth considering in that situation.

Initial Focus Magnification (Movies)

This option is similar to the one with the same name for still images, discussed in Chapter 4. This menu item is different from that one because the magnification factor for the Focus Magnifier can only be x1.0 or x4.0 for movies, rather than the greater levels of magnification that are available when shooting still images.

Audio Recording

The Audio Recording menu option can be set either on or off. If you are certain you won't need the sound recorded by the camera, you can turn this option off. I never turn it off, because I can always turn down the volume of the recorded sound when playing the video. Or, if I am editing the video on a computer, I can delete the sound and replace it as needed—but there is no way to recapture the original audio after the fact if this option was turned off during the recording.

Audio Recording Level

This last option on screen 2 of the Camera Settings2 menu is available for selection only when the mode dial is set to Movie mode. If you record movies by pressing the Movie button in any other shooting mode, the camera will set the level for recording sound, and you cannot control it. In Movie mode, you can control the recording sound level using this menu option.

Figure 9-11. Audio Recording Level Menu Screen

When you select this option, the camera displays a screen like that in Figure 9-11, with a scale of values from 0 to 31. While the scale is highlighted by the orange box, use the control wheel, control dial, or the Left and Right buttons to select your desired value on the scale. If you highlight the Reset block and press the Center button, the level will be reset to the default value of 26. You can check the level of the sound by watching the audio level meters on the screen for setting the volume level.

Once the adjustment is made, press the Center button to exit to the live view. The new setting will be reflected in the behavior of the volume meters on the screen, when those meters are displayed, as shown in Figure 9-12.

Figure 9-12. **Audio Level Meters on Recording Screen**

The meters will be displayed only when the Audio Level Display option is turned on through screen 3 of the Camera Settings2 menu. If that menu option is turned on, the meters will appear on the screen during video recording in any shooting mode and they also will appear on the screen before the recording begins when the camera is in Movie mode.

When the screen in Figure 9-12 is shown, the audio level meters will react to sounds you make, so, in Movie mode, you can test the sound level before the recording starts. For example, before you start recording an interview, you can ask your subject to speak normally to test the level. You should try to adjust the level so the green bars never extend all the way to the right sides of the meters; if the bars reach into the red zones, the result is likely to be distorted sound.

No matter what level is set, the camera uses a limiter—an electronic circuit that keeps the volume from getting excessively loud.

The audio recording level meters will operate when you

are using the built-in microphone or when using an external microphone, as discussed in Appendix A.

Audio Level Display

This option controls whether audio level meters appear during movie recording in any shooting mode and before recording a video when the camera is set to Movie mode. The meters have green indicators that move farther to the right to indicate increases in the volume of audio, as shown in Figure 9-12.

The meters appear on detailed information screens; if this option is on and you don't see the meters when recording a video, press the Display button to call up one of the other screens. Also, check to see if the Audio Recording menu option, discussed above, is turned on; if that option is turned off, the meters will not be displayed. I generally leave this option turned on; seeing the movement of the audio levels on the meters reassures me that the audio is being recorded successfully.

Wind Noise Reduction

This option, if turned on, activates an electronic filter designed to reduce the volume of sounds in the frequencies of wind noise. I recommend not activating this feature unless the wind is strong, because it limits the sounds that are recorded. With video (or audio) editing software, you can remove sounds in the frequencies that may cause problems for the sound track, but using this built-in wind noise filter may permanently remove or alter some wanted sounds. This option does not affect recordings with an external microphone.

Marker Display

This option, which can be turned either on or off, determines whether or not various informative guidelines, called "markers," are displayed on the camera's screen for movie recording. There are four special markers available, which outline the aspect ratio and other areas on the screen. Any or all of them can be selected for use with the Marker Settings menu option, directly after this one on this menu screen. If you turn Marker Display on, then any of the four markers that you have selected will be displayed on the shooting screen while a movie is being recorded in any mode. The markers also will be displayed while the mode dial is set to the Movie mode position or the S & Q position, even before recording starts.

If this option is turned on, the selected markers will

display on the camera's display screen, but they will not be recorded with the movie.

Marker Settings

This menu option works together with the Marker Display option, discussed above. This option lets you activate any or all of the four available markers—Center, Aspect, Safety Zone, and Guideframe.

If you turn on the Center marker, it places a cross in the center of the display, as illustrated in Figure 9-13. If you are shooting video in a busy or hectic environment, this marker may help you keep the main subject centered in the display so you don't cut it off.

Figure 9-13. Center Marker in Use

The Aspect marker can be off or set to any one of seven settings: 4:3, 13:9, 14:9, 15:9, 1.66:1, 1.85:1, or 2.35:1. Figure 9-14 shows the display with the 13:9 setting.

Figure 9-14. Aspect Marker 13:9 in Use

This setting places vertical white lines at the sides of the frame or horizontal white lines at the top and bottom of the frame, to outline the shape of the movie frame for the chosen aspect ratio. These lines are useful if you plan to alter the aspect ratio of your footage in post-production, to show what parts of the image will be cut off and help you frame your shots accordingly.

The Safety Zone marker can be off, or set to outline

either 80% or 90% of the area of the display. The purpose of this marker's guidelines is to provide a margin for safety, because the average consumer television set may not display the entire video signal provided to it. If you set these lines to mark a safety zone, you can make sure your important subjects are included in the area that definitely will be displayed on most television sets. Figure 9-15 shows the display with the 90% safety zone activated.

Figure 9-15. Safety Zone 90% in Use

Finally, the Guideframe option, if turned on, displays a grid that is similar to the Rule of Thirds grid available with the Grid Line option, discussed in Chapter 5. That option uses thin, black lines, which may be hard to see when you are shooting video under difficult conditions. The bold, white lines of the Guideframe setting may be more useful for video shooting. You cannot use both options at the same time; Grid Line is not available when Marker Display is turned on. Figure 9-16 shows the Guideframe option in use.

Figure 9-16. Guideframe in Use

Movie with Shutter

This final option on screen 3 of the Camera Settings2 menu can be turned either on or off. If it is turned on, you can start and stop movie recording by pressing the shutter button when the camera is set to Movie mode or S & Q Motion mode. If it is left off, you have to press the red Movie button to start or stop movie recording. (You also can set a control button to the Movie option using the Custom Key options on screen 8 of the Camera Settings2 menu.) Some people find it more natural to use the shutter button to control the recording process, because the button is directly under the right index finger.

Turning this option on does not reduce the functionality of the shutter button for taking still images, because you cannot take still images when the mode dial is at the Movie or S & Q position. However, it does remove the ability to cause the camera to focus by pressing the shutter button during movie recording.

Custom Key (Movies)

This option, on screen 8 of the Camera Settings2 menu, is quite useful for movie recording. It lets you assign a movie-related function to each of several control buttons, so you can call up that function while recording a movie, when the mode dial is set to either the Movie or the S & Q Motion position. The items that can be assigned were discussed in Chapter 5.

Movie Button

This item on screen 9 of the Camera Settings2 menu is the final video-related option to be discussed here. As discussed earlier, you can set this option to Always or Movie Mode Only, to control whether the red Movie button (or another button assigned to the same function) can start and stop a movie recording with the mode dial at any position, or only when the mode dial is at the Movie or S & Q Motion position. I generally leave it set to Always.

Effects of Mode Dial Position on Recording Movies

The second category of setting that affects video recording with the a6400 is the position of the mode dial. As I discussed above, you can shoot normal-speed movies with the dial in any position except S & Q Motion (if the Movie Button menu option is set that way), and you can get access to many movie-related menu items no matter what position the dial is in. However, as I noted above, the shooting mode does make some difference for your movie options.

First, the position you select on the mode dial determines whether you can adjust the aperture and/

or shutter speed for your movies. If the dial is set to the Auto, Scene, Program, or Sweep Panorama modes, the camera will set both aperture and shutter speed automatically. However, if the dial is set to the Aperture Priority, Shutter Priority, or Manual exposure position, you will be able to adjust the aperture, shutter speed, or both aperture and shutter speed, just as you can when shooting still images. The range of available shutter speeds is different for movies than for still images, but you can make those adjustments at any time.

You also can make those adjustments when the mode dial is set to the Movie position and you select one of the more advanced exposure modes using the Exposure Mode item on screen 1 of the Camera Settings2 menu. For example, as discussed earlier in this chapter, if you select Manual Exposure for Exposure Mode with the mode dial at the Movie position, you can adjust both aperture and shutter speed for your movies, in the same way as if the mode dial were set to the M position. (If you set the mode dial to the S & Q Motion setting, you can shoot slow-motion or quick-motion movies. I will discuss those options in an S & Q Motion section later in this chapter.)

Because of the ability to adjust aperture and shutter speed in the advanced still-shooting modes, you might wonder why you would ever use the Movie position on the dial—why not just set the dial to A, S, or M if you want to adjust aperture and/or shutter speed while recording a movie, or to P if you want the camera to set the aperture and shutter speed automatically?

The answer is that several options or settings are available only when the mode dial is at the Movie position. For one thing, you will see how the video recording will be framed before you press the Movie button to start recording. If the mode dial is at a still-oriented position such as Auto, Scene, or a PASM mode, the display will show the live view according to the current setting for Aspect Ratio on screen 1 of the Camera Settings1 menu. If the setting is 3:2 or 1:1, it will not correspond to the framing of the video, which will be recorded in widescreen format, until you press the Movie button to start recording. (If Aspect Ratio is set to 16:9, the framing will show approximately how the framing will look before you press the Movie button.)

When the mode dial is at the Movie position, the camera adjusts the live view to show how the video will look before you press the Movie button, so you will know before you start the recording how to set up the shot to include all of the needed background and foreground elements.

In addition, when the mode dial is at the Movie position, you can take advantage of the Movie Button menu option, on screen 9 of the Camera Settings2 menu, to limit normal-speed video recording to that one shooting mode. In this way, you can make it impossible to start a recording accidentally by pressing the Movie button when the mode dial is set to a still-oriented mode such as Auto, Scene, or one of the PASM modes. If that setting is turned on, you will need to turn the mode dial to the Movie position in order to record a video.

Moreover, several menu options are not available unless the mode dial is at the Movie position (or, in some cases, the S & Q Motion position). In particular, on screen 4 of the Setup menu, the 4K Output Select option is not available, nor are most of the sub-settings of the TC/UB Settings option. All of these settings can be useful when recording to an external video recorder.

In addition, the Marker Display option on screen 3 of the Camera Settings2 menu can be selected in any shooting mode, but any marker you have selected for display will not appear in still-oriented modes until you actually start recording a video. When the mode dial is at the Movie position (or the S & Q position), you will see the marker on the display before the recording starts, so you can set up your composition ahead of time.

You also can use the Audio Recording Level option on screen 2 of the Camera Settings2 menu to set the audio input level, which cannot be controlled in other shooting modes.

Also, the camera's shooting mode has an effect on what options are available on the Camera Settings1 menu and with the control buttons, as discussed in following sections of this chapter. For example, if the mode dial is set to Auto, Sweep Panorama, or Scene, the Camera Settings1 menu options are limited. If the mode dial is set to Program, Aperture Priority, Shutter Priority, or Manual exposure, the options are greater. This point is important for video shooting because, as discussed below, several important Camera Settings1 menu options carry over to movie recording.

If the camera is set to Program mode (P on the mode dial), you can make several settings that will affect the recording of videos while the mode dial is in that position. The camera will set the aperture and shutter speed automatically, as it does with still-image shooting. You can use exposure compensation to vary the exposure, but only within the range of plus or minus 2 EV, instead of the 5-EV positive or negative range for still shooting.

If the camera is set to Aperture Priority mode (A on the mode dial), you will have the same Camera Settings1 menu options as in Program mode, and you can also set the aperture; the camera will set the shutter speed automatically, but the range of available shutter speeds will be somewhat different than for still images. That range is also affected by the Record Setting option selected and the setting of the Auto Slow Shutter menu option, as discussed earlier in this chapter.

If the camera is set to Shutter Priority mode (S on the mode dial), you will have the same Camera Settings1 menu options as in Program mode, and you can also set the shutter speed. You can set it anywhere from 1/4 second (the camera's slowest setting for movies) to 1/4000 second (the camera's fastest setting for movies), regardless of the Record Setting or Auto Slow Shutter settings, with one exception. The one exception is that the slowest setting available is 1/125 second when Record Setting is set to either of the 120p settings (100p for the PAL system), which are available when File Format is set to XAVC S HD.

If the camera is set to Manual exposure mode (M on the mode dial), you will have the same Camera Settings1 menu options as before. You can set both shutter speed and aperture, with the same restrictions for shutter speed settings noted above for Shutter Priority mode.

If the camera is set to Sweep Panorama mode, it will act largely as if it were set to Movie mode with the Program Auto exposure mode selected. If it is set to Scene mode, it will shoot movies as if it were set to Intelligent Auto mode, in which limited menu options are available. It will not recognize any specific scene settings, such as Portrait, Sports Action, or Sunset.

There is a lot of information involved in outlining the differences in the a6400's behavior for video recording in different shooting modes, so I am including here a table that lays out the more important differences, for reference.

Table 9-1.   BEHAVIOR OF A6400 FOR VIDEO RECORDING IN VARIOUS SHOOTING MODES

SHOOTING MODE:	AUTO	SCENE	PANORAMA	S & Q MOTION	MOVIE	M	S	A	P
ADJUST APERTURE DURING VIDEO RECORDING	No	No	No	DEPENDS ON EXPOSURE MODE (S & Q) MENU OPTION SETTING	DEPENDS ON EXPOSURE MODE (MOVIE) MENU OPTION SETTING	YES	No	YES	No
ADJUST SHUTTER SPEED DURING VIDEO RECORDING	No	No	No	DEPENDS ON EXPOSURE MODE (S & Q) MENU OPTION	DEPENDS ON EXPOSURE MODE (MOVIE) MENU OPTION SETTING	YES	YES	No	No
SEE VIDEO FRAMING BEFORE RECORDING STARTS	No	No	No	YES	YES	No	No	No	No
USE 4K OUTPUT SELECT	No	No	No	No	YES	No	No	No	No
USE ALL TC/UB SETTINGS OPTIONS	No	No	No	ALL EXCEPT TC RUN	YES	No	No	No	No
ADJUST AUDIO RECORDING LEVEL	No	No	No	No	YES	No	No	No	No
SEE MARKER DISPLAY ITEMS BEFORE RECORDING STARTS	No	No	No	YES	YES	No	No	No	No
USE 120P/100P RECORD SETTINGS OPTIONS	No	No	YES	S & Q VIDEO ONLY	YES	YES	YES	YES	YES
CAN RECORD VIDEO IF MOVIE BUTTON MENU OPTION IS SET TO MOVIE MODE ONLY	No	No	No	S & Q VIDEO ONLY	YES	No	No	No	No

Effects of Camera Settings1 Menu Settings on Recording Movies

Although the settings on the Camera Settings1 menu are largely oriented toward still images, several of them affect the recording of movies. I will discuss those options in this section.

One of the main reasons the shooting mode is important for movies is that, just as with still photography, some menu options are not available in some modes. For example, in an advanced still-shooting mode like Aperture Priority or Program, video recording is affected by the settings for Focus Area, ISO, Metering Mode, White Balance, DRO, Creative Style, Picture Effect, Picture Profile, Focus Magnifier, and Face/Eye AF Settings. In some cases, you can adjust these settings while the video is being recorded.

You cannot get access to the Camera Settings1 menu (or any menu) by pressing the Menu button during video recording; you have to use a control button, the Function menu, or the control dial or wheel to call up the item to adjust. Of course, you have to have that setting assigned to the button, menu, dial, or wheel ahead of time.

For example, you can adjust ISO while recording a video, but only if you have assigned ISO to the control wheel, the control dial, or one of the control buttons using the Custom Key (Still Images) menu option on screen 8 of the Camera Settings2 menu, or to the Function menu. (For the dial and wheel to be assigned, you would need to use other menu options also, such as My Dial Settings or Dial/Wheel EV Compensation.)

Another option from the Camera Settings1 menu that is particularly useful for video recording is Picture Profile, found on screen 11 of that menu. Although Picture Profile is applicable for both still images and video recording, it is really oriented for shooting video. I discussed the details of its settings in Chapter 4. If you want to have the greatest amount of dynamic range available in your video sequences and are willing to go through the effort of color grading your clips with post-processing software, you can choose PP7, PP8, PP9, or PP10 for the Picture Profile setting, to take advantage of the S-Log2, S-Log3, or HLG setting for gamma curve. Otherwise, choose one of the lower-numbered profiles, or no profile at all. If you want to get involved with parameters such as gamma, black level, detail, and knee, you can create your own profile with settings you prefer.

If you want to experiment with different Picture Profile settings, you can assign this menu option to one of the control buttons using the Custom Key options on the

Camera Settings2 menu or to the Function menu. You can then call up different Picture Profile settings while recording a video, to see how they affect the recording.

If you use a profile that includes the S-Log2, S-Log 3, or HLG gamma setting, you can use the Gamma Display Assist option, discussed in Chapter 8, to increase the apparent contrast of the footage as it is displayed by the camera during recording and playback, so it will be easier to judge composition, exposure, and focus, etc.

Table 9-2 provides information about the options on the Camera Settings1 menu that are the most useful for video recording, showing which of these settings carry over to video recording if set before recording starts, and which of those also can be adjusted while a video recording is in progress, when the camera is set to a shooting mode in which that adjustment is possible. (This table does not include some technical options that have no effect on your images and videos, such as Circulation of Focus Point, Display Continuous AF Area, and others of that nature.)

Table 9-2. **Camera Settings1 Menu Items that Affect Movies and Can Be Adjusted Before or During Video Recording**

Camera Settings1 Menu Item	Carries Over to Video if Adjusted Before Video Recording	Can Adjust During Video Recording
Focus Mode	Yes	Yes
Focus Area	Yes (Tracking not available)	Yes
Face/Eye Priority in AF	Yes	No
Subject Detection	Yes	Yes
Right/Left Eye Select	No	No
Face Detection Frame Display	Yes	No
Exposure Compensation	Yes	Yes
ISO Setting	Yes	Yes
Metering Mode	Yes	No
Face Priority in Multi Metering	Yes	No
Spot Metering Point	Yes	No
White Balance	Yes	No
DRO/Auto HDR	Yes (DRO only)	No
Creative Style	Yes	No
Picture Effect	Yes	No
Picture Profile	Yes	Yes
Focus Magnifier	N/A	Yes
Peaking Display Select	Yes	Yes

There are built-in limitations with some of these settings. Exposure compensation can be adjusted to plus or minus 2.0EV only, rather than the 5.0EV range for still images. The ISO range includes Auto ISO and specific values from 100 to 32000, omitting several of the highest settings.

Also, you cannot set ISO to Multi Frame Noise Reduction, which would cause the camera to take multiple shots. With Picture Effect, you can use some of the sub-settings, but not all. The settings that are unavailable for movie recording are Soft Focus, HDR Painting, Rich-tone Monochrome, Miniature, Watercolor, and Illustration. (As noted on the table, you cannot get access to the Picture Effect settings during video recording.)

There are some other options on the Camera Settings1 menu that have no effect for recording movies. Some of these settings are clearly incompatible with shooting movies, such as Drive Mode, Flash Mode, and Auto Object Framing. Some are less obvious, including AF Illuminator and Scene Selection.

There are two other points to make about using Camera Settings1 menu settings for movies. First, you have a great deal of flexibility in choosing settings for your movies, even when the camera is not set to the Movie position on the mode dial. You can set up the camera with the ISO, Metering Mode, White Balance, Creative Style, Picture Effect (to some extent), or other settings of your choice, and then press the Movie button to record using those settings. In this way, you could, for example, record a black-and-white movie in a dark environment using a high ISO setting. Or, you could record a movie that is monochrome except for a broad selection of red objects, using the Partial Color-Red effect from the Picture Effect option, with the red color expanded using the color axis adjustments of the White Balance setting. (Note that you can't use Creative Style and Picture Effect settings at the same time.)

Second, you have to be careful to check the settings that are in effect for still photos before you press the Movie button. For example, if you have been shooting stills using the Posterization setting from the Picture Effect menu option and then suddenly see an event that you want to record on video, if you press the Movie button, the movie will be recorded using the Posterization effect, making the resulting footage practically impossible to use as a clear record of the events.

Of course, you may notice this problem as you record the video, but it takes time to stop the recording, change the menu setting to turn off the Picture Effect option, and then press the Movie button again, and you may have missed a crucial part of the action by the time you start recording again.

One way to lessen the risk of recording video with unwanted Camera Settings1 menu options is to switch the mode dial to the Auto position before pressing the Movie button. That action will cause the camera to use more automatic settings and will disable the Creative Style and Picture Effect options altogether. (Of course, you have to have the Movie Button item on screen 9 of the Camera Settings2 menu set to Always for this approach to work.)

Effects of Physical Controls When Recording Movies

Other settings that carry over to some extent from shooting stills to video recording are those set by the physical controls. In this case, as with Camera Settings1 menu items, there are differences depending on the position of the mode dial. I will not try to describe every possible combination of shooting mode and physical control, but I will discuss some settings to be aware of.

First, you can use the focus mode switch on the lens (if the lens has one) to change between autofocus and manual focus modes while recording a movie. The only two modes available for video recording with the a6400 are continuous autofocus and manual focus. If you set a focus switch on the lens to the AF position, the camera will use continuous autofocus. If you set the switch to the MF position, the camera will use manual focus.

Second, the touch screen operates during video recording, but in a somewhat different way than it does for shooting still images, assuming touch screen features are turned on through the Touch Operation item on screen 3 of the Setup menu.

If Focus Area is set to Wide, Zone, or Center, you can touch the screen to select a focus point, and the camera will direct its focus to that point. It will not display a focus frame, but the focus will become sharp at that point. At the same time, the camera will switch the

focus mode to manual focus so the focus will stay locked at that spot. It stays in manual focus mode until you touch the screen at another point, or touch the finger icon with an X that turns off the Touch Focus feature. You can use this feature, which Sony calls "spot focus," to carry out a "pull-focus" operation by touching one subject and then another. The speed of that operation is governed by the setting for AF Drive Speed on screen 2 of the Camera Settings2 menu.

If Focus Area is set to Flexible Spot or Expand Flexible Spot, you can drag the focus frame to a new location, and the camera will focus at the new point. You can use this operation for a "pull focus" effect by dragging the focus frame from one subject to another. You also can tap any spot to set a new focus frame, but the camera does not switch to manual focus as it does when Focus Area is set to Wide, Zone, or Center, as discussed above.

If manual focus mode is in use, you can tap twice on the screen to enlarge the view. However, if the Initial Focus Magnification (Movies) option on screen 2 of the Camera Settings2 menu is set to x1.0, the double-tap will just turn on the Focus Magnifier frame; you then have to press the Center button to enlarge the view.

Next, you can adjust exposure compensation while recording movies when the mode dial is set to the P, A, S, M, Movie, S & Q, or Sweep Panorama setting. That setting is not available during video recording in the Auto or Scene modes. The range of exposure compensation for movies is plus or minus 2.0 EV, rather than the plus or minus 5.0 EV for still images. If you set exposure compensation to a value greater than 2.0 (plus or minus), the camera will set it back to 2.0 after you press the Movie button to start shooting a movie.

Also, the Function button operates normally. For example, if the mode dial is set to P for Program mode, then, after you press the Movie button to start recording a movie, you can press the Function button and the Function menu will appear on the screen. This menu will let you control only those items that can be controlled under current conditions.

If you start recording a movie while the mode dial is set to a mode such as Auto in which most options on the Function Button menu are not available, the a6400 will display the menu, but few items will be available for selection.

If you assign a control button to carry out an operation using the Custom Key (Still Images) or Custom Key (Movies) option on screen 8 of the Camera Settings2 menu, you can use that button to perform the operation while recording a movie if the action is compatible with movie recording in the current shooting mode. The situation is similar if you assign exposure compensation to the control wheel or dial using the Dial/Wheel EV Compensation option on screen 9 of the Camera Settings2 menu, or if you assign temporary settings to the control wheel and/or dial using the My Dial options on screen 8 of the Camera Settings2 menu.

There are numerous options that can be assigned to a control button that will function during video recording, if the current context permits that control. For example, if the Right button is set to control ISO and you are shooting a movie with the mode dial set to P, pressing the Right button will bring up the ISO menu and you can select a value while the movie is recording. If the mode dial is set to Auto, though, pressing the button will have no effect during recording, because ISO cannot be adjusted in that shooting mode.

If the Center button (or another button) is assigned the Focus Standard setting through the Custom Key (Still Images) or Custom Key (Movies) menu option, you can press the button during video recording to activate a movable focus frame or to cause the camera to focus in the center of the frame, depending on the current Focus Area setting. Of course, to use either of those options, the camera must be set to use autofocus rather than manual focus.

If you set the AEL button (or some other button) to the AEL Hold or AEL Toggle function, you can press that control while recording a movie to lock the exposure setting. This ability can be useful when recording a movie, when you don't want the exposure to change as you move the camera over different areas of a scene.

Following is a list of functions that can be assigned to one of the control buttons, dial, or wheel, or to the Function menu, and that can be controlled during video recording by using the assigned control:

- Self-timer During Bracketing
- Focus Mode
- AF/MF Control Hold
- AF/MF Control Toggle
- Focus Standard
- Focus Area
- Switch Focus Area
- Subject Detection
- AF On
- Focus Hold
- Exposure Compensation
- ISO Setting
- AEL Hold
- AEL Toggle
- Spot AEL Hold
- Spot AEL Toggle
- AWB Lock Hold
- AWB Lock Toggle
- Picture Profile
- Focus Magnifier
- Peaking Display Select
- Peaking Level
- Peaking Color
- In-Camera Guide (provides help for Function menu items during recording)
- Movie (button operates to start/stop video recording)
- S & Q Frame Rate
- Audio Recording Level
- Audio Level Display
- Marker Display Select
- SteadyShot
- Zoom
- Finder/Monitor Select

- Finder Frame Rate

- Zebra Display Select

- Zebra Level

- Grid Line

- My Dial 1/2/3 During Hold

- My Dial 1—2—3

- Toggle My Dial 1/2/3

- Audio Signals

- Gamma Display Assist

- Touch Operation Select

- TC/UB Display Switch (switches among counter, time code, and user bit displays)

One item on this list, Self-timer During Bracketing, is not useful during video recording. However, Sony for some reason has made that item available for use with an assigned button during movie recording, so I have included it on the list.

Slow and Quick Motion Recording

The a6400 camera can record video at a higher-than-normal frame rate, which results in slow-motion sequences when played back at a normal rate, or at a lower-than-normal rate, resulting in a speeded-up movie. If you are using the NTSC system, you can record at a rate as high as 120 frames per second (fps) or as low as 1 fps; with the PAL system, you can record at up to 100 fps or as low as 1 fps.

With the NTSC system, you can create a video sequence to be played back in the camera at up to five times slower or 60 times faster than normal; with PAL, the limits are four times slower and 50 times faster. Because there are several settings and steps to be taken to use this feature, I will provide a step-by-step guide.

1. Set the mode dial to S & Q, as shown in Figure 9-17.

Figure 9-17. Mode Dial at S & Q Position

2. On screen 1 of the Camera Settings2 menu, highlight the second option, Exposure Mode (S & Q), and select one of the available exposure modes, as shown in Figure 9-18—Program Auto, Aperture Priority, Shutter Priority, or Manual Exposure.

Figure 9-18. Exposure Mode (S & Q) Menu Options Screen

These modes are similar to those for normal-speed movie shooting, discussed earlier in this chapter. If you choose S or M, the shutter speed that can be set will depend on the Frame Rate setting you make in Step 8. For example, if you select 120 fps for the Frame Rate, the shutter speed will have to be 1/125 second or faster.

3. Make any control or menu adjustments that are needed. For example, if you selected Aperture Priority for the exposure mode, set the aperture. Also set ISO, Metering Mode, White Balance, and any other available settings, if needed. Set the focus mode using the Focus Mode menu option. Select the zoom amount for the lens (if using a zoom lens) and adjust the focus for your subject.

4. On screen 1 of the Camera Settings2 menu, highlight S & Q Settings and press the Center button. You will see a screen like that in Figure 9-19.

Figure 9-19. S & Q Settings Menu Options Screen

5. On this screen, set Record Setting as you want it. This setting is not the same as Record Setting on the Camera Settings2 menu screen, which applies for normal video recording. This setting sets the video quality for your S & Q Motion videos, and determines the frame rate for playback of those videos. If your camera is set for the NTSC system, the choices for Record Setting are 60p, 30p, or 24p. The bit rate is set at 50M for each of the three settings. The video will be recorded using the XAVC S HD format. For highest quality of the final video, select 60p. For the greatest amount of slowing down of the final video, select 24p. (The 60p setting is not available if Frame Rate is set to 120 fps.)

6. Go back to the S & Q Settings options and select Frame Rate. The choices are 120 fps, 60 fps, 30 fps, 15 fps, 8 fps, 4 fps, 2 fps, or 1 fps. You can determine how slow the slow-motion footage will be by dividing this number by the Record Setting figure. For example, if Frame Rate is 120 and Record Setting is 30, the final video will be slowed down four times when played back in the camera.

7. If Frame Rate is greater than Record Setting, the final movie will be in slow motion. If Frame Rate is smaller than Record Setting, the final movie will be in speeded-up motion, like an old-time silent movie, or, at the lowest Frame Rate settings, such as 1 fps, similar to a time-lapse movie. If the two values are equal, the video will play back at normal speed, but (like all S & Q movies) with no sound.

8. When you are ready to start recording, press the Movie button.

9. The final movie can be played back like any other movie. Movies recorded in S & Q mode are recorded with no sound.

Recording to an External Video Recorder

For recording everyday videos such as clips of vacations or family events, the a6400 will serve you well. However, the camera has some options that are useful for professional video production. Several of these options control how the camera sends video to an external video recorder. I will not discuss all possible scenarios for using the a6400 with a recorder, but I will describe the steps I took to record video with the camera connected to an Atomos Shogun 4K recorder, discussed in Appendix A, with the caveat that there undoubtedly are other approaches that will work; this is one that worked for me.

First, make sure the Shogun is powered by a battery or power supply and has a formatted storage disk installed. I used a SanDisk Extreme Pro 480 GB solid state drive (SSD). Connect headphones to monitor sound. On the Input menu, enable HDMI input and HDMI Trigger. I selected Apple ProRes HQ as the recording format.

Connect the HDMI input port of the Shogun to the HDMI output port of the a6400 using a micro HDMI cable. Make sure the camera has an SDHC or SDXC memory card rated at least in Class 10 or UHS Speed Class 1. Then turn on both the camera and the recorder and make the settings on the camera shown in Table 9-3. Set the camera's mode dial to the Movie position. Set Focus Mode to the AF-S, AF-A, AF-C, or DMF so the camera will use autofocus, unless you prefer to use manual focus.

Table 9-3. Recommended Settings on a6400 Camera for Recording 4K Video to an Atomos Shogun Recorder

CAMERA SETTINGS1 MENU	
FOCUS MODE	CONTINUOUS AF
FOCUS AREA	WIDE
SWITCH V/H AF AREA	OFF
FACE/EYE AF SETTINGS: FACE/EYE PRIORITY IN AF	ON IF RECORDING FACES
FACE/EYE AF SETTINGS: SUBJECT DETECTION	HUMAN, UNLESS RECORDING PETS
FACE/EYE AF SETTINGS: FACE DETECTION FRAME DISPLAY	OFF UNLESS NEEDED

FACE/EYE AF SETTINGS:	
ANIMAL EYE DISPLAY	OFF UNLESS NEEDED
EXPOSURE COMPENSATION	ADJUST AS NEEDED
ISO SETTING	AUTO, OR ADJUST AS NEEDED
METERING MODE	MULTI
FACE PRIORITY IN MULTI METERING	ON IF RECORDING FACES
SPOT METERING POINT	FOCUS POINT LINK IF NEEDED
WHITE BALANCE	AUTO WHITE BALANCE
PRIORITY SET IN AWB	STANDARD
DRO/AUTO HDR	DRO IF NEEDED
CREATIVE STYLE	STANDARD
PICTURE EFFECT	OFF
PICTURE PROFILE	PP1, OR OTHER PREFERRED

CAMERA SETTINGS2 MENU

EXPOSURE MODE (MOVIES)	PROGRAM AUTO
FILE FORMAT	XAVC S 4K
RECORD SETTING	30P 60M
PROXY RECORDING	OFF
AF DRIVE SPEED	NORMAL
AF TRACKING SENSITIVITY	STANDARD
AUTO SLOW SHUTTER	OFF
INITIAL FOCUS MAGNIFICATION	X1.0
AUDIO RECORDING	ON
AUDIO RECORDING LEVEL	26, OR AS NEEDED
AUDIO LEVEL DISPLAY	ON
WIND NOISE REDUCTION	OFF
MARKER DISPLAY	ON IF NEEDED
MARKER SETTINGS	AS NEEDED
MOVIE W/SHUTTER	ON IF DESIRED
RELEASE W/O LENS	DISABLE
RELEASE W/O CARD	DISABLE
STEADYSHOT	ON UNLESS USING TRIPOD
ZOOM	(NOT AVAILABLE)
ZOOM SETTING	OPTICAL ZOOM ONLY
ZEBRA SETTING	SET IF NEEDED
GRID LINE	OFF UNLESS NEEDED
EXPOSURE SETTINGS GUIDE	OFF

SETUP MENU

GAMMA DISPLAY ASSIST	OFF UNLESS USING S-LOG OR HLG SETTING
NTSC/PAL SELECTOR	NTSC (IN U.S., ETC.)
TOUCH OPERATION	ON
TOUCH PANEL/PAD	TOUCH PANEL ONLY (UNLESS USING VIEWFINDER)

SETUP MENU: TC/UB SETTINGS

TC/UB DISPLAY SETTING	TC
TC PRESET	00:00:00:00
UB PRESET	00 00 00 00
TC FORMAT	DF
TC RUN	REC RUN
TC MAKE	PRESET
UB TIME REC	OFF

SETUP MENU: HDMI SETTINGS

HDMI RESOLUTION	AUTO
24P/60P OUTPUT	60P
HDMI INFO DISPLAY	OFF (NOT AVAILABLE)
TC OUTPUT	ON
REC CONTROL	ON
CTRL FOR HDMI	OFF
4K OUTPUT SELECT	MEMORY CARD + HDMI

Some of the above settings are optional or unnecessary and some, such as White Balance and Metering Mode, can be changed according to your preferences. The important ones are File Format, Record Setting, the TC/UB settings, and the HDMI settings. I have not listed some other settings that are unlikely to be needed, such as USB Connection and several others.

Once the connections and settings are made, press the Movie button on the a6400. The screen on the Shogun recorder should indicate that the recording has begun. Use the controls on the camera to zoom or adjust settings as needed. When you are ready to stop the recording, press the Movie button again, and the recorder should stop.

I also tried a modified version of these settings with no memory card in the camera, setting 4K Output Select on the Setup menu to HDMI Only (30p). The Shogun recorded the video as expected and the resulting file imported readily into Adobe Premiere Pro CC for viewing and editing.

Capturing Still Images from Video Recording

The a6400 cannot shoot still images while recording a video sequence. If you want to save a still frame from a video sequence, you can use a good video editing program, such as Adobe Premiere Pro CC, or others. However, there is a way to capture a still frame in the camera itself—by using the Photo Capture feature, as discussed in Chapter 7. For example, if you record video using the XAVC S 4K format, the video clips will have the relatively high resolution of 4K video (about 8 megapixels), giving you the option to save a still frame that is of high enough quality to stand on its own. If you use an exposure mode that lets you set the shutter speed, you can choose a fast shutter speed to stop action, and use this technique as a type of super burst shooting. Figure 7-28 in Chapter 7 and Figure B-2 in Appendix B are examples using this approach.

Summary of Options for Recording Movies

As I have discussed, there is some complication in trying to explain all of the relationships among the controls and settings of the a6400 for recording movies. To simplify matters, I will provide a summary of options for recording movies with the a6400.

To record a video clip with standard settings, set the mode dial to the Auto or Scene position and press the Movie button. The camera will adjust exposure automatically, and you can use either continuous autofocus (set for video recording using the AF-S, AF-A, AF-C, or DMF setting for the focus mode) or manual focus (MF setting). In those shooting modes, you cannot adjust many shooting options, such as ISO, White Balance, DRO, Creative Style, or Picture Effect. You can use options such as Focus Magnifier, Peaking, and SteadyShot (if the lens you are using is designated OSS, for Optical SteadyShot). You can choose File Format and Record Setting options to control the video quality.

For more control over video shooting, set the mode dial to the P, A, S, or M position. Then you can control several additional Camera Settings1 menu options, including ISO, White Balance, Metering Mode, Creative Style, and Picture Effect, among others. You can choose continuous autofocus or manual focus in the same way as for the more automatic shooting modes. You can adjust aperture, shutter speed, or both, or let the camera set them, depending on which shooting mode you select.

For maximum control over movie recording, set the mode dial to the movie film icon for Movie mode. Then select an option for the movie exposure mode from the Exposure Mode (Movies) item on screen 1 of the Camera Settings2 menu. To control aperture, choose Aperture Priority; to control shutter speed, choose Shutter Priority; to control both aperture and shutter

speed, choose Manual Exposure. Other options can be selected from the Camera Settings1 menu.

Control buttons and dials operate during movie recording if the context permits, as discussed earlier. If you want a set of functions tailored for video recording, use the list in Table 9-4 to start, and adjust it for your own needs. Remember that you may need to use two menu options to make these assignments: Custom Key (Single Images) if you will be recording video with the mode dial at a position other than Movie mode; and Custom Key (Movies) if you will be recording with the mode dial at the Movie position.

Table 9-4. **Suggested Control Assignments for Movie Recording**

CONTROL	FUNCTION
CUSTOM BUTTON 1	FOCUS MODE
CUSTOM BUTTON 2	FOCUS AREA
CENTER BUTTON	FOCUS STANDARD
LEFT BUTTON	ZEBRA DISPLAY SELECT
RIGHT BUTTON	ISO
DOWN BUTTON	EXPOSURE COMPENSATION
AF/MF BUTTON	FOCUS MAGNIFIER
AEL BUTTON	PEAKING DISPLAY SELECT
FOCUS HOLD BUTTON (IF ANY)	FOCUS HOLD

To record good, standard video footage at a moment's notice without having to remember a lot of settings, I recommend that you set up one of the seven registers of the Memory Recall shooting mode with a solid set of movie-recording settings. Table 9-5 lists one group of settings to consider. (Settings not listed here can be set however you like.) The Record Setting option and the Picture Profile setting in this table make some other settings unavailable, as noted in the table. If you want to use those settings, turn Picture Profile off and use a different option for Record Setting. I am assuming the mode dial is at the Movie position.

Table 9-5. **Suggested Menu Settings for Recording Movies in Movie Mode**

CAMERA SETTINGS1 MENU	
FOCUS MODE	AF-S, AF-A, AF-C, OR DMF
FOCUS AREA	WIDE
FACE/EYE AF SETTINGS: FACE/EYE PRIORITY IN AF	ON, IF RECORDING PEOPLE
FACE/EYE AF SETTINGS: SUBJECT DETECTION	HUMAN

ISO	ISO Auto
Metering Mode	Multi
Face Priority in Multi Metering	On
White Balance	Auto White Balance
Priority Set in AWB	Standard
DRO	Not available with Picture Profile Activated
Creative Style	Not available with Picture Profile Activated
Picture Effect	Not available with Picture Profile Activated
Picture Profile	PP1 or other as needed
Camera Settings2 Menu	
Exposure Mode (Movie)	Program Auto
File Format	XAVC S HD
Record Setting	30p 50M
Proxy Recording	Off
AF Drive Speed	Normal
AF Tracking Sensitivity	Standard
Auto Slow Shutter	Off unless needed
Audio Recording	On
Audio Recording Level	Adjust as needed
Audio Level Display	On
Wind Noise Reduction	Off unless needed
Marker Display	Off unless needed
Marker Settings	All off unless needed
Movie w/Shutter	Off
SteadyShot (If supported by lens)	On; Off if using tripod
Zoom Setting	Optical Zoom Only
Zebra Setting	Use as needed
Grid Line	Off
Exposure Settings Guide	Off

Other Settings and Controls for Movies

There are several other points to be made about recording and playing back videos that don't concern the Camera Settings1 or Camera Settings2 menu or the major physical controls. Here are brief notes about these issues.

The Display button operates normally to change the information that is viewed during video recording. The screens that are displayed are controlled by the Display Button option on screen 6 of the Camera Settings2 menu. However, the For Viewfinder screen does not

appear for video shooting, even if it was selected through that menu option.

In playback mode, the Display button operates normally for movies. The screen with space for a histogram will display, but the spaces for histogram and other information will be blank.

The MF Assist option on screen 13 of the Camera Settings1 menu does not operate for video recording, so the camera will not magnify the display when you turn the focus ring to adjust manual focus. However, you can assign the Focus Magnifier function to one of the control buttons and use that capability to enlarge the screen when using manual focus (or autofocus).

After you press the assigned control button to put the orange Focus Magnifier frame on the display, press the Center button to enlarge the area within the frame to 4.0 times normal. (This is less than the 5.9x enlargement factor for still shooting.) Then turn the focus ring or press the shutter button halfway to adjust the focus. Half-press the shutter button to dismiss the Focus Magnifier frame. (If the Initial Focus Magnification (Movies) option on screen 2 of the Camera Settings2 menu is set to x4.0, the screen will be magnified as soon as you press the assigned control button to activate Focus Magnifier.)

The Setting Effect Off choice for the Live View Display option on screen 7 of the Camera Settings2 menu does not function for video recording; the Setting Effect On choice is locked in. So, for example, if you are shooting movies in Movie mode using Manual Exposure for the Exposure Mode setting and you have the aperture and shutter speed set for strong underexposure, you cannot adjust this option to make the display more visible.

Program Shift does not function during video recording. If you turn the control dial while the camera is set to Program mode, the exposure settings will not change while the camera is recording a movie. The menu button and Playback button do not operate during video recording.

Finally, when Focus Mode is set to MF for manual focus and Touch Operation is turned on through screen 3 of the Setup menu, you can tap the LCD screen twice during video recording to bring the Focus Magnifier frame onto the monitor, as discussed above. You can drag the magnified image around the display with a finger, and you can tap twice again to return the screen to its normal viewing size.

Movie Playback

As with still images, you can transfer movies to a computer for editing and playback or play them back in the camera, either on the camera's display or on a TV connected to the camera.

If you want to play your movies in the camera, there is one feature of the a6400 to be mindful of. As I discussed in Chapter 7, the View Mode option on screen 3 of the Playback menu controls what images or videos you will see in playback mode. If you don't see the video you are looking for, check to make sure that menu option is set to display all files from a certain date (Date View), AVCHD View, XAVC S HD View, or XAVC S 4K View.

Once you have selected a proper mode to view your video, navigate to that file by pressing the direction buttons or turning the control wheel or control dial. When the first frame of the selected video is displayed on the screen, you will see a playback triangle inside a circle, as shown in Figure 9-20. In the lower right corner of the screen will be a Play prompt with a white circle icon indicating that you can press the Center button to play the video. (If you don't see that prompt, press the Display button one or more times until it appears.)

Figure 9-20. Movie Ready for Playback in Camera

After you press the Center button to start playback, you will see more icons at the bottom of the screen, as shown in Figure 9-21. From the left, these icons indicate: Rewind/Fast Forward; Pause; Open Control Panel; and Exit. From this screen, you can press the Left or Right button repeatedly to play the movie rapidly forward or backward; multiple presses increase the speed up to four times.

Figure 9-21. Initial Movie Playback Control Icons

When the movie is paused, the icons change, as shown in Figure 9-22, to indicate Previous File or Next File; Play; Open Control Panel; and Exit.

Figure 9-22. Initial Movie Playback Control Icons When Paused

While the video is playing or paused, press the Down button, and you will see a new line of controls at the bottom of the screen, as shown in Figure 9-23. When the movie is playing, these icons indicate, from left to right: Previous File; Fast Reverse; Pause; Fast Forward; Next File; Photo Capture; Volume Setting; Exit.

Figure 9-23. Movie Control Panel Icons When Playing

When the movie is paused, the icons change, as seen in Figure 9-24. Those icons indicate, from left to right: Previous Frame; Reverse Slow Playback; Normal Playback; Forward Slow Playback; Next Frame; Photo Capture; Volume Setting; and Exit.

Figure 9-24. Movie Control Panel Icons When Paused

On any of these screens, move through the icons with the Left and Right buttons, and press the Center button to select the function for the selected icon.

When a movie is playing, you can fast-forward or fast-reverse through it at increasing speeds by turning the control wheel or control dial right or left or by pressing the Right or Left button.

Editing Movies

The a6400 cannot edit movies in the camera. If you want to do any editing, you need to use a computer. For Windows, you can use software such as the Photos app that comes with Windows 10. If you are using a Mac, you can use iMovie or any other movie editing software that can deal with AVCHD files and XAVC S files. I use Adobe Premiere Pro CC on my Mac, and it handles these file types well.

You also can use the PlayMemories Home software that is available from Sony for use with the a6400. To install PlayMemories Home, you need to download the software from the internet at http://www.sony.net/pm/. This software is updated with new features periodically, so be sure to keep checking the website for updates. You also can refer to the list of programs for editing 4K video provided by Sony at https://support.d-imaging.sony.co.jp/www/support/application/nle/en.html.

Chapter 10: Wi-Fi, Bluetooth, and Other Topics

Wi-Fi Features

The a6400 can connect to computers, smartphones, and tablets using a Wi-Fi network. With some devices, the a6400 can use NFC (near field communication) technology to establish a Wi-Fi connection without going through all the steps that are ordinarily required. Note, though, that the a6400, unlike some other Sony camera, does not have the ability to download and use camera apps. The camera also can use a Bluetooth connection to be operated by a remote control device and to add location data to images. I will discuss these features in this chapter.

First, here is one note to remember when using any of the camera's Wi-Fi and Bluetooth features: The Network menu, marked by a globe icon, has an option called Airplane Mode near the bottom of its first screen. If that option is turned on, no wireless features will work. Make sure that menu setting is turned off when using the wireless options.

Sending Images to a Computer

Although you can edit and print images and edit videos to some extent using a smartphone or tablet, the easiest way to work with them is to transfer them to a computer. The traditional ways to do this are to connect the camera to the computer with the camera's USB cable or to use a memory card reader. However, there is a way to transfer your images and videos from the a6400 to a computer over a wireless network, eliminating the need to use a USB connection or a card reader.

To do this, you can use the Send to Computer menu option to transfer images and videos from the camera's memory card over a network. Here are the steps to set up the camera and computer:

1. Install Sony's PlayMemories Home software on the computer. For both Macs and Windows-based computers, the software is available for download at http://www.sony.net/pm/.

2. On the camera, set USB Connection on Screen 4 of the Setup menu to Mass Storage.

3. Register the Wi-Fi access point that you want to use to send images and videos to your computer. To do this, go to screen 1 of the Network menu and choose Wi-Fi Settings. On the next screen, choose WPS Push or Access Point Settings, and follow the directions on the camera's screen to register your Wi-Fi access point with the camera.

4. Run the software you downloaded in Step 1. If it does not automatically prompt you to set up your computer for wireless import, do this manually, using the steps below.

5. On a PC using Windows 10, start the PlayMemories Home program, then connect the a6400 camera to the computer using the USB cable. When the computer displays a dialog box recognizing the camera, answer Yes when the computer asks if you want to see options for cameras, such as Import Media Files. The computer then will display a screen with several options. Select the option for Wi-Fi Import Settings. Follow the prompts to set up this computer to receive files wirelessly from the a6400. Then disconnect the camera from the computer, using the proper procedure for safe disconnection.

-or-

On a Macintosh, go to the PlayMemories Home menu. Select Preferences, then Wireless Auto Import, and select the option to set this computer as the destination for importing images. When prompted, connect the camera to the computer with the camera's USB cable. Follow further prompts, then disconnect the camera from the computer, using the proper procedure to eject the camera from the computer safely.

6. On the camera's Network menu, select Send to Computer, as shown in Figure 10-1.

Figure 10-1. Send to Computer Highlighted on Network Menu

7. The camera will display a screen like that in Figure 10-2, reporting the name of the computer it is connecting to.

Figure 10-2. Camera Screen Reporting Connection to Computer

8. The computer will eventually display an Import dialog box showing thumbnails of the images and videos being imported. The images and videos will be uploaded to a folder on your computer. You can designate that folder using the software installed in Step 1. The default folder is the Pictures folder; the computer places the images and videos in a sub-folder bearing the date of the transfer.

The camera will only transfer images and videos that have not previously been transferred wirelessly to the computer, but there is no way to select which items will be transferred. The transfer may take a long time, especially if the transfer includes XAVC S videos using the HD or 4K setting for File Format.

If you have difficulty in using this option to transfer files wirelessly, see Sony's technical support information at https://www.sony.com/electronics/support/articles/00047471.

If you have a fast Wi-Fi network available, this option can be a convenient way to transfer images and videos.

SENDING IMAGES TO A SMARTPHONE

If you don't need to print your images or do heavy editing, you may want to transfer them to a smartphone or tablet so you can share them on social networks, display them on the larger screen of your tablet, or otherwise enjoy them.

You can transfer images wirelessly from the a6400 to a smartphone or tablet that uses the iOS (iPhone and iPad) or Android operating system, but you cannot transfer AVCHD videos. For XAVC S 4K videos or XAVC S HD videos recorded with the 120p/100p Record Setting option, you can transfer proxy versions but not the full-sized files. With iOS, you have to use the camera's menu system to connect. With some Android devices, you can use NFC technology, which establishes a Wi-Fi connection automatically when the camera is touched against the smartphone or tablet.

Here are the steps for connecting using the menu system, using an iPhone as an illustration:

1. Install Sony's Imaging Edge Mobile app on the phone; it can be downloaded from the App Store for the iPhone or from Google Play for Android devices. Figure 10-3 shows the app's icon on an iPhone.

2. Put the camera into playback mode and display an image or video to be transferred to the phone.

3. On the Network menu, select Send to Smartphone Function, then, on the next screen, Send to Smartphone. From that option choose Select on This Device. On the next screen, you can choose to transfer This Image, All with this Date, or Multiple Images.

4. On the next screen, as shown in Figure 10-4, the camera will display the SSID (name) of the Wi-Fi network it is generating.

Figure 10-3. Icon for Imaging Edge Mobile App on iPhone

Figure 10-4. Camera Screen Showing ID of its Network

5. On the phone, go to the Settings app, select Wi-Fi, and select the network displayed on the camera's screen, as shown in Figure 10-5. The first time you connect to that network, you will have to scan the QR code on the camera's screen with the phone, in the Imaging Edge Mobile app. Or, if you prefer, you can press the C2/Delete button to go to a screen that displays the network password, which you can enter in the phone. After that initial connection, you can connect to that network without entering the password.

6. The camera will display a message saying "Connecting." At this point, launch the Imaging Edge Mobile app, unless it was already started so you could scan the QR code from the camera's screen.

7. The phone will display a message saying it is copying the images or videos from the camera, and will confirm the copying with a screen like that in

Figure 10-6. The images or videos will appear in the Camera Roll area on an iPhone.

Figure 10-5. Network ID of Camera Selected on iPhone

Figure 10-6. Message on iPhone When Images are Copied

If you prefer, you can initiate the Send to Smartphone process by pressing the Function button when the camera is in playback mode, assuming that button is assigned to that operation. (The Function button is assigned to Send to Smartphone by default, but that operation can be assigned to a different button using the Custom Key (Playback) option on screen 8 of the Camera Settings2 menu.)

CONNECTING WITH NFC

If you are using an Android device with NFC, the steps for connecting that device to the a6400 are different. I tested the procedure using a Sony Xperia XA2 phone, but the same process should work with other Android devices that have NFC included. Here are the steps:

1. On the Android device, go to the Google Play Store and find and install the Imaging Edge Mobile app.

2. On the Android device, go to the Settings app, and find the settings for NFC. On the device I used for this test, it was under Settings—Device Connection—Connection Preferences—NFC. Make sure the setting for NFC data transfer is turned on, as shown in Figure 10-7.

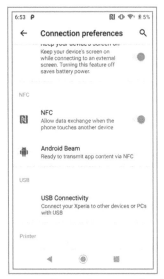

Figure 10-7. NFC Turned on on Android Phone

3. Put the a6400 into playback mode and display an image you want to send to the Android device.

4. Find the NFC icon on the right side of the camera, which looks like a fancy "N," as shown in Figure 10-8.

Figure 10-8. NFC Area on Camera

5. While both devices are active, touch the N on the camera to the NFC area on the Android device. (On the Sony Xperia XA2 that I used, this area is on the back,

just below the main camera.) Be sure the two areas touch; you cannot have the two NFC spots separated by more than about a millimeter, if that.

6. Hold the devices together, and within a few seconds you may hear a sound, depending on settings, and the camera will transfer the image to the Android device; you may see a message on the camera as the connection is established. You may see a message to select an option on the phone such as Connect to Camera to complete the operation. However, if you wait a few seconds, the camera and phone should complete the connection and transfer the image without any further action on your part.

7. If you want to transfer multiple images, select that option from the camera's menu before touching the camera to the Android device to start the transfer.

By default, when you transfer images to a smartphone or tablet, the maximum image size will be 2 MP. If the image originally was larger than that, it will be reduced to that size. You can change this setting to send the images at their original size or at the smaller VGA size. To do that on your device, find the settings for the Imaging Edge Mobile app, then the Copy Image Size setting. On an iPhone, go to Settings, then scroll to find Imaging Edge Mobile. On an Android device, open Imaging Edge Mobile, then tap the Settings icon. If the images were taken with Raw quality, they will be converted to JPEG format before being transferred to the smartphone or tablet, even if the device is set for transfer at the original size.

Using a Smartphone or Tablet as a Remote Control

You can use a smartphone or tablet as a remote control to operate the a6400 from a distance of up to about 33 feet (10 meters), as long as the devices are in sight of each other. Here are the steps to do this with an iPhone:

1. Go to the camera's Network menu, marked by a Globe icon, select Control with Smartphone, and set it to On. Then make a selection for Always Connected, either On or Off. (I recommend Off.) Then highlight the Connection option and press the Center button. The camera will initiate a connection to the phone.

2. The camera will display a screen with the identification information for its own Wi-Fi

network, along with a QR code for scanning and a message saying to press the C2/Delete button to use a password.

3. On the phone, you can open the Imaging Edge Mobile app and choose Scan QR Code of the Camera, or you can go to the Wi-Fi tab of the Settings app and select the network ID displayed by the camera, as shown earlier in Figure 10-5. If this is the first time you are making this connection, you will have to press the C2/Delete button on the camera to see the password, and enter the network password on the phone; you will not have to enter the password for future connections unless the network ID is changed. You may be prompted on the phone to install a profile. If so, follow the prompts.

4. Set up the camera on a tripod or just place it where you want it, aiming at your intended subject.

5. Open the Imaging Edge Mobile app on the iPhone, if it is not already open.

6. The camera will display a screen with an icon in the upper middle of the display showing that the camera can now be controlled from the phone, as shown in Figure 10-9.

Figure 10-9. Camera Screen When Under Remote Control

7. The phone will display a screen like that in Figure 10-10, showing the view from the camera's lens and several control icons.

8. Using these controls, you can adjust various settings, including exposure compensation, White Balance, ISO, aperture, shutter speed, continuous shooting, and self-timer, depending on the shooting mode. You also can adjust several options using the camera's controls. You can take a still image by tapping the large white circle at the bottom center of the screen.

Figure 10-10. Remote Control Screen in App on iPhone

9. You can tap the Menu icon on the app to get access to a menu that includes options such as Flash Mode, White Balance, self-timer, and others, as shown in Figure 10-11. You can tap the DISP icon in the lower right corner of the app to remove the icons from the screen, leaving only the live view. The Save Option item lets you set whether the camera sends still images you take remotely to the phone after shooting.

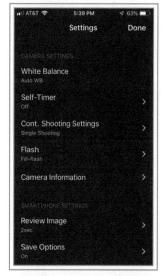

Figure 10-11. Menu Options for Remote Control in App

10. If you turn the camera's mode dial to the Movie position, the circle at the bottom of the app changes to a red dot, which you can tap to record a movie. You can change the Exposure Mode setting for movies on the camera by tapping the mode icon on the app. You can change the format for movie recording by tapping the Menu icon, giving access

to those settings and others. You can record S & Q Motion movies if you turn the mode dial to S & Q.

11. By default, images saved to the phone will be resized down to 2 MP unless they already were that small or smaller. Movies will be saved only to the camera; they cannot be displayed on the phone.

12. When you have set up the shot as you want it, press the camera icon on the iPhone app to take the picture or the red icon to start the video recording.

13. If you are using an Android device with NFC capability, you should be able to connect to the camera by touching the device to the camera, as discussed above in connection with transferring images. First, turn on the camera with Control with Smartphone turned on on the Network menu, and put the camera into shooting mode, then touch the two devices together at their NFC areas.

14. Once the connection has been made, you can separate the devices to the standard remote-control distance of up to about 33 feet (10 meters). If you have difficulty making an NFC connection, start the Imaging Edge Mobile App on the Android device before touching the camera to that device. The camera can then be controlled using the Imaging Edge Mobile app on the Android device, as noted in the numbered steps above.

You can use the remote-control setup if you want to place your camera on a tripod in an area where birds or other wildlife may appear, so you can control the camera from a distance without disturbing the animals. (The wireless remote will work through glass if you are indoors behind a window.)

Bluetooth Features

As discussed above, the a6400 can use a Wi-Fi connection to transfer images to a smartphone, tablet, or computer, or to control the camera remotely. In addition, the camera can use a Bluetooth connection to receive geographical location information from a compatible smartphone or tablet or to connect to a Bluetooth remote control device.

Bluetooth, like Wi-Fi, is a system for establishing a wireless connection between devices. One advantage of using Bluetooth instead of Wi-Fi is that Bluetooth consumes very little power, so a Bluetooth connection

can remain active for a relatively long time without draining the camera's battery excessively.

The steps to take for setting up a Bluetooth connection to gather location information with the a6400 are set forth below.

1. Install the Imaging Edge Mobile app on your smartphone, and use it to transfer at least one image from the camera to the phone, as discussed earlier in this chapter. After that procedure has been done, the Location Information Linkage item will appear on the main page of the app, as shown in Figure 10-12.

Figure 10-12. Location Information Linkage Item on App Screen

2. Make sure the Bluetooth setting is turned on on the smartphone. On an iPhone, go to Settings—Bluetooth—On.

3. On the a6400, go to screen 2 of the Network menu, select Bluetooth Settings, and, on the next screen, set Bluetooth Function to On, as shown in Figure 10-13.

Figure 10-13. Bluetooth Function Option Turned On

4. On the a6400, on the Bluetooth Settings screen, select Pairing.

5. On the phone, launch the Imaging Edge Mobile app and tap Location Information Linkage on the main page. Then tap the button for that setting to the On position, so a green circle appears.

6. On the phone, select the option to Set the Camera, then select the name of the a6400 camera from the list on the app's screen.

7. When the camera displays a message prompting you to allow the connection from the a6400, select OK. The app also may ask you to confirm the pairing operation.

8. On the a6400, go to screen 2 of the Network menu, select Location Information Link Setting, and set it to On. The phone and camera will then be paired.

9. The phone may prompt you to go to the settings within the Imaging Edge Mobile app and set location access to Always. If so, follow that step, as shown for the iPhone in Figure 10-14.

Figure 10-14. Location Access Set to Always on iPhone

10. As the camera shoots images, it will obtain location information from the smartphone via the Bluetooth connection. As it obtains information, the camera will display a small icon in the upper right corner of the display that looks like a pin sticking up out of a map, as shown in Figure 10-15. It will also display a Bluetooth icon to the right of that icon.

Figure 10-15. Map Pin Icon on Shooting Screen of Camera

11. You can view the location information using various software programs, such as Adobe Bridge and the Viewer module of Sony's Imaging Edge software. In PlayMemories Home, each image will have a GPS satellite icon displayed in the upper right corner, and the latitude and longitude can be read using the Properties panel.

Once the Location Information Link has been established between the smartphone and the camera, you can continue to take pictures and the smartphone will gather location information, as long as the app is running, even in the background. It may take a while for the phone to transmit the GPS data to the camera when the camera is turned on after having been turned off for a while. If you don't need to gather location information for a time, you can save battery power by turning off the Bluetooth settings on the camera.

The Network Menu

I have discussed some of the items on the Network menu, but there are several other options to discuss. Following is information about each of the items on this menu, whose first screen is shown in Figure 10-16.

Figure 10-16. Screen 1 of Network Menu

SEND TO SMARTPHONE FUNCTION

This first Network menu option lets you transfer images or videos to a smartphone or tablet. This menu item has two sub-options: Send to Smartphone and Sending Target, as shown in Figure 10-17. I discussed the steps for using the Send to Smartphone option earlier in this chapter. You also can press the Function button (or other button assigned to this option) when the camera is in playback mode, to carry out this action.

Figure 10-17. Send to Smartphone Function Menu Options Screen

The Sending Target option lets you choose how to transfer movies recorded with the XAVC S HD format—specifically, whether to transfer the original video file, the proxy file, or both. (Proxy recording is turned on with the Proxy Recording item on screen 1 of the Camera Settings2 menu; it creates a smaller version of a video file as the file is recorded.)

You cannot transfer AVCHD movies or XAVC S 4K movies, and you cannot transfer XAVC S HD movies recorded with either of the 120p/100p settings for Record Setting. So, this option controls only the way the camera transfers XAVC S HD movies recorded with a 60p, 30p, or 24p value for Record Setting.

The choices for this option are Proxy Only, Original Only, or Proxy & Original.

Make this choice according to your own preference and needs. If you just want to view a particular video on your smartphone, Proxy Only will make the transfer go more rapidly and should be sufficient. Otherwise, select the original, with or without the proxy.

SEND TO COMPUTER

This next option lets you send your images and movies directly from the a6400 to your computer via a Wi-Fi network. I discussed the steps for this process earlier in

this chapter.

VIEW ON TV

This option sets up the a6400 to transmit still images (not movies) wirelessly to a Wi-Fi–enabled TV, such as a Sony Bravia TV. The procedure will vary with the TV set you are using. Once the connection is established, you can browse through the images using the controls on the camera or the remote control of the TV if the TV is compatible with this setup.

This is a useful option once it is working properly, but it can be difficult to set up, depending on the TV you are using. With this camera, I eventually was able to connect to a device called WD TV Live, by Western Digital. I connected that device to an HDTV using an HDMI cable and connected the WD TV Live device to the same network my a6400 was connected to, through the Wi-Fi Settings/Access Point Settings option on the Network menu. Then, with the View on TV option, the camera was able to find and connect to the WD TV Live, as shown in Figure 10-18.

Figure 10-18. WD TV Live Device Found by Camera

After that connection was established, the camera sent still images to the TV through the wireless network. The camera showed the screen in Figure 10-19, with a few control icons at the bottom.

Once this screen appeared, I pressed the Center button to pause the transmission, and pressed the Down button to display a screen with additional options, including 4K display mode, found under the Playback Image Size option.

If you have a "smart" TV or are familiar with setting up a media server, this option may be useful for you. Otherwise, I recommend that you view your images on a TV using an HDMI cable, a USB flash drive, or some other direct connection.

Figure 10-19. View on TV Screen - Sending Images to TV

CONTROL WITH SMARTPHONE

I discussed this menu option earlier in this chapter, when I discussed the steps for controlling the camera using the Imaging Edge Mobile app on a smartphone. The first sub-option, Control with Smartphone, needs to be turned on; you then establish a connection using the Connection sub-option. The third sub-option, Always Connected, can be turned on or off. If it is turned on, the connection between the phone and camera will stay in place and will not need to be re-established. That setting uses up power more rapidly than letting the connection end, so I recommend not enabling the persistent connection unless you have a definite need to do so. Also, note that the Control with Smartphone option interferes with some other camera operations, such as the USB Connection menu item, so it is a good idea to turn off Control with Smartphone when you won't be using it for a while.

AIRPLANE MODE

This option is a quick way to disable all of the camera's wireless network connection functions, including the camera's internal Wi-Fi network and its Bluetooth connectivity. As indicated by its name, this option is useful when you are on an airplane and you are required to disable electronic devices. In addition, this setting can save battery power, so it may be worthwhile to activate it when you are on an outing with the camera and you won't need to use any Wi-Fi or Bluetooth capabilities for a period of time.

If you try to use any of the camera's Wi-Fi or Bluetooth functions such as Send to Smartphone or Send to Computer and notice that the menu options are dimmed, it may be because this option is turned on.

Turn it off and the Wi-Fi and Bluetooth options should be available again.

WI-FI SETTINGS

This last option on screen 1 of the Network menu has several sub-options, as discussed below.

WPS Push

The WPS Push option gives you an easy way to set up your camera to connect to a computer or other devices over a Wi-Fi network. Ordinarily, to connect to a wireless network, you have to use the Access Point Settings option and then enter the network password into the camera to establish the connection. The WPS Push option gives you a shortcut if the wireless access point or wireless router you are connecting to has a WPS button. That option, if it is present, is likely to be a small button on the back or top of the router, and it is likely to have the WPS label next to it or on it.

If the router has a WPS button, you will not have to make any manual settings or enter a password. All you have to do is select the WPS Push menu option on the a6400, and then within two minutes after that, press the WPS button on the router. If the operation is successful, the camera's display screen will show that the connection has been established.

Once that connection has been made, you will be able to connect your camera to a computer on that network to transfer images using the Send to Computer option or the View on TV option.

If the connection does not succeed using WPS Push, you will need to use the Access Point Settings option, the second sub-option for the Wi-Fi Settings menu item.

Access Point Settings

This option is for connecting the camera to a Wi-Fi router if WPS Push, discussed above, is not available or does not work. I discussed the use of this option earlier in this chapter, in connection with sending images and videos to a computer wirelessly.

Display MAC Address

This menu option causes the camera to display a screen like that in Figure 10-20, which shows your camera's MAC address. MAC stands for media access control.

The MAC address is a string of characters that identifies

a device that can connect to a network. In some cases, a router can be configured to reject or accept devices with specified MAC addresses. If you are having difficulty connecting your camera to a Wi-Fi router using the options discussed above, you can try configuring the router to recognize the MAC address of your camera, as reported by this menu item. I have not had to use this option, but it is available in case it is needed.

Figure 10-20. Display MAC Address Screen

SSID/PW Reset

When you connect your a6400 to a smartphone or tablet, either to transfer images or to control the camera remotely with the other device, the camera generates its own Wi-Fi network internally. With this option, whose main screen is shown in Figure 10-21, you can force the camera to change the SSID (name) and password of its own wireless network.

Figure 10-21. SSID/PW Reset Main Options Screen

You might want to do this if, for example, you have attended a conference where you allowed other people to connect their smartphones to your camera, and now you want to reset the camera's network ID so they will no longer have access to the camera's network.

The second and final screen of the Network menu is shown in Figure 10-22.

Figure 10-22. Screen 2 of Network Menu

BLUETOOTH SETTINGS

I discussed this menu option in connection with the procedure for sending GPS location information to the camera from a smartphone. You use this menu option to turn on or off the camera's Bluetooth functionality and to pair it with a smartphone. You also can use the Display Device Address option to show the BD address, or Bluetooth Device address, of the camera, in case you need that information for troubleshooting or other purposes.

LOCATION INFORMATION LINK SETTING

I discussed this option earlier, in connection with setting up the camera to receive location information. Once you have paired the camera with a smartphone through Bluetooth, you need to turn on the Location Information Link sub-option to cause the phone to send GPS data to the camera. You can also turn on the Auto Time Correction and Auto Area Adjustment sub-options, if you want the camera to obtain updated time and location information from the phone.

EDIT DEVICE NAME

This next option, shown in Figure 10-23, lets you change the name of your camera as it is displayed on the network. The default name is ILCE-6400, and I have found no reason to change it.

This option could be useful, though, if you are in an environment where other a6400 cameras are present and you need to distinguish one camera from another by using different names.

Figure 10-23. Edit Device Name Screen

RESET NETWORK SETTINGS

This next option on the Network menu lets you reset all of the camera's network settings, not just the camera's Wi-Fi SSID and password. This option is useful if you are having problems and need to get a fresh start with the wireless functions, if you are switching to a new wireless network where you use the camera, or if you are selling the camera and want to erase these settings.

BLUETOOTH REMOTE CONTROL

This final item on the Network menu lets you set up the camera to be operated by Sony's Bluetooth Remote Commander, model number RMT-P1BT. (Note that this option is not available unless the camera has been upgraded to firmware version 2.00.) Here are the steps to take to use that device:

1. On the a6400 camera, on screen 2 of the Network menu, select Bluetooth Settings, and turn on the Bluetooth Function sub-option.

2. On the same screen of the Network menu, select Location Information Link Settings, and make sure the Location Information Link sub-option is turned off.

3. On the same screen of the Network menu, select Bluetooth Remote Control, and turn it on.

4. On the same screen, select Bluetooth Settings, then select the Pairing sub-option. Select OK when the camera prompts you to confirm the pairing of the camera to the remote control.

5. Use the remote control to shoot stills or videos. You also can zoom the lens using the plus and minus buttons, if you are using a power zoom lens (with the PZ indication as part of its name), or a non-power zoom lens with Clear Image Zoom, Digital Zoom, or Smart Zoom turned on. If you move the Zoom/Focus switch on the remote to the Focus position, you can focus a power zoom lens when it is in manual focus mode, using the plus and minus buttons. You can press the C1 button to call up an option that has been assigned to that button on the camera using the Custom Key (Still Images), Custom Key (Movies), or Custom Key (Playback) menu option.

6. If you plan on using that button, it would be advisable to program a function that switches between various settings with each button press, rather than one that requires you to scroll through menu options, which you would not be able to do without using the camera's controls. For example, you might want to assign the C1 button a function such as AEL Hold, AF On, AF/MF Control Toggle, or Peaking Display Select. You probably should not assign it a function such as White Balance, which requires selecting one of several choices on a menu.

7. When you press the zoom controls (plus and minus buttons) on the remote when the camera is in playback mode with a still image on the display, the image will be enlarged or reduced with each button press. (The Zoom/Focus switch must be set to the Zoom position for this function to operate.)

8. Note that, as reflected in the steps above, you cannot have the Bluetooth Remote Control option turned on at the same time as the Location Information Link option. So, if one of those options is not working properly, check to see if the other one is turned on.

Other Topics

STREET PHOTOGRAPHY

The a6400 is well suited for street photography—that is, shooting candid pictures in public settings, often without the subject being aware of your activity. You can use a wide-angle lens that takes in a broad field of view, so you can shoot from the hip without framing the image carefully on the screen. You can tilt up the LCD screen and look down at it to frame your shot, which lets you take photographs without attracting attention to yourself. The camera performs well at high ISO settings, so you can use a fast shutter speed to avoid motion blur. You can silence the camera by turning off its beeps and shutter sounds using the Silent Shooting and Audio Signals menu options.

The settings you use depend in part on your style of shooting. One technique that some photographers use is to shoot in Raw, and then use post-processing software such as Photoshop or Lightroom to convert their images to black and white, along with any other effects they are looking for, such as extra grain to achieve a gritty look. (Of course, you don't have to produce your street photography in black and white, but that is a common practice.)

If you decide to shoot using Raw quality, you can't take advantage of the image-altering settings of the Picture Effect menu option. You can, however, use the Creative Style option on the Camera Settings1 menu. (You may have to use Sony's Imaging Edge software for the Creative Style setting to be effective with Raw images.) You might want to try using the Black and White setting; you can tweak it further by increasing contrast and sharpening if you want. Also, try turning on continuous shooting, so you'll get several images to choose from for each shutter press.

You also can experiment with exposure settings. I recommend you shoot in Shutter Priority mode at a fairly fast shutter speed, 1/100 second or faster, to stop action on the street and to avoid blur from camera movement. You can set ISO to Auto, or use a high ISO setting, in the range of 800 or so, if you don't mind some noise.

Or, you can set the image type to JPEG at Large size and Extra Fine quality to take advantage of the camera's image-processing capabilities. To get a gritty "street" look, try using the High Contrast Monochrome setting of the Picture Effect item on the Camera Settings1 menu, with ISO set in the range of 800 or above, to include some grain in the image while boosting sensitivity enough to stop action with a fast shutter speed.

For Figure 10-24, I used Intelligent Auto mode with high-speed continuous shooting turned on, to catch this image of a man walking along the pedestrian bridge over the river toward me.

Another possibility is to take advantage of the camera's ability to shoot 4K video. You can shoot video using an exposure mode such as Shutter Priority that lets you use a fast shutter speed to avoid motion blur, and record a street scene for several seconds, or even a minute

or more. You can then use video-editing software or the camera's Photo Capture feature to extract a single frame. Because of the relatively high resolution of 4K video, the quality is likely to be quite acceptable. I used that technique for Figure 7-28, discussed in Chapter 7 in connection with Photo Capture.

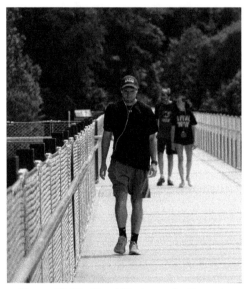

Figure 10-24. **Street Photography Example**

INFRARED PHOTOGRAPHY

The a6400 can take infrared photographs if you use a filter, such as a Hoya R72 infrared filter, of the right size to fit on the lens you are using.

Of course, the camera is not designed for infrared photography, so you need to use long shutter speeds to let enough infrared light in through the dark red filter. Therefore, this type of photography is really only suited for stationary subjects such as landscapes. It works best with green trees, grass, and the like, along with blue skies and clouds. An example is shown in Figure 10-25, which I took with the a6400 in Manual exposure mode with a shutter speed of 15 seconds at f/1.8 and ISO set to 640. I used a Hoya R72 infrared filter on the Sony DT 50mm f/1.8 lens and had the camera on a tripod.

Figure 10-25. Infrared Image

ASTROPHOTOGRAPHY AND DIGISCOPING

Astrophotography involves photographing sky objects with a camera connected to (or aiming through) a telescope. Digiscoping is the practice of using a digital camera with a spotting scope to get shots of distant objects such as birds and other wildlife.

There are many types of scope and several ways to align a scope with the a6400's lens. I will not describe all of the methods; I will discuss the approach I used and hope it gives you enough guidance to explore the area further.

I used a Meade ETX-90/AT telescope with the a6400 connected to it directly, without an eyepiece, using the "prime focus" method of connecting. To make that connection, you need an adapter to connect the a6400 camera's body to the telescope. I purchased an astrophotography adapter kit, model BNEX, from telescopeadapters.com, which included a T-ring as well as another adapter that was useful for digiscoping, discussed below.

I took the image of the moon in Figure 10-26 with the a6400 connected to the telescope using the T-ring adapter. I set the camera to Manual exposure mode with the shutter speed set to 1/3200 second. I needed a fast shutter speed to avoid motion blur from the unsteadiness of the telescope. I used manual focus, adjusting the telescope's focus control until the image was sharp on the camera's LCD. I used Auto ISO and the camera set the ISO to 16000.

At first I used the MF Assist option so I could fine-tune the focus with an enlarged view of the moon's craters. After some experimenting, I found I got better results using the Peaking Level function at High, and Peaking Color set to red. When focus was sharp, I saw a bright, red outline on the outer edge of the moon, which made focusing much easier than relying on the

normal manual focus mechanism, even with MF Assist activated.

Figure 10-26. Moon Image Taken Through Telescope

I set the self-timer to five seconds to minimize camera shake. I set Quality to Raw & JPEG so I would have a Raw image to give extra latitude in case the exposure seemed incorrect. As you can see in Figure 10-26, the a6400 did a good job of capturing the full moon. Because of the relatively large sensor and high resolution of the a6400, this image can be enlarged to a fair degree without deteriorating.

I tried the same setup for digiscoping, attaching the a6400 to a Celestron Regal 80F-ED spotting scope, using the same adapter I used with the telescope, but I was not able to get that setup to focus on any subject. I then tried using a standard telescope eyepiece in conjunction with the adapter, using a "projection body" that was part of the adapter kit I had purchased. With that setup, I was able to get the image in focus by adjusting focus on the scope. The result was Figure 10-27. As you can see, there is considerable vignetting, and the overall quality is not great, but at least I was able to get a magnified shot of the bird.

Figure 10-27. Digiscoping Example

CONNECTING TO A TELEVISION SET

The a6400 can play back its still images and videos on an external television set, as long as the TV has an HDMI input jack. The camera does not come with any audio-video cable as standard equipment, so you have to purchase your own cable, with a micro HDMI connector at the camera end and a standard HDMI connector at the TV end. These cables are available through online retailers.

To connect the cable to the camera, you need to open the door covering the ports on the left side of the camera and plug the micro HDMI connector into the middle port underneath that flap, as shown in Figure 10-28.

Figure 10-28. **Camera Connected to HDMI Cable**

Then connect the large connector at the other end of the cable to an HDMI input port on an HDTV set.

Once you have connected the camera to the set, the camera not only can play back images and videos; it also can record. When the a6400 is hooked up to a TV while in recording mode, you can see on the TV screen the live image being seen by the camera. In that way, you can use the TV as a large monitor to help you compose your photographs and videos.

You also can use this port and cable to output a "clean" video signal to another device, such as a video recorder. To do that, you have to turn off the HDMI Information Display option under the HDMI Settings item on screen 4 of the Setup menu, as discussed in Chapters 8 and 9.

As noted earlier in this chapter, the a6400 also has an option on the Network menu called View on TV, which lets you view your images on a Wi-Fi–enabled TV. As I discussed in that chapter, that option can be difficult to use effectively. Unless you are familiar with using media servers and sharing files over a network, I recommend that you stick to using an HDMI cable for the connection.

Appendix A: Lenses and Accessories

Lenses

The a6400 camera uses Sony's E-mount system for attaching a lens to the camera's body. There are several categories of lenses available for this camera: E-mount lenses designed for the a6400 and similar Sony cameras, such as the a6000, a6300, and a6500, which use an APS-C sensor; E-mount lenses designed for the a9, a7 series, and similar Sony cameras, which use a full-frame sensor; A-mount lenses designed for older Sony camera, such as the a99 II; and lenses made by other manufacturers, such as Sigma, Canon, Leica, and others.

Lenses from the first two categories can be mounted directly on the a6400 with no need for an adapter. Lenses from the A-mount category require the use of an adapter, discussed later in this section. Lenses from other manufacturers require the use of other adapters. You can find information about adapters for such lenses at sites such as https://briansmith.com/gear/sony-lens-adapters/.

E-mount Lenses for APS-C Sensor Cameras

These lenses could be considered "native" lenses for the a6400, because they are designed for use on the a6400 and other models with an APS-C sized sensor. The two most common examples are the "kit" lenses that are often sold in a bundle with the a6400 camera: the Sony E PZ 16-50mm f/3.5-5.6 OSS Lens and the Sony E 18-135mm f/3.5-5.6 OSS Lens, shown in Figure A-1.

There is a good deal of information to be learned from the names of these lenses. For example, with the 16-50mm lens, the E in its name means it uses the E-mount system. The PZ in its name means that it is a "power zoom" lens whose zooming is achieved with a built-in motor that can be controlled electronically by a remote control or other switch. Power zoom is a feature that is

useful for video recording, because it allows you to zoom the lens at a steady rate for smooth zoom shots.

Figure A-1. Sony Kit Lenses for a6400 Camera: 16-50mm on Left; 18-135mm on Right

The focal length range, 16-50mm, is stated in terms of the actual focal length of the lens. Because the a6400 uses an APS-C sensor that is smaller than full-frame, the 35mm-equivalent focal length of the lens when used on the a6400 is about 1.5 times those figures, or, in this case, 24-75mm. The f/stop (aperture) range shows the maximum (widest) aperture the lens provides.

When, as with this lens, there are two numbers listed for the maximum aperture (f/3.5-5.6), the first one (f/3.5) is the maximum aperture when the lens is zoomed back to its full wide-angle focal length of 16mm; the second (f/5.6) is the maximum aperture when the lens is zoomed in to its highest focal length of 50mm.

The OSS designation means that the lens has optical SteadyShot (image stabilization) built in. That is an important feature for a lens to be used with the a6400 camera, because this camera, unlike some other Sony models, does not have in-body image stabilization, so the only way to get that sort of steadying feature is to use a lens that includes it. If the OSS designation is not present, be prepared to shoot with higher shutter speeds, use a tripod, or take other measures to avoid motion blur from camera shake.

There are several other lenses made specifically for

Sony's E-mount APS-C cameras. I will mention just a few of them, to illustrate the variety available. One option is the Sony E PZ 18-105mm f/4 G OSS lens. In this case, the letter G included in the name stands for Gold, and designates what Sony considers to be an especially high-quality lens. In addition, even though this is a zoom lens, it has only a single aperture listed, f/4. That means that the lens maintains a constant aperture of f/4 even when zoomed in to its highest focal lengths. With this sort of lens, you can maintain the widest aperture at all times, thereby letting in plenty of light and having a good ability to achieve a blurred background.

Another possibility is the Sony E 16mm f/2.8 lens. This is an example of a prime lens, meaning it has only a single focal length (16mm), and therefore does not zoom. This lens is also considered to be a "pancake" lens, although that is not part of its official designation. That means that it has a particularly thin structure, so it could be a good choice when you want to keep down the weight and bulk of the camera and lens combination, and plan to shoot wide-angle images, possibly for landscape or street photography.

There also are quite a few E-mount lenses for Sony APS-C cameras that are made by other manufacturers. One example is the Sigma 16mm f/1.4 DC DN Contemporary Lens for Sony E, which offers a very wide aperture of f/1.4. A "fisheye" lens with a very short focal length that provides a distorted super-wide-angle view is the Meike MK-6.5mm f/2 Circular Fisheye Lens for Sony E. This is an inexpensive, manual focus lens. Other lenses are available from Rokinon, Samyang, Neewer, and others.

E-mount Lenses for Full-frame Cameras

The next category is lenses designed for use with Sony's full-frame cameras, such as the a9 and the a7 series. These lenses, when made by Sony, have the FE designation in their names. One example is the Sony FE 100-400mm f/4.5-f.6 GM OSS lens, shown on the a6400 in Figure A-2.

The GM designation stands for "G Master," a category that Sony says is higher than the G category, discussed above. These lenses are supposed to have very high quality, and definitely have a very high price. This particular model currently sells new for

about $2,500.00. This lens, designed presumably for professional sports photographers using full-frame cameras, is quite large and heavy, but it fits nicely with the a6400 and can yield excellent images. The focal length as listed is the actual focal length; when attached to the a6400, this type of lens, like the APS-C lenses discussed earlier, has a crop factor of about 1.5, so the effective focal length of the lens on the a6400 is 200mm to 600mm.

Figure A-2. Sony FE 100-400mm f/4.5-5.6 GM OSS Lens

There are many lenses available in this category. Some other examples are the Sony FE 90mm f/2.8 Macro G OSS lens, a macro lens designed for closeup shots of small items, the Sony FE 85mm f/1.8 lens, and the Sigma 35mm f/1.4 DG HSM Art Lens for Sony E.

A-mount Lenses

The final category to be discussed is lenses designed for Sony's older A-mount system. Use of these lenses requires an adapter, which is fairly expensive and rather bulky, so I don't recommend this approach unless you already own, or have access to, one or more good A-mount lenses. However, you may find that in some cases there is an A-mount lens that works better for your application than the other lenses available. Some photographers have a very favorable view, for example, of the Sony DT 16-50mm f/2.8 SSM lens. DT stands for "digital technology," and designates a lens designed for an APS-C sensor camera; SSM stands for SuperSonic Motor, a particular type of focusing motor. Another good option is the Sony FE 50mm f/2.8 Macro lens.

For any A-mount lens you need to use an adapter to mount it on the a6400. Sony currently makes two adapters, called Mount Adaptors, the LA-EA2 and the LA-EA4. The LA-EA4 is shown on the a6400 in Figure A-3, with the Sony DT 50mm f/1.8 SAM lens attached to the adapter. (SAM stands for Smooth Autofocus

Motor, a type of motor used on less-expensive Sony lenses.)

Figure A-3. Sony DT 50mm f/1.8 SAM Lens with Adapter

This lens, like the E-mount lenses discussed above, has a focal length of 1.5 times its actual value when used with an APS-C sensor, so it has an effective focal length of 75mm on the a6400.

Some A-mount lenses do not support the DMF (direct manual focus) mode for autofocus, including the 50mm lens shown above. In addition, when you are using one of these lenses with the Mount Adaptor on the a6400, the AF Illuminator will not illuminate for autofocus, even if the AF Illuminator menu option is set to Auto. Also, there is no focus distance scale on the camera's display when using an A-mount lens on the a6400 in manual focus mode, and MF Assist does not work. Touch Tracking does not function properly, although a tracking frame will appear on the display. The AF in Focus Magnification option also does not function when using the Mount Adaptor.

On the other hand, two menu options, Eye-Start AF and AF Micro Adjustment, are available only when using an A-mount lens with the Mount Adaptor.

You can refer to the following Sony website for more information about what lenses are compatible with the a6400 camera: https://support.d-imaging.sony. co.jp/www/cscs/lens_body/index.php?mdl=ILCE-6400&area=gb&lang=en.

Cases

You don't have to get a case for your a6400, but I always use one when I'm going out for a photo session, so I can carry along filters, extra batteries, and other items. I will discuss a few of the many possible choices.

Figure A-4. Ruggard Hunter 25 Bag with a6400

One option that works well for the a6400 with the 18-135mm kits lens attached is the Ruggard Hunter 25 Holster Bag, shown with the camera inside it in Figure A-4. This is a "top-loading" case, meaning the camera is placed in it with the lens facing down, so you can quickly grab the camera in its shooting position. This case protects the camera well, and has room for small items such as filters, batteries, and memory cards, but not for another lens.

A larger option is the Lowepro Passport Sling, shown in Figure A-5. This bag easily can hold the a6400 with the 18-135mm lens, as well as a second lens and various accessories. There are more recent versions since this one was released a few years ago, but they are similar in size and features. I like this bag for the convenience of carrying it over one shoulder and its flexibility for holding numerous small items.

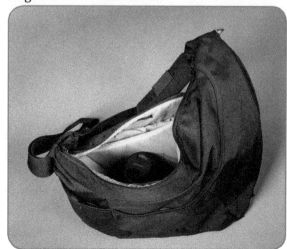

Figure A-5. Lowepro Passport Sling Bag with a6400

There are many other options available, such as the Lowepro Apex 110 AW, or, if you are using a smaller lens, the Lowepro Apex 100 AW. Beyond those, you can find backpacks, other sling packs, and many traditional cases.

Batteries and Chargers

These are items I recommend you purchase when you get the camera or soon afterward. I use the camera heavily, and I find it runs through batteries fairly quickly. You can't use disposable batteries, so if you're out taking pictures and the battery dies, you're out of luck unless you have a spare battery, or you can plug the camera's charging cable into a power outlet or USB port. You can get a spare Sony battery, model number NP-FW50, for about $50 as I write this. It won't do you a great deal of good by itself, though, because the battery is designed to be charged in the camera.

There is an easy solution to this problem. You can find generic replacement batteries, as well as chargers to charge the batteries outside the camera, inexpensively from eBay, B&H Photo, and elsewhere. Figure A-6 shows a Vivitar external charger and replacement battery, which have worked well with my a6400. As I write this, you can purchase a similar generic charger with two batteries for about $32. I also have used replacement batteries by Wasabi Power with good results.

Figure A-6. Vivitar Replacement Battery and Charger

One option if you need additional shooting time is to use a battery grip like the Vello BG-S4 grip, shown in Figures A-7 and A-8, attached to the a6400. This accessory holds two batteries, giving double the length of time for powering the camera. When one battery runs down, the device automatically switches to the other battery. The grip also gives you a very solid hold on the camera on two sides, and lets you position the camera vertically, with a second shutter button on

the bottom area, for shooting with the camera held sideways. Of course, this item adds considerable bulk and weight to the camera, but it can be useful if you need to keep the camera powered up for an extended period of time.

Figure A-7. Vello BG-S4 Battery Grip with a6400

Figure A-8. Vello Battery Grip, Showing Second Shutter Button

AC Adapters and Other Power Sources

As I discussed in Chapter 1, the battery charger that comes with the camera, model no. AC-UUD12 in the United States, can be used as an AC adapter as well as a battery charger. If you plug the camera's USB cable into that charger and into the camera's Multi port, and then plug the charger into an electrical outlet, the camera will be powered by the charger when the camera is turned on, as long as there is a battery in the camera. If you turn the camera off, the charger will charge the battery inside the camera. However, you cannot use the supplied charger to power the camera if you are using the Multi port for some other purpose, such as uploading images and videos to a computer, or if you have connected a wired remote control to the camera. In those situations, an optional AC adapter would be quite useful.

Sony sells an AC adapter, Model No. AC-PW20, as an optional accessory. As you can see in Figure A-9, this item is quite cumbersome. It consists of a power brick with a separate cord that plugs into an AC outlet, and a smaller cord that terminates in a block shaped like the camera's battery. That block is inserted into the camera, and the cord is routed through a small flap in the battery compartment door. You have to pull that flap out to leave room for the cord, so the door can be closed and latched. All this accessory does is power the camera. It does not recharge the battery, because the battery has to be removed from the camera in order to use this setup.

Figure A-9. Sony AC-PW20 AC Adapter

A more flexible type of external power supply is the Tether Tools Case Relay external power system, shown connected to the camera in Figure A-10. This system, like the Sony adapter discussed above, uses a "dummy battery" that is inserted into the camera's battery compartment, and connects to the power adapter with a cord.

Figure A-10. Tether Tools Case Relay Power Adapter

That cord has to be routed through the small channel in the camera's battery compartment door, as shown in Figure A-11.

Figure A-11. Tether Tools Power Adapter Cord Connected to a6400

The difference with this accessory from the Sony version is that it provides an "infinite" power supply. That means that it has its own internal battery, which supplies power to the camera and that can be recharged constantly from an external power source, such as a portable USB battery or a USB wall charger. If you use a USB battery, you can "hot-swap" a new one as an old one loses its charge. In this way, you could keep the camera powered on for many hours or days, while recording time-lapse sequences or carrying out other long processes.

Another device that is useful for providing power for the a6400 is the Anker 40-watt desktop USB charger, shown in Figure A-12, which has 5 slots for charging devices such as smartphones and tablets.

Figure A-12. Anker 40-Watt Desktop USB Charger

I use it to charge my iPhone and iPad, and it does a good job of charging the Sony battery inside the a6400 camera at the same time, or powering the camera when

I am using it near my desk. You also can use this device to charge the Tether Tools Case Relay, discussed above. There are many other USB chargers available from companies such as Aukey and RAVPower.

One more option for an external power supply is a portable USB battery like the Mophie PowerStation XL, shown in Figure A-13, which can be recharged from a USB wall charger and can provide power to the camera using the camera's micro USB cable or any standard micro USB cable. Again, devices like this are available from various manufacturers, such as Aukey, RAVPower, Anker, and Poweradd.

This device has two standard-sized USB ports. You can plug the camera's USB cable into one of those ports and connect the other end to the camera to provide a long-lasting source of power, or to charge the camera's battery. You can charge the power supply through its own micro USB port, using any compatible AC adapter. In fact, you can use the a6400's own AC adapter to recharge the Mophie device. The Mophie device is not very large and weighs about 7.65 ounces (217 grams).

Figure A-13. **Mophie PowerStation XL USB Battery**

External Flash Units and Flash Triggers

The a6400 is equipped with Sony's special Multi Interface Shoe, where you can attach an external flash unit, among other items. The most obvious choice for using external flash is to use one of the units offered by Sony. The smallest Sony flash for use with the a6400 is model number HVL-F20M, shown in Figure A-14.

This unit fits with the camera nicely. It has a guide number of up to 20 at f/2.8 and ISO 800, meaning it can reach up to 20 meters (66 feet) with those settings; it

has a shorter range at higher apertures and with lower ISO values. It has a Bounce switch, which rotates the flash head upward by 75 degrees to let you bounce the flash off a ceiling or high wall.

Figure A-14. **Sony HVL-F20M Flash**

The F20M is capable of acting as the trigger unit for Sony's optical wireless flash control system. As discussed in Chapter 4, the a6400's built-in flash unit does not provide that function. So, if you want to fire other flash units remotely using Sony's optical wireless system, the F20M is the least expensive option for that purpose. Note, though, that the F20M cannot be fired remotely using that system; it can act as the master unit, but not as a slave unit.

The next step up with Sony's external flash options is a considerably larger unit, the HVL-F32M, shown in Figure A-15. This powerful flash can act as either the trigger unit or a remote unit with Sony's optical wireless flash system.

Figure A-15. **Sony HVL-F32M Flash**

The next model, HVL-F43M, not shown here, also can assume either role for optical wireless flash and includes a video light that can provide continuous illumination.

The HVL-F45RM, shown in Figure A-16, has built-in capabilities as both a wireless commander unit and a wireless receiver unit for both of Sony's remote flash systems—optical and radio. I will discuss it again below, when I discuss radio flash triggers.

Figure A-17. Neewer NW320 Flash for Sony

Figure A-16. Sony HVL-F45RM Flash

Or, you can opt for the largest unit, the Sony HVL-F60M, not shown here, which can perform optical (but not radio) wireless functions.

Another option is to use an older Sony flash that was not designed for the Multi Interface Shoe. In that case, you need Sony's shoe adapter, model number ADP-MAA, so the flash will work automatically with the a6400. Note that not all older Sony flash units will work with the a6400, even with this adapter. In particular, I have been advised that the Sony HVL-F32X flash will not work with newer cameras, even with the adapter.

You also can use a non-Sony flash that is designed to be compatible with the Multi Interface Shoe. One example is the Neewer NW320, shown in Figure A-17, which works with the a6400 to provide automatic flash output. You need to be sure to purchase the version of this flash designed for the Sony Multi Interface Shoe.

Another third-party flash unit that is compatible with the a6400 is the Godox TT350 for Sony, shown in Figure A-18.

Figure A-18. Godox TT350 Flash for Sony

There are some other non-Sony flash units that work with the hot shoe of the a6400 and fire whenever the camera's shutter button is pressed. However, with these units, there is no communication with the flash unit through the camera's accessory shoe. Therefore, you have to set both the camera and the flash to their manual modes and determine the exposure through trial and error or by measuring the light with a meter.

I have tested two non-Sony units that fire reliably from the flash shoe of the a6400—the Yongnuo YN560-IV and the LumoPro LP180. Both of those units also have the ability to act as optical slave units, triggered by the light of the a6400's built-in flash. They both have various optical slave settings, so they can be set to ignore the pre-flash bursts from the camera's flash, and fire only when the camera's main flash is fired.

If you are not using the built-in flash or a Sony external flash, you probably will want to set the camera's White Balance to its Flash setting, because the Auto White

Balance setting will not take account of the use of flash unless the flash communicates with the camera.

Here is one other issue you need to be aware of when using a non-Sony external flash unit. When you set the camera to Manual exposure mode, the camera's display screen is likely to be black or very dark because the Manual exposure settings would result in a dark image if you were not using flash, and the camera will not "know" about the effects of the non-Sony flash. Therefore, it may be difficult to compose the shot.

The a6400 has a menu option that deals with this type of situation—the Live View Display option on screen 7 of the Camera Settings2 menu. If you select the Setting Effect Off option for that menu item, then, when you use Manual exposure mode, the camera's display will not show the dark image that would result from the shot without flash; instead, the display will show the image with normal brightness (if there is enough ambient light), so you can compose the shot with a clear view of the scene in front of the camera.

Another way to use external flash units with the a6400 is to fire them with a radio flash trigger system. Sony offers a radio triggering unit and a matching receiver that work well with the a6400 camera for this purpose. These units are the Sony Wireless Radio Commander, model number FA-WRC1M, shown in Figure A-19, and the Wireless Radio Receiver, model number FA-WRR1, shown in Figure A-20.

Figure A-19. Sony Wireless Radio Commander, FA-WRC1M

I won't discuss the details of their use here, but I tested them and they worked well, as discussed in Chapter 4. I attached a Sony HVL-F32M flash to the receiver, and attached the commander to the Multi Interface Shoe on

top of the a6400. After I followed the steps to pair the two devices, when I pressed the shutter button on the camera, the flash fired in its remote position.

Figure A-20. Sony Wireless Radio Receiver, FA-WRR1

I also tested the commander unit using the Sony HVL-F45RM flash as the remote unit. That flash unit has a built-in radio receiver, so there was no need to use the separate radio receiver unit. This setup also worked as expected, with the HVL-F45RM firing when I pressed the shutter button on the camera, with the commander unit attached to the Multi Interface Shoe.

Finally, there is an added benefit to be had from the Wireless Radio Commander and Receiver. You also can use those units to trigger the a6400 camera remotely, using a slightly different setup. In order to do that, you attach the receiver to the flash shoe on the camera. Then, because the shoe on the bottom of the receiver does not communicate with the camera, you need to obtain another item—the Sony Multi Terminal Connecting Cable, model number VMC-MM1.

That cable plugs into a Multi Terminal port on the receiver and into the Multi port on the a6400. Then, after you have paired the two devices and set up the commander in Release mode, you can press the Shutter button on the commander to trigger the shutter on the camera. (To get the unit into Release mode, press the Fn button, then the center button in the main controller, then select Release from the options that appear.)

This system is rated to work at a distance of about 100 feet (30 meters), so it can be a useful alternative to other remote control options. You also could attach the commander to the Multi Interface Shoe on one a6400 and press the shutter button on that camera to trigger the shutters of other cameras remotely.

I also have used other radio triggers, such as model number RF603N II, by Yongnuo. I purchased these in a pair, each of which can act as either a transmitter or a receiver, by moving a switch on its side. As seen in Figure A-21, I mounted the transmitter unit in the camera's accessory shoe. I attached the receiver unit to the LumoPro LP180, an external flash unit discussed above, which I placed on a small stand. With the flash set to its Manual mode and the camera's flash mode set to Fill-flash, when I pressed the shutter button, the external flash fired.

Figure A-21. Yongnuo RF603N II Radio Flash Trigger on a6400

With this system, you can use any flash unit that is compatible with the receiver. I have found that you need to use a flash that has a Manual mode, like the LumoPro unit. External flash units that have only automatic (TTL) exposure systems do not work, in my experience.

I also tested another radio transmitter, the Hensel Strobe Wizard Plus, not shown here, which I use for triggering monolight flash units for photography with a DSLR. It worked well in the accessory shoe of the a6400, triggering the monolights perfectly.

Finally, another item that lets you use off-camera flash, not shown here, is the Meike TTL Off-Camera Cord, model number MK-FA02. You need to specify the version for Sony cameras. This accessory includes an attachment that fits into the camera's Multi Interface Shoe and that connects to a cord that is about 18 inches (45 cm) long when coiled, but that can stretch to about twice that length. The other end has a Multi Interface Shoe that can hold a Sony or compatible flash, and that can be attached to a tripod or other support to hold the flash.

Remote Controls

In several situations, it is useful to control the camera remotely. For example, when you are using slow shutter speeds, holding the shutter open with the Bulb setting, or doing closeup photography, any camera motion during the exposure is likely to blur the image. If you control the camera remotely, you lessen the risk of blurred images from moving the camera as you press the shutter button. Remote control also is helpful when you need to be located away from the camera, as for taking self-portraits or images of wildlife. You also can place the camera on a long pole for a sort of aerial photography; see polepixie.com for details.

As I discussed in Chapter 10, the a6400 has a built-in Wi-Fi capability for connecting a computer, smartphone, or tablet to the camera wirelessly. Besides using that feature to transfer images from the camera to the other device, you can use a smartphone or tablet as a wireless remote control. However, it can be tricky to establish and maintain the connection between the camera and the phone or tablet.

Fortunately, Sony offers several remote controls that are compatible with the a6400 camera. Sony's model number RM-VPR1 is shown in Figure A-22.

Figure A-22. Sony Remote Control, RM-VPR1

You connect this device to the Multi port on the left side of the camera. You can half-press the remote's shutter button to cause the autofocus system to operate (if the camera is in an autofocus mode), and press the button fully to take a still picture. You can press the shutter button down and then slide it back toward the other controls to lock it in place. This locking is useful when you are taking continuous shots using the Drive Mode settings, or when you want to hold the shutter open using the Bulb setting in Manual exposure mode. Press the shutter button back up in its original direction to release it.

The red button labeled Start/Stop is similar to the Movie button on the a6400 camera. Press it once to start recording a movie and press it again to stop the recording.

The power button on the side of the remote control can also be used with the a6400, although it does not duplicate the functions of the camera's own power switch. You have to have the camera's power switch in the On position for the remote to work, and it cannot turn the camera completely off; it can only place it into power-saving mode or wake it up.

A more sophisticated remote, Sony model number RMT-VP1K, is shown in Figure A-23.

Figure A-23. Sony Remote Control, RMT-VP1K

This remote comes with an infrared receiver with a cable that plugs into the camera's Multi port. The receiver, shaped like a small cylinder, has a foot for attaching to the camera's flash shoe.

The remote control itself is similar to the wired remote discussed earlier, RM-VPR1, though there are some differences. You can press the shutter button, and you can lock it down for Bulb shooting. You can zoom the lens (if the lens is able to be zoomed) and start and stop a video recording. The remote also has a slide switch labeled TC Reset on the left side. You can operate that switch to reset the camera's time code to zero.

With the camera's mode dial at the Movie position, just press the TC Reset switch on the remote, and the time code displayed in the lower left corner of the display will be reset to the zero point. The way to accomplish this reset in the camera is to go to the TC Preset option under TC/UB Settings on screen 3 of the Setup menu. With TC Preset highlighted, press the Center button to bring up the screen showing the values of the current time code. While that screen is displayed, press the C2/Delete button, and the time code will be reset. It is considerably easier to just press the TC Reset button on the remote if you need to reset the time code.

Figure A-24. Sony Remote Control, RM-SPR1

Figure A-24 shows another option, Sony model number RM-SPR1. This device is a very simple wired remote that also connects to the Multi port. It has only one large button, which acts as a remote shutter button. You can press it halfway to evaluate focus and exposure, press it all the way to take a still image, or hold it down to fire a burst of shots if Drive Mode is set for continuous shooting. You cannot use this remote to record a movie or carry out any other functions.

Figure A-25. Sony Remote Control, RMT-DSLR2

Another option from Sony is the RMT-DSLR2, shown in figure A-25, a very small remote control unit with a considerable amount of usefulness. With this device, you can control the camera's shutter, start and stop video recording, and perform several other functions using the buttons on the device, including a button for the two-second self-timer, a Menu button, Display button, cursor buttons, a Playback button, Delete button, and others. You can also zoom the lens, if the camera is using a lens with power zoom, or if non-optical zoom functions are enabled on the camera. In order to use this device, you have to have the IR Remote Control option turned on on screen 4 of the Setup menu.

Sony also offers the RMT-P1BT, a Bluetooth remote, which I discussed in Chapter 10. That device, shown in Figure A-26, can control the shutter, movie recording, and zoom, and it has a C1 button. It is activated through the Bluetooth Remote Control option on screen 2 of the Network menu. You have to have at least version 2.00 of the camera's firmware installed for this device to work with the a6400 camera.

Figure A-26. Sony Remote Control, RMT-P1BT

Another device offered by Sony is the VCT-SGR1 Shooting Grip. This remote control consists of a handle that can expand into a small tabletop tripod, as shown in Figure A-27. It has built into it controls for shutter, video recording, and zoom, all of which are within easy reach of your thumb when holding the handle in its folded position. It has a cable built into the device for connecting to the camera's Multi terminal, so it can provide its remote control functions. This control is quite convenient if you hold the camera with the LCD monitor rotated toward you for vlogging.

Figure A-27. Sony Shooting Grip, VCT-SGR1

One more device, which has greater functionality than an ordinary remote control, is the Vello Wireless ShutterBoss, model number RCW-3-S2 for Sony Multi

terminal connection, shown in Figure A-28.

Figure A-28. Vello Wireless ShutterBoss

This device comes with a cord for connecting its receiver to the camera's Multi port. The remote transmitter can then send commands wirelessly to the camera from a distance of up to 250 feet (76 m). It can act as a remote control, similar to the Sony devices discussed above. In addition, it has several timer options, and it can serve as an intervalometer for recording a time-lapse sequence.

Using the controls and the small LCD screen on the device, you can set up a sequence of up to 999 shots, or an indefinite series, until you command it to stop. You can set the interval between shots to any value from one second up to 99 hours, 59 minutes, and 59 seconds. If you purchase this item, you need to specify the model for the Sony Multi Terminal. Vello also makes the ShutterBoss II, a similar device that is wired directly to the camera's Multi port.

Also, as discussed above in connection with flash triggers, you can use the Sony Wireless Radio Commander and Wireless Radio Receiver to trigger the shutter of the a6400 from a distance of up to about 100 feet (30 meters).

External LCD Monitor

There is another accessory to consider for viewing live and recorded images with the a6400. The Sony Clip-On LCD Monitor, model number CLM-FHD5, is an add-on unit with a 5-inch (12-cm) screen. This small monitor, shown in Figure A-29, comes with a foot that attaches securely to the accessory shoe of the a6400.

Figure A-29. Sony LCD Monitor, CLM-FHD5

The unit includes a short HDMI cable that ends in a micro HDMI plug at the camera end, for connecting to the HDMI port of the camera.

This monitor works well with the a6400. It adds visibility for viewing the shooting screen and for playing back images and videos. The screen can rotate 180 degrees, so you can view the scene from the front of the camera for self-portraits. It also can tilt up or down for viewing from high or low angles. The monitor has numerous controls for settings such as Peaking, brightness, and contrast, and it has a special display mode for boosting the contrast when you are using the S-Log2 or S-Log 3 gamma curve, whose use produces dark footage that is hard to see before it has been processed with a computer.

This unit costs about $700 at the time of this writing, but if you need the extra screen size or versatility, it is worth looking into. It does not come with a battery, but it can use any one of several Sony batteries, including the NP-FW50 battery used by the a6400, with an adapter that is included with the monitor.

One reader suggested an alternative, the FlySight RC801 HD monitor, which is intended for use in monitoring drone flights, and is much less expensive than the Sony monitor, at about $150.00. I have not tested this unit, but it looks as if it could be a good alternative to the more expensive one.

External Microphones

The a6400 camera has two features that enable the use of an external microphone—a standard 3.5mm audio input port on the left side of the camera, and the

Multi Interface Shoe, which allows a compatible Sony microphone to get its power from that shoe.

One problem with using an external microphone with the a6400 is that placing a microphone (or other accessory) in the shoe blocks the view of the LCD monitor when it is rotated all the way forward, for vlogging or selfies.

One relatively inexpensive microphone that connects through the camera's special interface shoe is Sony's model number ECM-XYST1M, shown in Figure A-30.

Figure A-30. Sony Microphone, ECM-XYST1M

This compact device has two microphone units that can be kept together or separated by 120 degrees, as shown here, to pick up sounds from different directions.

Another option, which provides wireless capability, is Sony's Bluetooth microphone, model number ECM-W1M, shown in Figure A-31. With this unit, you attach a small receiver to the camera's Multi Interface Shoe as shown here. You then can clip the separate microphone to a shirt pocket or any other location, and the camera will pick up sounds from the microphone within a range of about 300 feet or 100 meters.

Figure A-31. Sony Microphone, ECM-W1M

If you want a shotgun-style microphone, Sony offers model number ECM-GZ1M, shown in Figure A-32. It comes with a windscreen that you can slip over the microphone; that accessory is shown here lying beside the camera.

Figure A-32. Sony Microphone, ECM-GZ1M

Sony also offers a more expensive and sophisticated option for using external microphones—the XLR-K2M adapter kit, shown in Figure A-33.

Figure A-33. Sony Microphone Kit, XLR-K2M

The kit connects to the camera's Multi Interface Shoe and provides inputs for two professional-quality XLR microphones. That type of microphone provides balanced input, resulting in lower noise and cleaner sound.

The kit includes a single Sony shotgun microphone with an XLR connection and an adapter for attaching the kit to the camera, as well as a connector for another microphone and controls for both inputs.

You may not want to spend $600.00 to add this capability to a compact camera, but, given the a6400's excellent video features, it could be a worthwhile expense if you use the camera heavily for video production.

You also can use any of a multitude of other external microphones with the a6400, as long as the microphone has a cable that terminates in a standard 3.5mm stereo plug. One example from Sony is another shotgun mic, model number ECM-CG50. You also can use third-party mics, such as the Rode VideoMic Pro, or various models from Shure or Audio-Technica. Figure A-34 shows a Rode microphone attached to the camera.

Figure A-34. Rode VideoMic Pro Attached to a6400 with Bracket

One problem with using external microphones is that they block the LCD monitor when it is flipped up in self-portrait position. One solution to that problem is to use a bracket that lets you attach the microphone to the side of the camera, as shown in Figure A-34. In this case, I used a bracket from UURig, model number R006, called the Quick Release L Plate for Sony A6400, shown in Figure A-35. That bracket, which is solidly constructed, leaves space for access to the camera's ports, and has a convenient shoe where you can attach a microphone, as well as several tripod sockets for attaching various other items.

Figure A-35. UURig Quick Release L Plate for Sony A6400

External Video Recorder

In Chapter 9, I discussed how to take advantage of the a6400's video features to output its 4K video signal via the HDMI port to an external video recorder. Using this system, you can record 4K video without having to obtain an especially fast memory card for the camera; you can record with no memory card in the camera at all.

The recorder I used for this process is the Atomos Shogun 4K recorder. In Figure A-36, the recorder is mounted to the side of the a6400, on a Manfrotto accessory arm, model number 131DDB. The combination of a6400 and Shogun performed well in producing high-quality 4K video files. The menu system is easy to work with and the recorder produces high-quality files. At the highest quality, the files can be extremely large (more than 220 GB in one of my tests), so be prepared with a strong computer capability for editing. There are more recent 4K video recorders by

Atomos and other brands that are less expensive, but I have not tested any of those with the a6400 camera.

Figure A-36. Atomos Shogun 4K Recorder with a6400

APPENDIX B: QUICK TIPS

This section includes tips and facts that might be useful as reminders. My goal is to provide information that might help you in certain situations or that might not be obvious to everyone. I have tried to include points you might not remember from day to day, especially if you don't use the a6400 constantly.

Be aware of the optical stabilization ability of your lens. The a6400 does not have optical stabilization built into the camera body, so, if you need stabilization to reduce the effects of camera motion, you need to use a lens with stabilization built into it. Sony lenses with this feature have the OSS designation as part of their names. If it doesn't say OSS, you will have to use other ways to stabilize the camera, if you are shooting in conditions where camera shake is an issue. If the lens does have OSS, use the SteadyShot option on screen 4 of the Camera Settings2 menu to activate it.

Use continuous shooting settings. Consider turning continuous shooting on as a matter of routine, unless you are running out of storage space or battery power, or have another reason not to use it. Even with portraits, you may get the perfect expression on your subject's face with the fourth or fifth shot. Call up Drive Mode, scroll to Continuous Shooting, and select it. Continuous shooting is not available when the camera is set to the Sweep Panorama mode or any Scene mode setting other than Sports Action. It also is incompatible with the last six Picture Effect settings, Multi Frame Noise Reduction, Smile Shutter, and Auto HDR.

Use autofocus and autoexposure with continuous shooting. With the a6400, you can do high-speed continuous shooting, even with File Format (Still Images) set to Raw, and still have the camera adjust focus and exposure for each shot. To do that, after turning on continuous shooting through the Drive Mode menu, set Focus Mode to AF-C for continuous autofocus. For exposure adjustments, go to screen 9 of the Camera Settings1 menu and set AEL w/Shutter to Auto or Off. To maximize the camera's ability to focus sharply, go to screen 5 of the Camera Settings1 menu and set Priority Set in AF-C to AF.

Use shortcuts. You can speed up access to many settings by placing them on the Function menu for recall with a press of the Function button. You can assign your most-used settings to a control button using the Custom Key (Still Images) option on screen 8 of the Camera Settings2 menu. Speed through the menus by using the control wheel to move rapidly through the items on each screen, and use the Right and Left buttons or the control dial to move through the menu system a full screen at a time. In shooting mode, use the control dial to change scene types in Scene mode and to change panorama direction in Sweep Panorama mode.

Use the Register Custom Shooting Settings option to recall settings quickly. This powerful feature lets you call up temporarily a group of basic shooting settings, including shutter speed, aperture, ISO, Focus Mode, and others, at the press of one button. To use this feature, go to the Register Custom Shooting Settings item on screen 4 of the Camera Settings1 menu, and register a group of settings to Recall Custom Hold 1, 2, or 3. Then go to the Custom Key (Still Images) option on screen 8 of the Camera Settings2 menu and assign a control button to the Recall Custom Hold slot you chose.

Use the Memory Recall shooting mode. MR position on the mode dial gives you a powerful way to customize the a6400 by storing seven groups of settings. You also can use it for more specific purposes. One thing I like to do is have one slot set up to remove all "special" settings, such as Creative Style, Picture Effect, Picture Profile, and Drive Mode, so I can quickly set up the camera to take a shot with no surprises.

Use the extra settings for White Balance and Creative Style. When you set White Balance, even with the Auto White Balance setting, you can press the Right button to use the amber-blue and green-magenta axes to further adjust the color of your shots. This setting is not obvious on the menu screen, but it gives you a useful tool to alter color settings. Just remember to undo any color shift when you no longer need it. Also, you can press the Right button or turn the control dial after selecting a Creative Style option and then adjust the contrast, saturation, and sharpness settings. (Saturation is not adjustable for the Black and White or Sepia setting.)

Use the touch screen features. These are summarized in Chapter 6, in the discussion of the LCD screen. You can tap to choose a focus point when shooting stills or movies. You can tap the screen twice to enlarge it in playback mode, and you can also tap twice to enlarge it when shooting stills or movies in manual focus mode. You can turn on the Touch Shutter function to take still images by just tapping the LCD monitor.

Diffuse your flash. If the built-in flash produces light that's too harsh for macro or other shots, use translucent plastic pieces from milk jugs or broken ping-pong balls as homemade diffusers. Position the plastic between the flash and the subject. When using Fill-flash outdoors, try using the Flash Compensation setting on screen 10 of the Camera Settings1 menu to reduce the intensity of the flash by -2/3 EV.

Use the self-timer to avoid camera shake. The self-timer is not just for group portraits; you can use the two-second or five-second self-timer whenever you use a slow shutter speed and need to avoid camera shake. It also is useful for macro photography. Don't forget that you can set the self-timer to take multiple shots, which can increase your chances of getting more usable images.

Be aware of conflicting settings. There are times when a feature will not operate because a conflicting setting is in place. One excellent feature of the a6400 is that it often will explain the conflict when you try to select the feature. For example, if you have Picture Effect turned on and then try to select Creative Style, when you press the Center button to select it, the a6400 will display an error message about the conflict. There are many such conflicts; one is that you cannot take still images when the mode dial is set to Movie or S & Q Motion mode. Also, the Control with Smartphone option on screen 1 of the Network menu, when turned on, interferes with items such as USB Connection on screen 4 of the Setup menu.

Use Flexible Spot for the Focus Area setting. With this option, you can move the focus frame around the display. To use the feature most efficiently, set the Center button or one of the other control buttons to Focus Standard with the Custom Key (Still Images) menu option. Then, just press the assigned button in shooting mode to make the focus frame movable. You also can drag the frame with your finger if Touch Operation is enabled through screen 3 of the Setup menu.

Touch Tracking works where the Tracking settings for Focus Area do not. The Tracking settings for Focus Area are not available for use with video recording on the a6400 or with any setting for Focus Mode other than continuous autofocus. However, the Touch Tracking setting works with video recording and with all Focus Mode settings other than manual focus. To use Touch Tracking, turn on Touch Operation on screen 3 of the Setup menu and turn on Touch Tracking through the Function of Touch Operation item on screen 9 of the Camera Settings2 menu.

Take advantage of functions available only by assigning a button. The a6400 has several features that do not appear on any menu and that can be used only if you use the Custom Key options on screen 8 of the Camera Settings2 menu to assign them to a button. These include AEL Hold or Toggle; AF/MF Control Hold or Toggle; Recall Custom Hold; Register AF Area Hold; Eye AF; AF On; In-camera Guide; Focus Hold; and FEL Lock Hold or Toggle. In-camera Guide is very helpful in explaining the use of menu options and settings. I assign it to the C2 button on my camera.

Take advantage of two shooting modes that are hidden in menus. The Superior Auto shooting mode is not on the mode dial; to set it you have to set the mode dial to Intelligent Auto mode, then use the Auto Mode menu option to select Superior Auto, which adds the capability of taking bursts of shots to create composite images with improved quality. To get to the Multi Frame Noise Reduction setting, which involves bursts of shots to reduce noise, you have to use the ISO menu option. With MFNR, you normally would want to set the ISO level to a high value or Auto, but you also can use that option with a low ISO value to get higher image quality from the composite image.

Use DMF for focusing. Set Focus Mode to DMF for direct manual focus. Then you can use autofocus, but still turn the focusing ring for further adjustments with manual focus. You have to half-press the shutter button to adjust the focus when DMF is in effect. If you set Focus Mode to DMF when recording video, the camera will use continuous autofocus. DMF is not available with all lenses.

Use Auto ISO in Manual exposure mode. Not all cameras allow this. With this setting, you can set aperture and shutter speed as you want for a particular effect, and let the camera adjust the exposure by setting the ISO automatically. This works when shooting either still images or movies.

Try time-lapse photography. With time-lapse photography, a camera takes a series of still images at regular intervals, several seconds, minutes, or even hours apart, to record a slow-moving event such as the rising or setting of the moon or sun or the opening of a flower. The images are played back at a much faster rate to show the whole event unfolding quickly. You can do time-lapse photography using the Interval Shooting Function option on screen 3 of the Camera Settings1 menu; the interval-shooting features of Sony's Imaging Edge software when the a6400 is tethered to a computer; or with an external device such as the Vello Wireless Shutterboss, discussed in Appendix A.

Use the self-timer for bracketed exposures. To do this, use the Bracket Settings option on screen 3 of the Camera Settings1 menu and select the first sub-option, Self-timer During Bracket.

Use the camera's automatic HDR option. To do this, go to screen 11 of the Camera Settings1 menu, select DRO/Auto HDR, then Auto HDR. You cannot use certain other settings with Auto HDR, including Raw for File Format (Still Images), Picture Effect, or Picture Profile.

Use the Picture Profile feature to full advantage. If you are serious about getting the maximum benefit from the Picture Profile feature, especially PP7, PP8, and PP9 with their use of the S-Log2 and S-Log3 gamma curve settings, or PP10 with its use of an HLG setting, you need to use color-grading software. A good software package can take advantage of the profiles and bring out the colors, contrast, and other aspects of your video files in the way you intend. One powerful program is DaVinci Resolve 16, which is available in a free version as well as a professional one. See https://www.blackmagicdesign.com/products/davinciresolve.

Use tethered shooting. Go to the USB Connection option on screen 4 of the Setup menu and choose the PC Remote setting. Then use a micro USB cable to connect the camera to a computer that has Sony's Imaging Edge software installed, and run the Remote module of that software. Using the icons in the window that appears on the computer, you can control several settings on the camera and capture images directly to a directory on the computer. You also can do time-lapse shooting with the software's built-in interval timer.

Capture images of birds. The a6400, with its excellent autofocus and continuous-shooting features, is well suited for photographing birds. Here are some suggested settings to start with. Some of them can be saved to a Recall Custom Hold slot, as discussed earlier in the Quick Tips section. Use Spot metering, with the Standard or Large setting for the spot size, depending on how large the subject is. Use continuous shooting, with high speed or medium speed. Set Focus Mode to AF-C and AEL w/ Shutter to Auto on screen 9 of the Camera Settings1 menu. Use Shutter Priority mode with ISO Auto with shutter speed set to 1/1000 second or faster. Set Focus Area to Tracking: Flexible Spot M. For another perspective on this sort of shooting see the following link: https://petapixel.com/2017/11/25/tips-photographing-birds-flight/.

Figure B-1 is an example I captured using continuous shooting. I used the Sony FE 100-400mm f/4.5-5.6 GM OSS lens with high-speed continuous shooting turned on. The shutter speed was 1/1000 second at f/4.5 and ISO 10000.

Figure B-1. Bird Image Captured with Continuous Shooting

Use the Photo Capture option to save a frame from a 4K video. This feature is not all that obvious, but it can yield excellent results as another way to get shots of elusive birds and other wildlife, among other subjects. Put the camera into Movie mode with File Format set to XAVC S 4K and Exposure Mode set to Shutter Priority. Set the shutter speed to a high value, such as 1/1000 second or faster. Record a movie of birds in flight or another subject with lots of motion. When you have finished, use the Photo Capture option on screen 2 of the Playback menu to find and save some of the best frames from the movie as individual images. Because of the fast shutter speed, the shots should not suffer from too much motion blur.

Figure B-2 is an example of a shot saved with the Photo Capture option.

Figure B-2. Image Saved Using Photo Capture Option

Appendix C: Resources for Further Information

Websites and Videos

It's impossible to compile a list of sites that discuss the a6400 that will be accurate far into the future. I will include here a list of some sites or links I have found useful, with the caveat that some of them may not be accessible by the time you read this.

Digital Photography Review

Listed below is the current web address for the "Sony Alpha / NEX E-mount (APS-C) Talk" forum within the dpreview.com site. Dpreview.com is one of the most established and authoritative sites for reviews, discussion forums, technical information, and other resources concerning digital cameras.

https://www.dpreview.com/forums/1042

Reviews and Demonstrations of the a6400

The links below lead to reviews or previews of the a6400 by dpreview.com, photographyblog.com, and others.

https://www.dpreview.com/reviews/sony-a6400-review

https://www.imaging-resource.com/PRODS/sony-a6400/sony-a6400A.HTM

https://www.cameralabs.com/sony-alpha-a6400-review/

https://www.photographyblog.com/reviews/sony_a6400_review

https://www.tomsguide.com/us/sony-a6400-mirrorless-camera,review-6420.html

https://www.pcmag.com/review/366036/sony-a6400

https://www.pocket-lint.com/cameras/reviews/sony/147500-sony-a6400-review-mirrorless-camera

https://www.thephoblographer.com/2019/04/08/review-sony-a6400-the-sony-a9-with-an-aps-c-sensor/

White Knight Press

My own site, White Knight Press, provides updates about this book and other books, offers support for download of PDFs and eBooks, and provides a way for readers or potential readers to contact me with questions or comments.

http://www.whiteknightpress.com

The Official Sony Site

The United States arm of Sony provides resources on its website, including the downloadable version of the user's manual for the a6400 and other technical information.

http://esupport.sony.com

https://www.sony.com/electronics/support/e-mount-body-ilce-6000-series/ilce-6400m

https://www.sony.com/electronics/support/e-mount-body-ilce-6000-series/ilce-6400m/manuals

https://helpguide.sony.net/ilc/1810/v1/en/index.html

https://www.sony.com/electronics/support/e-mount-body-ilce-6000-series/ilce-6400m/specifications

https://www.sony.com/electronics/interchangeable-lens-cameras/ilce-6400

The link below has a list of software that Sony says can be used to edit 4K video files:

http://support.d-imaging.sony.co.jp/www/support/application/nle/en.html

The next link is to a guide for using the Picture Profile

feature with the a6400:

http://helpguide.sony.net/di/pp/v1/en/index.html

The link below is to the operating instructions for the Imaging Edge Mobile app for Android and iOS:

http://support.d-imaging.sony.co.jp/www/disoft/int/playmemories-mobile/en/operation/index.html

The link below leads to a site with information about using the location information linking features of the camera with the Imaging Edge Mobile app:

http://support.d-imaging.sony.co.jp/www/disoft/int/playmemories-mobile/en/location/index.html?id=hg_stl.

The next link points to a page with information about Sony accessories.

http://support.d-imaging.sony.co.jp/www/cscs/accessories/?area=gb&lang=en

The link below leads to the site where you can download PlayMemories Home and Imaging Edge software for use with the a6400:

https://support.d-imaging.sony.co.jp/app/disoft/en/

The link below has instructions for using the Remote module for tethered shooting with Imaging Edge software:

http://support.d-imaging.sony.co.jp/app/imagingedge/en/instruction/

Other Resources

The link below points to a video review of the a6400:

https://youtu.be/MamvBBsBbck

This next link leads to a video review of the a6400 being used with the Atomos Ninja V video recorder:

https://youtu.be/oy0Sxzvd_LU

This next link provides some technical information about the S-Log 2 gamma curve:

http://blog.abelcine.com/2013/01/18/sonys-s-log2-and-dynamic-range-percentages/

The link below provides a detailed analysis of the

differences between S-Log2 and S-Log3.

http://www.xdcam-user.com/2016/12/the-great-s-log2-or-s-log3-debate/

The next link is to a video comparison of the a6400 and the a6500:

https://youtu.be/nxmCWZkYL_8

The link below is to an article on why you might want to record video using an external video recorder:

https://www.dpreview.com/articles/3388025881/why-would-i-want-an-external-recorder-monitor

The link below provides information about settings that can be adjusted for Picture Profiles:

http://www.xdcam-user.com/picture-profile-guide/

The links below provide information about lenses available for Sony E-mount cameras such as the a6400:

https://www.alphashooters.com/cameras/a6400/lenses/

https://www.sonyalphalab.com

https://briansmith.com/aps-e-mount-lenses-for-sony-mirrorless-cameras/

https://thewirecutter.com/reviews/first-sony-e-mount-lenses-to-buy/

https://www.dpreview.com/reviews/buying-guide-best-lenses-for-sony-mirrorless

https://www.digitalcameraworld.com/buying-guides/the-best-sony-lenses

https://www.borrowlenses.com/blog/best-lenses-for-the-sony-a6500-6300-and-6000/

The next link points to a site with a good discussion of many accessories that are available for the a6400.

https://www.alphashooters.com/cameras/a6400/accessories/

Index